10698

Y

PATG 95- B7917

Music Matters

MUSIC
MATTERS

*A New Philosophy of
Music Education*

DAVID J. ELLIOTT

New York   Oxford
Oxford University Press
1995

Oxford University Press

Oxford   New York   Toronto
Delhi   Bombay   Calcutta   Madras   Karachi
Kuala Lumpur   Singapore   Hong Kong   Tokyo
Nairobi   Dar es Salaam   Cape Town
Melbourne   Auckland   Madrid

and associated companies in
Berlin   Ibadan

Published by Oxford University Press, Inc.,
200 Madison Avenue, New York, New York 10016

Oxford is a registered trademark of Oxford University Press

Library of Congress Cataloging-in-Publication Data
Elliott, David James.
Music matters : a new philosophy of music education /
David J. Elliott.
p.   cm.
Includes bibliographical references and index.
ISBN 0-19-509171-X
1. Music—Instruction and study—Philosophy.
MT1.E435   1995   780'.7—dc20   94-3815

2 4 6 8 9 7 5 3 1
Printed in the United States of America
on acid-free paper

To my father,
James William Elliott

Preface

This book examines the nature and significance of music and music education. Through the development of critical discussions and practical principles, it aims to construct a philosophical foundation for educating people toward the fullest understanding and enjoyment of music making and music listening.

The book unfolds in three parts. Part I probes past and present relationships between philosophy and music education. Part II builds a philosophy of music education based on a new way of thinking about the nature and significance of music: new in the sense that it provides new reasons to believe that music is one of the most consequential, dynamic, and practical pursuits in the human repertoire and, therefore, fundamental to the full development of the individual and the collective self. Part III proposes a new concept of music curriculum development for music teaching and learning.

Music Matters is primarily intended for senior undergraduate and graduate music education students and in-service music educators. I hope that it will encourage changes in the philosophy and practice of music education by serving as a catalyst for critical thinking and individual philosophy building. Indeed, this book offers a philosophy not in the popular but mistaken sense of a canon to live and die for, but as one possible view and, therefore, as a tool—as a means of initiating, stimulating, guiding, and supporting the efforts of music teachers (administrators, parents, and others) as they tackle the many theoretical and practical issues involved in music education. Moreover, it is my hope that this tool will be refined in the future with the help of those who use it to teach, learn, and reflect.

The motivation for this book is fourfold. First, I wish to contribute to the improvement of music teaching and learning. Second, I am discontent with conventional thinking; after studying and teaching the traditional philosophy of music education as aesthetic education for many years, I have become more and more convinced of its logical and practical flaws. Third, I have also become persuaded that a more analytic and contextual approach to the philosophical problems of music education, combined with insights from contemporary scholars in the philosophy of music, music cognition, education, and psychology, holds important opportunities to advance music teaching and learning. Fourth, having searched in vain for a text to meet my needs as a teacher of music education philosophy and foundations, I decided to write my own. In doing so, I have been encouraged by the enthusiasm and advice of students, teachers, and colleagues at several university music schools during the last seven years, including the University of Toronto, Indiana University, Northwestern University, and the University of Cape Town.

When I think back to the people who prepared the way for me to write this book, five teachers stand out. My father's active pursuit and lifelong love of music making has been a continuous source of insight, inspiration, and support. My early formal education included school music classes with Glen Wood, an exemplary artist-teacher whose example crystallized my decision to follow a certain way of life in music and music education. Robert Cringan offered me unlimited opportunities to perform, conduct, compose, arrange, and teach my peers in the rich context of my secondary school music program. Gordon Delamont provided an inspiring model of musicianship and musical creativity during my advanced studies of music theory and composition. Fortunately for me, all four men held a deep and abiding interest in the nature and value of music and an enthusiasm for sharing their ideas. Finally, although I disagree with the philosophy he avows, I count my doctoral studies with Professor Bennett Reimer among the important steps I have taken toward the present view.

This preface would be incomplete without recognition of the many friends and colleagues who supported this effort in a variety of ways. Vernon Howard, Philip Alperson, Francis Sparshott, and Timothy Rice encouraged my early thoughts and plans for this book during many stimulating discussions. Carl Bereiter, F. Michael Connelly, Brent Kilbourn, Michael Fullan, Chris Olsen, Mihalyi Csikszentmihalyi, Eric McLuhan, and James Kippen provided invaluable advice during its intermediate stages. Vernon Howard, Philip Alperson, Wayne Bowman, Doreen Rao, Lee Bartel, and Lori-Anne Dolloff offered many helpful comments on the draft manuscript. Robert Cutietta and Charles Fowler contributed importantly to the momentum of this project in its final stages.

To the many undergraduate and graduate students who tested the manuscript and offered valuable feedback in and out of our classes—especially Laura Houghton, John Stewart, and Debra Bradley—my thankfulness.

I owe a special debt to Glenn Fretz for his discerning and patient assistance in the design and production of the diagrams in these pages.

To Maribeth Anderson Payne, my sincere appreciation for her enthusiastic endorsement and editorial expertise as she guided this book smoothly into production and print at Oxford University Press. Also, I should like to acknowledge the acumen and efficiency of Paul Schlotthauer, associate editor.

In terms of research support, the preparation of this book was aided immeasurably by a generous award from the Social Sciences and Humanities Research Council of Canada and by a sabbatical leave from the Faculty of Music, University of Toronto.

Above all, I reserve my most heartfelt gratitude to Doreen Rao for her wisdom, encouragement, patience, and loving support throughout this project.

Harshaw, Wisc.   D. J. E.
April 1994

Acknowledgments

Some of the issues and proposals in this book were first introduced in journal articles and book chapters. I am grateful to the editors and publishers who have granted permission to use portions of the following material in the present volume:

"Music as Culture: Toward a Multicultural Concept of Arts Education," *Journal of Aesthetic Education* 24, no. 1 (Spring 1990): 147–66.

"Music as Knowledge," *Journal of Aesthetic Education* 25, no. 3 (Fall 1991): 21–40.

"When I Sing: The Nature and Value of Choral Music Education," *Choral Journal* 33, no. 8 (March 1993): 11–17. Portions reprinted by permission of the American Choral Directors Association.

"Musicing, Listening and Musical Understanding," *Contributions to Music Education*, no. 20 (1993): 64–83.

"On the Values of Music and Music Education," *Philosophy of Music Education Review* 1, no. 2 (Fall 1993): 81–93.

Winds of Change: A Colloquium in Music Education with Charles Fowler and David J. Elliott, ed. Marie McCarthy. New York: ACA Books, American Council for the Arts in cooperation with the University of Maryland at College Park, 1994. Portions reprinted by permission of the University of Maryland at College Park.

I am also grateful to HarperCollins Publishers Inc., for permission to make adaptations (see Figures 5.2 and 5.3) of the figure from page 74 of *Flow: The Psychology of Optimal Experience*, copyright © 1990 by Mihalyi Csikszentmihalyi.

Contents

II   MUSIC AND MUSIC EDUCATION

III   MUSIC TEACHING AND LEARNING

I

INTRODUCTION

It is not easy to determine the nature of music,
or why anyone should have a knowledge of it.
ARISTOTLE, *Politics*

1

Philosophy and Music Education

- What is music? Is music significant in human life? If so, why?

- What is music education? Does music education deserve a secure place in general education? Why?

- If cogent answers to these questions could be developed, what would this mean for the organization and conduct of music teaching and learning?

Although it is directed first to pre-service and practicing music teachers, this book is for anyone who takes a serious interest in the above matters. Why the serious interest? The question is fair. For at first glance, the nature and significance of music education are straightforward. Consider the following:

In Seattle it's 8:15 A.M. Members of a high school wind ensemble listen to their conductor as she sings a passage from Bernstein's *Candide*. "Do you hear how I build each motive toward the cadence?" The teacher asks the principal flautist, seventeen-year-old Clara Nette, to model the proper phrasing for the rest of the ensemble.

In Chicago it's mid-morning. Thirteen-year-old Tim Pani listens to a recording of *God Bless the Child* in his general music class. Tim's teacher calls out a sequence of numbers as the recording proceeds: "One . . . two. . . ." Tim finds number two on his listening chart and reads the following: "Melody *a:* short phrases; ostinato continues in low keyboard; chords in winds; drums punctuate."[1]

In Toronto it's nearly lunchtime at Maple Leaf Elementary School. A ten-year-old singer named Sara Band improvises a pentatonic melody. Her classmates perform an accompaniment to Sara's improvisation on the school's Orff instruments.

In London it's early evening. The London Philharmonic is about to perform a children's concert. The conductor steps on the podium, turns to his young audience, and describes the paintings related to each section of the upcoming work: *Pictures at an Exhibition*.

In a small city in southeastern Europe, it's later the same evening. A renowned Bulgarian bagpiper sits in his favorite chair by the fire. He listens carefully as his young student plays a *ruchenitsa* (a popular folk dance in '7'). The boy hesitates momentarily in the middle of a difficult passage. He stops. A short silence follows. No words are spoken.

The master stands. He raises his bagpipe. His fingers begin to whirl in rapid bursts; his feet begin to tap; a torrent of notes tumbles from his instrument. Suddenly he stops. A short silence follows.

The boy raises his bagpipe. His fingers begin to whirl; his feet begin to tap; he flies through the difficult passage in a torrent of notes.

Most people would be surprised if a world inventory of music education excluded any of these examples. People would be even more surprised if such an inventory did not list dozens more. It seems, therefore, that although it can take many forms, there is nothing about music education that invites or demands thoughtful concern. People everywhere find music rewarding, and everywhere we find people engaged in formal and nonformal efforts to teach and learn music.[2] It should be plain to everyone what music education is. And it should be obvious that it is good; the proof lies in the fact that people find it so. How could anything as clear-cut become problematic, let alone a focus for philosophy?

1. Serious Matters

Eight problems come to mind straightaway. First, although we might glean a basic sense of what music education is (or ought to be) by observing what music teachers do, observations alone are incomplete. A sampling of approaches offers no assurance that what we select is comprehensive, let alone acceptable in form and content. To determine the nature of music education requires systematic thinking about a host of related issues that cannot be settled entirely by observations and experiments.

Second, we often hear music teachers claim that music is a good thing, or that music education offers something that other school subjects do not. But what could these goods or values be? Good for what and whom? And when and how?

Third, some people suggest that what music teachers do is similar to yet different from what teachers in other subjects do. If so, what are these similarities and differences? And on what grounds shall we decide?

Fourth, whenever people engage in something they care about, they tend to reflect on what they do in order to do it better the next time. Improving as a music educator involves the thoughtful examination of aims, goals, strategies, standards, and plans in relation to a rigorous professional belief system.

Fifth, music teachers today teach under intense public scrutiny. Our profession is frequently required to justify its efforts in relation to a shifting array of educational, economic, political, and social priorities. This outside pressure often leads to an inside desire for deeper understandings about the grounding ideas of our field, including the concepts of music, education, schooling, teaching, learning, performing, listening, creativity, curriculum, assessment, and evaluation. Evidence of our collective need for such understandings lies in the fact that music teachers everywhere debate these concepts continually and with great passion. We do so privately and publicly. And we do so with a wide range of ability. We will no doubt continue to do so for some time.

These five points provide sufficient reasons to believe that music education involves many challenging issues and concepts and that music teacher education ought to make an important place for their careful consideration. But there is more.

Sixth, consider that the conceptual foundations of music education have already been laid. A field of inquiry called music education philosophy already exists. Our profession owes a large debt to a small group of scholars in this field, including Peter Dykema, Karl Gehrkens, James Mursell, Lilla Belle Pitts, Charles Leonhard, Harry Broudy, Abraham Schwadron, Bennett Reimer, and Keith Swanwick. But to suppose that all thinking that falls under the heading "music education philosophy" is equally valid is probably to assume too much. Systematic thinking about our philosophical inheritance is therefore imperative if professional practice intends to avoid misdirection and atrophy.

Indeed, a closer look reveals that while music education philosophy is well established, it is not well developed. At the time of this writing, philosophical thinking about music education consists in a small number of variations on one set of beliefs that has dominated the efforts of many scholars and teachers for more than fifty years.[3] This set of beliefs is commonly known as the philosophy of "music education as aesthetic education," or MEAE, for short. Unfortunately, there are compelling reasons to believe that the MEAE philosophy is theoretically and practically unsound, as several philosophers now argue[4] (and as I explain in Chapter 2).

Seventh, and more broadly, although every culture we know has something people would reasonably call music, many policymakers continue to deny music education a secure place in public schooling. Some claim that music is only important for a few "talented" children. Others claim that music has no real importance in human life and should therefore have no place in general education. These claims provide further incentives to think carefully about the nature and significance of music education.

Eighth, the questions raised by music teaching and learning form a kind of philosophical hub at the center of practical life. Like the spokes of a wheel, they take us to the heart of what it means to be human. They raise complex issues of knowing, meaning, thinking, feeling, teaching, learning, acting, and believing. (As Aristotle emphasized centuries ago: "It is not easy to determine the nature of music, or why anyone should have a knowledge of it."[5]) Accordingly, whatever people ultimately decide to say about human nature itself must make an important place for what people decide to say about music education.

Taken together, these eight points underline the fact that music and music education are serious matters that invite and demand critical thinking. But if this is so, then philosophy and music education have a necessary and important relationship. For critical thinking lies at the heart of what philosophy is.

2. Philosophy

Many people have a general idea of what *philosophy* means. The word pops up everywhere in a rough-and-ready way. We often hear it used in such familiar phrases as "my philosophy of life" or "the philosophy of the time." In this sense, philosophy refers to a grounding network of beliefs about this or that which people may find enlightening or inspiring. Music education's customary use of the term follows this tradition: "philosophy—some underlying set of beliefs about the nature and value of one's field."[6] Other people use the word more loosely to mean a basic set of operating principles or an overarching policy, as this advertising slogan suggests: "Our philosophy is to make a hamburger that's better than the other guy's." Then again, teachers will sometimes say things like "My philosophy is to teach children, not music" or "My philosophy of discipline is to be friendly but not familiar." In these circumstances, philosophy seems to connote a personal attitude, savvy, or sentiment that lies beyond the reach of formal scrutiny.

Most common notions of philosophy (including these) stem from a standard translation of the Greek word *philosophia* as "love of wisdom," from *philos* ("loving") and *sophia* ("wisdom"). But as John Passmore explains, the Greek sense of *sophia* was broader than our modern English sense of "wisdom."[7] To the Greeks, the verb *philosophein* also meant "to find out." Thus, says Passmore, "*philosophia* etymologically connotes the love of exercising one's curiosity and intelligence rather than the love of wisdom."[8]

Philosophers today tend to view philosophy as both a body of inherited knowledge and, more actively, the sustained, systematic, and critical examination of belief. Philosophy is not simply a collection of venerable ideas and arguments. Philosophy is something that people do by means of the strategies involved in systematic doubting, logical analysis, or critical thinking.

The "critical" thinker is the Greek *kritikos:* the person who acts as a careful judge of reasoning and belief to separate right claims from wrong. A critical thinker is a person who has both the disposition and the ability to assess the reasons people give in support of their concepts, claims, and actions. Consider the following conversation among three precocious children.

> *Jennifer:* You know, Rajeev, I've been thinking about whether there is a God, and I believe there is.
> *Rajeev:* I agree, Jennifer, but let me say why. Whenever I go out into the world I'm struck by the order and beauty I see. Everything seems carefully designed. This makes me think there must be a supreme designer. Furthermore, Jennifer, I know there's a God because my Uncle Charlie told me so!
> *Harry:* But Rajeev, when I look at the world I see many things that make me doubt there is any order at all. There are mosquitos, floods, out-of-tune singing, and aleatoric music. What I see is chaos, not design. There don't seem to be any good reasons to believe in a supreme designer. And furthermore, Rajeev, I know your Uncle Charlie, and he's a born liar!

Who is beginning to think critically in this discussion? Not Jennifer. She simply voices her opinion. In contrast, Rajeev and Harry are making an effort to supply reasons for their competing conclusions. The glaring exception is Harry's unsubstantiated accusation against Uncle Charlie. This is critical thinking in the vulgar sense of unsupported fault finding.

Like Jennifer, many people think in ways they never bother to examine. People acquire assumptions and beliefs from various types of authority: parents, peers, teachers, television, textbooks, and other sources. Belief *x* is absorbed passively, without scrutiny, and added to an unexamined set of beliefs *a, b,* and *c.*

In contrast, a philosophically minded person takes belief *x* and asks, "What grounds are there for holding this belief?" Among the first questions a philosophical person wants to have answered are these: "What do you mean?" and "How do you know?" Being philosophical is a matter of being precise, probing, analytical, skeptical, and discriminating. In short, an uncritical philosopher is no philosopher at all.

Wayne Bowman sums the essence of philosophy this way:

> Philosophy works to render the implicit explicit, with the ultimate intent of enriching both understanding and perception. Among its greatest allies is a persistent curiosity. Its enemies are the habitual, the stereotypical, the unexamined, the acritical, the "common sense" assumption or assertion. The philosophical mind critically challenges and explores received doctrine, renounces the security and comfort of dogma, exposes inconsistencies, weighs and evaluates alternatives. It explores, probes, and questions, taking very little for granted.[9]

Additionally, however, the philosophically minded person strives to balance systematic criticism with systematic understanding. For without a sincere effort to hear and believe what others are trying to explain, it is easy to play the doubting game on other people's beliefs alone, without playing it on our own beliefs. Suspending our disbelief long enough to give full consideration to another view has an essential purpose: it allows the force of another person's doubts about our assumptions to act with full effect.

Peter Elbow elaborates:

> [M]ethodological doubt is only half of what we need. Yes, we need the systematic, disciplined, and conscious attempt to criticize everything no matter how compelling it might seem—to find flaws or contradictions we might otherwise miss. But thinking is not trustworthy unless it also includes methodological belief: the equally systematic, disciplined, and conscious attempt to *believe* everything . . . to find virtues or strengths we might otherwise miss. . . .
>
> Methodological doubt caters too comfortably to our natural impulse to protect and retain the views we already hold. Methodological belief comes to the rescue at this point by forcing us genuinely to enter into unfamiliar or threatening ideas instead of just arguing against them without experiencing them or feeling their force. It thus carries us *further* in our developmental journey away from mere credulity.[10]

Many people make a practice of being philosophical about all sorts of meanings and meaningful pursuits. Accordingly, we find philosophies of most human phenomena, including philosophies of medicine, mind, law, education, emotion, sport, knowledge, literature, science, religion, mathematics, history, dance, music, legal education, medical education, mathematics education, science education—and, of course, music education.

3. Characteristics of Philosophical Inquiry

Philosophy is distinguished from other sorts of inquiry by particular kinds of goals, emphases, and strategies. There is no single thread that connects all philosophical efforts. Philosophers weave distinctive thought patterns using several typical threads, including the following:

1. *Philosophical inquiries are typically concerned with the "big picture."* This big-picture way of thinking is both a means and an end. It is a strategy for answering specific questions by considering them together, in relation, toward developing a comprehensive view of a problem or concept.
2. *Although philosophical thinking includes reflections on particular kinds of actions, situations, individuals, and objects, philosophy is primarily concerned with issues that cannot be addressed by observation, description, or experiment alone.* Philosophers tackle the reasons and methods for formulating claims and beliefs. In doing so, they attempt to clarify past and present understandings and to find ways of integrating knowledge acquired in different fields.
3. *The products of good philosophizing are not new facts but new perspectives on the assumptions, beliefs, meanings, and definitions that inhabit our thoughts and actions.* Philosophers deploy and develop methods of logical argument to make new connections, expose false assumptions, and refine specific problems over time. (The discovery and verification of new facts through observation and experiment belongs chiefly to science.) From this perspective, a philosophy of something does not simply rearrange what we already know. It casts existing understandings in new lights to derive new meanings and implications.
4. *Philosophers often synthesize and criticize past philosophical thinking on a topic to discover why others have been correct or mistaken.* Philosophers demonstrate the inadequacy of previous discussions by exposing the flaws in a thinker's basic assumptions; locating logical weaknesses in structured arguments; explaining a theory's omissions, oversights, or lack of comprehensiveness; and finding unjustified lapses in common sense. From this perspective, past philosophy is an important means for doing philosophy in the present. It provides a shared body of concepts, arguments, and supports—a priceless sourcebook on what other philosophers have held (rightly and wrongly) and why.
5. *Philosophy is not an independent field of inquiry in the same way that physics and chemistry are.* Philosophy presupposes a fund of expressed meanings and problems from other areas of human experience. These meanings and problems provide the departure points and targets for philosophical investigations. In this sense, philosophy is a helping enterprise. It makes the concerns of other fields its own concerns. And depending on the philosophers and the fields involved, a philosophical inquiry may also include recommendations for action.

In this book, I interlace these five threads to clarify the conceptual and practical fundamentals of music education. Indeed, philosophy has a practical target here. This is appropriate and unexceptional. It is appropriate because music education philosophy owes its existence and allegiance to the practical endeavors of music teaching and learning. It is unexceptional because for Socrates, as for Aristotle and many other philosophers, criticizing and building philosophical arguments was linked to the idea of living a good life. The goal, in part, was to contribute to society by developing understandings that would guide people's actions and reveal the natures of various social institutions toward improving them.

4. An Analogy

Although many teachers understand the benefits of a close working relationship between philosophy and music education, some do not. Some dismiss philosophy as ivory-tower conjecture on the far side of an unbridgeable gulf from classroom practice. Others oppose pre-service and in-service studies of music education philosophy in the belief that methods courses are the keys to professional success, or that serious thinking is unnecessary to the artistry of music teaching and learning. As one suspicious colleague put it: "Philosophy is like a pigeon: it's something to admire, as long as it isn't directly over your head."

Some criticisms of music education philosophy are justified. For philosophical thinking (like any form of inquiry) can be well or poorly done. Thus teachers are correct to reject illogical claims, arcane arguments, and dogmatic pronouncements. Additionally, philosophy can be well or poorly taught. Hence student teachers are correct to resist foundations courses that fail to make a central place for the development of critical strategies and reasoned principles through balanced investigations of competing views.

However, aside from these problems, there is no defence for the view that well-informed reflections on the basic concepts and issues of music education are unimportant in teacher education and professional development. Let me reinforce the link between philosophy and music education with the help of an analogy.

A philosophy is like a map, and doing philosophy is like map making. A map provides a comprehensive overview of a territory. It gives us our bearings. It helps us decide where to go and how to get there. Like a good map, a good philosophy can show us the best routes to our destinations based on careful considerations of the territory we want to travel. It may also point us to routes and destinations we never considered.

Of course, a map of Switzerland cannot give us the experience of living in Switzerland. It cannot even give us the details of the Swiss countryside we may want to see. But these are not good reasons for burning maps or shooting map-makers. A map will not tell you what it is like to live in Switzerland, but neither will living in Switzerland tell you what a map tells you. Maps are not useless things just because they are flat in comparison to the rich contours of actual experience. And surely map making is not a useless activity, even if it takes time and effort.

Some teachers who dismiss music education philosophy fail to acknowledge that a philosophy, like a map, has legitimate practical limitations. A map is not intended to atomize every feature it pinpoints. For example, the symbol used to mark the location to Zurich on a map is not expected to describe the condition of its streets. So while it is right to expect a map to provide guidance in conceptualizing and traveling a given territory, it is unreasonable to complain that a map omits to warn travelers of potholes in the road.

The parallel in educational terms is that even the best philosophy cannot be expected to predict or describe every contingency in every teaching–learning situation. No philosophy can be perfectly applicable to all practical situations. On the general nature of theories and their applications, the philosopher Kant said this: "[A] set of rules presented in a certain generality and with disregard of particular circumstances is called a Theory. . . . [T]he practitioner must exercise his judgement to decide whether a case falls under a general rule."[11] In other words, anyone who wants to develop or use a philosophy must be prepared to query its general directions in relation to daily details. The application of a philosophy to a practical situation is not a passive process of carrying out suggestions; it is an active process of asking questions about practicalities with the guidance of critically reasoned principles. As Harold Entwistle observes: "The job of a theory is to evoke judgement rather than rote obedience. The application of theory to practice is the bringing to bear of critical intelligence upon practical tasks rather than the implementation of good advice."[12]

Experienced teachers who reject philosophy often have an inborn fear of testing their practical procedures by reference to critically developed principles. Their main concern is the quality of the roads they travel in the classroom each day (that is, the nature of their teaching methods and materials). But however good teachers may be at using or building roads, it is essential that these roads take students to the right places. To suggest otherwise is to abdicate one's responsibility to think intelligently about why and how one ought to educate people.

The professional implications are clear. Pre-service and in-service teacher education programs ought to involve teachers in critical thinking and philosophy building in close connection with other fundamental aspects of their professional development. Indeed, pre-service teachers who are obliged to focus on methods courses at the complete expense of philosophical thinking are analogous to novice travelers who are given several pairs of shoes but no maps. How shall first time visitors find their way in New York? By sketching their maps as they walk? By asking fellow pedestrians about alternative destinations and routes? A mapless approach to New York is slow, unreliable, and dangerous. Both common sense and logic suggest a more reasonable way: orient travelers before their journey by examining reliable maps, discussing important destinations, planning appropriate routes, and identifying problem areas. Each traveler may then go on to refine his or her map as knowledge and experience accrue.

5. Three Intersections

The characteristics we have described begin to explain how philosophy can intersect music education on at least three related levels: the personal, the public, and the professional.[13]

Level One

To anchor, organize, maintain, improve, and explain music education requires *a* philosophy: a critically reasoned network of concepts and beliefs about the nature and significance of music education. Building and maintaining a philosophy requires critical thinking strategies and a personal disposition to use these strategies continuously. From this perspective, philosophy is for making up minds, not mending hearts, or curing cynicism, or filling one's soul with inner peace. In fact, being philosophical can be disturbing at times. For it is not easy to scrutinize cherished assumptions. And once begun, there is no guarantee that the quest for reasonable answers will follow familiar paths or lead back home to old beliefs.

At the same time, a philosophy can illuminate in ways that are inspirational. Getting the big picture can be uplifting. Raising one's vision from the trees to the forest can and does strike chords in people. In the words of Jonas Soltis, a philosophy is "both the engine that drives a person's commitment to educating and the rails that guide the way."[14]

Level Two

Various members of the public hold beliefs about the form and the content of music education. However vague or explicit, public beliefs are frequently packaged as promotional advertising or formalized in "mission statements" by governing bodies (for example, school boards, federal policymakers, and parent organizations).

It is in this second dimension that advocacy and philosophy can overlap. Philosophy seeks to explain the nature and the significance of music education through critically reasoned arguments. Advocacy seeks to build political and financial support for music education through calculated methods of persuasion. Advocacy is necessary, in part, because public policymakers do not always understand rational arguments and because the processes of public decision making are rarely free of irrational influences. Advocates can and should look to music education philosophy for logical arguments about the nature and the import of music education. In the end, however, winning political and financial support for school and community music programs often depends more on political savvy and marketing expertise than on a cogent philosophy.

It follows, then, that the quality of a philosophy of music education cannot and should not be assessed according to how well it translates into pep talks, bumper stickers, or television ads. The quality of a philosophy depends on its logical consistency in relation to the natures and values of music and education, and to the professional practice of music education.

Being philosophical at the intersection of music education and public policy means having the disposition and the ability to scrutinize claims made for and against music education and to garner support through logical argument whenever possible.

Level Three

There is a small but growing number of music education philosophers dedicated to critical thinking about the concepts, beliefs, policies, practices, and achievements of our field. Music education philosophers analyze professional discourse, probe past and present assumptions, scrutinize methodologies, and make curricular recommendations in relation to each of these dimensions. As a specific field of inquiry, then, the philosophy of music education is the sustained, systematic, and reasoned effort to examine the grounding ideas and ideals of music teaching and learning.

6. Aims

This book has three aims. The first is to develop a philosophy of music education—a critically reasoned concept of the nature and significance of music education. The second is to explain what this philosophy means (in general terms) for the organization and conduct of formal efforts to develop musical understanding. The third is to encourage a disposition in teachers to think philosophically as a regular part of their daily professional efforts.

Clearly, this book is not a how-to-do-it guide. It may be informative in this way. But its purpose is different. By developing a philosophy of music education, *Music Matters* offers something more fundamental and, therefore, more practical in the long term.

7. Premises

To map a territory, mapmakers must first take their bearings north, south, east, and west. The philosophical equivalents of compass points are orienting premises.

The premises of this book are two. The first is that the nature of music education depends on the nature of music. The second is that the significance of music education depends on the significance of music in human life. In other words, the most reasonable way to explain the nature and value of music education is to begin with an explanation of the nature and significance of music. If we can develop a cogent concept of what music is and why it matters, we can offer a reasonable explanation of what music education is and why it matters. Let me outline the thinking behind these premises.

Any term taking the form "*x* education" has at least four basic meanings: (1) education in *x*; (2) education about *x*; (3) education for *x*; and (4) education by means of *x*. By replacing *x* with "music," we arrive at four basic senses of the term *music education*.

1. Education *in* music involves the teaching and learning[15] of music making and music listening.

2. Education *about* music involves teaching and learning formal knowledge (or verbal information) about, for example, music making, music listening, music history, and music theory.
3. Education *for* music may be taken in two ways: either teaching and learning as preparation for beginning to do music or teaching and learning as preparation for a career as a performer, composer, historian, critic, researcher, or teacher.
4. Education *by means of* music overlaps with the first three senses since each can be carried out in direct or indirect relation to goals such as improving one's health, mind, soul, or bank account.

A fifth meaning of *music education* arises by construing *education* as a professional endeavor. A person earns credentials as a music educator and may thereby earn a reputation as well as a living. In this sense, *music education* indicates the professional practice of imparting knowledge in, about, for, or through music, depending upon one's beliefs about whether one, some, or all these senses are important.

Of course, these five senses only begin to address the complexities of music education. For taken by themselves, and in combination, they suggest many possible aims and goals for music teaching and learning. Some of these aims and goals are complementary; some conflict directly with others. If we add these complications to the possibility that music education may have other meanings, it becomes clear that philosophical inquiry has a central role to play in explaining what music education is and ought to be.

Where do we start? An obvious possibility is to begin by deciding the nature and value of education. Once we decide that, the place of music in the development of people might become clear. The history of music education philosophy contains several examples of this approach. But it has a fatal flaw. For the most important differences between, for example, science education, mathematics education, and music education lie not in what education makes of them but in the differences among and between science, mathematics, and music. In other words, without a prior sense of the nature and significance of music it is impossible to justify the place of music teaching and learning in any educational scheme, let alone explain how the values of music should be realized.

Another reason for beginning with a critically reasoned concept of music has to do with several important differences between *education* and *schooling* that theorists often overlook. As I explain in Chapter 12, schooling may be thought of as the medium of education. But because all forms of media influence what they convey, teachers need ways to monitor the extent to which local manifestations of schooling may be supporting or subverting their educational aims and efforts. A good philosophy of music education provides teachers with an aerial view of the relationships among music, teaching, learning, education, and schooling. Achieving such a viewpoint is a vital first step toward understanding and, perhaps, modifying the ways in which the functions, principles, and corollaries of schooling affect one's daily efforts on behalf of music education.

Again, then, the basic premises of this book are that in order to explain the nature of music education and why it matters, we must first understand what music is and why music matters.

8. Looking Ahead

Continuing on from the preliminary issues discussed in this chapter, Chapter 2 addresses the problems involved in explaining what music is. In the process, Chapter 2 also offers a brief analysis of the conventional aesthetic concept of music and music education. Until recently, the MEAE philosophy has largely escaped critical examination. In fairness to MEAE and to music education, we feel an obligation to help correct this situation. In addition, just as a strong visual background may help to clarify a foreground, a critical review of past thinking may help to clarify the new proposals put forth here. It also may explain why many philosophers and teachers today see a need for new philosophies of music education.

The seven chapters of Part II develop a philosophy of music as a basis for explaining the nature and significance of music education. The main line of argument in Part II proposes a multidimensional concept of music. Among other things, this concept contends that music making and music listening are unique forms of thinking and unique sources of the most important kinds of knowledge human beings can gain. The reasoning that supports these propositions allows music educators to affirm to themselves and others that music—as a unique form of thinking and knowing—deserves a central place in the education of all people.

An appropriate shorthand term for the philosophy developed in this book is a *praxial* philosophy of music education. The noun *praxis* derives from the verb *prasso,* meaning (among other things) "to do" or "to act purposefully." But when we use *prasso* intransitively its meaning shifts from action alone to the idea of action in a situation.[16] As Aristotle used the word in his *Poetics,*[17] *praxis* connotes action that is embedded in, responsive to, and reflective of a specific context of effort.

By calling this a praxial philosophy I intend to highlight the importance it places on music as a particular form of action that is purposeful and situated and, therefore, revealing of one's self and one's relationship with others in a community. The term *praxial* emphasizes that music ought to be understood in relation to the meanings and values evidenced in actual music making and music listening in specific cultural contexts.

Thus, and in contrast to conventional music education philosophy, this book refutes the belief that music is best understood in terms of the aesthetic qualities of pieces of music alone. Accordingly, *Music Matters* not only examines several aspects of music that the aesthetic philosophy fails to acknowledge, it recognizes several dimensions of musical works that MEAE overlooks altogether. In short, this praxial philosophy is fundamentally different from and incompatible with music education's official aesthetic philosophy. As such, it offers music educators a clear alternative to past thinking.

On the basis of the philosophy developed in Part II, Part III proposes a new concept of curriculum and curriculum making for music teaching and learning. The book ends with a broad perspective on the relationships between music education and schooling.

9. Using the Book

Since *Music Matters* hopes to spur critical thinking and individual philosophy building, it will work best if readers debate its contents carefully by internal dialogue and by discussion with others. To facilitate these efforts, I have divided the chapters of this book into numbered sections. As shown in the table of contents, this numbering outlines the logical development of the discussion. In addition, each chapter ends with several questions that you, the reader, may find useful for individual or group reflection, orientation, review, and discussion after (or before) examining the contents of that chapter. Also, the final pages of each chapter provide an annotated list of supplementary sources that you may wish to consult for further reflections on key ideas in the main text.

Since this book intends to further music education, I will sometimes explain my practical proposals in relation to the three typical music students (Clara Nette, Tim Pani, and Sara Band) introduced at the beginning of this chapter. In doing so, I hope to encourage you to relate the themes of this philosophy to individual students and teaching situations in your own experience.

Last, please note that the concepts and arguments in this book unfold gradually. There are several lines and layers of thinking that continue to develop from chapter to chapter, as one might expect with any topic as rich and complex as music education. In the case of musical performing, for example, Chapter 3 introduces several lines of thought that continue to develop in Chapters 5, 7, and 9. Similarly, Chapter 4 introduces a concept of music listening that is elaborated in Chapters 5, 6, and 8. Thus, the complete pattern of thinking will come into view only if the reader steps back and considers the discussion as a whole, at the end of the book, isolating no details prematurely as more or less important than the others.

10. End of the Beginning

What already exists in music education philosophy has been accomplished by scholars whose dedication is well known. Accordingly, neither the aims nor the sincerity of this book's intentions are distinctive. Moreover, what is put forth here is unlikely to replace completely what has already been done, let alone discourage others from producing alternatives. Still, within these admissions is the hope as well as the conviction that this philosophy will, like a good map, lead where others mislead and therefore help you on your way (instead of up the creek).

Questions for Discussion and Review

1. Give eight reasons (or more) why music education demands and deserves critical thinking. (For further reflections on this topic, see the discussions by Jorgensen and Sparshott listed below).

2. Examine newspapers, advertisements, journal articles, television or radio programs, and so on for three contrasting uses of the term *philosophy*. What *is* philosophy? What distinguishes philosophy from other forms of systematic inquiry?

3. Distinguish between (1) the philosophy of music education and (2) a philosophy of music education. How can a philosophy of music education benefit music teachers? music students? school administrators? parents? school boards? others?

4. Should music teacher education programs include courses in music education philosophy? Why?

5. Explain the advantages and disadvantages of grounding a philosophy of music education in (1) a philosophy of music and (2) a philosophy of education.

6. State five possible meanings of the term *music education*. What does each meaning imply for music teaching and learning?

7. What philosophical viewpoint has dominated music education for several decades? Why is it important to think critically about past and present contributions to music education philosophy?

8. What does the term *praxial* forecast about this book's concept of music and music education?

Supplementary Sources

Estelle Jorgensen. "On Philosophical Method." In *Handbook of Research on Music Teaching and Learning,* ed. Richard Colwell, pp. 91–101. New York: Schirmer Books, 1992. Jorgensen examines the nature and value of philosophy in relation to music education.

Wayne Bowman. "Philosophy, Criticism, and Music Education: Some Tentative Steps Down a Less Travelled Road." *Bulletin of the Council for Research in Music Education,* no. 114 (Fall 1992): 1–19. Bowman makes a strong case for *being* philosophical about music teaching and learning.

Francis E. Sparshott. "Education in Music: Conceptual Aspects." In *The New Grove Dictionary of Music and Musicians,* vol. 6, ed. Stanley Sadie, pp. 54–58. London: Macmillan, 1980. A perceptive summary of the issues and problems involved in the concept of music education.

James R. Johnson. "Joy and Process: A Philosophical Inquiry." *The Quarterly Journal of Music Teaching and Learning* 2, no. 3 (Fall 1991): 22–29. Johnson probes the characteristics of philosophy conceived as a process of inquiry.

Jay F. Rosenberg. *The Practice of Philosophy: A Handbook for Beginners.* Englewood Cliffs, N.J.: Prentice Hall, 1984. Chapter 1, "The Character of Philosophy," offers an engaging discussion of philosophical thinking.

Jonas F. Soltis. *An Introduction to the Analysis of Educational Concepts.* Lanham, Md.: University Press of America, 1985. An excellent primer of philosophical analysis.

2

Toward a New Philosophy

What is music? The question is more difficult than any within its scope. Yet some systematic answer must be given. A philosophical concept of music is the logical prerequisite to any philosophy of music education.

But where do we begin to say what music is? And how do we proceed? In Chapter 2 I attempt to answer these questions in five steps. Step 1 reviews three basic problems facing anyone who wants to develop a philosophical concept of anything. Step 2 clarifies what we need to say about music. Step 3 considers alternate ways of saying what music is. Step 4 examines the way past music education philosophers have said what music is. Finally, Step 5 explains this book's starting point and procedure.

1. Three Problems

Ideally, the process of developing a philosophy should be regulated by a strict concern for comprehensiveness, objectivity, and methodological purity. But these ideals are problematic in several ways.

First, no philosophy can be comprehensive in the omnipotent sense of providing the whole truth and nothing but the truth. A philosophy can never say all there is to say about something. At the same time, however, a philosophy can and should explain what something is all about. What this means in the present case is that the professional practice of music education ought to rest upon a philosophical concept of music that is constructed from as many logically related perspectives as possible. If such a concept were to be developed, it would have an important advantage: it would take priority over narrower concepts of music and over the philosophies of music education built upon them. This does not mean that all disputes about music and music education would automatically dissolve. Being more comprehensive (and therefore logically prior to something else) is not a guarantee of superiority. It is only an assurance that the concept includes as many considerations as it is reasonable to include.

Practically speaking, then, what comprehensiveness really amounts to is a pledge to develop (1) a range of guiding questions that ensures as wide a scope as possible, and (2) a consistent network of answers that addresses the full range of problems raised by these questions. In this view, a comprehensive philosophical concept of music is something we can and should strive for.

Objectivity is a more difficult problem. In philosophy, as in science, objectivity is an ideal, not a reality. How so? We tend to view scientific research as the epitome of objective inquiry: concrete, impartial, and dispassionate. The media depict scientists as purveyors of cold, hard, facts. But these portrayals are inaccurate. Scientists, like philosophers, have individual attachments, goals, and beliefs. Researchers of all kinds work in relation to past and present theories, traditions, and priorities. Personal interests inform each investigator's choice and definition of a problem, as well as his or her assumptions, methods, and results. This explains, in part, how different scientists working on the same problem can (and often do) produce dramatically different experimental results.

This book's philosophy of music and music education is not perfectly objective. For it is unlikely that just anyone would make a public point of asking "What is music?" and "What is music education?" As the philosopher Francis Sparshott suggests, any reader who picks up a book like this one already understands (or has the right to expect) that the person doing the asking has a serious interest in the questions under discussion and a sense of what the answers might be.[1] The reader expects that the author is asking these questions to underline the importance of asking, or to suggest that there may be problems with the initial questions, or to prepare the reader for new possibilities. In sum, no philosophy can be completely objective because a philosophy of something (no less than a scientific theory of something) can never be without personal and professional interests.

In terms of procedure, the ideal way to build a philosophy of music education would be to select a method that includes both a starting point and a series of steps to follow. Unfortunately, while methods of conceptual analysis and logical argument exist, none provides everything we need. As Sparshott points out, "[T]here is no method for selecting methods."[2] In addition, no method will tell us where to begin. We must figure this out for ourselves. Last, a method, like a bicycle, does not steer itself. Decisions must be made about the direction and the application of any set of strategies as different problems arise. So, in developing a philosophy, the best one can do is highlight one's assumptions, note why certain lines of thought are followed, why others are abandoned, and why succeeding lines of thought are or are not taken up.

2. Explaining Music

The first task of this inquiry is to say what music is all about. Let us make "all about" more precise. There are at least six different things we need to say about music somewhere in this discussion.

The first thing we need to explain is the nature of music. We must explain what we mean when we call something *music*. In doing so, we must be careful to distinguish between the question "What is music?" and the question "What is a work of music?" Most discussions falsely assume that these two questions are the same. As the philosopher Jerrold Levinson reminds us, saying what music *is* does not depend on saying first what kind of thing a *work* of music is: "We can determine what it is to count something as an instance or occasion of music without deciding precisely what ontological characterization pieces of music should receive."[3] Second, there is the *significance* of music: what is it about music that qualifies it for a role in human existence? Third, as Sparshott suggests,[4] we need to consider what people think of as "music," and what people tend to think of music *as*. Fourth, what is it that we loosely and comfortably call music, although we know very well that it does not fit exactly what most people mean by the word? Fifth, we need to examine the grounds for the decisions we make about whether to call something music depending on the context in which it takes place.[5] What is it that sometimes causes us to call something music instead of communication, invocation, entertainment, worship, background, or protest? Sixth, we also might want to say something about why we are troubled when people call something music, even though we have a vague sense of what they might mean.

It follows from these reflections that although *music* is a word, and although most people have some sense of what it means, the question of what music is will not be answered satisfactorily by a concise definition. Requests to reduce complex phenomena such as music to simple descriptions are as absurd as they are common. They ignore the fact that the things to which we assign words do not all take the same form. Although language makes it seem so, there is no one way to capture everything in our verbal nets by applying clear-cut rules of classification. Some things, like an apple, have a core; some, like an onion, do not. Some things, like a tree, follow branching patterns; some, like a butterfly, transform. Some, like music, are conceptually delicate and intricate, like branching trees and transforming butterflies.

3. Beginning and Proceeding

There are several ways of beginning and proceeding to explain the nature of music. Twelve come to mind at the outset. Since some of these ways are more theoretical than others, and since a full discussion of each would slow our progress unduly, I will concentrate on four of the most common.[6]

The most familiar way of beginning is to assume that music is a matter of humanly organized sounds and silences. But, as Levinson suggests,[7] while sounds and silences are a necessary dimension of music, they are not sufficient. The reason for this is that although my speaking voice and the ticking of a clock (and the throbbing of an engine and the babbling of a two-year-old) are all instances of humanly organized sounds and silences, they are not examples of what most people count as music.

A second way to begin is to say that music is a matter of humanly organized musical sounds and silences in the sense of deliberately designed melodic, harmonic, rhythmic, timbral, and textural patterns. This starting point won't do for two reasons. First, although melody, harmony, and the other qualities may be typical features of some music, they are not necessary features of all music.[8] For example, the *kete* drumming of the Asante people of Ghana has nothing Westerners would call melody, but it surely counts as music. The same holds for *Ionisation* by Edgar Varèse. Then again, a typical lullaby sung by the Zuni Indians of western New Mexico has nothing Westerners would call harmony, but it surely counts as music. So too with examples of, among other possibilities, psalmodic plainsong. In other words, the specific auditory means and ends of music around the world are inherently unstable. The audible features of musical achievements often evolve to the point of producing new ways of thinking about music and new means of music making. As a result, this second way of beginning is too ambiguous. It fails to provide the solid launching pad we need.

A third way of beginning is to decide what most people seem to take as the key to their personal experiences of music listening. The most popular version of this approach is to assume that all music everywhere is a matter of humanly organized sounds and silences that evoke or express human feelings. The objection to this approach is that while our experiences of music often involve feelings in one way or another, so do many other aural experiences, including the sounds of a child in pain or the sorrowful words of a bereaved father. Accordingly, neither the evocation nor the expression of emotion is a necessary or sufficient feature of all music. As Levinson suggests, something like George Crumb's *Makrokosmos* "seems neither the embodiment of a creator's inner state nor a stimulus to emotional response in hearers, but rather an abstract configuration of sounds in motion and/or a reflection of some nonindividual—or even nonhuman—aspect of things."[9] Whether Levinson is correct about *Makrokosmos*, his main point remains: "[M]usic cannot be defined by some special relation to emotional life; no such relation holds for *all* music and *only* for music."[10]

A fourth way of beginning and proceeding is to assume that music is aesthetic in its nature and value. At root, the aesthetic concept of music is an elaborate combination of the three problematic notions we have so far reviewed. Because the aesthetic concept has dominated music education philosophy for so long, it is important to unpack its grounding assumptions rather carefully now. In the process, I will also attempt a brief summary of the origin and development of aesthetics.

4. The Aesthetic Concept of Music

People often use the words *aesthetic* and *aesthetics* interchangeably to refer to beauty, fine art, and the theoretical study of beauty and fine art. In fact, the original meaning of *aesthetic* (sometimes spelled esthetic) had little if any link to the idea of beauty. It derives from the Greek word *aisthesis*, meaning "sense experience," or perception.[11] Thus, as Ralph Smith explains, "the term aesthetic . . . suggests the perception and contemplation of things rather than their creation—looking, listening, or reading rather than making."[12] The idea of aesthetics as a philosophical or scientific enterprise developed from a scholarly interest in this perceptual interest.[13]

The term *aesthetics* was coined in 1735 by a young German philosopher, A. G. Baumgarten (1714–1762).[14] By aesthetics Baumgarten meant something more definite than the philosophical study of beauty. Baumgarten wanted to establish and name a new field of inquiry that would do for the analysis of poetic imagery what logic had done for the analysis of conventional reasoning.[15] From an initial concern with poetry, the boundaries of aesthetics widened rapidly during the eighteenth and nineteenth centuries to include the study of the visual images and objects of painting, the effectiveness of music conceived as "works" and, eventually, all natural things (for example, sunsets, flowers, and landscapes). Theorists who considered the beauty of poems, paintings, and other artistic creations to be no different from examples of natural beauty deemed aesthetics the study of beauty.[16] Theorists who considered the beauty of poems, paintings, and musical works important because of what differentiated such beauty from natural beauty deemed aesthetics the theory of the arts.[17]

Of course, the philosophical study of artistic pursuits was ongoing long before Baumgarten's arrival. Western philosophical thinking about music began with the Greeks. But the Greeks had a different concern from Baumgarten (1714–1762), Lord Shaftesbury (1671–1713), Francis Hutcheson (1694–1746), and other European thinkers who contributed to the development of aesthetics.[18] The Greek concern is rooted in Plato's *Symposium*. Plato, who was interested in people's attraction to so-called impractical pursuits, focused on the nature of this attraction and what it revealed about human nature in general. The idea of music, painting, and poetry as products, objects, or "works" was not central in Plato's thinking. In fact, the original Greek meaning of *art* had much more to do with process than with product. To the Greeks, *art* meant *an organized set of informed actions and understandings directed to making changes of certain kinds in materials of a certain kind.*[19] But when the issue of people's attraction to impractical things was taken up again in the eighteenth century, art took on a different meaning and art objects or "works of art" became the focus of concern.

How so? Until the middle of the eighteenth century, there was no such thing as the grouping people now call the "fine arts": painting, sculpture, architecture, music, and poetry.[20] Part of the reason for this was that prior to the founding of aesthetics in the eighteenth century there was no theoretical basis for uniting these otherwise distinct pursuits. Aesthetics provided the required theory. According to the aesthetic concept, painting, sculpture, architecture, music, and poetry are collections of objects, works, or *aesthetic objects* that exist to be contemplated in one special way—with a "disinterested" (or nonpractical and distanced) attitude of *aesthetic perception*. To look at or listen to something *aesthetically* means to focus exclusively on its structural or *aesthetic qualities*, in abstraction from the object's context of social use and production. To what end? To achieve a special kind of experience called *aesthetic experience*.

The term *fine arts* originally meant "arts of beauty": arts devoted to producing beautiful objects. In this context, beauty means "that of which the very apprehension gives pleasure."[21] The value of fine art objects therefore lies wholly in their

aesthetic qualities as contemplated. From this we see that the defining characteristics of the fine arts overlap with the defining assumptions of the aesthetic concept
to the point that the fine arts may also be called the arts of the aesthetic.[22] In sum,
the original Greek sense of art was gradually overshadowed by the aesthetic notion
of art as fine art, meaning a class of special objects to which one directs aesthetic
perception.

Let me recast the above discussion in terms of music. The aesthetic concept of
music rests on four basic assumptions. The first assumption is that music is a
collection of objects or *works*. The second assumption is that musical works exist
to be listened to in one and only one way: aesthetically. To listen to musical works
aesthetically means to focus exclusively on their so-called aesthetic qualities, the
elements or structural properties of musical works: melody, harmony, rhythm, timbre, dynamics, and texture and the organizational processes (e.g., variation, repetition) that give form to these qualities. The third assumption of the aesthetic
concept is that the value of musical works is always intrinsic or internal. Most (but
not all) aesthetic theorists believe that the value of music lies exclusively in the
structural properties of musical works alone. The fourth assumption is that if listeners listen to pieces of music aesthetically, they will achieve (or undergo) an
aesthetic experience. The term *aesthetic experience* refers to a special kind of emotional happening or disinterested pleasure that supposedly arises from a listener's
exclusive concentration on the aesthetic qualities of a musical work, apart from
any moral, social, religious, political, personal, or otherwise practical connection
these qualities may embody, point to, or represent.

5. The Aesthetic Concept in Context

Consider, next, that the aesthetic concept of art (as fine art) is not based solely on
philosophical thinking about artistic pursuits. It belongs to something larger. Coincident with the aesthetic concept of art was the social transformation of European
society, a transformation that began around the turn of the eighteenth century in
Great Britain and Germany. The assumptions anchoring aesthetics, both then and
now, are inseparable from the Romantic ideology that emerged from and influenced
the social changes surrounding the decline of the European aristocracy and the rise
of the new middle class. As Terry Eagleton explains in *The Ideology of the Aesthetic* (1990), ''[t]he construction of the modern notion of the aesthetic artefact is
. . . inseparable from the construction of the dominant ideological forms of modern
class society.''[23]

At the heart of this new age and ideology was the belief that all men (but not
women) were free, equal, and self-sufficient. The old social order, based on inherited wealth and privilege, was being overturned. The new ideology emphasized the
autonomy of the individual and, therefore, the irrelevance of an individual's background. What counted in the new social order was not social or material inheritance
(context) but inner worth. Whereas European society had previously been controlled by arbitrary laws handed down from the aristocracy, social harmony came

to rest increasingly in the individual's personal sensibilities, taste, and self-discipline.

The heavy emphasis that past and present aesthetic theories of music place on the acontextual, intrinsic, "distanced" contemplation of objects duplicates the basic tenets of this social ideology. The autonomous musical work (like the autonomous individual) was to be valued in terms of innate properties alone. Eagleton puts it this way: "Like the work of art as defined by the discourse of aesthetics, the bourgeois subject is autonomous and self-determining."[24]

In summary, the assumptions underlying the aesthetic concept of music belong to a particular period of Western history and a definite ideology that saw its full flowering in the Romanticism of nineteenth-century Europe.

Let me connect this perspective to key aspects of Western music history. As I have already said, the Greeks did not think of music as a product-centered art but as a performance art. Musical performances in antiquity were valued as powerful forms of social, moral, and political expression.[25] Among the consequences of this sociopolitical concept of music was the subordination of instrumental music to vocal music. For in the Greek view, the sounds of instrumental music had an important deficit: they had no discernable way to convey meanings and, therefore, no means of making a worthy contribution to a rational and moral society.

This view continued long past antiquity into the Enlightenment. Until the last decades of the eighteenth century, music was understood chiefly as a performer's art geared to the functional demands of the wealthy patrons and institutions that supported and controlled the musicians of the time. Indeed, most composers before 1800 had little control over decisions affecting the music they produced for church and court functions, including decisions about instrumentation, text, and form.[26] Moreover, because the conditions of their employment required a steady stream of adaptable music, composers frequently combined original, reworked, and borrowed musical ideas in the form of incomplete scores and parts that they or their fellow performers would fill in on the spot during performances.[27] Accordingly, composers before 1800 did not usually think in terms of producing precisely notated scores for the preservation and perfect performance of their original musical ideas, and performers did not think in terms of instantiating completely formed and enduring creations.

The upshot is that prior to the late 1700s most European musicians had neither the intent nor the opportunity to pursue music as an independent, product-centered art.[28] Thus there was no standard way of referring to musical achievements. More importantly, as Lydia Goehr details in *The Imaginary Museum of Musical Works* (1992), the idea of a *work* of music—a fixed creation existing independently of its many possible performances—had limited (if any) influence in European musical practices.[29]

These circumstances began to change in the mid- to late-eighteenth century when several factors combined to produce a new concept of music as a nonfunctional, commodity-based art. As the social transformation of Europe gathered momentum, musicians developed aspirations for artistic and economic independence, including a desire to elevate instrumental music to a more respectable level of worth. These desires intensified as musicians gained freedom from prevailing guild restrictions and the powerful restraints of ecclesiastical and aristocratic patrons. Alongside these developments, the search was on for a theory that would explain the nature and value of instrumental music as a self-sufficient yet serious art form.[30]

The product-centered aesthetic theory, which was grounded in a concern for the literary and visual arts, provided a way of liberating music from its long association with intangible performances and social values. Aesthetic theorists reconstructed the achievements of instrumental music in terms of a hypothetical object called the *musical work,* a permanent yet ideal entity that exists above and beyond its physical score and any single performance of that score.

Goehr elaborates:

> [M]usic had to find a plastic or equivalent commodity, a valuable and permanently existing product, that could be treated in the same way as the objects of the already respectable fine arts. Music would have to find an object that could be divorced from everyday contexts, form part of a collection of works of art, and be contemplated purely aesthetically. Neither transitory performances nor incomplete scores would serve this purpose since, apart from anything else, they were worldly or at least transitory and concrete items. So an object was found through projection. . . . The object was called "the work."[31]

The work-concept of music not only provided musicians with a theoretical equivalent to the tangible and highly valued objects of painting and sculpture, it served to conceal music's social and performative aspects by diverting attention away from musical processes to musical outcomes conceived as autonomous objects. In these ways, music gained a place among the commodity-based fine arts.

The aesthetic theory also provided a way to elevate the artistic and economic status of instrumental music. Instrumental sounds were recast as the purest of aesthetic qualities because they seemed to lack any connection with the ordinary world. Theorists deemed instrumental music the ultimate aesthetic art because its sonic materials transcended all worldly matters and, therefore, offered listeners direct transport to the Sublime, the Infinite, or Beauty in the sense of pure aesthetic emotion. Nineteenth-century theorists touted the formal purity of instrumental music as divine: as embodying a higher form of Truth. In this view, instrumental music was not a functional means to an end, but an end in itself.

To further purify the nature and value of music-as-works, theorists invented a number of subsidiary concepts. Composers were conceived as divinely inspired geniuses whose creations exist in an ideal world that performers strive to enter by being faithful to a work's written score.[32] These principles of ideal permanence and separability from the world were reinforced by the notion of aesthetic perception, a code of listening that obliged nineteenth-century audiences to cooperate with musicians in stripping musical sounds of their social and practical links with the world for the purpose of entering the quasi-religious realm of aesthetic experience.[33]

In sum, the most accurate use of the term *musical work* is in relation to so-called serious or classical instrumental music of nineteenth-century Europe. The work concept is one component of the aesthetic concept of music as a product-centered art. It posits a fictional object that exists in an ideal world apart from any physical score and any single performance of that score. Thus to think of musical achievements as works of music is to import a cluster of specific theoretic assumptions, including the idea that music is a matter of fixed, fully formed, and enduring objects that require exact notation, perfect performance, and aesthetic perception.

Since the late 1700s, the aesthetic concept of music as a work- or object-centered art has become so familiar that many people (including many philosophers) fail to recognize its historicity, let alone its force. They assume that it is natural to think of all music everywhere as works of music. They then proceed to analyze and evaluate the outcomes of all music making (including jazz, African drumming, and Baroque choral singing) as musical works in the Romantic aesthetic sense.[34]

To end this section of the discussion, let me return to the word *aesthetics* which floats among several meanings like a boat without an anchor. Today *aesthetics* is commonly used in three different ways: broadly, loosely, and tightly. Broadly, aesthetics is an umbrella term for all philosophical and scientific inquiries even remotely concerned with the existence of beautiful things, with people's response to beauty, and with artistic efforts and people's responses to them.[35] Loosely, aesthetics is used as a synonym for the philosophy of art. Tightly, aesthetics refers to that large collection of philosophical theories that embraces the grounding assumptions of the aesthetic concept.

Aesthetics, in this third sense, names a doctrine. It identifies a particular way of thinking about music, painting, dance, and so on. As I have outlined, the aesthetic way of thinking depends on the eighteenth-century axioms of (1) aesthetic object, (2) aesthetic perception, (3) aesthetic qualities, and (4) aesthetic experience and their corollaries: the notions of fine art, taste, connoisseurship, aesthetic emotion, and autonomous works. Granted, there have been countless variations on the aesthetic concept during the past two hundred years or so. But its central themes remain largely intact. Thus, the more precise meaning of aesthetics is "that branch of philosophy that is concerned with the analysis of concepts and the solution of problems that arise when one contemplates aesthetic objects."[36]

Properly understood, then, aesthetics is not a synonym for the philosophy of art (or the philosophy of music), as commonly believed. In the case of music, there is a long line of Western philosophical thinking that originated with the Greeks and flourishes today unencumbered by the eighteenth- and nineteenth-century assumptions of the aesthetic concept.[37] Nevertheless, these assumptions have become so well established in the philosophical literature that they have acquired doctrinal status.

The same is true for the philosophical literature of music education. Most music education philosophers have embraced the aesthetic concept of music wholly and uncritically. Accordingly, our main philosophical inheritance is nothing more or less than a series of variations on these same aesthetic themes. Although it is beyond the scope of this chapter to examine every variation (the subject of this book is a philosophy of music education, not a history of music education philosophy), it is quite possible to trace the long-standing domination of aesthetic assumptions through a brief survey of important writings in the field.[38]

6. The Aesthetic Concept of Music Education

One of the first to conceptualize music education according to the aesthetic concept of music was the pioneering music education philosopher James Mursell (1893–1963). Mursell published twenty-three books and many articles between the late 1920s and the late 1950s. Although Mursell was inconsistent in his applications of aesthetic assumptions, his writings explain most tenets of what is now known as the philosophy of music education as aesthetic education.

In essence, Mursell held that if music was to yield its educational value, then "it must be taught and learned with a primary emphasis upon its esthetic aspects."[39] Mursell's concern was the development of aesthetic responsiveness through concentration on the aesthetic qualities of musical works. He believed that the value of music lies in the capacity of musical sound patterns to re-present or objectify human feeling. The following passage from Mursell's *Human Values in Music Education* (1934) summarizes his aesthetic beliefs:

> Music paints no picture, tells no story, stands for no system of articulate concepts. It does not directly symbolize anything at all beyond itself. It is design in sound. Often it seems to be just itself, and nothing else, and to have no outer meaning whatsoever. Yet this is not precisely true. The great creative artist, let us say, has some profoundly moving experience. In his music he does not, and indeed cannot, tell us of its detail. He does not paint for us the sunset, recount the love affair, tell the story of a tragic loss. But he takes the emotional essence of that experience and crystallizes it in tone. Of all the sensory media, tone is most closely connected with emotion. This is a psychological fact. Thus music is the most purely and typically emotional of all the arts. Here we find its essence. This must be our chief clue to its proper educational treatment, for it is the central secret of its human appeal and its power in the lives of men. Education in and through music must mean, first of all, participation in noble and humanizing emotion.[40]

Harry Broudy (1958) summarizes the aesthetic concept of music education in these words: "We are interested primarily in music as a type of aesthetic experience. In aesthetic experience we perceive objects in order to grasp their sensuous characteristics and not *primarily* to further knowledge or useful enterprises."[41]

In *Foundations and Principles of Music Education* (1959), Charles Leonhard and Robert House hold that the only basis for music education is the development of people's responsiveness to the aesthetic qualities of musical works.[42] In line with Mursell, Leonhard and House claim that musical patterns symbolize the general forms of feeling.[43] They conclude that music education ought to "carry the major load of aesthetic education in all organized general education"[44] by developing the ability of students to perceive and respond aesthetically.[45]

In his *Aesthetics: Dimensions for Music Education* (1967), Abraham Schwadron recommends that music educators concern themselves with the development of aesthetic perception and with fostering aesthetic experiences "so that such experiences may occur more often and at more subtle levels of response."[46] Although Schwadron takes a broader sociocultural view of music than most of his peers, his essential claims remain congruent with the axioms of MEAE.

To Keith Swanwick (1979), "music education is aesthetic education."[47] Swanwick believes that listening is a matter of relating to a musical object as an "aesthetic entity" through aesthetic experience.[48] In *Music, Mind and Education* (1988), Swanwick reaffirms his belief that music education ought to be primarily concerned with the "aesthetic raising of consciousness."[49]

G. David Peters and Robert Miller (1982) maintain that musical meaning is the result of perceiving and reacting aesthetically to the formal and technical qualities of musical objects.[50] Peters and Miller assert that "the best use of music in the schools and the best reasons for the inclusion of music in the curriculum stem from music as part of what has been known as 'aesthetic education.' "[51]

The most complete statement of the aesthetic concept of music education is Bennett Reimer's *A Philosophy of Music Education* (1970, 1989). Like his predecessors, Reimer conceives of music as a collection of "objects" or "art works."[52] The "aesthetic or expressive elements of music," says Reimer, "are rhythm, melody, harmony, tone color (including dynamics), texture, and form."[53] To Reimer, the meaning and value of musical works are internal: "They are functions of the aesthetic qualities themselves and how they are organized."[54] Accordingly, music education "must be so arranged that aesthetic experience is central."[55]

This persistent emphasis on the aesthetic way of thinking invites us to ask what the alleged value of aesthetic experience might be? Several theorists have formulated explanations during the past two hundred years. The explanation adopted by Mursell, Leonhard and House, Reimer, Swanwick, and most other music education philosophers in this century belongs to a theory of music developed by the esteemed philosopher Susanne K. Langer (1895–1985). Langer's key claim is that the aesthetic qualities of musical works capture and represent the *general* forms of human feelings (tension and resolution, motion and rest, rise and fall).[56] In this view, listening to music aesthetically provides listeners with a special kind of knowledge or "insight" into the general forms that feelings supposedly take. Langer defines art as the "creation of forms symbolic of human feeling."[57] She concludes that if "the arts objectify subjective reality," then "art education is the education of feeling."[58]

Leonhard and House rest their case for music education on Langer's central claim that "[m]usic bears a close similarity to the forms of human feeling and is the tonal analogue to the emotive life."[59] Following the same line of thought, Reimer repeats Langer's idea that the aesthetic qualities of musical works give listeners knowledge of "how feelings go."[60] Reimer continues: "[M]usic education is the education of human feeling, through the development of responsiveness to the aesthetic qualities of sound."[61] Similarly, Swanwick holds that music "helps us *explore* feelings" because music "structures feeling."[62] In his *Music, Mind and Education,* Swanwick credits the importance of Langer's theory to his own work during the past thirty years and notes his continuing enthusiasm for her idea that "music is a way of knowing the life of feeling."[63]

In summary, past music education philosophy is remarkably consistent. And its lineage is clear. It is grounded in the eighteenth- and nineteenth-century assumptions of the aesthetic concept generally and in Langer's theory particularly.

7. Against the Aesthetic Concept of Music Education

Viewed historically, it seems fair to say that the philosophy of music education as aesthetic education is one of the most influential formulations in the development of our field. Moreover, in the process of refining MEAE its founders and advocates not only advanced systematic thinking in music education but carved a central place for philosophy in the theory and practice of music teaching and learning. In particular, Bennett Reimer's many contributions made MEAE the focus of inquiries differing widely in purpose, motivation, and method during the 1970s and '80s. As a result, generations of music teachers have been reared on its beliefs, countless research publications have assumed or repeated its aesthetic claims, and numerous music curricula have incorporated its recommendations.

But while MEAE's place in history is not in dispute, its value as a philosophy certainly is. During the past thirty years, the decline of the aesthetic concept has been steady and dramatic among scholars in the philosophy of music, the sociology of music, musicology, ethnomusicology, curriculum theory, and (more recently) in music education. Included among those who oppose the aesthetic doctrine (in whole or in part) are Francis Sparshott, Arnold Berleant, Philip Alperson, Wayne Bowman, Landon E. Beyer, Arthur Danto, Susan McClary, Rose Rosengard Subotnick, John Shepherd, and Nicholas Wolterstorff.[64]

To Arnold Berleant, the notions of aesthetic object, aesthetic perception, and aesthetic experience are "anachronistic" and "manifestly unsatisfactory" in accounting for most examples of music and the other arts during the twentieth century.[65] Moreover, says Berleant, they are misleading even when applied to the artistic pursuits of earlier periods. Landon Beyer urges us to reject the reductionist notion of aesthetic perception[66] and the "empty aesthetic doctrine"[67] of aesthetic experience that diminishes the meaning of artistic products. Arthur Danto suggests that the aesthetic concept segregates artistic pursuits from life "in a manner curiously parallel to the way in which calling woman the *fair* sex is an institutional way of putting woman at an aesthetic distance—on a kind of moral pedestal which extrudes her from a world it is hoped she has no longer any business in."[68] To Danto, the aesthetic concept is as "savage" and indefensible as the old view that women as "ladies" belong in parlors "doing things that seemed like purposive labor without specific purpose—viz., embroidery, watercolor, knitting: essentially frivolous beings, there for an oppressor's pleasure disguised as disinterested."[69]

For what reasons do scholars object to the aesthetic concept of music? A full answer would fill several books. I focus on three notions that affect music education directly: the notions of music-as-object, aesthetic perception, and aesthetic experience. In doing so, I am aware that I am not providing an exhaustive account of all writings that support and oppose the aesthetic concept of music education.[70] I am also aware that I often combine variations on the MEAE philosophy that may deserve to be separated. I suggest, however, that the thrust of contemporary thinking in the philosophy of music and music education tends to support the arguments below.

Music-as-Object

Aesthetic theories mistakenly assume that the question "What is music?" is the same as the question "What is a work of music?" Indeed, as Carl Dahlhaus points out, "the idea that music is exemplified in works, no matter how firmly it has become rooted in the past century and a half, is far from self-evident."[71] Nicholas Wolterstorff agrees: "[T]he presence of music in a society requires neither composition nor works . . . before ever there were *works* of music, there was music."[72] Even in Western cultures, where composing and compositions are conspicuous features of our musical traditions, compositions do not exist in isolation from performing and improvising but rather exist in direct relation to the elaboration and development of music performance and improvisation.

Pieces of music are a central part of what music is. But it is unreasonable to assume from the outset that an explanation of musical works (in any sense of the term) will yield a comprehensive understanding of the nature and value of music. Beginning with this assumption only invites the possibility of producing a narrow and implausible concept of music and, therefore, a narrow and implausible philosophy of music education. Such is the case, I believe, with the MEAE philosophy. Its myopic focus on autonomous works is problematic in several theoretical and practical ways.

First, past music education philosophy consistently fails to provide critically reasoned explanations of the nature of music making in general (performing, improvising, composing, arranging, and conducting) and performing in particular. Its narrow concentration on musical works causes it to underthink and, therefore, to undervalue the process dimension of music: the actions of artistic and creative music making. (Recall that the aesthetic concern is "the perception and contemplation of things rather than their creation—looking, listening, or reading rather than making."[73]) In place of critically argued explanations, past philosophy offers inconsistent and unsubstantiated opinions about these fundamental aspects of music and music education.

The writings of Leonhard and House, Broudy, and Reimer typify this deficiency. For example, at the outset of *Foundations and Principles of Music Education* Leonhard and House claim that faulty music education programs include those "with undue emphasis on performance."[74] This theme has been echoed by many advocates of the MEAE philosophy. But what logical arguments ground this assertion? What is the nature of musical performing? And what does it mean to perform music well? Past philosophers fail to provide reasonable answers to these basic questions. To Leonhard and House, performing is a matter of "skill" and "technique" rather than musical knowledge.[75] But what are the meanings of these terms and the grounds for these alleged distinctions? Why and how is performing skill different from musical knowledge? Leonhard and House neglect to explain.

Broudy holds that as an end in itself, performance is merely "skill training."[76] By skill he means "using a wrench or piling brick upon brick."[77] But Broudy omits to support these problematic claims. Without logical foundation, he proceeds to recommend that if music educators are serious about making teaching a genuine profession, then performing ought to be viewed as a *means* to musical understanding rather than as an end in itself.[78]

Reimer echoes Broudy. Singing and playing instruments, says Reimer, are educational "means behaviors,"[79] even in performance-based programs. In Reimer's version of MEAE, performing is deemed "*the* major means for musical experience" in the performance program; in the general music classroom, performing is viewed as "*a* major means."[80] Not surprisingly, then, Reimer decries the strong emphasis that music educators place on musical performance in some general music programs and in Kodály and Orff programs.[81] He claims that music education's traditional emphasis on excellent performing ensembles is askew—the unfortunate result of teacher education programs that place a strong emphasis on applied studio lessons, expert performers, strong performing ensembles, and excellent concerts.[82] Reimer urges music educators not to be "sucked into this professional whirlpool."[83]

Bowman disagrees:

> This [Reimer's] remarkable metaphor is far from benign. Not only does it raise unfortunate questions about school music's commitment to musical excellence, it erects barriers where bridges are needed: surely a great deal of extraordinarily effective *musical education* goes on in the applied studio and in the ensemble experience. In fact, one dares suggest it is in precisely these settings that many of our most enduring and profound musical learnings occur.[84]

To Swanwick, "musical objects are the focus of musical experience and therefore of music education."[85] Here again, the music-as-product focus leads to fuzzy notions of performing. "Performance," says Swanwick, "involves a sense of presence, the presence of a vital musical object, developing and on the move; . . . The performer's special role is to mediate directly between the work and its auditors."[86] In a more recent discussion, Swanwick tells us only that "performance skills . . . are essentially imitative in emphasis."[87] In short, Swanwick also neglects to develop a critically reasoned concept of music performance.[88]

This lack of critical thinking about performing (and all other forms of music making) extends to the related concept of musical creativity. Music education philosophers tend to substitute murky Romantic reflections for systematic analyses of this important concept.[89] To Reimer, for example, creativity is a matter of "exploring" and "discovering" expressiveness in relationship to "feelingful qualities."[90] He claims that when music students are making musical decisions while performing, they deserve to be called creative: "When they are sharing in the making of musical decisions . . . they will be producing music creatively."[91] Reimer believes that even novice music students who produce three tones together are involved in "creating" and "creative tasks" because they are making personal decisions about how their tones ought to go.[92]

In this view, a beginner's toots are as creative as a solo by Wynton Marsalis. Is it reasonable to claim that anyone who makes a musical decision while singing or playing, or explores feelingful qualities (whatever this means), is automatically "creative"? I think not. As I explain in Chapter 9, aesthetic notions of creativity fail the tests of logic and common sense. More practically, they fail to provide realistic goals and guidelines for music educators faced with the daily challenges of teaching children to make music "creatively."

Consider, next, that the aesthetic notion of music-as-object encourages an educational emphasis on musical consumption rather than active and artistic music making. The educational aim of conventional philosophy is not to develop every student's musicianship or musicality. The aim is to develop every student's ability to listen to music in one particular way: aesthetically.[93] Thus, aesthetic education curricula focus on the development of aesthetic perception and reaction (or aesthetic sensitivity) primarily through listening lessons keyed to recordings.[94] "Teacher-proof" lesson plans are organized and sequenced in relation to verbal concepts about the aesthetic qualities of *musical works* in the nineteenth-century aesthetic sense. The MEAE philosophy views general music students not as active music makers, not as future "amateurs," but (in Reimer's words) as "consumers of music."[95] In addition, and without probing the cognitive connections between listening and performing, past theorists tend to separate perceiving and producing in discussions of the general music curriculum, as if the ability to listen to music intelligently were unrelated to the ability to perform music intelligently, and vice versa.

But as I explain in this book, listening and performing are intimately related, both cognitively and educationally. Past music education philosophy severely underestimates what it takes to listen to and to make music well because it fails to examine the intricate relationships among listening, performing, and the performative nature of music. Moreover, and contrary to the aesthetic philosophy, I shall argue that the ability to cognize the structural properties and designs of musical works is only one dimension of the musical understanding students require to achieve the values of music and music education.

Because of its focus on the consumption of aesthetic objects, past philosophy also promotes an illogical educational dichotomy. On one hand, says Reimer, there ought to be listening-based general music programs for the majority of students.[96] On the other hand, there ought to be elective performance-based programs for others. The MEAE philosophy assumes that musical performing is not a viable educational end for all children. A musical double standard is taken for granted: one kind of music curriculum for the majority of students, another for the rest.

Using an entirely different concept of musical understanding, I argue in Chapters 10 and 11 of this book that achieving the values of music and music education requires that all music students develop the same kinds of musical knowings in essentially the same kind of curricular context. I shall argue for a particular kind of "situated" music curriculum and curriculum-making process that counters the conventional divisions between so-called general music students and performance students.

In summary, past music education philosophy is remarkably weak in a fundamental regard: it neglects to consider the nature and importance of music making. Its educational pronouncements have been put forth in the absence of critically reasoned positions on musical performing, improvising, composing, arranging, and conducting; on the relationships between music making and music listening; and on the nature of musical creativity. As Estelle Jorgensen suggests, rigorous distinction making "has been less evident than it should be in music education."[97] Music education philosophers, says Jorgensen, "need to better clarify the meaning of the concepts they employ, and make more penetrating distinctions than they have in the past."[98]

Is it possible to argue that music is more than a collection of autonomous aesthetic objects? It is not only possible, it is essential to a comprehensive understanding of music and music education. Is it reasonable to argue that authentic music making is a viable educational end for all students? I believe it is. For upon analysis, performing, improvising, composing, arranging, and conducting are much more than skills or "means behaviors." This praxial philosophy will argue that *all forms of music making involve a multidimensional form of thinking that is also a unique source of one of the most important kinds of knowledge human beings can gain.* In particular, I shall argue that musical performing ought to be a central educational and musical end for all students (so-called general music students and otherwise). I shall also propose that becoming a creative music maker involves a special kind of learning process that students can both engage in and learn how to deploy themselves.

Aesthetic Perception

The aesthetic concept of music education is reductionistic in two basic senses. As I have explained, it begins with the implausible claim that music is a collection of objects. It then proceeds to narrow our musical understandings and experiences even further by insisting that listeners always listen aesthetically—with exclusive attention to the formal designs of musical works (in the nineteenth-century sense). For an experience to be truly musical, says Reimer, listeners must perceive and respond to the aesthetic qualities of music alone.[99] In this view, listening for relationships between musical patterns and matters of a religious, moral, social, cultural, historical, political, practical, or otherwise nonstructural nature is to listen "nonmusically."[100] Aesthetic listening is a matter of "immaculate perception."[101]

Notice that the aesthetic philosophy defines listening via a negative norm. To listen aesthetically is not to connect musical sounds to other human concerns. Reimer adopts the semitechnical language of eighteenth-century aesthetics to say the same thing: our disposition as listeners must be "intrinsic," "disinterested," and "distanced."[102] As Sally Markowitz suggests, the aesthetic doctrine directs listeners to act like musical microbiologists by placing the musical object against a blank background before focusing clinically on its structural properties alone.[103] In addition, the MEAE philosophy insists that all music everywhere—all music across all cultures—ought to be listened to in the same narrow way.[104]

It seems clear enough from this discussion that teaching music students to "perceive and react" aesthetically amounts to inculcating the ethnocentric ideology of a bygone age. It involves homogenizing the diversity of musical endeavors and musical products worldwide by (1) imputing a single purpose to all of them, (2) imposing a single mode of response on all their listeners, and (3) attributing a single motivation to all music makers and music listeners everywhere.

But the imposition of a uniform method of listening on the music of all times and places is the antithesis of what is most observable about the production and experience of music: its diversity, nonuniformity, and ambiguity—even with respect to its cognition. MEAE's claim that listening aesthetically is the most valuable, appropriate, or "musical" way of listening promotes a normative rather than a descriptive paradigm of listening.[105] It is analogous to claiming that Puritanism is the one true form of religious understanding.

I have no quarrel with the notion that music listening is related in a central way to the cognition of musical patterns (melody, harmony, and so on). What I shall argue in later chapters, however, is that truly knowledgeable listening is never a matter of listening to structural patterns alone. I propose to explain that works of music always involve several interrelated dimensions of musical meaning. Accordingly, there is no one way to listen for all musical works, as past music education philosophers typically maintain.

In other words, I propose to overhaul the aesthetic concept of musical works. This is necessary for several reasons. First, it is useful to have a general term that stands for the several kinds of musical achievements that music makers produce across cultures. Second, it is important to keep the term *musical works* because it provides a connection with what we most need to change in the conventional philosophy of music education.[106] Third, because the original notion of musical works is weak and ambiguous in several obvious ways, the pathway to change is reasonably clear.

Indeed, there are numerous counter-examples to the norms and characteristics claimed by the aesthetic notion of musical works. For example, where is the ideal and permanent work-object in jazz? In most cases, jazz musicians do not seek to comply with a precise score. Instead, the traditions and obligations of jazz performance usually require noncompliance in the sense of original deviations from and improvisations on melodic themes and harmonic patterns. In short, jazz improvisation makes it impossible to speak of one and the same ideal work being instantiated in different performances. The same holds for many kinds of folk music and avant-garde productions that allow performers various opportunities to participate in the realization, elaboration, decoration, and origination of musical patterns.

Now consider the claim that musical works are abstract entities because they are not susceptible to definitive performances. Rock and pop musicians would disagree. Hit songs are often conceived and produced as unambiguous and meticulously recorded performances that their originators often duplicate exactly in live performances.

What shall we say about the aesthetic corollaries of the work-concept? Clearly, European musical practices before the late 1700s did not conceptualize music making and music listening in terms of aesthetic objects, aesthetic qualities, aesthetic perception, or aesthetic experience. Not even Bach's music was made or listened to under aesthetic descriptions.

In summary, to apply the work-concept and its aesthetic corollaries to the production, audition, or teaching of music outside nineteenth-century European instrumental music is to impose a set of alien concepts that misrepresent the natures and values of these achievements. It is tantamount to what Lydia Goehr calls "conceptual imperialism.''[107] As I shall explain later, the work-concept and its aesthetic corollaries also diminish the richness and complexity of the nineteenth-century instrumental achievements they were originally intended to serve.

How can we modify the aesthetic idea of works to achieve a more reasonable concept of musical products? The process is already under way. We have begun to open and neutralize the aesthetic notion of works by confronting its basic assumptions and by challenging its claim of universal and absolute validity. From this point on I shall use the term *musical work* to indicate neither a real nor an ideal object but any *audible* musical achievement, such as a heard musical performance, an improvisation, or a rendition. The next step (which I begin in Chapter 4) is to develop a new content for the musical work-concept based on a range of flexible dimensions that provide for the possibility that different kinds of music may involve different kinds and combinations of musical expression, meaning, or information (in the broadest sense of the term).

Indeed, because of its devotion to aesthetic perception and the Romantic concept of works, past music education philosophy fails to provide music teachers with reasonable answers to three important sets of questions: (1) Can musical sounds be expressive of specific emotions (such as happiness or sadness)? If so, how? If not, why? (2) Can musical sound patterns characterize people, places, and things? If so, how? If not, why not? (3) Is it possible for music to influence or be influenced by its cultural contexts? If so, how? If not, why not?

Reimer attempts a partial answer. He claims that although musical meaning and value are always internal to the aesthetic qualities of music,[108] it is still possible for so-called extramusical references (''the words of songs, the story in program music''[109]) to become part of the ''internal form'' of a work. Reimer claims that extramusical references are ''always transformed'' by being ''dissolved'' in or ''swallowed''[110] by musical elements ''[a]s salt adds flavor to a stew, losing its character as grains of salt but adding a particular flavor to the stew.''[111]

Reimer's claim that the meaning and value of music are always internal yet not always internal (not referential, but sometimes referential) defies logic and common sense. But even if we grant the possibility that outside references are somehow dissolved in or swallowed by musical sounds, how do listeners identify and understand these references in their dissolved or swallowed states? Reimer neglects to explain.

Swanwick offers a more plausible view of the musical expression of emotions. He acknowledges that musical sounds can be charged with affective meanings. He then attempts to support his claim by invoking a theory of resemblances between human movements and the characteristics of musical patterns.[112] But while Swanwick's explanation makes sense as far as it goes, it fails to explain the larger issues of why and how such expressions ''stir and move people.''

Some aesthetic educators acknowledge the failure of MEAE in this area. For example, while Leonhard and House and Reimer maintain that listening for ''outside'' references in musical works is nonmusical, Peters and Miller[113] argue that musical sounds are concerned with carrying ''concrete information'' and that listening for such meanings is musical. In saying so, however, Peters and Miller open a very large can of worms. For their acknowledgment only underlines what opponents of MEAE already argue: that the notion of aesthetic perception is illogically restrictive and that the meanings and values of musical works may be largely (if not entirely) nonaesthetic. Wayne Bowman puts the point directly:

> I do not believe, personally, that music (or anything else for that matter) has "intrinsic" value, but that all value is grounded. As such, I conceive musical education as a quest fundamentally committed to the illumination, recognition, and understanding of musical values: values which are multiple, diverse, divergent, and often indeterminate.[114]

These thoughts begin to explain why the notion of aesthetic perception is, at best, suspicious.

Aesthetic Experience

The chief characteristic of aesthetic experience is that its value is intrinsic: "the value of the experience comes from its own, intrinsic, self-sufficient nature."[115] Reimer continues: "Aesthetic experience serves no utilitarian purpose. It is experience for the sake of experience in and of itself."[116]

The theoretical notion of aesthetic experience is problematic in several ways. First, it rests on a logical contradiction that Leonhard, Reimer, and others have decided to overlook. On one hand, these writers insist that the aesthetic experience is self-sufficient, disinterested, and impractical. On the other hand, they claim that the primary value of aesthetic experience (and aesthetic education) is knowledge of human feeling—an extrinsic benefit. As Philip Alperson observes, "the main justification for music education [as aesthetic education] ends up being the eminently practical functions of the acquisition of knowledge and the improvement of sensibility."[117] In short, past philosophy holds, illogically, that aesthetic experience is and is not utilitarian.

Second, as Landon Beyer notes, the disinterested and distanced nature of aesthetic experience "has the latent effect of producing people who regard experiences as pregiven, predefined, and something to be responded to rather than constructed."[118] This is so because "disinterested" conduct is depersonalized. Both aesthetic perception and aesthetic experience require listeners to divest themselves of all individual, social, and practical concerns. Beyer explains the consequences of disinterested and distanced perception:

> In separating aesthetic experiences from our other activities and interactions . . . we are doing something more than affording them some special status: we are also lessening the possibility of their being a life force, in the sense of providing insight into situations, events, and circumstances, that can redirect our thoughts and actions. . . . [119]

The effect of this approach to aesthetic experience is to produce rather passive, disengaged percipients, who have as their central posture the need to let the isolated, disconnected object dominate experience. The role of the aesthetic participant is one of passive recipient of images and surface features, a role which places little emphasis on the active construction of meanings in an interaction with the object itself. The work of art as object—in its ahistorical, asocial abstractness—is dominant and controlling, the aesthetic participant rather passive and restrained.[120]

A third problem concerns the alleged value of the aesthetic experience. Recall from my discussion earlier in this chapter that MEAE depends heavily on Susanne Langer's theory of music. Langer claims that musical works are a special kind of symbol that represent the *general* forms that feelings take.[121] To perceive and respond to the aesthetic qualities of musical works (and other works of art) is to gain a special kind of knowledge or insight into how feelings go. In this view, the aesthetic qualities of music are the one and only source of its singular value and, therefore, the proper focus of educational efforts. (Recall that Langer is also the source of MEAE's pivotal slogan: that "music education is the education of human feeling."[122])

At a distance, Langer's theory is attractive. But on close inspection, even sympathetic critics acknowledge major flaws in the logic of its main ideas.[123] (Since extensive criticisms of Langer's theory are available elsewhere,[124] I will not detail another one here.) In brief, I believe Langer's theory is correct to the limited extent that some listeners may hear some musical patterns as expressive of tension and release (or conflict and resolution). But this does not begin to explain the nature and value of musical works (let alone *music* in the more comprehensive sense I examine later in this chapter). For why would anyone want or need insight into the general forms of feeling? There is nothing to distinguish these general forms from any number of natural and artificial patterns, including the ebb and flow of waves on a beach, the expansion and contraction of a rubber band, or, as Reimer suggests, "the gathering storm, its energy, its dissolution."[125]

In other words (as several scholars maintain), musical sound patterns are by no means unique in doing what Langer and her followers claim. Hence there are no logical grounds for Langer's most basic assumption that music (every piece of music everywhere!) is a unique type of "unconsummated symbol" that "educates" listeners about general forms of feelings.[126]

Moreover, Langer and her followers ask us to accept the dubious claim that the insight (or education) that people apparently seek and gain in music listening vanishes from the mind and cannot be retained by human memory in the absence of musical sounds. If this were so, then music listening would be eminently frustrating and, therefore, something that most people would avoid. But this is not what we find. Many music listeners seem to experience genuine enjoyment while listening to music (another point that Langer fails to explain).

In sum, music education's traditional explanation of musical value falls flat. At best, it comes to little more than this: musical sound patterns represent the general patterns of an infinite number of indistinguishable natural and artificial processes that are already available in countless objective forms. Such a weak and implausible "explanation" does little to secure and guide music education.

The last problem concerns a fundamental issue of musical experience. Do musical sounds arouse actual feelings in listeners? Past philosophy is logically confused about the answer. On one hand, Leonhard and Reimer (and their followers) repeat the central themes of Langer's theory that denies that music can arouse affect. All music can do, says Langer, is reflect the general forms of feeling.[127] ("Music," says Langer, "is not the cause or cure of feelings."[128]) On the other hand, these same music educators repeat the themes of an early book by Leonard B. Meyer (*Emotion and Meaning in Music*, 1956) that claims the exact opposite: that musical sound patterns do arouse affect in listeners.[129]

This basic contradiction puts music educators in an awkward position. Do we believe past philosophers when they tell us (via Langer) that music listening does not arouse actual affect? Or do we believe them when they tell us (via Meyer) that music listening does arouse affect?

And there is yet another problem. For Meyer's theory (like Langer's) is also logically flawed. (Again, since extended criticisms of Meyer are available elsewhere,[130] I will not take the time to impart another one here.) Suffice it to say that Meyer relies on several incomplete (if not false) assumptions about the nature of emotion and the conditions that produce it. Most important, Meyer claims that emotion is aroused when a tendency to respond is inhibited and (by extension) that musical affect is aroused when a listener's musical expectations are frustrated.[131]

But as the philosopher Malcolm Budd and others point out, the frustration of an expectation is neither a necessary nor a sufficient condition for the arousal of emotion.[132] And even if we grant that the frustration of musical expectations may account for certain instances of musical disappointment or surprise, the inherent negativity of Meyer's main claim fails to explain the positive affect that performers and listeners often seem to experience while making and listening to music. For these and many other reasons, Meyer's *Emotion and Meaning in Music* does not provide a reasonable explanation of the nature and value of musical works (let alone music considered in a more comprehensive sense).

I suggest that during several decades the conventional philosophy of music education as aesthetic education has developed into a highly systematic set of beliefs. Yet, as I have attempted to explain, several basic assumptions and principles of the MEAE philosophy are logically suspicious, if not invalid. If so, then an important issue arises. For, as James Borhek and Richard Curtis point out, if even one basic principle in a highly systematic set of beliefs is invalid, then all the others must be considered suspicious, if not invalid:

> For highly systematic belief, any attack upon any of its principles is an attack upon the system itself; if one principle is abandoned, all the others must be, too. Therefore, the greater the degree of system, the greater the importance of negative evidence for the whole belief system. . . . In consequence, a systematic belief system is at the mercy of its weakest element.[133]

In summary, I suggest there are several good reasons to believe that music education's traditional doctrine of music education as aesthetic education fails to provide a logical and comprehensive philosophical foundation for music teaching and learning.

8. Toward a New Philosophy

If past ways of explaining music are unsatisfactory, what other choices do we have? Where do we start, and how do we proceed to explain the nature and significance of music?

I wish to suggest that there is a self-evident principle lying behind, beneath, and around our musical involvements that provides us with an indisputable starting point for building a comprehensive concept of music. This principle has been hit upon directly and indirectly in centuries of writing and thinking about music. It is implicit in the repertoire of procedures and guiding questions Aristotle used to address difficult questions. Nicolai Listenius touches upon it in his *Musica* (1537).[134] Carl Dahlhaus underlines it in his reflections on the nature and value of music.[135] And several contemporary philosophers, including Sparshott, Wolterstorff, Alperson, and Walhout, state the idea directly.[136]

This self-evident principle is best expressed as an orienting question that Aristotle might have used to get an inquiry such as this under way. Regarding the human phenomenon we call music, let us ask ourselves the following: Is there any sense in which music is a human activity? Both common sense and logic answer yes. Without some form of intentional human activity, there can be neither musical sounds nor works of musical sound. In short, *what music is, at root, is a human activity.* Here is a certain starting point that leads to a multipart way of explaining what music is and why it matters. Let me elaborate.

In the case of Beethoven's "Eroica" Symphony, or the *kete* drumming of the Asante people, or a Zuni lullaby, or Duke Ellington's *Cotton Tail,* and in every example of a musical product that comes to mind, what we are presented with is more than a piece of music, a composition, an improvisation, a performance, or a "work" in the aesthetic sense. What we are presented with is the outcome of a particular kind of intentional human activity. Music is not simply a collection of products or objects. *Fundamentally, music is something that people do.*

In the case of the "Eroica," a human being named Ludwig van Beethoven did something. What he did was to compose and conduct something in the context of a specific time and place and a specific kind of music making. In the case of *Cotton Tail,* a person named Duke Ellington did something. What he did was to compose, arrange, perform, improvise, and record something in the context of another time and place and another kind of music making.

More broadly still, recall that it is entirely possible to have musical sounds without notated compositions, as a glance around the world will quickly confirm. In many cultures, music is not a matter of revered pieces, as Westerners tend to think; music is a matter of singing and playing instruments. And even in the West, where composers and compositions are the norm, there are many kinds of musical situations in which the actions of singing and playing (in the intentional sense) take precedence over music in the narrow sense of esteemed works.[137]

Several points follow from these conclusions. First, if music is essentially a form of intentional human activity, then music must necessarily involve at least three dimensions: a doer or maker, the product he or she makes, and the activity whereby he or she makes the product. But this is obviously incomplete. For in any

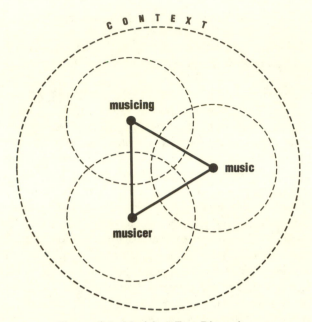

FIGURE 2.1. Musicing: Four Dimensions

instance of human activity, doers do what they do in a specific context. ("Context" comes from *contexere*, meaning "to interweave, join, or weave together." By "context" I shall mean the total of ideas, associations, and circumstances that surround, shape, frame, and influence something and our understanding of that something.)

Music, then, is a four-dimensional concept at least (Figure 2.1). Music is a tetrad of complementary dimensions involving (1) a doer, (2) some kind of doing, (3) something done, and (4) the complete context in which doers do what they do. Let us refer to musical doers as *musicers*,[138] to musical doing as *musicing*, and to the musical "something done" as *music* in the sense of performances, improvisations, and other kinds of audible musical achievements. (Please note that the term *musicing* is a contraction of music making. I shall most often use *musicing* in the collective sense to mean all five forms of music making: performing, improvising, composing, arranging, and conducting. On some occasions, however, I shall make it plain from the context of the discussion that I am using *musicing* as a synonym for performing or for one of the other four kinds of music making.)

Recall, now, that what we are in the middle of building is not a theory of music but a comprehensive way of proceeding to say what music is. Proceed how? Our four-dimensional approach can be enriched a further four times by looking at each of the original four dimensions from four different directions: head-on, in back, in front, and around. For example, we can look straight at what is done (Figure 2.2, Beethoven's "Eroica"), and in front of it (what it leads to), and in back of it (where it comes from), and around it (the immediate context of its use and production).

Similarly, the musicing itself (including the composing, performing, and conducting of the "Eroica") may be looked at (1) head-on, as the outcome of system-

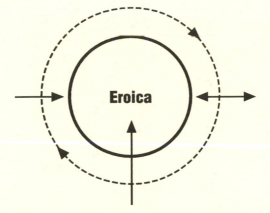

FIGURE 2.2. Four Directions of Investigation

atic action on its own, (2) in back, in terms of motivated action, (3) in front, as goal-directed action, and (4) around, as action in a context of similar actions. This procedure can be repeated for the musicer(s) and for the immediate contexts pertaining to the musicer, the musicing, and the musical work done, as well as for the complete context itself (Figure 2.3).

We now have a multipart way of proceeding to say what music is. We have four related dimensions of music as a human activity. Each dimension can be considered from four different perspectives. The word *related* is crucial. For in addition to having natures and values of their own, each dimension has an inevitable link with all the other dimensions. In fact, these four dimensions are not merely linked; they form a dynamic system of dialectic relationships. Musicers act and react in relation to the musical feedback inherent in the quality of their own music making. They evaluate their musicing and musical works in relation to the context of their actions: the accomplishments and reflections of mentors and peers past and present. And because the relationships formed between and among these four musical dimensions require the intersection of contexts that are social (at least in part), we can expect these relationships to generate beliefs and controversies about who counts as a good musicer, about what counts as good music making, and so on. This last point leads to our next line of thought.

We just said that the four basic dimensions of music are not merely linked. They form a dynamic system of exchange and feedback: doers are influenced by the musical consequences of what they do and make, as well as by what their mentors and peers think about what they do. Clearly, then, musical doing always includes another kind of doing called music listening. Music makers listen to what they do and make and to what other musicers do and make. The kind of doing we call music listening is therefore an essential thread that binds musicers, musicing, and musical products together.

But there is more. Linked to each kind of music making is a group of people who act specifically as listeners (auditors, or audiences) for the musical products of that kind of musicing. In the case of Bulgarian bagpiping, there are Bulgarian

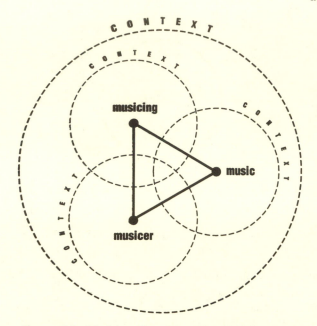

FIGURE 2.3. Musicing: Four Dimensions with Contexts

bagpipe listeners; for Baroque choral singing there are Baroque choral audiences; for dixieland jazz there are dixieland fans. Viewed in context, music makers are influenced by why and how their audiences (including themselves) listen to what they do. Conversely, listeners are influenced by why, what, and how musicers do what they do.

It follows from this that the intentional human activity of music listening forms another four-dimensional set of relationships (Figure 2.4). Musicers and/or listeners are doers of another sort who engage in another kind of doing called music listening. What listeners "get done" (or mentally construct) in the cognitive act of listening are the auditory experiences we call music, or what Sparshott dubs listenables (sounds to listen for).[139] Again, each of these four dimensions and their contexts can be considered from four different perspectives: head-on, in back, in front, and around.

Consider how far we have traveled. Beginning with the self-evident principle that music is a human activity, we have arrived at the more elaborated view that music is a multidimensional human phenomenon involving two interlocking forms of intentional human activity: music making and music listening. These activities are not merely linked; they are mutually defining and reinforcing. Let us call the human reality formed by this interlocking relationship a *musical practice* (Figure 2.5).

By "practice" I mean not the rehearsing and refining that goes on in practice studios but "practice" in the larger sense of a shared human endeavor. A human practice is something a group of people organizes toward some kind of practical end. Human practices pivot on shared ways of thinking and shared traditions and standards of effort. A human practice, says Sparshott, is "something that people

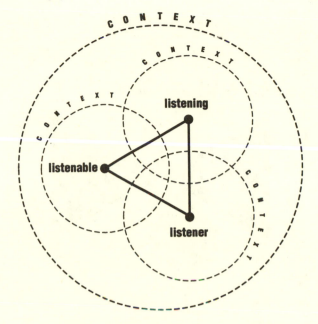

FIGURE 2.4. Music Listening: Four Dimensions

do, and know they do, and are known to do."[140] For example, whereas precise surgical cutting is not a practice, heart surgery is; and whereas singing pitches in tune is not a practice, operatic singing is (and blues singing is, and so on).

Physicians, teachers, lawyers, athletes, and music makers are practitioners who engage in the practices of medicine, education, law, sports, and music. More specifically, we often talk about physicians as surgeons, pediatricians, ophthalmologists, and radiologists. Physicians are practitioners of a practice called MEDICINE that has various subpractices, subspecialities, or "arts" of medicine.

Similarly (but not exactly), musicers are practitioners of a human practice called MUSIC that has various subpractices, subspecialities, or arts of music that go by such names as jazz, choral music, rock music, and opera. The subdivisions, of course, continue. For example, what we commonly call jazz is really a cluster of related musical subpractices that go by such names as dixieland, swing, bebop, cool, and hard bop. (We could follow a similar process of subdivision for choral practices, opera, rock, and so on). And of course, MUSIC, like many practices, is something people can do (and learn to do) without being or becoming licensed professionals.

The fundamental theme I wish to draw from this discussion, and emphasize strongly, is the following: MUSIC *is a diverse human practice.* Worldwide, there are many (many!) musical practices, or "Musics." Each musical practice pivots on the shared understandings and efforts of musicers who are practitioners (amateur or professional) of that practice. As a result, each musical practice produces music in the sense of specific kinds of musical products, musical works, or listenables. These products are identifiable as the outcomes of particular musical practices because they *evince* (manifest, or demonstrate) the shared principles and standards of

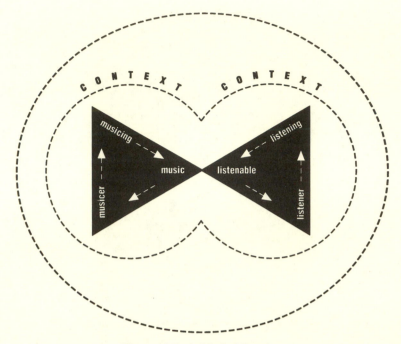

FIGURE 2.5. A Musical Practice

the musical practitioners who make them. This is how we know Baroque choral
singing, bebop jazz improvisation, Balinese *kĕbyar,* and Korean *kayagûm sanjo*
when we hear them: by the stylistic features manifested in the musical sound patterns themselves. Specific musical practices eventuate in distinct musical styles.

A musical *style* is a body of musical products that share certain auditory features
in common. These commonalties are explained by the fact that the musicers and
listeners of a musical practice share a certain set of musical beliefs, understandings,
and preferences in common.[141] Again, for example, bebop musicians may be seen
as musical practitioners who produce a specific body of music (performances, improvisations, compositions, and arrangements) in relation to bebop understandings,
standards, and traditions. (And of course, bebop-ers may or may not know how to
make the music of many other musical practices.)

Clearly, some musical practices are much more closely related than others. For
example, most jazz practices pivot on the principles of Western tonal music. Accordingly, most jazz practices exhibit several style characteristics in common with each
other and, more broadly, with many so-called Western European classical practices.

A useful way to tie these thoughts together is to alter the visual form of the
word music in three different ways—MUSIC, Music, and music. MUSIC is a diverse
human practice consisting in many different musical practices or Musics. Each and
every musical practice (or Music) involves the two corresponding and mutually reinforcing activities of music making and music listening. This is what I have attempted to capture visually in the interlocking triangle forms in Figures 2.5 and 2.6.
The word music (lowercase) refers to the audible sound events, works, or listen-

FIGURE 2.6. MUSIC: A Diverse Human Practice

ables that eventuate from the efforts of musical practitioners in the contexts of particular practices.

In conclusion, the springboard principle of music as a human activity provides a self-evident way of beginning to explain the concept of music in all its dimensions, as well as several related ways of proceeding. Which ways shall we select? We have no choice. To select any one direction of thought over another would bias our inquiry from the outset. We must use them all. We must consider all these dimensions and their interrelationships as they contribute to our understanding of the nature and significance of MUSIC as a diverse human practice. Taken together, these various dimensions and directions of thought provide a blueprint for constructing a philosophy of MUSIC on which to base a philosophy of MUSIC education. This is the task of the next seven chapters.

Questions for Discussion and Review

1. Explain three basic problems involved in developing a philosophy of music and music education.

2. Outline four (six, eight, ten, twelve, or more) ways of beginning and proceeding to explain the concept of music. What problems inhere in each approach? (In addition to reviewing sections of this chapter, consult footnote 6).

3. What does the term *aesthetic* mean and imply? Outline the origins of aesthetics. Distinguish between the Greek sense of art and the eighteenth-century European concept of art as fine art.

4. Summarize the basic assumptions of the aesthetic concept of music.

5. Is it correct to say that the aesthetic concept of music has dominated music education philosophy for several decades? How so?

6. Is it reasonable to conclude that the traditional philosophy of music education as aesthetic education fails to provide a solid philosophical foundation for music teaching and learning? If so, why? If not, why not?

7. What self-evident principle does this book use to launch its inquiry into music? How does this principle unfold into a multipart blueprint for explaining the nature and significance of music?

8. Explain the concept of a "musical practice." What does it mean to say that MUSIC is a diverse human practice? Name five (ten, twenty) musical practices (or Musics). Distinguish between a musical practice and a musical style.

Supplementary Sources

Arnold Berleant. "The Historicity of Aesthetics: Parts 1 and 2." *British Journal of Aesthetics* 26, no. 2 & 3 (1986): 101–11; 195–203. A clear overview and criticism of the aesthetic concept.

Lydia Goehr. *The Imaginary Museum of Musical Works: An Essay in the Philosophy of Music*. Oxford: Clarendon Press, 1992. Chapters 5 and 6 of this book trace the evolution of the aesthetic concept of music with special attention to the work-concept.

Philip A. Alperson. "What Should One Expect from a Philosophy of Music Education?" *Journal of Aesthetic Education* 25, no. 3 (Fall 1991): 215–42. A cogent review of past and present directions in music education philosophy.

David J. Elliott. "Music Education as Aesthetic Education: A Critical Inquiry." *The Quarterly Journal of Music Teaching and Learning* 2, no. 3 (Fall 1991): 48–66. A detailed criticism of the philosophy of MEAE.

Wayne Bowman. "An Essay Review of Bennett Reimer's *A Philosophy of Music Education*." *The Quarterly Journal of Music Teaching and Learning* 2, no. 3 (Fall 1991): 76–87. A detailed criticism of MEAE.

Roberta Lamb. "Aria Senza Accompagnamento: A Woman Behind the Theory." *The Quarterly Journal of Music Teaching and Learning* 4, no. 4, and 5, no. 1 (Winter 1993 and Spring 1994): 5–20. This article includes a feminist perspective on MEAE.

Bennett Reimer and Jeffrey E. Wright, eds. *On the Nature of Musical Experience*. Niwot: University Press of Colorado, 1992. This book includes concise summaries of Langer's and Meyer's theories.

Malcolm Budd. *Music and the Emotions: The Philosophical Theories*. London: Routledge and Kegan Paul, 1985. Chapter 6 of this book offers a detailed criticism of Langer's theory of music, Chapter 8 analyzes Meyer's theory.

II

MUSIC AND
MUSIC EDUCATION

3

Musicing

To have "music" in the familiar sense of audible performances, someone must first take action to make music or "music!" Musical works are not only a matter of sounds, they are also a matter of *actions*. Put another way, musicing is an inceptional property of music as an auditory presence.[1]

The word *musicing* may sound odd at first. This is understandable. The aesthetic concept of music-as-object obscures the more fundamental reality of "music!" as a form of deliberate doing and making. But consider how easily people speak of dancing, drawing, or painting, or how we use the word *dance* in multiple ways to mean the dancing a dancer does, a gathering of dancers, or the outcome of a dancer's dancing.

Musicing is an important term. It serves to remind (and re-mind) us that long before there were musical compositions there was music making in the sense of singing and playing remembered renditions and improvisations; that many cultures still view music as something people do; and that even in the West where composers and composing are essential aspects of the musical tradition, compositions remain silent until interpreted and performed by music makers. Most of all, musicing reminds us that performing and improvising through singing and playing instruments lies at the heart of MUSIC as a diverse human practice. As the philosopher Nicholas Wolterstorff insists, "the basic reality of music is not works nor the composition of works but music making."[2]

From this viewpoint, the question "What is music?" subdivides first into two closely related questions: (1) What is the nature of musicing? and (2) What does it mean to be a music maker? This chapter begins to answer both questions. But since we cannot say everything at once, and since improvising is a kind of performing, and since composing, arranging, and conducting usually imply the presence of musical performers, it seems reasonable to start with an emphasis on performing. (Thus, I shall often use *musicing* interchangeably with *performing* in this chapter.) Note, however, that most themes in my discussion apply to all forms of music making. Later chapters will develop these themes in relation to improvising, composing, arranging, and conducting.

1. Orientation

When people such as Jessye Norman or our imaginary students Clara, Sara, and Tim perform a composition by singing or playing an instrument, what is occurring? To say they are engaged in an activity is not precise enough. A person can be active and still get nothing done. Doing implies intention; the word *activity* alone does not. When Clara, Sara, Tim, and Jessye Norman perform a composition, they are not acting aimlessly or accidentally, nor are they acting musically in the sense that someone might be acting impatiently. They are doing something intentionally, and they are getting something done. Performing involves doing and making. For to make something is always to do something, and doing something always involves making a difference of some kind in a situation or condition.[3]

The key word above is *intention*. In thinking about the nature of performing we must differentiate immediately between (1) involuntary physical movements, reflexes, and manifestations of character (e.g., "acting impatiently") and (2) intentional actions. To act is not merely to move or exhibit behavior. To act is to move deliberately, with control, to achieve intended ends. Actions are purpose-*full*. Actions include movements, but actions cannot be reduced to movements because movements can occur without intent (such as involuntary twitches, tics, and shudders[4]). As the philosopher Saul Ross puts it, "the characteristic of personal action is that it is the realization of intentions. Action is informed and determined by a conscious purpose."[5]

Musicing in the sense of musical performing is a particular form of intentional human action. Performing depends on the deliberate formulation of purposes in a definite context. A musicer acts by selecting a particular situation or condition with an intention in mind; by deploying, directing, and adjusting certain actions to make changes of certain kinds in sounds of a certain kind; and by judging when the intended changes have been achieved in relation to standards and traditions of musical practice. To perform music is to achieve intended changes of a musical kind through actions that are taken up deliberately, or at will.[6] What this means, in turn, is that *to perform music is to act thoughtfully and knowingly*. For selecting, deploying, directing, adjusting, and judging are definite forms of thinking and knowing.

In review, musical performing involves the following essential ingredients in combination:

1. a music maker, or music makers
2. some kind of knowledge that determines and informs the intentions of music makers, including knowledge of relevant standards and traditions of musical practice
3. the sounds that music makers make and act upon in relation to their musical knowledge
4. the instruments (including voices) of their work
5. the actions of performing (and/or improvising)
6. the musical product-in-view (i.e., a performance of a composition, or an improvisation)

7. the context (physical, cultural, and social) in which music makers interpret, perform, or improvise musical works

These reflections bring us to the central question of this chapter: Exactly what does it mean to act thoughtfully and knowingly as a music maker? To answer, we must address several fundamental matters of human *being,* including the concepts of consciousness, knowledge, and thought. In other words, we must begin with what it means to be a music maker in the most fundamental sense of an individual, conscious *self.*

2. Consciousness, Knowledge, and Thought

What is consciousness? Philosophers and cognitive scientists are not entirely sure. What is certain, however, is that while the traditional theory of consciousness called *dualism* is in wide disrepute, *materialism* is a theory of consciousness approaching consensus.[7] Among the assumptions of the old dualistic notion of consciousness are the following:[8]

1. Mind (or human consciousness) is mental and the body is physical. (Mind is composed of special "mental stuff" that is distinct from the "physical matter" of the brain.) Hence, mind and body are separate and distinct.
2. There is a central place in the mind where a Central Controller (or Mental Boss) sifts and sorts all information and directs all thinking.
3. Thinking and knowing are matters of speaking silently to oneself, or out loud, or in written symbols. Action is physical and therefore dumb.

In opposition to dualism, materialism holds that there is no special "mental stuff" distinct from the physical brain. The philosopher and cognitive scientist Daniel Dennett summarizes the basic tenet of materialism this way: "[T]he mind *is* the brain."[9] That is, the physical processes of the brain are responsible for all the characteristics of human consciousness, including thinking, knowing, feeling, imagining, attending, remembering, and intending. (Some readers may prefer the term *naturalism* to *materialism* because it captures the same idea more clearly: "that the mind-brain relationship is a natural one. Mental processes just are brain processes."[10]) Furthermore, there is likely no central place in the brain where all incoming and outgoing information is sifted, sorted, and interpreted by some kind of Central Controller. Instead, human consciousness is parallel and distributed; consciousness consists in many simultaneous streams of processing that operate throughout the brain.

Consciousness, then, is not an inscrutable process. It is neither a mystical power nor a secret compartment in the head. Consciousness is part of the human nervous system that, in turn, is the outcome of biological processes. As Mark Johnson suggests, it's not that the mind is in the body, it's that *the body is in the mind.*[11] Furthermore, as I detail later, each individual human consciousness (or self) is a product of both natural selection and cultural evolution.

The psychologist Mihalyi Csikszentmihalyi (pronounced Me-hi Chick-sent-me-

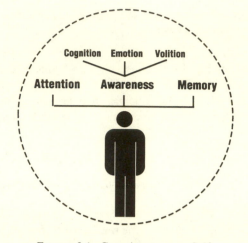

FIGURE 3.1. Consciousness, or Self

hi) maps consciousness in terms of three integrated subsystems: attention, awareness, and memory.[12] Awareness, in turn, consists in three capacities: cognition,
emotion, and volition (or intention). Cognition (from the Latin *cognoscere*, "to
know") means knowing in the widest sense of the term and includes all processes
involved in the verbal and nonverbal organization, retrieval, use, and application
of our apprehensions. Cognition refers to the various processes by which we recognize, relate, and deploy information from inside and outside ourselves. *Information* includes all the differentiated sights and sounds, all the recognized thoughts
and emotions, all the situations and events, that we encounter.[13] In sum, attention,
awareness, and memory constitute the human meaning-making system we call consciousness, and another word for human consciousness is *self*.

The "portrait" of the self in Figure 3.1 brings these thoughts together.

I wish to highlight three important themes. First, attention, awareness, and
memory interact. Our everyday phenomenological experience results from the integration of our powers of consciousness. There is likely no such thing as cognition
without emotion, emotion without cognition, or awareness without memory.

Second, every aspect of consciousness depends on attention. Attention is the
gateway to consciousness and is required to select, sort, retrieve, and evaluate all
overt and covert actions.[14] Csikszentmihalyi conceives attention as an energy supply that fuels thinking and knowing in all their various forms.[15] But there are
limitations on this energy supply.[16] We cannot pay attention to everything there is
to see, hear, or do.

Third, there is a consensus among scholars that thinking and knowing are not
one-dimensional phenomena: verbal expression is not the only form that thinking
and knowing can take. Instead, there are varieties of thinking and knowing. Aristotle made the same point long ago when he distinguished between theoretical
knowledge (*epistémé*), practical knowledge (*politiké*), and productive knowledge
(*techné*).[17] Aristotle believed that each form of knowledge depends on its own
dominant form of thinking and its own definite standards. In line with this tradition,

the philosopher Vernon Howard suggests that thinking exhibits itself in at least the following ways:[18] (1) in what people believe and assert; (2) in how people deliberate and decide; (3) in how people perform in various kinds of action; and (4) in how people generate and use images to guide and shape action. Moreover, says Howard, "whatever the dominant mode of thought, others inevitably get involved in surrounding and supporting ways."[19]

Contemporary theories of intelligence reflect this multidimensional view of thinking and knowing. For it stands to reason that if thinking and knowing come in a variety of forms, then human intelligence is not one-dimensional, but multidimensional. Howard Gardner's theory of multiple intelligences[20] (which posits musical intelligence as one of seven) and Robert Sternberg's triarchic theory of mind[21] are extensions of this multifarious way of thinking about thinking. "An intelligence," says Gardner, "is an ability to fashion products, or to solve problems, that are of significance within one or more cultural settings."[22] Part of Gardner's mission is to emphasize that abilities not typically considered intelligences in Western culture (e.g., musical and bodily-kinesthetic ones) should be counted on an equal footing with linguistic and mathematical abilities.[23] Gardner suggests that one helpful way to grasp his proposal "is to think of the various intelligences as *sets of know-how*—procedures for doing things."[24]

Gardner's reference to "know-how" echoes the writings of Jean Piaget and Gilbert Ryle, among others. In his influential book *The Concept of Mind*,[25] Ryle debunks dualism and its corollary that thinking and knowing are always and only verbal. In the process, Ryle makes important distinctions between nonverbal knowing-*how* (or procedural knowledge) and verbal knowing-*that* (or formal knowledge). These two basic classifications of knowledge are widely accepted by philosophers and cognitive scientists. Moreover, many scholars posit several additional categories of knowing.

In summary, the way has been opened for a more complete epistemology, one in which thinking and knowing (and intelligence) are not restricted to words and other symbols but are also manifested in *action*. With these ideas in mind, let us return to the nature of music making in general and performing in particular.

3. Musicianship

Music making is essentially a matter of *procedural* knowledge. I say "essentially" because it is reasonable to argue that at least four other kinds of musical knowledge contribute to the procedural essence of music making in a variety of ways. Following the cognitive psychologists Carl Bereiter and Marlene Scardamalia,[26] the names I shall give to these four kinds of knowing are: formal musical knowledge, informal musical knowledge, impressionistic musical knowledge, and supervisory musical knowledge. Taken together, these five forms of musical knowing constitute *musicianship*.

Let me rephrase what I have just written. Whenever a person (child through adult) is making music well, he or she is exhibiting a multidimensional form of knowledge called musicianship. Musicianship is demonstrated in actions, not

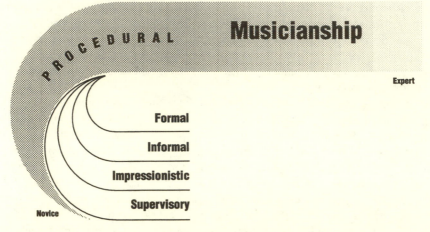

FIGURE 3.2. Musicianship

words. It is a form of practical knowledge, or reflective practice,[27] a matter of what
Donald Schön calls "thinking-in-action" and "knowing-in-action."[28] But while
musicianship is procedural in essence, four other kinds of musical knowledge contribute to this essence in surrounding and supporting ways.

A preliminary map of musicianship appears in Figure 3.2. More will be added
in later chapters, including an explanation of the relationships between music making and music-listening know-how (or *listenership*).

The next several sections of this chapter explain the procedural essence of
musicianship and the four other kinds of musical knowing that contribute to this
essence. Before I proceed, however, there are a few overarching points that need
highlighting.

In Chapter 2 I stated that MUSIC consists in many musical practices worldwide
and that each musical practice pivots on the shared understandings of the musicers
who are the practitioners of that practice. Thus, musicianship is not synonymous
with what it takes to make and listen for the music of any one musical practice.
Musicianship is practice-specific. That is to say, while the five kinds of knowledge
that make up musicianship likely hold across most (if not all) musical practices,
the precise contents of these knowledge categories are context-dependent. For example, the musicianship of a Dagomba master drummer differs in content (but not
in its five-dimensional structure) from the musicianship of (say) a North Indian
drummer, a jazz drummer, an opera singer, or a Bulgarian bagpiper. It is because
the five component knowings of musicianship are practice-specific (or "situated")
that musicianship differs from musical practice to practice.

What I am proposing, then, is that while musicianship is essentially local (or
context-dependent), it is global to the extent that most (if not all) forms of musicianship involve the same five *kinds* of musical knowing. Of course, musicianship
is also global in the most basic sense that all forms of music making are mainly
directed toward the construction of successive and simultaneous musical sound
patterns.[29] Music makers everywhere construct and chain musical patterns together,

make same-different comparisons among musical sound patterns, and vary, transform, and abstract musical patterns.[30] (This is not to say that musical works are merely sound patterns. On the contrary, as I explain in later chapters, musical works are always multilayered, or multidimensional. But all musical works obviously depend on auditory patterns of some kind.) In sum, musicianship is what music makers know how to do with practice-specific musical sound patterns in relation to practice-specific musical knowings.

Let us now examine each knowledge component of musicianship in turn.

4. The Procedural Essence of Musicianship

An understanding of musicianship begins with an understanding of its procedural nature. What does it mean to act thoughtfully and knowingly as a musical performer?

In the old dualistic view, actions follow from verbal thoughts in a two-step sequence of think-act, think-act, ad infinitum. The first event is mental (speaking silently to oneself), and the second event is physical (bodily movement). The dualistic assumption is that thinking and knowing are always verbal and that bodily actions are nonverbal, or dumb.

Most philosophers and cognitive scientists today deny the dualistic view. Actions do not proceed by (1) verbally theorizing to oneself and then (2) physically doing. If they did, says Ryle, then the first event (verbal thinking) would become an action that would itself require a preceding act of theorizing, thereby leading us to the absurdity (or infinite regress) that no one can act until he or she completes an infinite number of verbal thoughts.[31] In the contemporary view, *actions are nonverbal forms of thinking and knowing in and of themselves.* Ryle puts it this way: "Overt intelligent performances are not clues to the workings of minds; they are those workings."[32]

Consider the example of a surgeon operating on a patient. As Saul Ross explains, the surgeon's actions are theoretical and practical at the very same time:

> Each thrust of the scalpel, a movement which is done intentionally, is one wherein thought and action work together, not as two separate additive components nor as two consecutive events, one mental and the other material, but as one where the mental and the material components are interwoven. An action is a piece of overt behavior that cannot be detached or separated from the thought which motivates and directs it.[33]

John Macmurray agrees:

> The Self that reflects and the Self that acts is the same Self. . . . Action is not blind. When we turn reflection to action, we do not turn from consciousness to unconsciousness. When we act, sense, perception, and judgment are continuous activity, along with physical movement. . . . Action, then, is full concrete activity of the self in which all our capacities [all powers of consciousness] are employed.[34]

When we know how to do something competently, proficiently, or expertly, our knowledge is not manifested verbally but practically. During the continuous actions of singing or playing instruments *our musical knowledge is in our actions; our musical thinking and knowing are in our musical doing and making.* Thus, it is entirely appropriate to describe competent musical performers as thinking very hard and very deeply (but tacitly) as they perform (or improvise)—as they construct and chain musical patterns together; as they vary, transform, and abstract musical patterns; as they judge the quality of their musical constructions in relation to specific criteria and traditions of musical practice; and as they interpret the emotional expressiveness of musical patterns. In other words, a performer's musical understanding is exhibited not in what a performer says about what he or she does; a performer's musical understanding is exhibited in the quality of what she gets done in and through her actions of performing. Of course, it is entirely possible to reflect *on,* or speak to oneself about, one's actions as they proceed. Such "reflecting-on-action"[35] can and does occur. For the most part, however, performers think nonverbally *in* action, reflect-in-action, and know-in-action.

Let me develop these points through another example. If I tell you that I know how to ski, and if I explain the why-what-and-how of downhill skiing, will this convince you that I really know how to ski? I think not. You will want tangible proof of my skiing know-how. You will want to see me ski successfully on several occasions before you grant that, "Yes, David, you really do know how to ski." My words about skiing are not enough. The proof of my "skiership" lies in the effectiveness of my skiing actions.

The same holds for you as my evaluator. To understand and assess my performance as a downhill skier, you must also possess some degree of competency or proficiency in downhill skiing. As Gilbert Ryle insists: "[T]he knowledge that is required for understanding intelligent performances of a specific kind is some degree of competence in performances of that kind."[36] Knowing how to do something intelligently and knowing how to watch or listen to someone do something well are two sides of the same conscious coin: "The intelligent performer operates critically, the intelligent spectator follows critically. Roughly, execution and understanding are merely different exercises of knowledge of the tricks of the same trade. . . . [T]he capacity to appreciate a performance is one in type with the capacity to execute it."[37]

Note that the ability to follow an expert performance does not require the same *levels* of knowing involved in accomplishing that performance. (One need not be an Olympic-level skier to understand Olympic skiing.) What I am suggesting instead is that to understand and appreciate (or value knowledgeably) an intelligent performance, a spectator (or audience member) requires the same *kinds* of knowing as the performer(s), including a reasonable level of procedural knowledge in performances of that nature.[38]

Of course, nonparticipants may gain some knowledge and pleasure by reading about skiing, basketball, or cricket, or by watching these sports on television. But because sports are essentially concerned with athletic performances (or thinking-in-action), a discerning level of understanding and appreciation demands knowledge in kind. Without developing some competency in the procedural knowings that lie at the core of these pursuits, and a first hand knowledge of the circumstances in which these knowings apply, a spectator's perspectives on and relationships with these sports will remain moot in the most essential regard.

These ideas apply equally to musicianship. The proof of my musicianship lies in the quality of my music making, in what I get done as a performer (improviser, composer, arranger, or conductor). To understand and assess the quality of my musicianship as exhibited in my music making, my evaluators (and other listeners) must possess some degree of competency in musicing themselves. Rephrasing Ryle: Your capacity to understand (and therefore estimate properly the value of) my musical thinking-in-action is one in type with knowing how to think musically in action yourself.

Non–music makers may gain some knowledge and pleasure by reading about music or by listening to recordings. But as I shall continue to explain in this book, because the sounds of music are essentially a matter of artistic-cultural actions and performances, a discerning level of understanding and appreciation demands knowledge in kind. Without developing some competency in the procedural know-ings that lie at the core of musical practices and musical works, and a first hand knowledge of the circumstances in which these knowings apply, a listener's per-spectives on and relationships with music will remain moot in the most essential regard.

On the basis of the discussion so far, it seems fair to suggest that a person who knows how to do something competently possesses knowledge in the robust sense of a working understanding of a domain. Clearly, a working understanding includes known principles and the ability to make effective judgments about one's actions in relation to the applicable standards, traditions, obligations, and ethics of a given domain. But what shall we say about the role of verbal knowledge? Indeed, mention of "principles" and "judgments" implies the presence of verbal concepts.

This is partly correct—but only partly. For concepts need not be verbal. A concept (from *concipere,* "to conceive") is a thought or an idea of any degree of concreteness or abstraction. A concept is anything that enables consciousness to distinguish between and among phenomena, a cognitive unit that can manifest itself in words, in images of various kinds, or in practical actions. In short, our contem-porary understanding of the term *concept* goes well beyond the old classical notion of early psychology that restricts concepts to verbal abstractions alone.[39] Cogni-tive scientists now recognize various kinds of concepts, including verbal concepts, nonverbal practical concepts, fuzzy concepts, situational concepts, and social concepts.[40]

Jean Piaget foreshadowed these ideas in *The Origins of Intelligence in Children.* Piaget recognized that children make practical adaptations and judgments and solve problems in relation to their environments before they can speak or conceptualize in words.[41] In doing so, children develop and employ *practical* concepts, principles, and judgments. In Piaget's view, actions speak for themselves. Piaget elaborates: "There is no basic difference between verbal logic and the logic inherent in the coordination of actions, but the logic of actions is more profound and more prim-itive. It develops more rapidly and surmounts the difficulties it encounters more quickly, but they are the same difficulties of decentration as those which will appear later in the field of language."[42]

Practical concepts are far richer than words can capture. Compare bicycle riding to a written description of the physics involved in balancing a bike. The action of riding speaks more effectively than words about riding. More to the point, there is no reason to believe that riding a bicycle involves anything like speaking the laws of physics to ourselves while we ride along.

In musical terms, there is no reason to accept the dualistic supposition that musical performing involves anything like reading a set of rules in the mind before or during the actions of performing. As Hubert Dreyfus emphasizes, although a verbal explanation may enable the audience to conceive certain aspects of a performance for itself, a verbal formalization is "in no way an explanation of [a] performance."[43] At best, words can only describe what may be going on; they cannot explain what is actually going on in performers while they perform or improvise.

While it is true, then, that verbal concepts and principles play an important role in learning to make music (as I explain in the next section of this chapter), the actions of music making can be seen, fundamentally, as the "em-body-ment" of musical thinking, knowing, and understanding.

There is an important parallel here. Whereas the development of verbal thinking depends heavily on verbal concepts, practical thinking-in-action depends heavily on nonverbal, practical concepts. Just as verbal concepts emerge, develop, and are utilized in the realm of language, practical concepts emerge, develop, and are utilized in action.[44] This helps explain why models of action are so effective in learning how to do something. Models and demonstrations are practical concepts. Practical concepts inform the actions of students in much the same way that verbal concepts inform verbal thinking. Again, practical concepts can never be fully translated into verbal statements. They are too complex. This is why Sparshott emphasizes that the artist's procedural knowledge "is neither verbalizable nor mechanical, and hence neither reducible nor subordinated to propositional knowledge."[45] Sparshott continues: "It is the novice, and not the skilled practitioner, whose knowledge is contained in precepts he can recite, and many of his failures come about because his skill does not run beyond his grasp of general truths."[46]

In broader perspective, materialism holds that there is likely no hierarchy of commands at work in consciousness when we engage in ongoing actions.[47] Actions are not controlled with verbal messages sent by a Central Controller from a Central Command Center in the brain as dualistic theories maintain.[48] There are no grounds for believing in such things. Our conscious processes do not operate in linear, step-wise fashion. Again, consciousness is a matter of many parallel streams of processing in which multiple goals are simultaneously on the alert for means of expression.

"Means of expression" include actions as well as words. And means of expression are, themselves, on the alert for employment opportunities. Our conscious processes are a matter of back-and-forth interactions among the intentions we want to express, our individual ways of expressing these intentions, and the contexts in which we act. During the overall action of musical performing, consciousness makes a continuous series of parallel adjustments in relation to our musical knowledge (tacit and verbal) and the context in which we express our musical thinking-in-action.

I conclude this section with four supplementary reflections on the procedural dimension of musicianship and the kind of thinking-knowing it involves.

Consider that the actions of musical performers and improvisers (like the actions of surgeons and dancers) are not natural (or innate). They are cultural actions.[49] Cultural actions require the elaboration, extension, and very often the reconstruction of everyday movement patterns. For example, there is nothing routine about the way a musician holds a violin in Western classical practices, or the way an African master drummer uses his drumming hands, or the way a singer achieves bel canto. Ordinary efforts and movements become part of artistic musical actions by virtue of the thinking a performer does in and about his attempts to perform the musical works of a particular musical practice.

Second, the actions of musical performing involve different costs and benefits and different levels of risk for success. Performing therefore requires us to make personal judgments in action. Contrast this with a task that follows a predetermined set of steps. For example, preparing an aircraft for takeoff requires step-by-step algorithmic thinking in checklist fashion. (Similarly, some rudimentary aspects of musical performing require the integration of movement sequences through step-by-step reflecting-on-action, especially during the early stages of learning.) But a competent, proficient, or expert performer must continuously reflect upon, judge, and adjust his or her thinking-in-action on the basis of internalized sets of practical or heuristic understandings.

Third, the actions of performing are most often prepared, informed, or practiced before final public performances. (This also holds, to a large extent, for improvising.) Practice sessions and rehearsals may therefore be thought of in terms of bringing about and editing numerous "drafts" of a "final-draft" performance. As I explain in Chapters 7 and 9, each draft rehearsal of a composition involves generating, selecting, and refining one's concept or *interpretation* of a given musical composition as a whole. In other words, there is a substantial and critical difference between merely being able to produce tones and rhythms and knowing how to *perform* musical works. The difference, of course, is *musicianship*.

Fourth, while preparing a composition for performance, performers inevitably think deductively and inductively. For example, to decide the most effective bowings and articulations for an orchestral composition, a violinist employs deductive strategies. In addition, inferences must be drawn from particular details to similar instances. The same holds for a singer's analysis and interpretation of the relationships between a choral composition and its text. A performer accomplishes such thinking in relation to verbal and practical knowledge of the musical context concerned, including his or her previous experience in that practice. What this means, in turn, is that a *person's performance of a given composition is a robust representation of his or her level of musical understanding of that work and the musical practice of which it is a piece.*

In this view, differences in accuracy and interpretation across performances of a given composition reflect differences in individual musical thinking and knowing. In singing or playing a composition, performers think partly in relation to sound patterns and action patterns defined by a score (or a remembered performance). But they also think in relation to less clearly stipulated guidelines, including

histories and standards of musical practice, possibilities of interpretation, the feedback that arises in a specific context, and their own musical judgments and intui-
tions. Such judgments are more individualized than evaluations of, for example,
mathematical correctness, because part of the artistry (or deep musical understanding) we often expect from musical performers includes their ability to personal-
ize their performances by creating original and significant interpretations of given
compositions.

We can draw several conclusions at this point. First, an artistic performance of
a composition requires many forms of thinking and knowing, ranging on a wide
continuum from the most convergent to the most divergent, from the most tacit to
the most verbally explicit, from the most practical to the most abstract. Second,
performing musically in relation to the standards and traditions of a musical domain
engages a person's entire system of conscious powers: attention, awareness, cognition, emotion, intention, and memory. Third, although competent music making
demands many types of thinking and knowing, it is nonverbal and procedural in
essence. Knowing *how* to make music musically and knowing *that* performing
involves this-and-that are two different modes of knowing. Procedural knowledge
and formal knowledge are logically separable.[50] Artistic musical success validates
musicianship; logical evidence validates formal knowledge about music. Donald
Schön summarizes the differences between procedural knowledge and formal
knowledge:

> Whatever language we may employ . . . our descriptions of knowing-in-action are
> always *constructions*. They are always attempts to put into explicit, symbolic form
> a kind of intelligence that begins by being tacit and spontaneous. Our descriptions
> are conjectures that need to be tested against observation of their originals—which,
> in at least one respect, they are bound to distort. For knowing-in-action is dynamic,
> and "facts," "procedures," "rules," and "theories" are static.[51]

I have separated procedural musical knowledge from other forms of musical
knowing (including verbal knowledge) for the sake of clarity. I reconnect them
now.

5. Formal Musical Knowledge

Formal knowledge includes verbal facts, concepts, descriptions, theories—in short,
all textbook-type information about music. (Equivalent terms are propositional
knowledge, declarative knowledge, or knowing-*that*.)

In domains such as the performing arts and athletics, where thinking effectively
in action is what counts, the relationship between procedural knowledge and formal
knowledge can be highly variable. Many students grasp principles nonverbally in
the process of music making and in the course of seeing and hearing models (practical concepts) of how to perform artistically. Other students require "talk" before
they can think-in-action. Most students grasp principles both nonverbally and verbally. Some students will be full of verbal information about what they do; others
will advance their musicianship to a significant level without it.

Most musical practices are sufficiently complex that music makers (including teachers and students) must consult sources of formal musical knowledge at various times. Verbal concepts about music history, music theory, and vocal and instrumental performance practices can influence, guide, shape, and refine a learner's musical thinking-in-action. By itself, however, formal musical knowledge is inert and unmusical. It must be converted into procedural knowing-in-action to achieve its potential. Accordingly, verbal concepts about musical pieces and procedures ought to be viewed as nothing more or less than resource materials for improving the reliability, portability, accuracy, authenticity, sensitivity, and expressiveness of musical thinking-in-action. In this view, the issue of prime importance to music educators is not whether to make use of formal musical knowledge but when and how.

This praxial philosophy of music education holds that formal knowledge ought to be filtered into the teaching-learning situation parenthetically and contextually. Verbal concepts about musical works and music making ought to emerge from and be discussed in relation to ongoing efforts to solve authentic musical problems through active music making. This contextualization of formal knowledge enables students to understand its value immediately and artistically. This, in turn, enables students to convert formal musical knowledge into musical knowing-in-action. As procedural knowledge develops in educational settings that approximate genuine musical practices, actions come to embody formal knowledge, including knowledge of musical notation.

The issue of notation deserves separate comment. Part of the musicianship of many (but not all) musical practices worldwide is knowledge about notation and knowledge of how to decode and encode musical sound patterns in staff notation, graphic notation, hand signs, or rhythmic syllables. But "music literacy,"[52] or the ability to decode and encode a system of musical notation, is not equivalent to musicianship. It is only one part of the formal and procedural dimensions of musicianship. Moreover, literacy should also be taught and learned parenthetically and contextually—as a coding problem to be gradually reduced within the larger process of *musical* problem solving through active music making.

Speaking more broadly, imparting formal musical knowledge in the process of active musical problem solving requires the use of various "languages." As Vernon Howard suggests, the term "languages" includes everything from the theoretical and technical terminology of a musical practice to practice-specific jargon to similes and metaphors to diagrammatic conceptions.[53]

For example, at one point in my development as a young trombonist I recall my teacher setting me the musical problem (or challenge) of performing a slow jazz ballad. This ballad required a very smooth, legato style. With a few carefully chosen words about breath support and articulation (formal knowledge), and a brief model of legato playing (practical concept), my teacher coached me toward performing the ballad musically—that is, in relation to the criteria and traditions of the jazz practice (the musical whole) of which the selected ballad was a part. In the course of trying to solve this musical problem, I grasped the principles I needed to think-in-action by converting formal knowledge into procedural knowledge. This legato aspect of my musicianship developed as an aside (in parenthetical relation) to the central thrust of my effort: learning to make music artistically in relation to the norms and ideals of a specific musical practice. In other words, the larger wheel of thinking-in-action meshed with the smaller "legato wheel" to propel me forward in my musical efforts. Subsequent reflecting in and on my musical performing made this small but important part of my procedural knowledge effective, reliable, and tacit.

Clearly, the procedural essence of musicianship is not acquired by slavishly repeating movements or memorizing verbal concepts about musical works. Instead, and with the guidance of educated teachers, students learn to *reflect on* the causes of their musical successes and failures in the course of their focused actions. Students learn how to *target their attention* to different aspects of their musical thinking-in-action in relation to practical and formal concepts. As Donald Schön explains, such reflecting-on-action usually occurs in the medium of words spoken silently to oneself (or aloud to others).[54] In contrast, reflecting-in-action—monitoring the effectiveness of our musical thinking-in-action in the present moment—is a nonverbal form of critical thinking. It enables us to adjust our thinking-in-action in relation to our grasp of musical goals, standards, traditions, and working principles. Schön adds the following:

> Like knowing-in-action, reflection-in-action is a process we can deliver without being able to say what we are doing. . . . Clearly, it is one thing to be able to reflect-in-action and quite another to be able to reflect *on* our reflection-in-action so as to produce a good verbal description of it; and it is still another thing to be able to reflect on the resulting description.[55]

While reflecting on their musical actions, students compare their music making to that of other musicers (peers, teachers, and musical heroes past and present). Students notice (or should be encouraged to discern) why, when, and how music making proceeds well or poorly. Such discernments lead to further understandings (tacit and verbal) of principles, standards, and histories of music making.

It follows that while formal knowledge about music and music making is necessary to become a music teacher, critic, or musicologist, it is neither a necessary prerequisite nor a sufficient corequisite for achieving competent, proficient, or expert levels of musicianship. True, many brilliant performers (improvisers, composers) talk and write eloquently about music and musical artistry. But many others do not. In sum, the acquisition of formal musical knowledge is a proper but secondary goal of music education.

6. Informal Musical Knowledge

Although widely recognized by cognitive scientists, informal knowledge is just beginning to receive rigorous study. As Bereiter and Scardamalia explain it, informal knowledge is the savvy or practical common sense developed by people who know how to do things well in specific domains of practice.[56]

Many popular films rest on oversimplified contrasts between formal and informal knowledge. Typically, the informal knowledge of the old country doctor wins out over the bookish stupidity of the young hotshot fresh out of medical school. But formal knowledge is not at odds with informal knowledge; it is simply different. Bereiter and Scardamalia suggest that formal knowledge is to informal knowledge as the tip of an iceberg is to its foundation.[57] Indeed, informal knowledge is hard to get at. It is not available in textbooks. Even experts have difficulty saying how they know what they know in the informal sense. When questioned, experts often refer to this kind of knowledge loosely as "experience." But a closer look reveals that informal knowledge involves at least three related ingredients. In musical terms, these ingredients can be explained this way: Informal musical knowledge involves the ability to reflect *critically* in action. Reflecting critically depends, in turn, on knowing when and how to make musical *judgments*. And knowing how to make musical judgments depends on an understanding of the musical situation or *context:* the standards and traditions of practice that ground and surround a particular kind of music making and music listening.

Critical reflecting-in-action is fundamental to musicianship because music making is not a simple matter of habits, behaviors, routines, or physical skills. (These common ways of talking about musical performance are as inaccurate as they are widespread. They rest on a dualistic misunderstanding of the cognitive nature of music making.) Indeed, it is not the case that for every action of music making there is a verifiable principle that always works and that can always be reduced to words. Principles of music making, like chess strategies, do not guarantee success. They are always provisional. The effectiveness, flexibility, and portability of musicianship hinges on the critical selection and deployment of all forms of musical knowing.[58]

Underlying the critical selection and deployment of musical knowings is "strategic musical judgment" (Howard's term[59]): the disposition and the ability to make musical judgments in action. This ingredient of informal musical knowledge develops through active musical problem solving. It grows by listening intently for the musical sounds one is performing and interpreting; weighing musical choices in action; adjusting one's musical thinking-in-action according to one's choices; assessing the artistic results of one's choices; and considering alternative strategies during continuing efforts to make music well.[60]

To give these ideas a human face, consider the informal musical knowledge of an African master drummer. In his *African Rhythm and African Sensibility* (1979), John Miller Chernoff explains how the Dagomba drumming practiced in Ghana interweaves diverse rhythmic patterns in a complex polymetric structure. The way the drummers in a Dagomba drum ensemble repeat, accentuate, and improvise contrasting patterns exerts a kind of pressure on the many rhythmic parts that make up the musical whole. This pressure creates rhythmic tension and drive. At its best, African musicians call the music "sweet."[61]

Making the music "sweet," says Chernoff, is a matter of knowing how and learning how to be "cool."[62] Less successful drummers tend to be "hot." They play impulsively. In the terms I am using, they have yet to develop the informal knowledge component of Dagomba musicianship.

The master drummer knows how to be patient. He knows the importance of waiting for the right moment in the ongoing texture of rhythms to make his contribution.[63] He improvises with respect for what the other drummers are doing.[64] (The master drummer is the one who has "cooled his heart."[65]) He pays attention to what the dancers are dancing. In the terms of this book, the master drummer knows how to reflect critically in action. He makes strategic judgments on the basis of his "situated knowledge" of the standards and traditions of Dagomba drumming. He is in tune with both the musical and social occasion that he is influencing and motivating. He has achieved this situational savvy from making music (and from observing others make music) in the authentic contexts of his Dagomba practice. In addition, his music making reflects and informs the social practices of his community. For, as Chernoff says, "we should be conscious of the fact that music making in Africa is above all an occasion for the demonstration of character."[66]

(At this point, the reader may wish to stop and reflect on the ways that informal musical knowledge manifests itself differently in different musical practices.)

Informal musical knowledge derives from two sources. One source is a person's individual (and usually partial) interpretations of the formal knowledge of a musical practice (if such is available). But the most important source is one's own musical reflecting-in-action. The informal knowledge component of musicianship crystallizes in a student's efforts to develop practical solutions to realistic musical problems in relation to the standards, traditions, history, and lore of a musical context. The process resembles the way a chess player learns: not by repeating moves over and over in isolation but by solving real chess problems in the context of playing real chess games (or practice games).

In sum, informal musical knowledge (like procedural musical knowledge) is distinctive in being closely tied to learning and working in the local conditions of a practice. Informal musical knowledge is *situated* knowledge: it is knowledge that arises and develops chiefly from musical problem finding and musical problem solving in a genuine musical context, or a close approximation of a real musical practice.

7. Impressionistic Musical Knowledge

"Intuition" comes closest to what we mean by "impressionistic knowledge."[67] It is what experts know as a strongly felt sense that one line of action is better than another, or not quite right.

At root, impressionistic knowledge is a matter of cognitive emotions or knowledgeable feelings for a particular kind of doing and making. Israel Scheffler and Paul Wagner use the terms "cognitive emotion"[68] and "mindful feeling"[69] to break down the walls people tend to build between thinking and feeling. As I have emphasized, consciousness is integrated. There is likely no such thing as thinking without feeling or feeling without thinking. Thinking and feeling are hybrids, neither completely emotive nor completely cognitive in content. Accordingly, says Wagner, the words *emotion* and *feeling* are vague and clumsy ways of referring to a wide assortment of experiences and events.[70] (Psychologists prefer the term *affect*.)

For example, while fear can be induced through direct chemical intervention (fear as bodily sensation), fear is most often a cognitive emotion resulting from a cognitive evaluation (tacit or verbal) of a particular situation. Indeed, people often have good reasons for being afraid of someone or something.[71] (Recall that cognition does not always require or imply the presence of verbal thinking. Our integrated powers of consciousness can appraise our circumstances tacitly in action and in-the-moment.)

Generally speaking, emotions tend to be cognitive. Emotions such as surprise, sadness, anger, jealousy, pride, sorrow, certainty, and doubt are always *about* something. Emotions arise from our personal knowledge and beliefs (tacit and verbal) about people, objects, situations, events, and ideas. Thinking and feeling (cognition and affect) are interdependent.

Music makers acquire nonverbal impressions, or an affective sense of things, while doing, making, and reflecting in specific musical contexts. These impressions influence a student's subsequent efforts and decisions. To develop musicianship is, in part, to advance a student's feel for or affective awareness of what "counts" in musical situations. Musicianship includes educated or knowledgeable feelings for the nature of music making and the nature of musical works in the contexts of definite music cultures. This is what I mean by impressionistic musical knowledge.

Consider the example of a young singer like our student Sara Band who is learning how to perform Kabalevsky's song *Good Night*.[72] As an advanced beginner, Sara is starting to reflect in and on her musical actions. Implicit in Sara's musical thinking-in-action is an emerging sensibility about how her singing ought to be carried out. Her affective sense of what ought to be done musically (which is informed by her procedural, formal, and informal musical knowings) works for her as she sings. In other words (and following the previous work of Nelson Goodman, Israel Scheffler, and Paul Wagner), I suggest that cognitive musical emotions fulfill a selective function by facilitating choices among patterns and by "defining their salient features, focusing attention accordingly."[73] Cognitive emotions play an essential role in helping music makers evaluate, decide, judge, generate, and select musical options in the actions of music making.

Notice, again, that impressionistic musical knowledge (like procedural and informal knowledge) is situated knowledge. It cannot be taught or learned in abstraction from the actions and contexts of actual music making. Impressionistic musical knowledge develops through critical musical problem solving in relation to natural music making challenges (for example, compositions to interpret and perform, improvisations to make).

The concept of impressionistic musical knowledge helps explain why a proficient performer might well say that he or she "feels" how to sing a certain phrase in a certain way or "senses" what to do without being able to say exactly why. Impressionistic musical knowledge is no less rational or intelligent for being affective. It is about specific musical matters. In short, cognitive musical emotions are artistically thought-*full*.

Impressionistic musical knowledge makes an essential contribution to musicianship. It helps us assess, categorize, and "place" our musical actions. It contributes to the ability to reflect in and on our actions. And it is especially important in grounding our ability to make critical musical judgments in action.

8. Supervisory Musical Knowledge

Supervisory knowledge is sometimes called metaknowledge or metacognition. This form of musical knowing includes the disposition and ability to monitor, adjust, balance, manage, oversee, and otherwise regulate one's musical thinking both in action ("in-the-moment") and over the long-term development of one's musicianship.

The immediate importance of supervisory musical knowledge becomes clear when we compare musical performing and improvising to reading a book or adding a sum. In reading and arithmetic, thinking and knowing usually operate in predictable (or closed) contexts. In performing and improvising, thinking- and knowing-in-action usually occur in less certain (or open) circumstances. The same holds for other reflective practices (such as teaching and athletics) in which the ability to act appropriately and optimally under pressure (in balanced relation to guidance from one's overall assessment of a given situation) is essential to succeeding.

In broad terms, I suggest that supervisory musical knowledge (knowing how to manage, guide, and advance one's musicianship in and over time) combines the following: (1) an overarching sense of musical-personal judgment; (2) an understanding of (if not a devotion to) the musical obligations and ethics of a given practice (see Chapter 7); and (3) a particular kind of imagination that Vernon Howard calls "heuristic imagination":[74] the ability to project and hold pertinent images in one's mind before, during, and after one's musical efforts. Indeed, while "imagination" has several aspects (as I detail in Chapter 9), the practical process of musical image making (or "imagination in action"[75]) is a key component of supervisory musical knowledge. Howard offers several examples of this point:

> "mental rehearsal": going over things "in the mind's eye" before or after doing them; forming or holding particular ends-in-view such as ... the aural image of a desired sound, a game plan, or correction to be made in practice; metaphoric imagery—"Imagine the throat as a tall dome across which the voice travels," ...; and aspect perception— ... the hidden fifth in a musical progression. In these and many other ways, mental imagery constitutes a "mind set" or selective predilection to specific patterns of thought, action, and perception.[76]

Howard observes that imagination-in-action goes hand-in-glove with the ability and disposition to continuously retarget one's attention forward to new musical challenges (or ends) as one develops the ability (or means) to meet current challenges: "Improved facility at the keyboard, for example, enables one not only to perform a musical passage up to some preconceived [or imagined] standard of phraseology, but to reconceive the phraseology itself—to project [or imagine] a new standard."[77]

Finally, a student who uses heuristic imagination as part of his musical self-management procedures may be more likely to identify with, care for, and enjoy what and how he is musicing. This is so because holding appropriate musical images, goals, and standards in mind as references for the quality of one's moment-to-moment efforts prevents rehearsals and practice sessions from degenerating into mindless drill and drudgery. As Howard says:

The implicit distinction here is between critical foresight and mere preconception or slavish adherence to habit or routine. Only in imagination can we confront past experience with present challenge by holding ends *in* view as well as the past in *re*-view. In so doing, imagination focuses the whence and the whither of our efforts in critical overview, supporting the will by showing the way. . . .

[T]he imagination sustains critical hindsight and foresight, not so much as a matter of "inspiration," but rather as of *control* within a means-ends continuum linking the necessary skills to the propelling disposition to do well.[78]

Supervisory musical knowledge is yet another kind of situated knowledge. It develops primarily in educational contexts centered on musical actions, interactions, and transactions with life-like musical challenges. To some extent, supervisory knowledge also results from talking to one's teachers, peers, and oneself about the strengths and weaknesses of one's musicianship. But its ultimate application (and test) occurs during efforts to monitor and coordinate all other forms of musical knowing in the pursuit of artistic musical outcomes.

Notice, in review, that four of the five kinds of knowledge that constitute musicianship—procedural, informal, impressionistic, and supervisory musical knowledge—are essentially nonverbal and situated. These commonalities hold several important implications for music teaching and learning that I expand upon later. At this point I wish only to link and underline the following points.

To make and listen for music intelligently requires musicianship. Developing musicianship is essentially a matter of induction; students must enter and become part of the musical practices (or music cultures) they intend to learn. This is so because musicianship is context-dependent. The musicianship underlying any practice of music making and listening has its roots in specific communities of practitioners who share and advance a specific tradition of musical thinking. Musical practices swirl around the efforts of practitioners who originate, maintain, and refine established ways and means of musicing, as well as cherished musical histories, legends, and lore.

Of course, the extent to which practitioners formalize and regulate the criteria and traditions of their musical practices varies greatly around the world. Many musical practices survive orally and aurally. Many other practices depend on complex formal institutions (such as university music schools) to protect, maintain, research, teach, and certify practitioners in their traditions and standards of musicianship. Either way, effective music teaching and learning requires a definite type of teaching-learning situation that inducts learners into musical practices as authentically as possible (see Chapters 10 and 11). John Dewey placed a high value on teaching and learning conceived as "induction" in this sense: "The customs, methods, and working standards . . . of the calling constitute a 'tradition,' and . . . initiation into the tradition is the means by which the powers of learners are released and directed."[79]

Note Dewey's words: "released and directed." Standards and traditions of musical practice nurture musicianship, musical achievement, and musical enjoyment by releasing or pushing musical thinking forward as much as they define what communities of music makers and listeners currently understand and value. They mark the existing boundaries of musical practices. Even new musical practices depend on shared ways of making and listening for musical works, on shared norms and ideals, and on the tradition that begins to form around the initial musical works of innovative practitioners.

Standards and traditions define (formally and informally) what counts as musical in a specific context of musicing and listening. Thus, musical standards and traditions function in two ways. They ask musicers and listeners to respect and work within current boundaries. At the same time, they invite musicers and listeners to go beyond current understandings and values to create highly original musical works and, perhaps, whole new musical practices. Indeed, just as the real products of apple trees are not apples but new apple trees, the eventual outcomes of musical practices are not only new musical works but new musical practices.

9. Musicianship as Musical Understanding

Some people want to claim that musical understanding is distinct from knowing how to make music well. The claim is false. It rests on the dualistic assumption that verbal knowledge about music represents true understanding, while the ability to make music well is a mechanical skill or behavior. Such notions fail to appreciate the rich and complex nature of music making as knowledge-in-action. Howard Gardner agrees:

> A word about understanding in the arts is in order. If the notion of understanding is introduced in too literal a fashion in the arts, it may be taken as cognate to the mastery of certain concepts like "style" or "rhythm" or "the Renaissance." As I have noted throughout this book, however, any notion of understanding ought to center on the capacities exhibited and the operations carried out by masters of a domain, and each domain features its own characteristic constraints and opportunities.
>
> Such a perspective reveals that, in the arts, production ought to lie at the center of any artistic experience.[80]

This book's praxial philosophy of music education holds that musicianship equals musical understanding. Musicianship (which always includes listenership) is a form of working understanding. The word *understanding* points to something deeper than formal knowledge about musical works. It implies a related network of knowings, not always linear or verbal, but weblike and procedural in essence. The word *working* suggests a practical, situated form of knowing—knowing anchored in the contexts and purposes of specific musical practices.

David Perkins suggests that all forms of understanding share at least five characteristics.[81] Musicianship exhibits all five characteristics. First, musicianship is a *relational* form of knowing. It is gridlike. Competent, proficient, and artistic music makers know how different aspects of musicing relate to one another in terms of cause-effect, whole-part, form-function, comparison-contrast, and production-interpretation.[82] More broadly, to possess musicianship is to comprehend how the components of one's thinking and knowing relate to the goals, ideals, standards, and histories that define particular musical communities and thereby give one's musical efforts meaning.[83]

Second, musicianship is *coherent*. At an expert level, the various strands of tacit and verbal knowings that make up this multidimensional form of understanding weave together in a seamless fabric of fluid thinking-in-action. Musicianship is not only unified in itself, it is effective in achieving the practical ends of musical excellence and creativity as artistic music makers actually know them.[84]

Third, musicianship includes what Perkins calls "standards of coherence,"[85] or what this chapter calls *standards of practice*. Standards of musical excellence, originality, and significance anchor and define the contents of musicianship. In doing so, standards also serve to guide the development of musicianship. For as the various components of musicianship grow and weave together, knowledge of musical criteria directs music makers toward new goals and new possibilities of music making within a given genre.

Fourth, musicianship is a *productive* form of knowledge. As in all forms of working understanding, the relevant test of musicianship is the way it "plays out in action in response to the demands and opportunities of the moment."[86] What this chapter calls the *procedural* essence of musicianship David Perkins terms "generative use":[87] the demonstration of understanding in practical achievement.

Fifth, musicianship is *open*. Like all forms of genuine understanding, musicianship is not an end but a continuous process. It grows in the ways that a complex web weaves inward and outward. It develops as each of its five knowledge components mature and interweave with each other.

For all these reasons, I recommend *praxis* to summarize the essential nature of music making and musicianship. As I noted in Chapter 1, Aristotle used *praxis* to mean informed and deliberative "doing-action" in which doers (as ethical practitioners) are not merely concerned with completing tasks correctly (*techné*), but with "right action": enlightened, critical, and "situated" action. *Praxis* means action committed to achieving goals (*telos*) in relation to standards, traditions, images, and purposes (*eidos*) viewed as Ideals that are themselves open to renewal, reformulation, and improvement. In *praxis* (and in knowledgeable music making as I have attempted to describe it), the feedback that arises from one's reflections is used to improve one's expertise and to refine (or redefine) the goals that guide one's making and doing.[88] Put another way, to act artistically as a music maker is to engage in music making and music listening (and MUSIC) as *praxis*.

Contrast this praxial view with more common descriptions of music making as a skill, craft, technique, or psychomotor behavior. If laypeople understood the original meaning of "skill" (from the Old Norse *skil* for understanding, or competence), then we might make a case for retaining its usage. But the original sense of the word has been almost completely lost. Nowadays *skill* means many things, including manual dexterity, a trade, a general ability, a habit, a routine, or the ability to follow rules in algorithmic fashion. In short, *skill* fails to communicate the fact that competent music making depends on a legitimate and complex form of *knowledge* that partakes of consciousness as a whole (attention, cognition, emotion, intention, and memory).

More broadly, the tendency to describe music making in terms of knowledge *and* skill assumes a dualistic sense of mind. It implies, wrongly, that verbal knowledge is primary in music making, that musical actions always follow from verbal thoughts, and, therefore, that the actions of musicing are essentially mind-less.

Craft (from the German word *Kraft*) is ambiguous, suggesting strength, manual dexterity, and informed ability.[89] While it is true that *craft* is sometimes used in the larger sense of practical knowledge,[90] its old-fashioned association with manual dexterity persists. Accordingly, musical craftsmanship is inadequate to communicate the fact that music making depends on a wide range of tacit and verbal knowings, especially knowings of an informal, impressionistic, and supervisory kind.

The suggestion that music making pivots on techniques will not do either. Technique (from *techné*) is narrowly concerned with the technology of making. True, the procedural dimension of musicianship includes techniques, as well as routines, procedures, facilities, and abilities. But in music making done well, the procedural essence of musicianship always involves several other forms of thinking and knowing linked to specific goals, ideas, and values of musical doing and making (as *praxis* implies).

In summary, many common ways of conceiving music making and musicianship tend to misrepresent and diminish their true natures. This book's philosophy urges the view that musicianship equals musical understanding and that musicianship (which always includes listenership) is a multipartite form of working understanding (or *praxis*) that is procedural and situated in essence. Stated another way, artistic music making and intelligent music listening involve a multidimensional, relational, coherent, generative, open, and educable form of knowing called musicianship.

10. Levels of Musicianship

Because musicianship is open—because it is not an all-or-nothing matter—there must be various levels or stages of musicianship to achieve. Since the possibilities are numerous, and since *Music Matters* is a philosophy of music education (not a psychology of musical development), my only intent in the following is to supplement this discussion with a general outline of how musicianship may progress. In doing so, I combine the themes of this chapter with a five-level scheme of expertise suggested elsewhere by Dreyfus and Dreyfus.[91] Later chapters will reference this scheme as the concept of musicianship continues to unfold.

Before continuing, please note that the five-level progression I present is not tied to "age-level characteristics" as traditionally defined by mathematical, linguistic, or other kinds of nonmusical measures. Accordingly, a musical artist can be a child or adult, depending on what that person knows how to do musically. Note, also, that a person can evidence his or her level of musicianship in several ways: by performing, improvising, composing, arranging, and/or conducting (all of which involve listening). For ease of discussion, however, I describe the five levels—novice, advanced beginner, competency, proficiency, and expert— in terms of musical performing.

1. *Novices* may have some formal knowledge about musical works. They may

even possess a few tacit and verbal principles of action that they can follow in step-by-step fashion. But their musical thinking is essentially trial-and-error; it is not yet thinking-in-action. Novices have little (if any) informal, impressionistic, or supervisory musical knowledge because they have not yet had time to "situate" themselves in the context of the musical practice(s) they are striving to learn. As a result, novices are typically unable to see the musical forest for the trees. Their focus is local, not global. Novices tend to be so absorbed in *reducing* immediate problems that they have no attention left for musical problem *solving*. This local focus and lack of surplus attention prevents novices from making music in a reliable and reflective way.

2. Unlike the novice, an *advanced beginner* like Sara Band (see Chapter 1) has small degrees of musical knowledge in each of the five categories that make up musicianship. Sara has begun to weave these knowings together in action. (She has begun to *proceduralize* her musical knowings.) For these reasons, Sara has small amounts of surplus attention that she can deploy to move back and forth between local and global levels of musical thinking-in-action. But the advanced beginner cannot yet think reliably or fluently. Her reflecting-on-action still absorbs too much of her attention and awareness at the local level of detail.

3. The *competent* music student is one who has succeeded in proceduralizing a variety of tacit and verbal knowings from each of the five knowledge categories. He is able to reflect-in-action by monitoring the features and outcomes of what he is doing in relation to standards of musical practice. He understands these demands formally and informally. He can solve many musical problems if they are pointed out to him by his teacher.

The more global intents of students at the competent level of musicianship act like a magnet to draw their actions forward from in-front. (The local concerns of novices push them along from behind.) Still, a major part of what competent students lack is the ability to *find* musical problems on their own. Competent students have yet to develop the musical problem-finding ability they require to integrate and enhance their musicianship.

4. Someone like Clara Nette is said to possess a *proficient* level of musicianship. Her attention is almost completely free of reflections on her actions. Her musicing is characterized by fluent thinking-in-action and reflecting-in-action. Clara's informal, impressionistic, and supervisory musical knowings inform her thinking-in-action as she attends to the significant features of the compositions she is interpreting and performing.

5. The *musical expert or artist* possesses what Dreyfus and Dreyfus call "deep situational understanding."[92] An expert level of musicianship is distinguished by the full development and integration of procedural, formal, informal, impressionistic, and supervisory musical knowledge. The artist's level of thinking-in-action is so rich that he or she not only solves all problems of musical execution in a composition, she deliberately searches for and finds increasingly subtle opportunities for (or problems of) artistic expression. As I explain in Chapter 9, creative music makers develop what Bereiter and Scardamallia call knowledge of creative "promisingness"[93] and the disposition to use this aspect of their informal musical knowledge to achieve creative musical results.

11. Implications for Music Education

This chapter holds several implications for the why-what-and-how of music teaching and learning.

On the most fundamental level, it is clear that music making in the sense of singing and playing instruments lies at the heart of what MUSIC is and that music making is a matter of musical knowledge-in-action, or musicianship. Music education ought to be centrally concerned with teaching and learning musicianship, which, as I have explained, involves several related forms of thinking and knowing. In this sense, what music educators do is the same as what all teachers do. For thinking and knowing lie at the heart of all educational efforts. Teachers in every subject area focus on the outcomes of student thinking in relation to domain-specific standards of accuracy, appropriateness, and originality. At the same time, what music educators do is unique. For developing musicianship is a matter of teaching a multidimensional form of "sound-artistic" thinking that is procedural and context-dependent.

The next question, of course, is how we organize and carry out music teaching and learning in ways that are true to the nature and value of MUSIC and musicianship. It will take the whole of this book to answer. Let me begin by proposing several first principles of music teaching and learning that are implicit in the themes of this chapter. In doing so, I continue to focus on performing for ease of explanation, but the principles outlined apply to the development of musicianship as manifested in all forms of musicing.

• *The teaching-learning context.* The prime principle that follows from the philosophical themes of this chapter concerns the nature of the teaching-learning environment. Recall that musicianship is practice-specific and that four of its five knowledge components are essentially nonverbal and situational. What this means is that musicianship develops only through active music making in curricular situations that teachers deliberately design to approximate the salient conditions of genuine musical practices. The name I give to this kind of teaching-learning environment is *curriculum-as-practicum.* In Chapters 10 and 11 I detail the practicum concept of curriculum that follows from this praxial philosophy of music education. At this point it is enough to emphasize that the musical authenticity of the teaching-learning situation is a crucial determinate of what music students learn and how deeply they learn. In other words, knowledge cannot be separated from the context in which it is learned and used.[94] In essence, then, developing musicianship is a matter of inducting students into particular music cultures.

• *Progressive musical problem solving.* Inducting students into musical practices depends on selecting significant musical challenges that confront students with genuine musical problems to solve in context: in relation to the demands and traditions of carefully selected musical practices. By a musical challenge I mean an authentic and engaging musical work (or project) to be performed (improvised, composed, arranged, or conducted).

Musicianship advances and integrates to the degree that teachers require their students to meet increasingly significant musical challenges on a continuous basis. By increasingly significant musical challenges I mean either completely new compositions to perform (improvise, compose, arrange, or conduct) or aspects of musical works that are already familiar to learners in some respects but not yet in others. Progressive problem solving[95] requires students to take more and more musical details into account during successive encounters with familiar and unfamiliar challenges. To engage in progressive musical problem solving is to work at the edge of one's musicianship.

• *Targeting surplus attention.* Ericsson and Smith observe that "research on expertise may be one of the most rapidly expanding areas within cognitive psychology and cognitive science."[96] Recent contributions to this research suggest that most students can achieve the rudiments of most forms of know-how through repeated attempts and moderate effort.[97] But since competency, proficiency, and expertise occur less frequently, there is clearly something more involved in advancing beyond a novice level. What is this something more?

As the rudimentary knowings of musicianship begin to develop through active music making, more of the energy resource called attention is released for further investment. Bereiter and Scardamallia suggest that advancing beyond a novice level to competency, proficiency, and artistry depends on what students learn to do with the surplus attention that becomes available as their thinking-in-action improves.[98] Students have three choices. They can spend their surplus attention on: (1) issues unrelated to musicianship; (2) musical problem reduction; or (3) musical problem solving and problem finding.

Students who advance their musical thinking beyond a novice level are those who learn how to reinvest their surplus attention (and, therefore, their powers of cognition, emotion, intention, and memory) in progressive musical problem solving. Improving musicianship does not depend on the slavish repetition of isolated movements or the memorization of verbal concepts. Moving from beginning to advanced levels of musicianship depends on learning to target and solve significant problems in the music one is making and the ways one is making music through performing, improvising, composing, arranging, or conducting.

• *Problem finding.* Donald Schön points out that problem solving in ordinary talk assumes that there is already a well-defined problem that learners can identify and go about solving.[99] But this is not always the case in music making and music listening. An important part of what music students need to learn is how to locate what counts and what needs to be done musically in relation to a given musical challenge. Finding what counts depends, in turn, on learning the expectations and ideals of the musical practice that apply to one's musicing and listening.

• *Problem reduction.* There is an important distinction between problem reduction and problem solving. Suppose, for example, that Sara is having difficulty singing a particular composition because of the demands it makes on her breath control. To advance, Sara must reduce (or eliminate) her breath management problem in terms of the amount of attention it takes up in her conscious awareness. Suppose Sara starts to reduce her breath control problem with the help of practical and verbal concepts provided by her teacher. At this juncture, Sara has a choice to make. The wrong choice is to invest her surplus attention in further breath control management (problem reduction) instead of musical problem solving (e.g., learning to phrase a melodic line expressively).

Musical problem reduction is necessary and intelligent. But in order for musicianship to develop, problem reduction cannot be confused with musical problem solving.[100] Part of what music students need to learn is how to decide when to pursue problem reduction and when to pursue musical problem solving. In general, problem reduction can and should proceed parenthetically—as an aside to the ongoing process of learning to make music well.

It follows from this discussion (and from the research of Bereiter and Scardamallia in particular[101]) that the development of musicianship involves a specific kind of learning process that learners can both engage in and learn how to carry out themselves. This learning process depends on the pursuit of increasingly challenging musical projects using musicianship that is never quite sufficient to meet all the requirements of a given musical challenge. Within this process, students must learn when and how to invest their surplus attention in musical problem finding and problem solving.

Carefully chosen musical challenges expose what students do not yet know how to achieve. With the guidance of music teachers who have achieved competent, proficient, or expert levels of musicianship themselves, music students learn how to meet successive musical challenges by drawing upon and developing various dimensions of their own musicianship. This learning process is promoted by a learning context in which individual advances are observed and shared by students who are taught as (and who therefore learn to see themselves as) authentic music makers. In this context, students learn to expect members of their class and school music community to succeed not merely in problem reduction but in meaningful and significant music making.

Music educators who conceive the development of musicianship as a progressive process in which students and teachers engage in finding, solving, and meeting genuine musical challenges together will not find musical performing elitist. (The same holds for all forms of music making.) Teachers and students will find the achievement of competent, proficient, and expert levels of performing (improvising, composing, arranging, and conducting) central to the development of individual musicianship and, therefore, central to the individual self. A musically excellent teaching-learning community is one in which to pursue and comply with standards and traditions of musical artistry is to grow. What this means, in turn, is that the boundaries of musicianship are not limited to individuals. They also apply to musical organizations (e.g., class and school choirs, class and school wind ensembles, string orchestras, jazz ensembles, composition workshops, guitar ensembles, woodwind ensembles) and to school music education programs as a whole.

• *Music teachers and music students.* The philosophical themes of this chapter suggest that the music educator's role is principally one of mentoring, coaching, and modeling for music students conceived as apprentice musical practitioners. That is to say, all music students (including all general music students) ought to be viewed and taught in the same basic way: as reflective musical practitioners engaged in the kind of cognitive apprenticeship we call music education.[102] Indeed, the fundamental natures of MUSIC and MUSICIANSHIP point to the conclusion that authentic music making (which always involves listening intelligently for the music one is making) ought to be the focus of all music education curricula.

During the interactions of music teaching and learning, music teachers shift back and forth between the products and the processes of students' musical thinking. We analyze what and how our apprentice practitioners are thinking-in-action. Music educators are diagnosticians of musical thinking. We consider what our students are giving attention to, what they fail to notice and understand, what they find difficult to solve, what they feel right or wrong about musically, and so on. On the basis of these analyses, we target students' attention and guide their thinking-in-action by using different languages of instruction including modeling, demonstrating, explaining in words, gestures, diagrams, and metaphors.[103]

Implicit in this view of the music teacher and the music student is the conviction that musicianship is educable. Unless there are serious congenital deficiencies, it seems reasonable to posit that the innate powers of consciousness that contribute to musical intelligence make it possible for most students to learn how to make music to a competent (if not a proficient) degree. True, some children have extraordinary levels of musical intelligence that enable them to develop the musicianship of their music cultures more quickly, deeply, and broadly than others. But even a high level of innate musical intelligence does not promote musicianship. That is, a child with a high degree of musical intelligence can be, but still may not learn to be, musically competent.[104] To achieve a competent, proficient, or artistic level of musical thinking requires the development of a practice-specific form of understanding called musicianship.

• *Evaluation.* Like all forms of thinking and knowing, musicing can be done well or poorly, brilliantly or ineptly. In terms of evaluation, the primary point to make now is that a student's level of musical understanding demonstrates itself primarily in the quality of his or her music making, not in what a student can tell us about musical works. For example, if Clara knows how to perform a variety of compositions proficiently and reliably (according to relevant standards of musical practice), then Clara can be said to possess a proficient level of musicianship. The quality of Clara's music making evidences her musical understanding of the musical works she is interpreting and performing and her understanding of the musical practices of which these works are individual pieces.

The ability to generalize about a musical composition using verbal concepts often helps a student perform musically. But verbal information (or formal knowledge) about music is no substitute for the ultra-specific nonverbal conception of musical works that a student exhibits when he or she performs (improvises, composes, arranges, or conducts) intelligently. Having a concept of something is not limited to the ability to match a word with a phenomenon. Knowing musical concepts is something a student evidences practically in the consistency and quality of her musical thinking-in-action. (Just because musicing is nonverbal in essence does not mean it is nonconceptual.)

An unfortunate legacy of dualistic thinking is the false belief that to really possess musical understanding one must possess a storehouse of verbal information about musical works. The corollary of this belief is that pencil-and-paper tests of verbal concepts are measures of musicianship. This is also false. Tests of formal musical knowledge are just that: decontextualized gauges of one aspect of musicianship. And by itself, formal musical knowledge will not get any music making done.

I am not at all suggesting that verbal knowledge about music is unimportant in music education. Verbal explanations may alleviate or reveal students' misunderstandings and lead to improvements in their musical thinking-in-action. In addition, verbal explanations can help to contextualize the teaching and learning of musicianship. What I am urging, however, is that a musical performance ought to be valued for what it is: an embodiment of a student's musical understanding of a given work and its related practice. The same holds for all other kinds of musical outcomes (improvisations, compositions, and musical arrangements). As I detail in later chapters, a performance of a work is especially valuable in assessing musical achievement. This is so, I suggest, because a performance provides authentic and tangible evidence of a person's moment-to-moment musical understanding (including his or her music-listening ability) with regard to all relevant dimensions of a musical work and the musical practice in which it is embedded.

A full explanation of the values of music making in music education must wait for Chapter 5. But even at this point, one thing seems clear: The values of musicing in music education cannot be tied to its use as an educational means. Authentic music making is a valid and valuable educational end for all students. For in real life, people do not learn how to make music just to improve their ability to listen to music. Instead, music making is something people find worth doing for the sake of musicing itself.

Questions for Discussion and Review

1. What does *musicing* refer to in this chapter? Explain why music teachers may find *musicing* a helpful term and/or a problematic term.

2. Explain the basic distinctions between activity and action. What qualifies music performing as a specific form of action? Summarize the essential ingredients involved in any act of music performing.

3. What is consciousness? (Include a brief comparison between dualism and materialism). What other terms do scholars use for consciousness? What does this book mean by *information*? Explain the functions of attention and cognition.

4. This chapter proposes that musicianship involves at least five forms of musical thinking and knowing. Summarize the main characteristics of each. Explain why musicianship is procedural in essence. Explain why musicianship is "context-specific."

5. Explain the reasons behind this chapter's contention that musicianship equals musical understanding.

6. Analyze the words and concepts people use (in interviews, conversations, and commentaries) to explain how musicians, athletes, and other kinds of "reflective practitioners" do what they do. In what ways do these popular discussions match, conflict with, or extend the several kinds of knowing explained in this chapter?

7. Distinguish between (1) producing sounds and (2) performing music. Some people believe that musical performing is a skill, a technique, or a craft. Explain why you agree or disagree.

8. This chapter proposes several practical principles for the development of musicianship. Summarize five (or more) of these principles. On the basis of (1) your own music teaching experiences and/or (2) your observations of other music teachers in action and/or (3) your study of the videotape listed in the supplementary sources, give an example of each of these principles in action.

Supplementary Sources

V. A. Howard. "Introduction." In *Varieties of Thinking*, ed. V. A. Howard. New York: Routledge, 1990. A succinct overview of "thinking."

Gilbert Ryle. *The Concept of Mind*. New York: Penguin Books, 1949. Chapter 2 explains Ryle's classic distinction between knowing-how and knowing-that.

Mihalyi Csikszentmihalyi. *Flow: The Psychology of Optimal Experience*. New York: Harper and Row, 1990. Chapter 2 explains the "anatomy of consciousness."

V. A. Howard. *Learning By All Means: Lessons From the Arts*. New York: Peter Lang, 1992. Chapter 2, "Music as Educating Imagination," examines the role of imagination in music performance.

Doreen Rao. *ACDA on Location, Vol. 1: The Children's Choir*. Lawton, Okla.: American Choral Directors' Association, Educational Videotape Series, 1988. This video provides several examples of the "first principles" explained at the end of this chapter. Please keep in mind, however, that the philosophical themes and practical proposals explained thus far apply to all forms of music performing and, indeed, to the teaching and learning of most (if not all) forms of musicing. This video exemplifies just one of many (many!) possible ways of implementing just some of the themes in this chapter.

Eleanor V. Stubley. "Philosophical Foundations." In *Handbook of Research on Music Teaching and Learning,* ed. Richard Colwell, pp. 3–20. New York: Schirmer Books, 1992. A broad examination of knowledge in relation to music and music education.

John Seely Brown, Allan Collins, and Paul Duguid. "Situated Cognition and the Culture of Learning." *Educational Researcher* 18, no. 1 (January–February 1989): 32–42. An explanation of "situated cognition."

Daniel C. Dennett. *Consciousness Explained*. Boston: Little, Brown, 1991. Chapter 2, "Explaining Consciousness," offers a concise introduction to the case against dualism and the argument for materialism.

4

Music Listening

Musicing of whatever kind always includes another kind of doing called music listening. Music makers listen for what their thoughtful actions produce and for what other musicers do and make. In addition, each musical practice usually includes (or attracts) a group of people who act specifically as listeners or audiences for the musical works of that practice. Thus music listening is an essential thread that binds musicers, musicing, and musical works together. But how shall we explain the nature of music listening? And what does it mean to be a competent, proficient, or expert music listener?

1. Listening: Thought-less, or Thought-full?

In everyday life, nothing seems to come between ourselves and the sounds of our environment, including the sounds of tunes, loons, mosquitos, and spoken language. Listening seems direct and automatic. Perhaps we should say, then, that sounds come to us loaded with all the information we need for their complete and accurate understanding. If so, then sounds must be fully formed external objects that listeners merely "copy," or receive immediately (without any mediating cognitive processes).

Some "ecological" theories of perception advocate this immediate view of listening. They hold that all forms of perceiving involve the direct pickup of information from the environment.[1] In this view, hearing and seeing are controlled by the qualities or "affordances" of objects that fit our needs and goals. From this standpoint, listening is essentially thought-*less*.[2]

There are several basic reasons why the notion of thoughtless listening is untenable. First, although the information available to listeners at any given moment is infinite, we do not take in everything there is to hear. Human attention is highly selective. Recall from Chapter 3 that information arises in consciousness by means of attention. Attention is required to select, sort, retrieve, organize, and evaluate all covert and overt actions.[3] Even "instant" decision making requires attention.

But attention is a limited energy resource.[4] As a result, we cannot and do not process every detail of sound, sight, sensation, and emotion that comes our way. Instead, human consciousness engages in a continuous process of deciding and selecting where to spend attention. This is the most obvious reason why acts of listening and looking are "thought-full."

Second, consider what it actually means to see or hear something. As the philosopher John Heil points out, to see a bird the way a botanist or a bird-watcher sees it requires more than good eyesight or a pair of binoculars.[5] We must have knowledge of what we are gazing at. To pick up even the rudimentary information that what we are looking at is a bird, we must know and believe many things, including that this feathery thing is a living organism and not a decoration on a hunter's hat.

In aural terms, to pick up the rudimentary information that an auditory event has the timbral quality of a clarinet is to hear something *as* a clarinet tone. To hear that a clarinet is sounding is to hear that something is the case. And this is very close to saying that a person knows or believes that what he or she hears is a clarinet.

Let us extend these ideas by supposing now that Clara Nette and Tim Pani are at Symphony Hall in Boston. Suppose the Boston Pops Orchestra begins to perform an instrumental medley from Leonard Bernstein's *West Side Story*. Suppose that Clara and Tim recognize the song called "Maria." What are they doing?

At the very least, Clara and Tim are receiving acoustic signals. All sounds have physical properties, including pitch, duration, intensity, and timbre. Acoustic energy stimulates auditory nerves, and nerve firings are transmitted to the brain to cause sensations. But having sensations does not amount to recognizing "Maria." To do so, Clara and Tim must somehow recall the characteristic auditory patterns of this song from previous hearings for continuous comparison with the sonic patterns that they hear unfolding in the BPO's instrumental performance of this work and that they are also somehow cognizing intelligently. In short, Clara and Tim must *know* the auditory patterns called "Maria."

Clearly, to know "Maria" does not mean that Clara and Tim merely know *that* the title of these sounds is "Maria." For even if they mistakenly called the piece "Teresa," they could still be said to know "Maria" when they hear it. And to "know" this piece does not necessarily mean that Clara and Tim know that the orchestra is playing the notes C–F#–G and so on. Many people who know and love "Maria" don't know a C from a sea.

Instead (and at root), Clara and Tim can be said to know "Maria" if, upon hearing the initial patterns of this piece, they believe certain sound patterns will follow that do in fact follow. They are cognizant of this piece if they can detect variations, errors, or omissions in the Boston Pop's performance of "Maria." And, of course, they "know" it if they know how to sing, whistle, or hum along accurately as the BPO plays "Maria." Thus, and in the everyday act of recognizing this song, Clara and Tim "know" in a particular sense: they know *how* to discriminate, construct, and organize auditory events of the "Maria-kind." They know how these Western, tonal, orchestral, song-related kinds of auditory patterns tend to unfold in time. In the words of Mary Louise Serafine, such listeners possess "style-specific cognitive processes."[6]

Even these introductory reflections are enough to negate the thought-less notion

Audition
hearing . . . listening-to . . . listening-_for_

Vision
seeing . . . looking-at . . . looking-_for_

FIGURE 4.1. Degrees of Audition

of human listening. Listening is never direct or immediate. Personal understandings and beliefs (tacit and verbal) always mediate our auditory processes. Listening is thought-full and knowledgeable. What ecological theories fail to recognize, says Howard Gardner, is that "individuals are able to act appropriately in an environment because they make inferences about what they see [and hear], and because they have beliefs, goals, purposes, and other intentional states directed toward their percepts."[7] Indeed, if music listening were merely a matter of aural copying, then every child with fully functioning ears would apprehend everything in Beethoven's Ninth Symphony that the maestro James Levine apprehends, but this is simply not the case.

When we say that listening is thoughtful and knowledgeable we are not saying that listeners necessarily talk silently to themselves while listening. Intentional acts of listening are not two-step sequences of (1) mentally theorizing to oneself and then (2) listening. If they were, then the first event (talking silently to oneself) would become a covert action that would itself require a preceding act of theorizing, thereby involving us in an infinite regress.[8] Instead, listening is essentially a _covert_ form of thinking-in-action and knowing-in-action. Of course, we _can_ talk silently to ourselves while listening. We are capable of reflecting on our acts of listening to some extent, just as we reflect verbally on other forms of action. But it is not necessary to do so. For the most part, when I listen for something I am not doing two things (thinking and listening), I am doing one: I am thinking _in_ my tacit, covert acts of listening.

That hearing and seeing involve degrees of attention, awareness, and memory explains in part why people differ in the details of what they hear and see. Compare the three degrees of audition and vision illustrated in Figure 4.1. Within audition we can differentiate between passive hearing and active listening-_for_. Note the increasing level of personal involvement and knowledge as we move from merely seeing to looking-for, from merely hearing to listening-for.

Competent, proficient, and expert levels of music listening involve active listening-for. Intelligent music listening requires that we deploy our powers of consciousness deliberately to achieve an intention. In music listening, "getting something done" is a matter of thinking and knowing in relation to auditory events. Music listening is not equivalent to registering sounds the way a tape recorder captures a conversation or a recital. Music listening requires us to interpret and *construct* auditory information in relation to personal understandings and beliefs.

Harold Fiske agrees: "Music cognition is a construction process and not a copy process."[9] What we experience as musical patterns, says Fiske, "are the product of cognitive activity and not merely an aural 'photocopy' of material contained in sound objects."[10] Serafine puts it this way: "[M]usic is actively generated (even in perception), not simply 'processed.' "[11]

In the next two sections of this chapter I attempt to explain more precisely why and how music listening is cognitive and constructive. In the process, I explain why music listening is a covert (or internal) form of thinking-in-action and knowing-in-action that is *procedural* in essence. I say "in essence" because it is reasonable to argue that at least four other kinds of musical knowing contribute to the procedural essence of music listening in a variety of ways.

2. The Fundamentals of Music Listening

Although the sounds of speech and music may seem like crisp chunks of sound lined up like eggs in a row, they are not. Acoustic energy reaches our ears in waves. Acoustic waves are ambiguous smears of sound because every aspect of sound production spills over to influence all the others.[12] Each individual sound is influenced by the rate, duration, intensity (and so on) of past and present sounds and by the context in which acoustic energy originates. This influence spreads across a broad time span. Listening is especially temporal because it involves making sense of information that is never completely present before us all at once, like a picture. Our understanding of aural events depends on what we capture in a continuous "moving" stream of information. Accordingly, listening is a *context-dependent* process. What we hear comes to us not as neat little eggs in a row but as something more like scrambled eggs.[13] The complexity of listening is increased by the fact that attention is a finite resource and that auditory cognition has limits. (That is, some patterns of auditory information are easier for humans to cognize than others.)

Given these complexities, we might predict that listening would be an unreliable and haphazard process. But listening proceeds with an ease and an accuracy that are nothing less than miraculous. Most striking is the degree to which the physical properties and discrete units of acoustic information are subordinated in our experience to cohesive units. The atomistic segments of speech and music pass largely unnoticed, and smaller units become subsumed within larger patterns.[14] Our conscious awareness of sounds consists not in isolated elements heard one by one but in identifiable patterns clearly separated and organized into greetings, warnings, questions, statements, melodic phrases, and rhythms. As the data from spectrograms demonstrate, there is a vast difference between the continuous streams of acoustic energy we take in and what we experience in consciousness as the distinct and bounded patterns of sounds, including speech and music.[15] How is this possible?

Contemporary theories of consciousness suggest that all varieties of thought are accomplished in the brain by parallel, multitrack processes that interpret and elaborate sensory input.[16] These processes occur in countless streams of brain activity and at various locations in the brain. Acts of discrimination happen throughout the brain. There is no Central Controller doing all the work, no Central Control Booth where all processing takes place. The brain is not a one-thing-at-a-time machine; it is a many-things-at-a-time processor. As Daniel Dennett explains, the physical brain-mind is "massively parallel, with millions of simultaneously active channels of operation."[17]

During acts of listening and looking, we take in raw, one-sided information. Our conscious powers of attention, awareness, and memory produce revised and enhanced representations of this information. We do not directly experience what happens in our auditory nerves or on our retinas. What we experience is the result of many layered processes of interpretation. In Dennett's words, information entering consciousness is under continuous "editorial revision."[18] The multiple information processors distributed throughout the human brain continuously produce and edit multiple drafts of the information we bring in through our senses.[19] These editing processes, says Dennett, "occur over large fractions of a second during which time various additions, incorporations, emendations, and overwritings of content can occur, in various orders."[20]

In the case of listening, consciousness conducts a wholesale editing and restructuring of incoming acoustic information. The process is analogous to the way a recording studio's multichannel mixing board enhances, balances, edits, overlays, and variously adjusts the sounds made by live performers. More fundamentally, consciousness seems to have specialized auditory processing mechanisms dedicated to identifying, categorizing, and interpreting different types of sounds. For example, Fiske theorizes that auditory cognition may involve a three-component process. The first component of acoustic processing makes a speech-nonspeech distinction. The second component makes "interpattern relationships between identified speech patterns and non-speech patterns," and the third component (among other things) makes music-nonmusic decisions "based on the listener's culturally-determined beliefs and experiences."[21]

Although we do not yet have sophisticated models of how such multiple, superimposed functions actually work, one thing seems certain: the brain's comparing, judging, and editing processes do not occur in words.[22] As I have explained, thinking does not necessarily involve talking to oneself. In addition, because our conscious powers are distributed throughout the brain, there is no single moment when each event enters conscious awareness. Thus, while some theorists want to make a large separation between perception and cognition, the conscious acts of locating, identifying, interpreting, and understanding sights and sounds (and so on) are most likely coincident in consciousness, even though the brain's location and identification channels are located in different regions of the brain.[23] Dennett elaborates:

> There is no line that can be drawn across the causal "chain" from eyeball [or ear] through consciousness to subsequent behavior such that all reactions to x happen after it and consciousness of x does not happen before it. This is because it is not a simple causal chain, but a causal network, with multiple paths on which Multiple Drafts are being edited simultaneously and semi-independently.[24]

We begin to understand why musical works are not simply perceived or even processed by listeners. The combined powers of human consciousness actively *construct* the complex physical events we experience as musical sound patterns. In essence, music listening involves scanning acoustic waves for musical information, constructing cohesive musical patterns from this information (e.g., melodic patterns, rhythmic patterns, dynamic patterns), interpreting this information, and making comparisons among musical patterns.

The next major point in this examination of listening concerns the role of knowledge. All acts of attending, scanning, identifying, interpreting, constructing, and comparing occur as a result of innate and learned principles of musical pattern construction. The brain-mind's complex mixing board is guided fundamentally by procedural understandings: by nonverbal, practical, and practice-specific knowings that most people in most cultures use implicitly and begin to learn easily and early in life. Fiske supports the basic thrust of this view: "[T]he link between acoustic cues and the detection and identification of auditory (musical) patterns is a set of rules, known implicitly by both performer and listener, that guide the pattern construction and recognition process. The process is active (that is, it requires immediate involvement by the listener), and it is context dependent."[25]

These thoughts bring us back to the topic of musicianship. All forms of music making and music listening depend on practice-specific forms of musical knowing (both tacit and verbal) that musical practitioners and listeners learn informally and formally. Different music cultures pivot on different beliefs about, and principles of, musical pattern construction.

But as Serafine argues,[26] practice-specific principles of musical design suggest the existence of something more basic: a set of generic listening processes that all people have in common and that cut across and underlie most, if not all, practice-specific ways of musicing and music listening. For example, says Serafine,[27] while "come to rest at the tonic" is a common rule of Western melodic organization, this rule reflects more fundamental laws or tendencies of human audition that might be stated as follows: organize and cognize sound patterns in coherent units and divisible resting points. Serafine continues:

> We must assume that people employ such generic cognitive processes in the course of effecting a particular musical style, because they surely do not alter their minds every time a new style makes its appearance. Indeed, styles change continuously. . . . If there were no generic, pan-stylistic processes, we could only understand one style at a time, perhaps only one in a lifetime.[28]

In other words, if human infants did not share an innate set of auditory thinking processes in common, then how would people in different cultures ever learn to make sense of such radically different Musics as Chinese opera, North Indian drumming, Cape Breton fiddling, and Balinese gamelan music? Without a set of innate listening processes, human beings would not be able to produce or listen for musical sound patterns of any kind. But if this is so, then what can we say about these generic listening processes and the practice-specific knowings they support? Asked another way: What constitutes the procedural nature of music listening?

I begin my answer by drawing upon the original insights of Serafine and Fiske.

I emphasize "begin" because while I accept the thrust of their views, I shall argue that music listening is not restricted to cognizing purely sonic information. This is so, I suggest, because the auditory events that music makers produce and that listeners organize covertly as musical works are always context-dependent and therefore always include several kinds of information in addition to the purely acoustic data that human brains use to construct tonal-rhythmic structures. Indeed, most accounts of music cognition are problematic in two basic ways: they conceive music listening too narrowly as aural-cognitive activity alone[29] and (or because) they embrace the aesthetic fallacy that musical works consist in autonomous sound patterns (or sounds alone).[30]

But if it is reasonable to say that: (1) human consciousness is the outcome of genetic and cultural influences; (2) auditory cognition is one part of human consciousness as an integrated whole; (3) musical sound patterns are the result of practice-specific ways of thinking; and (4) music listening is context-dependent, then it is doubtful that music listening is strictly limited to the cognitive processes of purely aural pattern construction that I describe next in this chapter.[31]

In sum, I suggest that a listener's internal organization and experience of musical works includes several kinds of musical thinking and knowing (in addition to the core processes outlined next) because the sonic materials of musical works (including instrumental works) are always practice-specific and culture-specific constructions. Put another way, the material means of musical works are *artistic* in nature, not aesthetic, and therefore evince (manifest, or present) several dimensions of musical information for listeners to actively organize or listen for.

3. The Procedural Essence of Music Listening

Listening for music is analogous to constructing a moving jigsaw puzzle. Listeners do not simply listen from wholes-to-parts or parts-to-wholes because auditory parts and wholes coalesce. At the most basic level, says Serafine, listeners must identify, group, and chain short musical units together in time to form longer musical units, including melodic, rhythmic, timbral, and textural patterns.[32] Implicit in acts of identifying and grouping sound patterns are the additional processes of remembering musical patterns across short and long time spans and making same-different comparisons between and among consistent and inconsistent auditory patterns.

In addition to chaining successive auditory patterns horizontally, most (but not all) musical practices require the cognition of simultaneous events, including chords, superimposed melodic and rhythmic events, and combined timbres. For example, in listening to a singer with piano accompaniment, we parse acoustic waves into long and short time spans and simultaneous interwoven streams to construct contrasting foreground-background relationships such as melody-accompaniment and melody-countermelody.[33]

Of course, some aural patterns are much easier to grasp than others because their auditory features or designs are more congruent with the perceptual tendencies of consciousness. For example, consciousness tends to group elements together that are close in time, that are physically similar, or that seem to follow in the same direction. Consciousness also tends to connect and remember regular patterns more easily than irregular patterns.

Summing to this point, the procedural essence of music listening consists in such covert, nonverbal acts as constructing coherent musical patterns, chaining musical patterns together, making same-different comparisons among and between patterns, and parsing musical patterns into different types of textures. Serafine calls these kinds of thinking generic processes[34] because they likely pertain to the cognition of most, if not all, musical works. But these processes take on specific characteristics in specific musical practices. For example, in making decisions about the same-different relations among the melodic patterns of Wagner's "Liebestod," listeners deploy these thinking processes in relation to their tacit and verbal knowledge of Western musical practices in general, and Romantic practices in particular.

The procedural dimension of listening includes four other processes Serafine calls closure, abstraction, transformation, and hierarchic structuring. Following is a brief overview of these processes as Serafine conceives them.[35]

Every musical practice has specific principles and procedures for creating a sense of musical beginning, continuation, and closure. In many Western practices, closure might be created by a combination of patterns in the following way: a V_7–I harmonic pattern, a melodic pattern of leading tone to tonic, a *ritardando* and a *decrescendo*. These are all practical procedures for shaping closure. They reflect the practice-specific rules and working principles of Western tonal music. The musical practices of other cultures create closure in other ways.

Across musical practices, coherent musical patterns tend to become embedded in larger patterns. For example, a composer or improviser may remove a melodic motive from its original statement and relocate it as the germ of a different theme or a development section. This process, called *abstraction,* is pervasive across musical practices. The relocation of characteristic patterns across a wide time span is a basic way composers and improvisers unify musical works.[36] It is also a basic music listening process that listeners carry out. Implicit in this process is what Fiske calls same-different decision making in relation to the local and global features of unfolding musical patterns.[37]

Closely allied to the process of abstraction is *transformation.*[38] Music makers often vary or transform patterns when repeating or relocating them in a musical work. Common means of transformation include ornamentation, transposition, diminution, augmentation, inversion, and rhythmic alteration. Listeners must therefore make decisions about variations between and among patterns. This is not to say that listeners necessarily have verbal knowledge that a motive is in some way transformed. For the most part, listeners make nonverbal decisions about pattern similarities and differences across short and long time spans.[39]

Listeners also seem to engage in a decision making process called *hierarchic structuring*[40] that likely pertains to musicing and listening across music cultures. Although every detail of a musical work contributes to the design of the whole, not all patterns and relationships have equal importance in the structure of a work.

The same holds for the patterns of human speech. (Music is not a language, but musical patterns are like talk in this way). Some phrases are more important than others in giving us a sense of the context and meaning of a spoken sentence.[41] Key phrases cause a cognitive ripple effect. Like a pebble cast in a pond, a spoken phrase (such as, "in the ambulance") can prime our thinking and knowing. It contextualizes the information we hear and prompts us to think ahead to related concepts (accident, emergency, physician, nurse, trauma, hospital).

Similarly (but not exactly), some musical patterns prime our auditory thinking-in-action more than others. "Priming" facilitates our ability to pick out coherent musical units quickly and efficiently. For example, an awareness of "key" centers in the music of Western tonal practices enables listeners to unlock connections among and between melodic, harmonic, and contrapuntal patterns. Characteristic harmonic relationships (e.g., IV–I) activate and frame a listener's covert thinking-in-action. As a result, listeners are able to organize patterns into levels of importance in terms of background and foreground, focal tones and ornamental tones, and so on.

Note, finally, that if music listening involves such covert acts as chaining, comparing, and abstracting musical patterns over time, then listening must also include representing or "image-ing" previously heard musical patterns for future recall and comparison. For example, to decide whether the pattern we hear now is a melodic variation of an earlier pattern, we must make a relationship between an actual sound pattern and an aural representation or echoic image of a previously heard pattern. How does consciousness encode previously heard musical sounds? And how do people play back and self-generate (or imagine) musical patterns in their heads in the presence and absence of actual sounds? The topic of musical imagery has a long and complex history of investigation.[42] It is enough to say now that varieties of evidence affirm that: (1) human consciousness can image and recall auditory-like patterns; and (2) the ability to generate echoic images before, during, and after music listening episodes is an important aspect of musicianship. Moreover, listeners' auditory imaging abilities appear to develop as other forms of musical knowing increase through education.[43]

Our discussion sums to four closely related themes. We said, first, that the procedural dimension of music listening involves various cognitive processes. In the act of listening for a musical work, music makers and listeners *covertly* construct, chain, compare, order, abstract, transform, recall, and imagine auditory patterns. Of course, performers, improvisers, composers, arrangers, and conductors *overtly* construct coherent musical patterns, chain patterns together, abstract and transform musical patterns, and so on. In other words, *the procedural dimension of listenership and the procedural dimension of musicianship are two sides of the same coin.* Whereas all forms of music listening involve the constructive impression of musical relationships, all forms of music making involve the constructive expression of musical relationships. In this view, people who know how to listen expertly for the works of a particular musical practice possess musical knowings that overlap the knowings of its artistic practitioners.

Second, there is a reciprocal relationship between how human listening functions and what musicers make for people to listen for. That is, musical works are manifestations of generic human listening processes and the practice-specific ways that different cultures instantiate and develop these processes.

Third, the conscious experience of music is not a copy of a static object waiting "out there" to be picked like an apple on a tree. Music listening is a matter of minding. What we experience as a musical performance (live or recorded) is a matter of information that arises in consciousness through interactions between our powers of attention, cognition, emotion, volition, and memory (all of which include various musical knowings) and the artistically created aural patterns of a piece of music. Furthermore, because the mind *is* the physical brain and because our conscious powers are just as much part of the physical world as the musical sounds we listen for,[44] a musical work is neither all "out there" nor all "in the mind." Our musical experiences lie at the intersection of human consciousness and humanly made musical sounds.

Fourth, it seems clear from everything discussed to this point that musical experiences depend on cognizing very specific kinds of sound patterns in very specific ways. Musical performances and improvisations depend on practice-specific musical sound patterns. Both the auditory patterns we listen for as music and the ways we listen for these patterns are highly contextual. In short, *the sounds of music are not just any old sounds.* Accordingly, music-listening experiences always involve the cognition of *several* dimensions of practice-specific musical meaning. Put another way, listening for musical works includes the cognition of artistically and culturally determined information by means of artistically and culturally determined musical knowings (procedural, formal, informal, impressionistic, and supervisory). An example will begin to illustrate this point.

4. Tones-for-Us

How do we know that the sounds of Bach's Fifth "Brandenburg" Concerto are musical sounds and not the sounds of a siren? Our ability to distinguish the sounds of Western tonal music from other nonspeech sounds depends on our ability to differentiate and organize a particular category of sounds. More specifically, Fiske suggests that human cognition employs a set of implicit auditory processing rules that enable a listener to identify and organize nonspeech sounds as "music-intended" or "nonmusic-intended"[45] on the basis of their acoustic features and their function within a "listener-realized tonal-rhythmic order."[46]

For example, while the sounds of a siren go up and down, and while each pitch in a siren's range relates to at least two others (the pitches immediately above and below), each siren pitch taken alone has no coherent relationship with any other pitch in the siren's range.[47] Accordingly, if you listen to a siren wail up and down several times, and if you isolate one siren pitch, you cannot tell where it belongs in the siren's range. An isolated siren pitch lacks any sense of upward or downward direction in relation to other pitches in the siren's range.

What this means is that although the sounds of a siren and the performed sounds of Bach's Fifth "Brandenburg" Concerto both involve pitched sounds, the pitches of the concerto go up and down in relation to one another. This makes it possible for humans to grasp the concerto's successive and simultaneous patterns (melodic, harmonic, and contrapuntal). In contrast, the innate limitations of human listening make it impossible for us to construct coherent relations among the pitches of a siren.

In most cultures, works of music are made of a very small number of special sounds called musical tones. Tones share the audible qualities of pitch, duration, timbre, loudness, and attack with many other sounds in our environment. But tones have one special feature. They are not merely pitches. Tones are pitches-in-relation. A tone is a pitched sound that belongs to a special system of pitched sounds called a scale. Scales create relationships among pitches. These relationships are systematized differently from musical practice to practice and culture to culture, but the basic point remains: Scale-type relationships make it possible for sounds to be systematically and simultaneously alike, yet different. How?

Pitch is a phenomenon like few others. Music makers around the world tend to recognize that from "high to low" along the pitch continuum, every pitch duplicates itself almost exactly at regular intervals called *octaves*. Octaves function to frame a limited set of pitches. These pitches-in-relation are alike in that they are members of a set of tones between two equivalent tones. They are different in that each pitch within the octave is heard as occupying a particular place (or having a particular psychological weight) within the set of tones called a scale. Octave equivalence underlies scale construction and, therefore, tones and, therefore, "syntactic" musical relationships (as I explain later in this chapter).

Western scales are the outcomes of centuries of musical practice and theoretical reflection. They are practice-specific and culture-specific versions of generic listening processes. They are functionally useful because the human ability to identify and categorize auditory patterns has limits. Listeners cannot make reliable comparisons among the continuous sounds of all possible pitches in a siren. Our powers of attention, awareness, and memory are aided tremendously when music makers limit and differentiate the auditory materials of music. Tonal patterns provide a cognitive framework. They make it rather easy for most people to compare, categorize, organize, and remember musical events.

This brings us to two crucial observations. First, Western musical practices are not concerned with organizing and performing sounds per se. They are concerned, instead, with organizing very special sounds that have been "prepitched" or predetermined by careful calculation over centuries of practice and reflection. Indeed, most musical practices around the world pivot on the use of very particular sounds that are preorganized as musical tones according to different theoretical and practical systems. (With more time and space we could build similar arguments for the ways in which different musical practices preselect particular kinds of rhythmic, timbral, textural, and dynamic patterns.)

But while the musical practices of (say) China, India, and Arabia use sounds that are prepitched as tones-in-relation, many people in North America do not accept or understand these sounds as musical sounds. In other words, says Sparshott, when a listener hears (identifies or understands) certain sound patterns as musical sounds, he or she also cognizes this information culturally, as *tones-for-him-or-her*.[48] Listening is mediated by cultural beliefs, associations, and values. We understand particular sounds as tones-for-us (or not) because we construct musical patterns in relation to culture-specific principles of musicing and listening. We know Western music when we hear it because we learn how to think musically in relation to many practice-specific understandings. But we also know it the way we know (and feel) the cultural and psychological impact of a familiar word of English while walking alone through the unfamiliar streets of Teheran, or Kiev.

In other words, a pitch system like the Western tonal system (or the Indian system of *raga*s) involves more than is apparent at first. Its principles of auditory organization yield a distinctive aural character that becomes a tacit reference point in people's minds for accepting or rejecting the sounds of other musical practices as music. Specific practices of musical sound organization often come to be heard as belonging to this or that social group and as representing this or that set of cultural values.

The philosopher Joseph Margolis agrees: "Musical properties are culturally emergent *incarnate* properties."[49] The sounds of vocal and instrumental music are "*historically referential*": they always refer in the sense that they are "about some part of a pertinent [musical-cultural] history."[50] What is composed, arranged, performed, conducted, or improvised in the context of a particular musical practice is *musical* sound, not mere sound; music is not a "natural kind." Margolis sums up the point: "Music *possesses historied properties*—not merely properties (that is, ordered sound)—that are the precipitates of creative efforts that have their own history and intentional energy."[51]

Lucy Green advances similar ideas in her *Music on Deaf Ears* (1988). Green suggests that the musical sounds of different musical practices carry "delineated meanings."[52] Like a stone tossed into a pond, the music of a particular musical practice ripples and rings outward to form circles of social and cultural meanings around the auditory events themselves. Thus the characteristic sounds of a system of musical tones (timbres, rhythms, and so on) can invite or repel listeners because they implicate familiar or unfamiliar social contexts in which the musical practice is embedded.

In summary, underlying each musical practice is a shared body of beliefs, concepts, and principles for constructing and listening for musical patterns in certain ways. As a result, musical works are never a matter of purely sonic information alone. Even a performance of so-called pure instrumental music (such as Bach's Fifth "Brandenburg" Concerto) involves more than successive and simultaneous sound structures. Music listening includes attending to, being cognizant of, and remembering musical patterns as auditory information and as artistic and cultural "tones-for-us."[53] Stated another way, every musical performance of a musical work *evinces* culture-specific and practice-based norms of musical artistry. (I develop these ideas in more detail in Chapters 7 and 8.)

If this is so, then we must reconsider a conventional assumption about the structural properties of musical works.

5. Artistic Qualities versus Aesthetic Qualities

Philosophers of music (as well as of visual art and dance) make important distinctions between aesthetic qualities and artistic qualities.[54] Aesthetic qualities are usually thought of as attributes of things that are immediately perceptible.[55] They are qualities that belong to something and are directly noted, not supplied or constructed by listeners or observers. Aesthetic qualities are typically defined as attributes of things that do not manifest indications of their contextual embeddedness. In contrast, artistic qualities are usually defined as attributes of works that are directly reflective of the practices and traditions of which they are part, including "the influences they undergo or exert and their various relations . . . to other works of art."[56]

Most music education philosophers make no distinctions between aesthetic qualities and artistic qualities. Past thinking simply assumes that the structural properties of musical works—melody, harmony, rhythm, tone color, texture, dynamics, and the formal strategies of musical organization (e.g., repetition, variation, and development)—are aesthetic qualities.[57]

In my view, past thinking is false. There are important distinctions between aesthetic qualities and artistic qualities. Melody, harmony, rhythm, and so on are not rightly called aesthetic qualities. They are artistic qualities or musical qualities. I have three main reasons for saying so.

First, as I have explained, musical patterns are not merely given directly to listeners. Listeners must have practice-specific musical know-how to make sense of musical patterns. Second, and closely related to this first point, the sounds of music are not natural sounds but rather sounds organized by means of practice-specific standards and principles. Musical works may occasionally include natural sounds (such as bird sounds), but musical patterns are not usually made of such sounds. Music makers do not invent the materials of music each time they compose, improvise, perform, arrange, or conduct. In most cases, music makers begin with a delimited set of materials (pitches, timbres, durations, and intensities) that are already "musical" because they have been preselected and preorganized in relation to specific systems of pitch organization, rhythmic organization, and vocal and instrumental timbre traditions. The successive and simultaneous sound patterns Westerners call melody and harmony (and so on) depend on long traditions of music making. In other words, the basic characteristics of musical sound patterns are already "artistic" before musicians begin to use them. "The materials of music," says Kivy, "are in large part preformed artifacts." Kivy elaborates: "Composers do not start from scratch with some kind of palette of natural sounds. They work with melodies, melodic fragments, preformed patches of harmonic fabric . . . : in short, the materials of music are not natural sounds, but music already."[58]

Sparshott makes the same point in broader terms:

[M]usic is not, properly speaking, an art of sound, but an art of musical sound. . . . [M]usic, alone of the arts, is made from materials the very nature of which is derived from the principles of the art: musical materials, themes, and subjects, are of a piece with the procedures to which they are subjected. It is in this respect that it is said that all art aspires to the condition of music.[59]

Even the most fundamental details of melodic, harmonic, rhythmic, timbral, textural, and formal patterns indicate their contextual affiliations. Every auditory aspect of a musical work is inexorably tied to some artistic-musical-historical tradition. Hence, there is nothing innocent, self-contained, neutral, or ordinary about the sound patterns of musical works or the processes of listening for musical sound patterns. Philip Alperson agrees:

> [T]he question of what makes a property an "aesthetic" property is not an easy one. One reason for this is that there may be no such thing as a pure "aesthetic" judgment about a work of art. Our habits of perception are hardly innocent. They are affected, if not in large part determined, by historically and culturally specific conventions and expectations. . . . The sonata-allegro form, for example, is not a "natural" musical configuration which one perceives in a cultural vacuum but rather a culturally encoded musical form with a particular history. Learning to compose, perform, or appreciate fully music in which this form is an important compositional element is a matter of having learned to recognize, even if subconsciously, the features of that musical form which became part of the vocabulary of a particular musical culture at a particular time.[60]

The third reason that melody, harmony, and other musical patterns are rightly called artistic qualities is that MUSIC is a performing art. Each and every aspect of a musical work that we listen for is always the result of an individual or collective interpretation and performance of a composer's musical design, or an improvised design, or a performer's rendition of a remembered design. Thus, the auditory features of every musical work give evidence of or reveal some tradition of musical interpretation and performance. Put another way, the successive and simultaneous sound patterns of a musical work not only relate *intramusically* (to each other), they also relate *intermusically* by manifesting stylistic features in common with other works in the same tradition of practice. Consider Bach's Fifth "Brandenburg" Concerto as interpreted by Trevor Pinnock and the English Concert (and performed on original Baroque instruments).[61] The conscious act of listening for this performance involves cognizing a unique interpretation of a composition composed in relation to highly contextualized standards and traditions of musical knowledge. The knowledge involved in making and listening for these kinds of musical sounds is, in turn, dependent on a peculiarly Western (cultural) manifestation of generic listening processes.

For all the above reasons, this philosophy holds that MUSIC is neither an art of pure sound nor an aesthetic art. MUSIC is the human endeavor of making and listening for musical sounds that are culturally rooted and practice-specific and, therefore, artistic through and through. Accordingly, musical works are not rightly conceived as aesthetic objects. Musical works are not aesthetic in nature, and they are not physical objects.

Instead, and because the human experience of music lies at the intersection of human consciousness and humanly generated musical sounds, works of music are physical *events* of a special kind. Musical works are *performances:* physical events that are intentionally generated by the knowledgeable actions (overt and covert) of human agents (or musicers) to be intentionally conceived as such by other knowledgeable agents (musicers and/or listeners).[62] (I elaborate on this view in Chapters 7 and 8.) And as I shall continue to argue throughout this book, it is because musical works are so deeply rooted in human action and social practice that music making and music listening can be so powerful, so beautiful, so moving, and so significant in human life.

The last point in this section is directed to the reader who may still want to claim (following John Cage) that music is in the ear of the beholder, or that all sounds are music. As Levinson points out,[63] although it is possible to regard any sounds as if they are music, it does not follow from this that all sounds *are* musical sounds. (You can call a horse a cow if you like, but that doesn't make it so.) There is an important difference between what musical sounds are and what people can regard as musical sounds. The relativistic notion that any sounds can count as music denies the possibility of rational inquiry because it trashes a host of characteristics that are obviously central to MUSIC as we know it, including the intentional, artistic, practice-based characteristics of music making and music listening. In sum, a listener's attitude is an important consideration in deciding what to count as musical sounds. But it is by no means the only consideration.

6. Musical Works: Multidimensional Challenges

Everything to this point has prepared the way for the next key proposal of this philosophy, which I will introduce now and continue to develop through the next four chapters. The proposal is this. While intelligent music listening depends crucially on learning to cognize the structural patterns (or formal designs) of musical works, listening for structural patterns does not exhaust what music listening invites and demands. In other words, musical works are not one-dimensional constructions. A heard musical performance of a composition (or an improvisation) is a *multidimensional thought generator*. Musical works are intentionally generated *challenges* to our powers of consciousness.

How so? Given the preceding sections of this chapter, it is evident that musical works always involve (1) a performance/interpretation of (2) a composer's previously organized musical design, or an improvised design. And because dimensions (1) and (2) are made by and for people who share a certain type of musicianship, the audible features of musical works also evince (3) specific standards and traditions of musical practice.

The full proposal I build in the following chapters is that *musical works always involve at least four and often as many as six interrelated dimensions of musical information to listen for* (and, therefore, to teach and learn). That is, in addition to the three dimensions listed above, I argue (in Chapter 6) that some (but not all) musical works are (4) expressive of emotions and/or (5) representational in the sense that they describe or characterize subjects of various kinds, including people, places, and things. I then explain (in Chapter 8) why the cognition of all musical

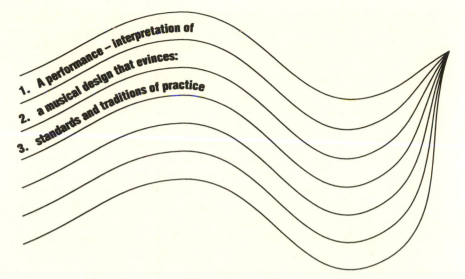

1. A performance – interpretation of

2. a musical design that evinces:

3. standards and traditions of practice

FIGURE 4.2. A Musical Work: Three Basic Dimensions

works involves (6) the apprehension of various kinds of cultural-ideological information.

Figure 4.2 offers a preliminary view of this book's multidimensional concept of musical works. Again, dimensions (4), (5), and (6) will be explained and filled in as we proceed.

With this larger perspective in mind, let us focus briefly on the structural or formal design dimension of musical works (dimension 2 of Figure 4.2). (Chapter 6 contains more about this dimension.)

7. Musical Works: The Design Dimension

The musical design dimension of musical works consists in patterns of melody, harmony, rhythm, timbre, texture, tempo, articulation, and dynamics. Leonard Meyer divides these musical qualities into two categories, called syntactic and nonsyntactic parameters.[64] The syntactic parameters of musical design include melody, harmony, and rhythm. The nonsyntactic parameters of musical design include timbre, texture, tempo, articulation, and dynamics.

Why make a distinction between syntactic and nonsyntactic parameters? Meyer explains that because of the nature of our generic listening processes, some attributes of sound can be divided into discrete relationships so that the similarities and differences between them are proportional. As I explained in my brief discussion of tones, pitch can be divided and cognized in this way. So too with the durations of musical sounds (as rhythmic patterns).[65] In contrast, musical patterns of timbre,

texture, tempo, articulation, and loudness cannot be segmented. There is no equivalent in timbre to a minor third or a dotted quarter note. Timbres can only be
brighter or darker in relation to other timbral patterns; dynamics can only be louder
and softer in relation to other dynamic patterns.

The pitch and rhythm parameters of music are called syntactic because their
elements can be organized into patterns that give a sense of musical movement—
a sense of tones relating to other tones and, therefore, a sense of musical com-
pleteness and closure.[66] Discussions of musical syntax are usually concerned with
practice-specific rules for the construction of syntactic patterns.

Nonsyntactic musical qualities also form relationships, but in different ways.
For example, a constant *allegro* tempo, a steady *crescendo,* and the continuing
timbre of a trumpet section are all examples of nonsyntactic patterns. Nonsyntactic
patterns tend to persist until they cease or alter, or until changes in syntactic dimensions (e.g., a cadence) signal a change.[67]

Music makers organize syntactic and nonsyntactic musical patterns in relation
to three levels of constraints that Meyer calls laws, rules, and strategies.[68] The term
laws refers to the generic principles governing human auditory processing. By *rules*
Meyer means the practice-specific knowings that music makers develop and follow
to organize sound patterns in characteristic ways (e.g., the harmonic rules of Western common practice). The term *strategies* refers to the individual choices that
musicians make in relation to the possibilities established by the rules of a practice. Indeed, new musical practices often result from the development of new
strategies.[69]

In summary, listening for the design dimension of a musical work involves
cognizing the ways syntactic and nonsyntactic musical patterns are organized, interpreted, and performed in relation to practice-based rules and strategies. Figure
4.3 offers a visual summary of this discussion.

8. Musicianship and Listenership

Worldwide, children begin to make sense of their culture's musical sounds early
in life and without formal education. Even very young children learn how to distinguish the sounds of their music from other sounds, how to separate their culture's
music from other Musics, how to identify and remember familiar musical patterns,
and how to tell when their music is just beginning, ending, or repeating.[70] (A similar
statement might also apply, with modifications, to the auditory capacities of the
human fetus.[71]) In other words, most children seem to achieve a novice level of
listenership (or music-listening know-how) through repeated contact with and casual exploration of musical sound patterns.

But since competent, proficient, and expert levels of music listening occur much
less frequently, there must be more involved in the development of listenership
than repeated contact with musical sounds and random explorations. What more?
To answer, let us compare a beginning listener with an expert listener in the specific
context of Baroque musical practices.

When Sara Band, a beginner, and conductor Nikolaus Harnoncourt, a Baroque

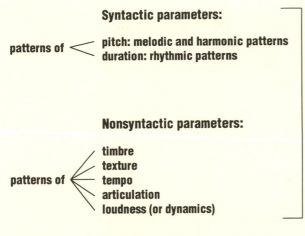

Syntactic parameters:

patterns of < pitch: melodic and harmonic patterns
duration: rhythmic patterns

Organized in relation to:

Generic listening processes or "laws"
Practice-specific rules or principles
Individual strategies

Nonsyntactic parameters:

patterns of < timbre
texture
tempo
articulation
loudness (or dynamics)

FIGURE 4.3. The Design Dimension of Musical Works

artist, are listening for Bach's Fifth "Brandenburg" Concerto, they are both engaged in covert thinking-in-action and knowing-in-action. How is Sara able to listen for this work? Sara has been raised in the context of Western culture. As a young singer, Sara has been learning to interpret and perform a variety of music in her class choir (including Bach's *Duet and Choral from Cantata No. 93*[72]). Thus Sara has already acquired many practice-specific ways of procedural thinking in relation to the Western tonal system. While listening to a performance of Bach's Fifth "Brandenburg," Sara is nonverbally constructing musical patterns (syntactic and nonsyntactic), comparing and contrasting musical patterns, and abstracting musical patterns. Sara does not possess a great deal of formal knowledge about Baroque music, but she recognizes informally that some patterns in this music repeat and echo and are "thick and thin" at times. Her teacher is helping her learn the formal terms for such details. In addition, Sara has acquired an impressionistic understanding that these sounds are tones-for-her and that the performers of this music are working in relation to valued traditions of musical practice. Principally because of her procedural, informal, and impressionistic knowings, Sara is able to construct enough patterns and relationships in the performance she is listening for to make sense of various portions of Bach's concerto.

What does Sara lack in comparison to an expert Baroque listener like Nikolaus Harnoncourt? She lacks formal knowledge about Baroque music. But this is not all. Nor is formal knowledge the most important factor separating Sara the beginner from Harnoncourt the expert. As a form of knowing-in-action, Harnoncourt's listening is highly discriminating in terms of the structural design of Bach's composition, the standards and traditions of practice embodied in Bach's design, the cultural and ideological values this work evinces, and the particular interpretation of these several dimensions expressed in the performance of Bach's concerto that Harnoncourt is currently listening for. His listening is deeply musical because it is informed by all the same kinds of musical knowings that a Baroque performer draws upon to interpret and perform Baroque music artistically. Harnoncourt is not

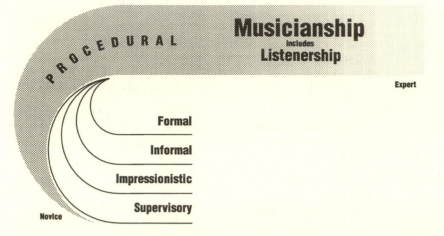

FIGURE 4.4. Musicianship—Listenership

an expert Baroque listener just because he knows more verbal concepts than Sara. His listenership is neither equivalent to nor reducible to his verbal knowledge about Baroque music.

Here is the main point: The kinds of musical knowing required to listen competently, proficiently, or expertly for the works of a given musical practice are the same kinds of knowing required to *make* the music of that practice: procedural, formal, informal, impressionistic, and supervisory musical knowledge. Let us revisit these five components of musicianship from the standpoint of the music listener.

9. Music Listening: Five Dimensions of Musical Knowing

We began this chapter by examining the procedural nature of listening. Our first concern was to explain such innate and learned abilities as identifying, constructing, grouping, chaining, and abstracting musical sound patterns. The following discussion links the procedural essence of music listening with the other four kinds of musical knowing introduced in Chapter 3. It also links music listening to the model of musicianship introduced in Chapter 3. This linkage is emphasized in Figure 4.4—that musicianship always includes listenership.

Formal Musical Knowledge

Music makers and listeners benefit from theoretical knowledge about the syntactic and nonsyntactic parameters of music. The technical languages used by music theorists and historians can be extremely useful in helping listeners identify, construct, organize, and analyze successive and simultaneous musical patterns. In addition, verbal information about practice-specific rules of interpretation, performance, composition, and improvisation contribute significantly to the depth and accuracy of a listener's covert thinking-in-action and a music maker's overt and covert thinking-in-action.

From an educational standpoint, however, formal musical knowledge is problematic in two ways. First, verbal knowledge is not the core knowledge of musicianship. Musicing and listening are procedural in essence. The basics of music are not melody, harmony, and so on; the basics of MUSIC are the practice-specific thinking processes that musicers and listeners use to construct musical patterns in their auditory, artistic, and contextual fullness.

It follows from this that the core knowledge of music education is not verbal concepts about melody, harmony, or anything else. The core knowledge of music education is action-based: it is knowledge-*how* to think musically *in* the actions of musicing and listening. This emphasis on listening as thinking-in-action may help teachers to keep verbal concepts about music and musicing in their proper place: as a supplement to but not a goal or an organizer of music teaching and learning. (I explain this point more fully in Chapters 10 and 11.)

Studied out of context, as an end in itself (and in isolation from the sounds and actions of music making), formal musical knowledge is inert and unmusical. To be of musical value (as opposed to purely scholastic value), and to be transformed into procedural knowledge, verbal knowledge ought to be employed parenthetically—as an adjunct to music making and listening.

Of course, formal musical knowledge may also take the form of analytical maps of musical structure, or traditional musical scores. As far as they go, such representations support the development of listenership. But neither scores, nor charts, nor maps of musical structure—none of these representations capture all there is to listen for in musical works. This is especially true of aesthetic listening guides (known as call charts or perception charts[73]). By focusing students' attention exclusively on the structural design dimension of musical works, aesthetic listening guides perpetuate the false notion that all musical works everywhere are one-dimensional aesthetic objects (or sounds alone).

Second, it is important for teachers to consider that talk about music can also be practice-specific. Different musical practices use different ways of describing the musical works they make and listen-for. Overall, it is not a question of whether to use multiple or alternative ways of describing musical patterns; it is a question of when. In the context of Western music, for example, there are several ways to talk about performances and compositions, depending on the practice and the musical work concerned. We can discuss musical works *systematically* (in terms of dominant, first subject, fugue, and so on), or *relatively,* by making comparisons among musical qualities (short-long; high-low; single line-multiple lines; consonant-dissonant; repeated-varied). In addition, we can talk *phenomenologically,* in terms of thick and thin sounds, dark and bright sounds and so on. Moreover, as I explain in Chapter 6, it is sometimes (but not always) legitimate to discuss musical works *descriptively,* as sounds of celebration, mourning, marching, "sounds-like-a-train," and so on. Finally, it is often (but not always) appropriate to talk about the artistic qualities of specific works *emotionally,* as being expressive of happiness, perhaps, or sadness, or melancholy.

Informal Musical Knowledge

Learning how to listen intelligently depends importantly on acquiring informal musical knowledge. This form of knowledge arises from the local conditions that swirl around the actions of goal-directed music making. It is the kind of knowledge that an expert like Nikolaus Harnoncourt has acquired while learning to make music artistically. It is the kind of knowledge Sara is beginning to develop through her active involvement in performing authentic works and solving real musical problems.

If music listening were a matter of listening for natural sounds, then listeners could learn to listen well without the informal knowledge that arises in the processes of reflective music making. And if musical works were only a matter of abstract patterns, then listeners could achieve a competent level of listening without acquiring the critical thinking abilities that arise in the course of learning to make music competently, proficiently, and expertly.

But works of musical sound are culture-specific constructions that are always presented to us as physical-temporal events of a special kind that we call musical performances. Musical performances, in turn, are individual or group interpretations that result from the critical decisions of reflective musical practitioners. An expert listener like Harnoncourt is a person whose listening is discriminating in relation to the kinds of musical decision making that music makers deploy in action. Thus an essential aspect of intelligent music listening is knowing how to listen critically—in relation to authoritative principles of musical interpretation and performance.

Recall from Chapter 3 that critical musical thinking and strategic musical judgment go hand-in-glove. Strategic judgment is part of one's informal musical knowledge as a music listener and a music maker. The critical and strategic core of informal knowledge crystallizes as students learn to listen for music from the inside of a practice—from the viewpoint of the music maker who dwells in a music culture as a practitioner of that particular art of music. (Informal musical knowledge does not develop from the outside viewpoint of the distanced and disinterested consumer of aesthetic objects.) Learning to listen critically, with strategic judgment, develops from listening for one's own efforts to make music well. It grows by making practical musical choices, assessing the outcomes of one's musical choices, testing alternative artistic strategies in musical problem solving, and developing personal accounts of these alternatives in relation to the artistic constraints of a musical practice.

Impressionistic Musical Knowledge

Becoming a competent listener includes developing a refined emotional sense or feel for what is musically appropriate, original, and artistically significant in the music one makes and listens for. Recall that impressionistic musical knowledge involves cognitive emotions; it involves educated feelings for particular kinds of musicing and listening.

Educated feelings for musicing and listening are not sensations that some people are born with and others are not. They arise from one's knowledge and beliefs about everything from the cultural meanings of tones-for-us to the most precise details of musical interpretation and compositional design. Hence, the development of impressionistic musical knowledge depends on coaching students to make appropriate appraisals regarding the standards and traditions of practice that apply to the musical works that students themselves are learning to interpret, perform, improvise, compose, arrange, and conduct. From this perspective, informal and impressionistic knowledge are closely allied. Critical thinking-in-action and strategic judgment give rise to educated feelings about music.

A music education curriculum based on systematic efforts to make music well places students at the center of the belief systems that ground different musical practices. A curricular emphasis on the progressive development of competent, proficient, and excellent music making instates the contexts, opportunities, and challenges that students require to develop their critical dispositions and educated feelings for the music of different musical communities.

Once again, impressionistic knowledge, like procedural and informal knowledge, is situated. Situated forms of knowing accrue in teaching-learning contexts that approximate viable music cultures. They grow in the actions of natural musical problem solving. General music programs geared to recorded music do not provide the proper conditions for developing the several kinds of knowledge required for intelligent listening because recordings place the student-as-listener outside the artistic decision-making process. A music curriculum based on recordings encourages passive listening-to. In contrast, music making places the student-as-listener inside the musical works and practices he or she is endeavoring to learn. The kind of music listening one engages in while performing, improvising, arranging, composing, and conducting is a matter of artistic listening-*for*. It is directed toward musical problem finding and problem solving. In sum, educating competent, proficient, and expert listeners for the future depends on the progressive education of competent, proficient, and artistic music makers in the present.

Peter Kivy concurs with this praxial view. Because of recordings, says Kivy, "listening to music has become a completely asocial pastime, neither bringing people together in a sense of ritual participation, nor bringing them, in its fullness, the sense of cooperatively wresting order from chaos, society from anarchy that a live performance might convey."[74]

Kivy also supports the strong emphasis this praxial philosophy places on teaching music listening through significant music making.

> For not only is the performing of music, in ensemble, a deep and rich communal experience in itself; it enriches as well in ways hard to convey to the nonperformer the experience of musical listening. It literally makes one able to hear what to others is inaudible. In particular, I would conjecture, it renders more audible just those qualities of music having the deepest ritualistic, "tribal" vibrations by a kind of sympathetic response to the performance that only someone who has experienced performance directly can have. At the risk of some exaggeration, to listen to music without having performed it at some level, as a singer or player, is like seeing *Romeo and Juliet* without ever having been in love.[75]

Supervisory Musical Knowledge

Recall from Chapter 3 that supervisory knowledge concerns knowing how to monitor, manage, and direct one's overt musical thinking- and knowing-in-action. What I wish to underline now is that music makers and listeners must also monitor and direct their listening in relation to the several dimensions of meaning or information that musical works evince. Indeed, the importance of supervisory musical knowledge becomes clearly apparent when we remind ourselves that *there is no one way to listen for all musical works everywhere*. Different musical practices produce listenables that emphasize different dimensions of musical meaning and different combinations of dimensions. The characteristic features of these strata differ across musical practices.

From the position of the listener, then, becoming competent, proficient, or expert involves learning why, how, and where one should focus one's thinking while listening for the several dimensions of different musical works. In the process of listening, educated listeners supervise the allocation of their musical knowings by reflecting in and on the progress of their listening. Educated listeners have the disposition and the ability to evaluate the effectiveness of their covert thinking-in-action. In this way, supervisory knowledge draws upon and feeds back to the other four knowledge components of one's musicianship-listenership.

One aspect of a listener's supervising knowledge deserves special mention. Recall that the procedural knowledge of music listening includes several kinds of cognition that depend, in turn, on relating an incoming pattern and an "echoic image": a previously heard and remembered musical pattern. What I suggest now is that proficient and expert listeners may develop an enhanced disposition and ability—a supervisory intention—to generate and use musical imagery while listening. For the ability to make accurate comparisons between real, remembered, and imagined musical patterns orients a listener's thinking-in-action within the bounds of a given practice and style. It also engages a listener (or musicer) in anticipating, hypothesizing, or listening ahead for the kinds of musical information that may (or should) be coming next in the moment-to-moment events that constitute a musical work. I suggest, also, that student listeners who learn to engage and generate auditory imagery as part of their musical self-management procedures may be more likely to identify with the music they are learning to cognize. This is so because relating pertinent musical images, goals, and standards to what one is listening for now is synonymous with the kind of artistic listening that musicers employ to balance musical ends and means and make music well.

In sum, aural imagining-in-action[76] is another kind of heuristic imagination (discussed in Chapter 3) and a key part of a listener's procedural and supervisory know-how. It goes hand-in-glove with the ability to continuously retarget one's attention forward to new details or problems in the music one is making or listening for.

How do students acquire supervisory musical knowledge? The primary way is by learning to target their powers of attention, cognition (including aural imagination), and musical memory during periods of progressive musical problem solving. Indeed, the presence or absence of supervisory knowledge (and musicianship in general) is conspicuous in the quality of a student's music making. An excellent interpretation and performance of a musical work or a significant portion of a work is concrete evidence that a student understands the relevant dimensions and features of that work and knows how to supervise his musical thinking-in-action. A second way to enhance supervisory knowledge is to encourage students to reflect verbally about what there is to interpret, express, and listen for in specific works. Learning to scrutinize one's musicing and listening in reflective and critical ways goes hand-in-hand with learning to target one's attention and awareness to more and more subtle details of musical works.

When artistic music making (which includes artistic music listening) is at the center of the music curriculum, then listening is properly contextualized. As a supplement to authentic music making, listening to recordings provides students with additional opportunities to develop supervisory musical knowledge.

10. Implications for Music Education

In Chapter 3 I emphasized that musicianship is a form of understanding that is situational and relational. It is web-like, coherent, and context-dependent. In Chapter 4 I have emphasized that musicianship includes listenership and that competent, proficient, and expert levels of music listening include all the same kinds of musical knowing required for intelligent music making. I suggest, also, that music listening is a multidimensional form of thinking and knowing that can be progressively developed to meet the demands made by the multidimensional nature of musical works. Musical patterns and musical works invite listeners to generate artistic and culture-specific meanings in combination with the cognitive generation of auditory relationships.

How do we organize and carry out music teaching and learning in ways that are true to the nature of music listening? In the concluding section of Chapter 3 I proposed several basic principles of music teaching and learning. These principles apply equally to the education of music listening. Let me revisit and amplify each of these principles now.

• *The teaching-learning context*. Recall that music listening is practice-centered and that four of its five knowledge components are nonverbal and situational. Accordingly, to educate music listening beyond a novice level requires that music students be inducted into and immersed in musical practices through meaningful music making. Listening artistically for the music one is making oneself (and with others) enables a student to understand how different aspects of musicing and listening relate to one another in terms of cause-effect, whole-part, form-function, comparison-contrast, and production-interpretation relations.[77] Learning to listen deeply and intelligently for the music of a particular practice requires that students learn music from inside musical practices, from the perspective of *reflective musical practitioners*.

Another way of putting this is to say that music listening ought to be taught and learned in classroom situations that music teachers deliberately design to approximate actual musical practices. As I mentioned in Chapter 3, the name for this kind of teaching-learning situation is curriculum-as-practicum. A music curriculum based on authentic music making serves to contextualize and situate listenership and its component knowings. In this view, artistic listening—listening for what one is attempting to achieve musically—is the primary form of listening in music education.

Contrast this praxial view of music listening with the notions of past philosophy.

Aesthetic educators insist that the primary focus of general music programs should be listening—listening in the peculiar sense of perceiving and reacting to recordings according to the axioms of aesthetic perception. But this focus is wrong for several reasons (in addition to what I have already noted about the failures of the aesthetic doctrine).

First, by positing record listening as the end behavior of music education, and by relegating music making to the status of an educational "means behavior," past philosophy not only negates the natures of MUSIC, musical works, and musical understanding, it negates the participatory nature of MUSIC as a performing art. As Peter Kivy argues, teaching people to listen musically is not the same as teaching people to read great literature. Reading is a private, passive activity, says Kivy, "[n]ot, of course, in the sense that the reader does not have to bring things to his or her reading of a text and do things conceptually to a text, but in the sense that the reader need not be a writer or a performer. To love, appreciate, and enjoy novels I hardly need also write them or read them aloud."[78]

In contrast, to love, appreciate, and enjoy musical performances, one needs to know MUSIC as performing art. To become an enthusiastic and knowledgeable listener requires knowing MUSIC as the interpretive and social art it is. As Kivy explains, recording technology creates the illusion that music listening is private and passive. But the illusion is false.[79] (Indeed, as valuable as recorded music can be, audio recordings, like all forms of media, tend to distort the information they convey. In particular, recordings create the false impression that music is a collection of autonomous sounds alone.) The reality of music listening for most people in most musical practices (and the reality that recordings depend upon but fail to reconstruct by themselves) is one in which people join together in the communal and ritual actions of listening, watching, and participating empathetically as music makers bring forth unique musical events and experiences.

Underlying the MEAE focus on record listening are the mistaken beliefs that "one need not compose in order to experience music" and "one need not perform in order to experience music."[80] Perhaps students can learn to experience music in the passive sense of becoming distanced and impersonal consumers without learning how to make music well. But achieving *an* experience of the special kind of event-performance we call a musical work requires an understanding of musical performing; it requires that students learn how to perform and improvise competently themselves, as well as to compose, arrange, and conduct.

The aesthetic philosophy assumes the wrong paradigm for music education. It assumes that teaching music is the same as teaching nonperforming arts such as literature, painting, and sculpture. Put another way, aesthetic curricula prepare students for what MUSIC is not: the isolated, asocial consumption of aesthetic objects. In sum, learning to perceive and react to the aesthetic qualities of recordings by following call charts listing bits of formal knowledge (e.g., first theme, second theme) will not lead to competent listenership, let alone musicianship.

Instead of teaching children wrongly that music is a matter of abstract, contentless aesthetic objects, the praxial philosophy urges educators to teach children through authentic music making that MUSIC is a diverse, human, participatory, social, and performing art.

Kivy agrees:

> To be able to sing or to play is a necessary part of musical literacy. It is . . . a necessary part of the full listening experience. . . .
> To be able to rattle off "first theme, second theme, closing theme" is a parlor trick not worth the trouble of acquiring. To have Beethoven's Third Symphony in one's blood and bones is a boon beyond compare: part of our rites of passage, part of our tribal identity, an important part, it seems to me, of what makes us human.[81]

Indeed, the self that makes music and the self that listens for music is the very same self. It is not that listening is mental and music making is physical and that one is separate from the other. Musicing and listening are possible only because of human consciousness, and consciousness is physical. The brain is the mind; the body is in the mind. The connection between listening and musicing is therefore intimate, to say the least. Music listening and music making are mutually interdependent; they are two sides of the same coin. Furthermore, as Doreen Rao suggests,[82] music making involves a special form of music listening in so far as a singer necessarily listens in two ways to her own singing voice: from the outside, the way her audience listens, and from the inside, the way her sung sounds feel and sound in her bodily actions. The same basic principle holds for instrumentalists.

Consider, also, that whereas listening to recordings excludes (or anesthetizes) part of the self, performing partakes of the self as a whole. Compared to the novice or the beginner, the expert's listening know-how is distinguished by its embeddedness in his or her expert actions of singing or playing. The expert's listening know-how is informed by his knowledgeable actions.

Finally, if the body is in the mind, then it makes perfect sense (as Dalcroze, Orff, and Kodály specialists maintain) that the kinds of moving involved in music making (including conducting) are essential to improving musical understanding, which, I have argued, is essentially procedural.

In summary, teaching students how to perform and improvise musically informs their music-listening abilities both now and in the future. Cognitive scientists use a single word for the same idea: *isotropy*.[83] Isotropy is a fundamental characteristic of consciousness that amounts to this: Anything we learn contributes to what is of present and future concern. Suppose, for example, that a proficient music student stops performing after high school graduation, or that a professional guitarist injures his hands and cannot continue to play. Neither person forfeits the essence of his or her musicianship. Listening for a performance of a familiar work, both listeners will still know how it should be interpreted and performed and how they would perform it if they could. And the musicianship they retain is not something they could detail fully in words. It is something they know tacitly, and feel, and live once again in the artistic actions of the musical performers they are listening for in the present.

Students have the rest of their lives to listen to recordings of musical performances after schooling is over. The best preparation for listening to musical performances in the future is full participation in music making in the present. Moving beyond a beginning level of listenership requires that students develop their musicianship by entering into the multidimensional nature of MUSIC as a reflective, artistic endeavor.

• *Progressive musical problem solving.* Advancing a listener's thinking-in-action depends on presenting him or her with carefully selected musical works that demand more and more advanced levels of musicianship. Progressive problem solving requires student listeners to take more and more dimensions and details of musical works into account during their efforts to make and listen for music artistically. Students who engage in progressive problem solving work at the edge of their listening competence.

• *Targeting surplus attention.* The development of listening beyond a beginning level depends on what students do with their surplus attention as they become more cognizant of the various dimensions and details that musical works present. Students have three choices: They can spend their surplus attention on matters unrelated to music listening and musical works (e.g., day-dreaming), or on the reduction of listening-related problems (e.g., interval identification, or atomistic pattern recognition), or on holistic musical problem solving. Clearly, students who advance their listenership learn to direct their surplus attention to more and more subtle problems in the music they are learning to make and listen for. Among the several dimensions of a musical work in which students must find and solve musical problems are the three dimensions introduced earlier in this chapter: (1) the performance-interpretation dimension, (2) the compositional design dimension, and (3) the dimension of practice-specific standards and traditions that all musical works evince. Reinvesting surplus attention in more and more advanced problem finding and problem solving is not only characteristic of what expert listeners and music makers do, it is characteristic of the process of becoming musically proficient and expert.

• *Problem reduction.* Reducing listening-related problems is a necessary part of teaching students how to listen expertly. For example, learning verbal facts about the structure of a fugue that students might be learning to perform is a problem that must be diminished in terms of the amount of attention it takes up in consciousness. But as formal knowledge about the fugue becomes proceduralized in the actions of musicing and listening, and as attention is freed up, students have a choice. The musical choice is to reinvest this attention in further artistic problem solving, not in the acquisition of more verbal information about fugues in isolation from music making. Musical problem reduction is the opposite of musical understanding.

Achieving competent, proficient, and expert levels of listening is the outcome of a process that learners can both engage in and learn by pursuing increasing musical challenges with musicianship that is never quite sufficient to solve all current problems. Drawing on their musicianship, music educators guide students' musical thinking by targeting their attention to specific details of the works they are making themselves, performing important parts of the works that students are making and listening for, and explaining in words, diagrams, charts, gestures, metaphors, and other symbols where and how students need to target their concentration.

• *Music teachers and music students.* This chapter's discussion of music listening and musical works reinforces another principle introduced in Chapter 3. Despite such common distinctions among instructors' titles as general music teacher, band director, and Kodály educator, the music educator's role is principally one of mentoring, coaching, and modeling for music students conceived as apprentice musical practitioners. All music students (general students, or otherwise) ought to be viewed and taught in the same basic way: as reflective musical practitioners engaged in the kind of cognitive apprenticeship we call music education.

• *Evaluation.* Like all forms of thinking, music listening can be carried on intelligently or ineptly. When listening is proceeding intelligently, the result is neither a written description nor a theoretical analysis of a musical score but a personally constructed understanding and experience of a musical work. The nature and quality of a listener's covert thinking-in-action lies in what his or her conscious powers accomplish in conscious awareness.

The covert nature of listening creates an obvious dilemma in terms of evaluation. For what a listener is able to say or write about the results of her aural thinking-in-action is, at best, a secondhand account of her listening ability. And it is not "intelligence-fair." For just as a student's ability to perform music may be above or below her ability to talk about what she knows how to do, her listening ability may be above or below her ability to verbalize the results of what she knows how to do as a listener. In short, paper-and-pencil tests of verbal knowledge about musical works are not evaluations of music listening. They are evaluations of the formal knowledge component of musicianship. Verbal and graphic descriptions of musical works have an important place in the teaching and assessment of listening. Students should be engaged in these forms of articulation. But music educators need to guard against the temptation to assess music listening solely in terms of students' formal musical understanding.

One of the most musical ways of assessing a student's listenership is to assess his or her performances of specific works (or relevant portions of works). An artistic performance is the ultimate nonverbal description of a work. Only in an artistic performance (rendition or improvisation) of a work do all its relevant dimensions come together as a whole. This is partly what we mean when we say that music is a performing art. A musical performance is a rich, nonverbal explanation of what a performer understands procedurally, formally, informally, impressionistically, and in supervisory ways about a particular example of music and the musical practice of which it is a piece. If I know how to interpret and perform a work well, then I understand it and I know how to listen for it. My knowing is in the actions of my artistic music making. Similarly, if I compose or arrange artistically—in relation to the relevant standards and traditions of a genre—then I have a working musical understanding of that practice, and I know how to listen for the works of that domain.

In conclusion, music listening is a complex form of thinking and knowing that can be taught and learned. Music students can achieve competent, proficient, and expert levels of music listening. But teaching and learning this kind of thinking effectively requires that its development be embedded in efforts to develop musicianship through performing, improvising, composing, arranging, and conducting.

Questions for Discussion and Review

1. Many people assume that listening occurs directly (or immediately), without any mediating cognitive processes. Give three basic reasons why you agree or disagree with this view.

2. What does it mean to say that consciousness is parallel and distributed?

3. There is a miraculous difference between physical acoustic signals and our experiences of the distinct and bounded patterns of music and speech. What characteristics of consciousness and auditory cognition account for this difference?

4. This chapter proposes that music-listening ability (or listenership) involves several forms of musical thinking and knowing. Summarize the main characteristics of each. Explain why music listening is procedural in essence. Explain why music listening is situated, or context-specific. Could listenership involve additional (or fewer) forms of knowing? If so, what forms of knowing could be added (or subtracted), and why?

5. Readers will find the phrase "performing and listening" throughout the literature of music education. Are performing and listening separate and distinct as the phrase implies? If not, why not? (Your answer should include your views on two related questions: It is possible to become an intelligent performer without becoming an intelligent music listener? Is it possible to become a competent, proficient, or expert music listener without developing some degree of competency or proficiency in music making?)

6. Summarize the concept of tones-for-us.

7. Are the structural properties of musical works (melody, harmony, and so on) properly termed artistic qualities or aesthetic qualities? Why? Does it make sense to call musical works aesthetic objects? Why, or why not?

8. What reasons does this chapter offer to support the view that musical works are multidimensional constructions?

9. What reasons does this chapter offer for the view that educating competent, proficient, and expert listeners for the future depends on the progressive education of competent, proficient, and artistic music makers in the present?

10. This chapter includes several practical principles for the education of music listenership. Summarize five (or more) of these principles. On the basis of (1) your

own music teaching experiences, and/or (2) your observations of other music teachers in action, and/or (3) your study of the videotape listed in the Supplementary Sources, give an example of each of these principles in action.

Supplementary Sources

Harold E. Fiske. "Structure of Cognition and Music Decision-Making." In *Handbook of Research on Music Teaching and Learning,* ed. Richard Colwell, pp. 360–376. New York: Schirmer Books, 1992. A clear discussion of music listening in the essential but restricted sense of tonal-rhythmic pattern construction and comparison.

Mary Louise Serafine. *Music as Cognition: The Development of Thought in Sound.* New York: Columbia University Press, 1988. Chapter 1, "The Problem," provides a concise review of past and present theories of music, including the premises of Serafine's important (but narrow) theory. Chapter 3, "Some Processes," explains many important aspects of music listening.

Harold E. Fiske. *Music Cognition and Aesthetic Attitudes.* Lewiston, N.Y.: Edwin Mellen Press, 1993. Chapter 3 explains Fiske's three-component model of speech and music processing. Chapter 5 analyzes the concept of musical imagery.

Jean-Jacques Nattiez. *Music and Discourse: Toward a Semiology of Music.* Princeton, N.J.: Princeton University Press, 1990. Chapter 2, "The Concept of Music," includes several ideas in support of my view that musicing, listening, and musical works involve social-cultural meanings.

Joseph Margolis. "Music as Ordered Sound: Some Complications Affecting Description and Interpretation." In *The Interpretation of Music: Philosophical Essays,* ed. Michael Krausz, pp. 141–53. Oxford: Clarendon Press, 1993. Margolis holds that musical sounds embody their contexts of musical and cultural production.

Peter Kivy. "Music and the Liberal Education." *Journal of Aesthetic Education* 25, 3 (Fall 1991): 79–93. A critique of music appreciation and a bold position on the place of music in liberal education.

Leonard B. Meyer. *Style and Music: Theory, History, and Ideology.* Philadelphia: University of Pennsylvania Press, 1989. Chapter 1, "Toward a Theory of Style," explains Meyer's recent views of musical parameters, laws, rules, and strategies.

Stephen Handel. *Listening: An Introduction to the Perception of Auditory Events.* Cambridge, Mass.: MIT Press, 1989. An extraordinarily detailed examination of listening that includes many discussions of music listening. If your time is short, examine several brief sections for key ideas: pp. 1–4; 180–89; 321–26; 379–82; 538–45; 547.

Doreen Rao. *ACDA on Location, Vol. 1: The Children's Choir*. Lawton, Okla.: American Choral Directors' Association, Educational Videotape Series, 1988. This videotape provides examples of several practical principles explained in this chapter.

Morton Hunt. *The Story of Psychology*. New York: Doubleday, 1993. Chapter 15 summarizes past and present perspectives on the nature of human affect.

5

Musicers, Listeners, and Musical Values

On the surface, music making and music listening are strangely impractical endeavors. There is no obvious biological reason for the existence of musical practices. At the same time, life without musicing and music listening would not be human as we know it. Homo sapiens is the species that "musics." In other words, that MUSIC is significant is not in dispute, only *why*.

This chapter lays the foundation for an explanation of the values of MUSIC as a diverse human practice. In doing so, it also prepares the way for an explanation of the values and aims of music education.

1. Human Tendencies and Human Interests

Three things seem clear at the outset. First, the fact that most (if not all) human societies have shown an interest in some form of musicing and music listening does not establish the presence of a specific human need for which musical practices are a necessary satisfaction. This fact establishes only the likely presence of specific human *tendencies*.[1] Second, in considering what tendencies might underpin MUSIC, both common sense and logic suggest that we are under no obligation to identify one overriding tendency. There may be several important human tendencies linked to a variety of musical interests. Third, in attempting to explain its significance, we must not lose sight of what is most obvious and curious about MUSIC: that the actions of music making and music listening often give rise to experiences of positive or satisfying affect. Indeed, even a quick glance around the world is enough to show that while some people make music chiefly for money, status, and other tangible rewards, most do not. Most musicers and listeners find the actions of musicing and listening rewarding in themselves.

The sum of these reflections can be stated in the following way. The keys to understanding the human values of MUSIC (including the values of musical works) are most likely to be found in the nature of human consciousness and the human tendencies it spawns. More specifically, to explain the significance of MUSIC it

seems reasonable to start by searching for one or more human tendencies (1) that
most (if not all) people have in common, (2) that are likely to promote human
efforts to make and listen for musical works, and (3) that are reflected in the musical
processes and products of musical practices.[2]

Such an approach to the values of musicing, listening, and musical works is
not unique to this book. It traces its roots to Aristotle, whose explanation of poetry
rests on a prior consideration of the human tendencies underlying its existence.[3]
Variations on Aristotle's way of thinking appear in the works of several contemporary scholars, including Francis Sparshott, Nicholas Wolterstorff, Daniel Dennett,
David Perkins, and Mihalyi Csikszentmihalyi. The next several sections of this
chapter draw principally from the work of these five scholars, with a special debt
to Csikszentmihalyi.

2. Consciousness Revisited

Recall from Chapter 3 that consciousness is part of the human nervous system,
which, in turn, is the outcome of biological processes. To identify the tendencies
of consciousness that might explain our human interests in musicing and listening,
we begin with a brief overview of the origins and development of consciousness.

Dennett suggests that in the earliest stage of our world there were simple replicators.[4] To survive, these replicators had to become concerned with self-
preservation. This concern marked the origin of boundaries (e.g., the walls of single
cells) and a primordial kind of self-ish concern. For when survival becomes a goal,
the distinction between self and not-self arises, and boundaries become important.

The next primordial problem was likely one of "fight or flight," or "Given
this threat, now what do I do?" During the long history of human evolution, there
came a point when some sort of anticipation ability was necessary for survival.
This need required the evolution of a nervous system that could track, evaluate,
and foresee important changes in the environment.[5] The modern brain-mind is, in
part, an exquisite anticipation device.

The next stage in the evolution of consciousness was a basic shift in the economy of survival. Organisms moved from simply monitoring and anticipating details
of their environment to actively exploring for pertinent information. Most mammals
demonstrate this hunger for information about the status of their surroundings and
their being. Dennett suggests that our early ancestors may have even found enjoyment in various forms of exploration, including self-exploration connected to information gathering.[6]

Over the vast time span of hominid brain evolution, the astonishing elaboration
and combination of these functions and motivations have brought us to what we
now know as human consciousness. Taken together, the innate specializations of
the modern human brain, its evolved patterns of neural activity, and its unique
plasticity make it possible for us to represent all sorts of things to ourselves and
therefore to learn and help others to learn.

Overall, then, human consciousness is the result of both natural selection and cultural evolution. In terms of natural selection, human reproduction has succeeded in moving genes from body to body to replicate evolutionary advances in brain structure. In addition to genes, and in terms of cultural evolution, there are memes—permanent units of cultural thinking, information, or knowledge produced by intentional human action.

The biologist Richard Dawkins originated the term *meme* to emphasize that just as the chemically coded instructions contained in a gene can be passed on from one generation to the next, ideas (and cultural products) can be passed on from one generation to the next through instruction, example, imitation, variation, and/or various forms of presentation and encoding.[7] The list of memes is endless and includes the following: 2 + 2, Paris, law, wheel, alphabet, calendar, triangle, story, painting, game, religion, H_2O, printing press, shelter making, free speech, faith, Beethoven's Symphony No. 5, computer.

Because of its predilection for information of all kinds, and because of its marvelous plasticity, human consciousness grows and adapts in relation to memes. As Dennett suggests, memes are what turn brains into minds.[8] Memes cohere and replicate in the brains of humans by being taught, learned, and passed around via languages, schools, books, artifacts, performances, and tools. Human beings grasp, generate, and modify memes. Human consciousness is a storehouse for memes, a repository of cultural values, beliefs, knowledge, and wisdom.

If this is so, then human consciousness is not isolated. Consciousness is of the world. It is situated, or context-dependent; it develops and functions in relation to its social-cultural location. Indeed, the cultures that human societies construct and maintain might also be thought of as "memospheres."[9]

Figure 5.1 elaborates on the earlier map of consciousness presented in Chapter 3 (see Figure 3.1) by emphasizing its social-culture nature and the interaction between genes and memes in the development of consciousness.

The ideas presented thus far bring the nature and functions of consciousness into sharper focus. As Csikszentmihalyi explains, consciousness functions to represent and coordinate information about occurrences inside and outside ourselves so that we can assess and act upon this information.[10] Consciousness mediates and prioritizes the often conflicting instructions that come from our basic survival drives on the one hand (our biological needs for food, safety, sex, and so on) and the controls imposed by societies to regulate the actions of individuals. Human consciousness functions as a mediator between our genetic instructions (or genes) and the cultural norms, rules, and ideas (or memes) we learn informally and formally.[11]

Since outside events do not exist without conscious attention and awareness, consciousness can also be thought of as our individual phenomenal experience of reality.[12] During the long process of evolution, human consciousness has become so complex that it is not only able to select, sort, and weigh the information our senses take in, it can develop its own meanings and create internal states. Consciousness is a matter of information that is intentionally ordered by our own individual powers of attention, cognition, emotion, intention, and memory.[13] To be conscious means that conscious events are taking place and that we have the capacity to guide, shape, and deploy these events (or information).[14] In sum, people

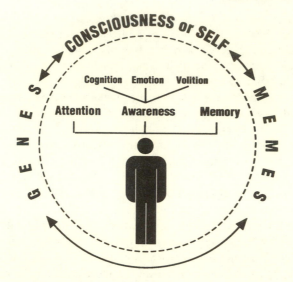

FIGURE 5.1. Consciousness Revisited: Genes and Memes

can modify their individual experiences of themselves and their circumstances by changing the contents of consciousness.[15] Dawkins puts it this way: "We have the power to defy the selfish genes of our birth and, if necessary, the selfish memes of our indoctrination.... We are built as gene machines and cultured as meme machines, but we have the power to turn against our creators."[16]

As each person develops and realizes his or her powers of attending, thinking, feeling, intending, and remembering, individual consciousness grows to the point of developing an independent status called the self. The self becomes "the symbol that stands for the full range of the individual's conscious processes—including those unconscious contents that occasionally surface in awareness."[17] The self, says Csikszentmihalyi, is an *"epiphenomenon . . . the result of consciousness becoming aware of itself."*[18]

As Dennett emphasizes, however, the need for self-knowledge does not stop at the basic need to know *what* we are doing. It extends to the need to know *how well* we are doing in our own circumstances (external and internal). Dennett continues:

> Thus do we build up a defining story about ourselves, organized around a sort of basic blip of self-representation. . . . It [this self-representation] gathers and organizes the information on the topic of *me* in the same way other structures in my brain keep track of information on Boston, or Reagan, or ice cream.
>
> And where is the thing your self-representation is *about?* It is wherever you are. And *what* is this thing? It's nothing more than, and nothing less than, your center of narrative gravity.[19]

As human beings, we are aware of only parts of our selves at any given time. This is because the self is the total of everything that an individual has seen, heard, thought, felt, imagined, intended, and decided. Each human self is a unique pattern of intentions and goals. The self determines when and where the energy of attention will be deployed and, therefore, what events and experiences will enter consciousness. The self is not linear but circular and dynamic. This is so because: (1) attention to outside and inside information determines conscious content; (2) conscious content shapes intentions and goals; and (3) intentions and goals determine the deployment of attention.[20] Outside events (triumph and tragedy, success and failure, change and lack of change) are taken in as information, interpreted in relation to the goals of the self, and assessed as supporting or threatening to the self. As a result, individuals regularly rise above their objective circumstances. People turn hopelessness into hope, misery into happiness, and failure into opportunity. (Of course, people also turn happiness into misery and opportunity into failure.)

This dynamic process points to a central tendency of the human species.

3. Self-Growth

In his *Metaphysics* and in his *Poetics,* Aristotle emphasizes that human beings possess the desire to know. Today, David Perkins reminds us that humans are sapient beings: "[W]e can know and come to know things."[21] We can represent our inside and outside experiences to ourselves; we have the power of understanding. Thus, humans not only have biological and social deficiency needs, human beings also have achievement needs: we desire to "play out our powerful motive as sapient organisms to operate our understanding system."[22] Human understanding, says Perkins, "has a life of its own as a human motive."[23] Accordingly, many human pursuits are taken up precisely because they engage our powers of understanding.[24]

In the same vein, Dennett and Csikszentmihalyi stress that our characteristic powers of consciousness are no accident. They exist to meet the needs of a self-aware, self-directed organism. In other words, there is a "teleonomy of the self":[25] human beings have a goal-seeking tendency. The central goal of each self is to order the self, or strengthen the self.

The themes thus far discussed converge as follows. As human beings, we have a powerful disposition to deploy our capacities of attention, awareness, and memory to shape our environment and our individual experiences of inside and outside realities. The evolution of human consciousness in general, and individual consciousness in particular, depends on and is motivated by a central human tendency that can be expressed in several overlapping ways. As human beings, we have a drive to know our own capacities, to bring order to consciousness, or to gain self-knowledge.[26] We strive to ensure the integrity and growth of the self.[27]

How do we order and strengthen the self? How do we gain self-knowledge? Let us first say what disorders or weakens the self. Csikszentmihalyi explains that when incoming information of any kind conflicts with the goals and intentions of the self, humans tend to experience this incongruity in various ways, including anxiety, fear, panic, anger, jealousy, disappointment, and frustration.[28] Among the kinds of events that may cause disorder in consciousness are the death of a loved one, divorce, loss of one's job, or culture shock. Each self interprets information individually, thereby investing it with personal values and meanings.

In contrast, when outside information is congruent with our self-goals we experience this congruence positively. There is no anxiety or disruption when consciousness is ordered by incoming information that matches the goals of the self. There is an affective experience of buoyant satisfaction. Such experiences are what Csikszentmihalyi variously calls "optimal experience, autotelic experience, or flow."[29]

I will have more to say about the characteristics of optimal experience in a moment. The key point now is that optimal experience results from the active engagement and extension of the self. The sort of information that orders consciousness and that human beings tend to assess as supportive of the self is that which arises when we take up challenges that match and extend our powers of consciousness. Such pursuits strengthen the self; they provide self-knowledge, or "constructive knowledge."[30] Jacob Bronowski proposes the same thesis in different words: "The most powerful drive in the ascent of man is his pleasure in his own skill. He loves to do what he does well and, having done it well, he loves to do it better."[31]

There is a fundamental circularity here. Humans engage in actions and pursuits that strengthen and order the self. We experience these pursuits as more satisfying, enjoyable, and absorbing than everyday activities because they are more demanding and more congruent with the goals of the self. And because we enjoy these endeavors, we continue to pursue them.[32]

Csikszentmihalyi suggests that by investing our powers of consciousness in pursuits that are not based exclusively on our purposeful drives for biological and social satisfaction, "we open up consciousness to experience new opportunities for being that lead to emergent structures of the self."[33] Our motivation is not any material reward. Our motivation is the enjoyment or "flow" that arises when we apply our conscious powers and knowings effectively in goal-directed action. *Enjoyment, then, is the affective concomitant of self-growth.* Csikszentmihalyi elaborates:

> Following a flow experience, the organization of the self is more *complex* than it had been before. It is by becoming increasingly complex that the self might be said to grow. Complexity is the result of two broad psychological processes: *differentiation* and *integration*. Differentiation implies a movement toward uniqueness, toward separating oneself from others. Integration refers to its opposite: a union with other people, with ideas and entities beyond the self. A complex self is one that succeeds in combining these opposite tendencies.[34]

4. Conditions of Self-Growth and Enjoyment

What conditions must be in place to achieve self-growth and enjoyment? Let us first consider what does not lead to self-growth. Some people attempt to order consciousness by satisfying their biological drives for pleasure and/or fulfilling their social drives for power, acceptance, or recognition. It is both normal and likely that most people follow these tendencies to some degree in shaping the self.[35] But problems arise when biological and social drives become goals of the self. As Csikszentmihalyi explains, the pursuit of pleasure, power, or recognition to nurture and shape the self not only has a negative impact on the welfare of others, it fails to order and strengthen the self.[36] This is so because the self is neither limited to nor controlled by biological drives and social needs.

This brings us to an important distinction between pleasure and enjoyment. When biological and social needs intrude into consciousness, the result is disorder. Order is restored in consciousness by satisfying these needs. When consciousness tells us that our biological needs or social expectations are satisfied, we experience pleasure.[37] Pleasure can occur with little or no conscious effort; enjoyment cannot. Pleasure can be stimulated electrically and chemically in the brain; enjoyment cannot. Enjoyment results not from satisfying basic biological and social needs but from moving forward in psychological growth and complexity. Enjoyment arises only from unusual investments of our conscious powers.[38]

On the basis of numerous worldwide research projects,[39] Csikszentmihalyi and his colleagues posit several conditions that they believe underlie the achievement of self-growth and enjoyment. First, two interlocking conditions must be in place: (1) something to do (a challenge) and (2) the capability to do it (know-how).[40] The universal prerequisite for self-growth and optimal experience is a *match*, or at least a *balance*, between something a person conceives or regards as a challenge and the know-how that person brings to the challenging situation. Csikszentmihalyi explains:

> In all the activities people in our study reported engaging in, enjoyment comes at a very specific point: whenever the opportunities for action perceived by the individual are equal to his or her capabilities. Playing tennis, for instance, is not enjoyable if the two opponents are mismatched. The less skilled player will feel anxious, and the better player will feel bored. The same is true of every other activity: a piece of music that is too simple relative to one's listening skills will be boring, while music that is too complex will be frustrating. Enjoyment appears at the boundary between boredom and anxiety, when the challenges are just balanced with the person's capacity to act.[41]

A challenge is what sets self-growth and enjoyment in motion. A challenge may take many forms: a mountain to climb, a chess game to play, a ski slope to ski, a poem to write or read. Clearly, challenges may also take musical forms: a composition to perform and listen for; an improvisation to improvise; a composition to compose; a performance to listen for as an audience member.

Any form of intentional action to which there is a corresponding form of know-how provides the basis for ordering consciousness and experiencing enjoyment. Enjoyment is not something that just happens; enjoyment is something that people make happen as a result of their efforts to meet the demands of something that they themselves deem a challenge.

Implicit in this two-part condition is another. The kinds of pursuits that lead to self-growth and enjoyment are those that involve goals and standards of achievement. (By "pursuits" I mean overt and covert forms of intentional action; by "know-how" I mean overt and covert forms of thinking-in-action and knowing-in-action). Goals and standards establish the foundation for feedback about how well a person is doing something and where that person stands in relation to achieving his or her goals. The actions of downhill skiing, sky diving, and heart surgery have clear goals. Feedback about the effectiveness of one's actions as a skydiver is immediate and unambiguous. (If at first you don't succeed, so much for sky diving!) In contrast, the goals of other pursuits (e.g., musical improvisation) may be less clear, especially to the casual observer. But to an experienced participant, what counts in the context of a particular endeavor (or human practice) is usually well known, if not recorded in written form (or in legends and lore). The key point here is that the feedback participants receive about their efforts is the information they need and use to assess the quality of their actions and, therefore, the effectiveness of their selves. Such information orders consciousness and structures each individual self.

Consider, next, that no endeavor can continue to provide self-growth and enjoyment for long unless both the challenges and the knowledge that define the pursuit become more complex over time.[42] For something to engage our attention and sustain our powers of consciousness, it must have an inner dynamism.[43] It must be capable of providing the participant with increasing levels of challenge to match the increasing levels of know-how that come from pursuing something one enjoys. It is this matching increase in the level of challenge and know-how that propels the self to higher levels of complexity, that results in self-growth, and that participants experience as an exhilarating and absorbing sense of "flow." All powers of consciousness—attention, cognition, emotion, intention, and memory—are propelled to higher levels of complexity and integration.

> The self becomes more differentiated as a result of flow because overcoming a challenge inevitably leaves a person feeling more capable, more skilled. . . . After each episode of flow a person becomes more of a unique individual, less predictable, possessed of rarer skills. . . .
> Flow helps to integrate the self because in that state of deep concentration consciousness is unusually well ordered. Thoughts, intentions, feelings, and all the senses are focused on the same goal.[44]

I shall argue that music making and music listening are unique and major ways of bringing order to consciousness and, therefore, unique and major ways of achieving self-growth and self-knowledge, or constructive knowledge. Stated in terms of affect: Dynamic musical practices provide the conditions necessary to attain optimal experience, "flow," or enjoyment. Before I elaborate on this argument, I wish to highlight several additional features of self-growth.

5. Characteristics and Consequences of Self-Growth

In studying the phenomenology of self-growth, Csikszentmihalyi and his colleagues found several characteristics that seem to cut across different pursuits and cultures.

First, the matching conditions of a particular kind of challenge and challenge-related knowledge create specific kinds of action contexts. Such contexts (sports, games, arts) amount to mini-worlds of effort that are differentiated from the randomness of ordinary events by their internal order. Because these contexts allow for the ordered balance of challenges and know-how, the enjoyment people experience includes a stronger than usual sense of control. As Csikszentmihalyi explains, it is not that people enjoy being in control of their actions as much as that they enjoy exercising control because of their know-how.[45] *Knowledge is the key to enjoyment and control* because know-how enables people to meet the challenges presented by a mountain to be climbed, a chess game to be played, or a musical work to be performed.

Second, optimal experiences are typically marked by a complete focus of concentration on one's actions, whether overt or covert. When the level of challenge and the level of know-how match within a definite context of action, the psychic energy of attention is fully taken up. The doer experiences a oneness with the doing of the action itself. When we are thinking-in-action effectively, events follow one another so smoothly, with such a feeling of flow, that our actions seem effortless, or spontaneous. But as we now understand, enjoyable experiences only seem effortless, thoughtless, and natural. In fact, the enjoyment that arises from successful actions is anything but effortless. Consciousness is ordered and enjoyment arises through learning how and knowing how to deploy one's knowledge in relation to particular contexts and criteria of action.

Third, a pursuit that offers clear goals and feedback within the context of a distinct tradition facilitates concentrated attention. Focused concentration, in turn, expedites the ordering of consciousness and the achievement of enjoyment.

Fourth, optimal experiences frequently include a loss of self-consciousness. There is no anxiety or disruption when consciousness is ordered by the incoming feedback that "I am this person who is doing this thing well." Paradoxically, when we are deeply involved in enjoyable endeavors that strengthen the self, we usually forget our selves, that is, we do not concentrate on our individual representations of our selves. This is because there is too little attention left for self-analysis or self-concern. While thinking-in-action, self-as-other becomes foreground, while self-as-oneself becomes background (less self-*ish*). The doer has a sense of "moving out" and becoming one with his or her chosen pursuit. By investing one's conscious powers in the efforts of a structured endeavor, one experiences a sense of being at the center of the action that flows from one's goal-directed powers of attention, awareness, and memory. Csikszentmihalyi continues:

> When a person invests all her psychic energy into an interaction—whether it is with another person, a boat, a mountain, a piece of music—she in effect becomes part of a system of action greater than what the individual self had been before. This system takes its form from the rules of the activity; its energy comes from the person's attention. But it is a real system—subjectively as real as being part of a family, a corporation, or a team—and the self that is part of it expands its boundaries and becomes more complex than what it had been.[46]

For all these reasons, we also tend to lose track of ordinary time during "flow experiences." We seem to enter another dimension where time has depth as well as length. The time we invest in meeting an absorbing challenge seems to pass either more quickly or more slowly than actual clock time. For example, although we may be engaged in performing or conducting a musical work for twenty minutes, the musical flow experience may seem like only a few seconds. On the other hand, something that takes only a minute, such as rewriting a sentence to get it just right, may seem to move in slow motion.

Finally, pursuits that order consciousness are usually actions that we engage in not primarily for money, fame, glory, or other material rewards but rather for their own sake, meaning *for the sake of the self*.[47] This last point is important. In all cases, human actions require human doers who are self-directed in relation to the traditions and standards of a pursuit. While it is characteristic of enjoyment or flow that it arises in the actions of doing something inherently or intrinsically rewarding, we cannot mean "intrinsic" in the absolute or pure sense of something completely unrelated to all real-life concerns. It would be illogical to make such a claim. For constructive knowledge and enjoyment are essential *life goals*.[48] They are personally and culturally anchored. What could be more practical, more useful, or more interesting to an individual than the self-growth and enjoyment he or she experiences in the actions of meeting a challenge by doing something that he or she personally knows how to do?

In sum, self-growth pursuits are forms of action (overt and covert) that we tend to do for the sake of the self-doing—for the sake of our selves. Our attention tends to be focused in and absorbed by the goal-directed actions of what we are doing. The self-directed action of doing something for its inherent value, for the sake of self-growth, is characteristically exhilarating, gratifying, uplifting—in a word, enjoyable.

6. Self-Esteem

One consequence of self-growth that deserves separate comment is self-esteem. To have self-esteem is to have an overarching awareness (an intrapersonal kind of supervisory knowledge) that one has achieved, or that one possesses, desirable qualities.[49]

Self-esteem can manifest itself verbally ("I'm doing well" or "I'm pleased with my effort") after deliberate reflection on one's effectiveness in meeting significant challenges. Most often, however, self-esteem manifests itself as an intrapersonal kind of impressionistic knowledge: as a feeling that one is successful, good, "together," capable, or productive.

For most people, self-esteem is not a steady state. It varies in relation to changes in the context and effectiveness of an individual's actions. During and immediately following flow experiences, people tend to report high self-esteem:

> [D]irectly after a person has been in flow, his or her self-esteem is higher than at other times. After being in flow people report being more successful, they feel better

about themselves, and they feel that they are living up more to their own and others' expectations. This finding has been replicated in several studies. . . .[50]

In addition, people who frequently achieve self-growth and flow seem to have higher overall levels of self-esteem than those who achieve flow infrequently.[51] Indeed, self-growth pursuits (and the flow that arises in these pursuits) have long term effects. Csikszentmihalyi offers several examples.

> Teenagers who report more flow tend to be happier, and they develop academic talents further than teens who are in flow less often. Adults who spend more time in flow work longer, yet are less prone to stress-related illness. . . . Individuals who cannot experience flow, or who enjoy only passive and simple activities, end up developing selves that are often in turmoil, riven by frustration and disappointment. Those, on the other hand, who master enough skills to find flow in more complex activities tend to develop selves that can transform everyday events . . . into meaningful experiences. In so doing they not only enjoy their own lives, but they contribute to the evolution of complexity for humanity as a whole.[52]

In summary, developing the knowledge required to meet significant challenges in a particular context or domain of effort leads to self-growth, self-knowledge, and enjoyment. These consequences contribute, in turn, to the development of self-esteem and happiness. One of the main reasons that flow is beneficial is that one's overall quality of life depends on it. As Aristotle recognized twenty-three hundred years ago, human beings seek self-esteem and happiness more than anything else. What we have realized more recently is that people are happier when they have the knowledge and the opportunities necessary to achieve flow.[53]

Note, however, that higher overall levels of self-esteem do not result from the simple addition of isolated flow experiences. Instead, self-esteem is intimately related to involving one's self more and more deeply in the challenges and complexities of an established domain of effort, or "in a system of meanings that gives purpose to one's being."[54]

I shall argue in a later section that most musical practices are dynamic "domains of effort," or "systems of meanings," or "certain ways of life" that provide the necessary and sufficient conditions for self-growth, self-knowledge, and flow and, therefore, for the ongoing development of self-esteem.

7. Human Tendencies and Human Interests Revisited

This overarching concept of human consciousness points to several interdependent human tendencies. These tendencies help to explain the interests that human beings take in music making and music listening.

First, it seems a characteristic tendency of human beings that we deploy our powers of consciousness not merely to survive but to understand. As Aristotle said, we "desire to know." Humans seek to understand who they are and what they are capable of doing. We have an innate propensity to bring order to consciousness and to gain self-knowledge.

Second, and closely related to this first tendency, we tend to enjoy pursuits that extend our capacities of consciousness. Humans enjoy (and seek further enjoyment in) pursuits that they find absorbing, demanding, and self-fulfilling. We are motivated to understand more about our capacities. We relish pursuits that challenge our abilities, that fully engage our powers of consciousness. It is characteristic of human beings that we do things for the sake of the self-growth that arises from investing our powers of consciousness in the actions of a challenging pursuit.

Before people can do things for self-growth and enjoyment, they first need things to do. These pursuits come from things that people already do. Humans have a tendency to elaborate aspects of ordinary life. Sparshott calls this "the tendency to make values out of necessities."[55] For example, it is easy to understand why people run or jump to escape danger. But many people run and jump for the sake of running and jumping, or as part of catching footballs and scoring points in basketball. Similarly, while eating and drinking are necessities, menus, banquets, tablecloths, restaurants, and waiters are not. Driving a car is essential for many commuters. But driving in rallies and races is not.

In all these examples, "necessary" activities spawn identifiable pursuits. Ordinary activities like running, dining, and driving become pursuits in and of themselves (or aspects of games, rituals and sports) with specific goals, rules, standards, traditions, heroes, legends, lore, and competitions. It would be most unusual if the same thing did not occur in relation to one of our most basic human necessities: the need to listen for sounds.

Fourth, we have already seen how consciousness is the result of both biological and cultural forces (genes and memes). Humans are simultaneously and inseparably physical, mental, biological, and social. Thus we should not be surprised to find human beings pursuing experiences and shaping consciousness in relation to biological or social drives or resonating with visual and auditory references to these drives, as reflected in sports, paintings, songs, and stories.

Look back now to the starting point of this chapter. It seems reasonable to suggest that the four human tendencies I have described are tendencies (1) that most people have in common, (2) that are likely to promote musicing and music listening, and (3) that are reflected in the processes and products of musical practices. The remainder of this chapter expands on points (2) and (3).

8. The Values of Music Making

On the most obvious level, performers, improvisers, composers, arrangers, and conductors make musical sounds for a variety of purposes including dancing, worshiping, celebrating, marching, mourning, socializing, teaching, and learning. In addition, as I explain in Chapter 6, musicers make musical works to be listened to for: (1) the intricacy of their intramusical designs, and/or (2) musical expressions of emotion, and/or (3) musical representations of people, places, and things, and/or (4) musical expressions of various kinds of beliefs (e.g., personal, political).

The central proposal I wish to make now is this. In addition to and underlying all the various purposes for which music is made are the central values of music making as a human pursuit: self-growth, self-knowledge, and enjoyment. Most musical practices offer music makers the two necessary conditions for achieving the life values of self-growth, self-knowledge, and optimal experience: (1) multidimensional musical challenges and (2) the musicianship required to meet the challenges of a given musical practice. All forms of music making depend on a multidimensional form of understanding called musicianship. The contents of musicianship vary across musical practices and correspond to specific repertoires of musical challenges (i.e., musical works to interpret, perform, improvise, compose, arrange, or conduct). Musicianship is the key to the values of music making. And musicianship can be taught and learned.

Most (but not all) musical practices are dynamic practices, because the musical works that make up the body of most music cultures spiral upward in complexity. Dynamic musical practices invite and require the progressive matching of increasingly complex musical challenges with increasing levels of musicianship.[56] And the traditions and standards of each musical practice determine what count as the proper artistic goals of music making in that practice.

For example, proficient jazz educators know the traditions and criteria of dixieland, swing, bebop, cool, jazz-rock fusion, and other forms of jazz. They know what counts as a good (very good and excellent) jazz improvisation in a particular jazz practice and, therefore, what the appropriate goals and benchmarks of student improvisers should be at beginning to expert levels. Part of a music educator's task is to develop the musical goal-setting abilities of students by teaching them the criteria for judging a truly musical jazz performance. Similarly, music educators who teach in the context of children's choirs know the traditions and standards of children's choral music. They know what counts as good (very good and excellent) choral singing in a particular practice and, therefore, what the appropriate ideals and standards of student singers should be at beginning to expert levels of development. By increasing students' strategic musical judgment abilities, music teachers enable their students to set short-term and long-term musical goals themselves. This, in turn, makes students independently able to recognize what counts as musical feedback and musical success.

In this praxial view, music making is inherently valuable. Performing, improvising, composing, arranging, conducting—all are worth doing for the doing itself, meaning "for the sake of the self." When a person's level of musicianship (beginner to expert) is matched with an appropriate level of musical challenge, this matching of knowledge and challenge brings order to consciousness. The affective concomitant of this matching relationship is experienced as musical enjoyment.

Music making is a unique and major source of self-growth, self-knowledge (or constructive knowledge), and flow. Even for students who are just beginning to internalize the standards of a musical practice and who are just beginning to deploy their musical thinking-in-action, performing in a practice-specific musical context provides second-by-second information about how well they are musicing. So too does music making provide proficient, competent, and expert music makers with feedback about how well they are musicing in relation to the goals and standards of the practices they know so well.

When a person's level of musicianship matches a given musical challenge, his or her powers of consciousness are completely engaged. Consciousness and

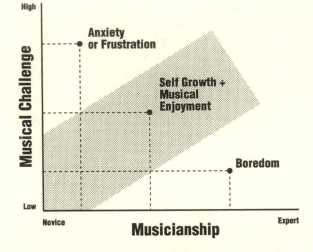

FIGURE 5.2. Musicianship × Musical Challenge = Musical Values

action merge to take us up into the actions of musicing. Music making done well (according to the artistic obligations of a musical practice) engages the whole self.

Music making is valuable and significant in itself because it propels the self to higher levels of complexity. As a student's level of musicianship progresses in complexity to meet the demands of increasingly intricate works, all aspects of consciousness are likewise propelled upward.

Much remains to be said about the nature of musical works as multidimensional constructs and the particular challenges involved in the performance, interpretation, and improvisation of musical works. These issues will be addressed in Chapters 6, 7, and 8. Suffice it to say, again, that musical works are never a matter of isolated sound patterns. It is also important to emphasize that everything we have said about music making in this section applies equally (but not in identical detail, of course) to performing, improvising, composing, arranging, and conducting.

In summary, music making is a unique and major way of gaining self-growth, self-knowledge, and optimal experience, both now and in the future. And to the extent that these values are achieved in and through the development of musicianship, musicing is also a unique and major way of developing self-esteem. For these reasons, music making is something worth learning to do well by *all* students.

In this praxial view, musicianship is not an end in itself. The task of music education is not to develop the various forms of musical knowledge as ends in themselves but *to develop the musicianship of learners through progressive musical problem solving in balanced relation to appropriate musical challenges every step of the way.* As pictured in Figure 5.2,[57] it is the balancing or matching of musicianship with carefully selected musical challenges that results in students' self-growth, enjoyment, and self-knowledge. *Self-growth, self-knowledge, and musical enjoyment are the aims of music education overall and the primary goals of every music teaching-learning episode.*

9. The Values of Music Listening

It is neither prudent nor typical of humans that we should merely hear or listen *to* sounds. To make our ways in the world we must also listen *for* sounds. Human consciousness continuously anticipates and seeks out information of all kinds. We often listen in order to predict what might be coming next. For example, we listen for the sounds of an infant crying at night, or for the sounds of unfamiliar footsteps on the stairs. On another level, we listen not only for the content of *what* a friend is saying but for *how* the emotional inflections in her voice inform us more fully about the meaning of her words.

Since humans already listen to sounds as a normal part of living in the world, and since humans tend to make values of necessities, and since auditory cognition is a multidimensional form of thinking and knowing, it should not be surprising to find that listening *for* a special category of *musical* sound patterns has become a valued human endeavor in its own right. If we combine these ideas with what we now understand about the human tendency toward self-growth, the diverse human practice of making a variety of musical challenges to be deliberately and thoughtfully listened for begins to make sense.

Each interlocking practice of music making and music listening provides listeners with the two necessary conditions for attaining self-growth and optimal experience: a repertoire of musical challenges to engage people's listening know-how, and increasing levels of musicianship to meet these challenges. When a listener's level of musicianship is equal to the overall challenge presented by the several kinds of information that constitute a heard musical performance, a listener experiences this matching of musicianship and challenge as optimal experience: as an enjoyable, absorbing flow experience (see Figure 5.2). If one's musicianship continues to improve, this development of personal competency propels the self to higher levels of complexity. Music listening spirals upward in relation to the cognitive challenges inherent in the musical works of a given practice.

Because music listening is a rich form of thinking and knowing, music listening is also a rich source of self-growth, self-knowledge, and enjoyment. Musicianship is the key to achieving these life values in the music-listening context. Accumulating verbal concepts about the designs of musical works contributes to the development of listening as knowing-in-action if and only if such formal knowledge becomes proceduralized. Neither musicianship nor listenership can be reduced to verbal knowing-that. Because music listening is procedural in essence, and because most children can achieve at least a novice level of listening know-how rather easily and early in life, most children have what they need to begin meeting the most basic musical pattern construction challenges presented by musical works. Accordingly, even novice listeners can begin to enjoy music listening at an early age.

Music educators are experts at enabling and promoting the kind of thinking we call music listening in relation to appropriate musical challenges. Music teachers know how to help students set listening goals and how to enable students to recognize when their thinking-in-action has succeeded. Indeed, until student listeners understand what sorts of things they might find to listen for in the works of different musical practices, they have no way of knowing what they are missing. Students who learn how to listen competently, proficiently, and expertly learn how to process second-by-second feedback about how well their covert thinking-in-action is proceeding.

Music listening is an absorbing form of thinking for students who learn how to listen intelligently. The reason, again, is that when a listener's musicianship matches the demands presented by a given musical performance, the resources of consciousness are fully concentrated. A listener's conscious focus and absorption are enhanced by the fact that music listening has integrity as a distinct endeavor in its own right. This is so because musical works are not autonomous aesthetic objects but highly contextualized artistic constructions that involve and compel many kinds of musical knowing. The integrity of music listening as a robust form of situated cognition separates it from the randomness of everyday life.

Nevertheless, says Csikszentmihalyi, "even greater rewards are open to those who learn to make music."[58] This is plausible because the challenges involved in making music well are more complex than those involved in listening alone, because music making usually involves clearer goals and feedback than listening alone, and because making music for and with other people generates the musical memes (works) that listeners need to achieve self-growth and musical enjoyment for themselves. For these reasons, music making can propel the self to the greater rewards of increased differentiation, integration, complexity, and flow.

In sum, music listening is a unique and major way that human beings bring order to consciousness. Enabling students to achieve self-growth, constructive knowledge, and flow in music listening depends on balancing the development of their musicianship with authentic musical challenges.

10. Musical Experience versus Aesthetic Experience

Past music education philosophers claim that an experience is musical if and only if it conforms to the theoretical characteristics of aesthetic experience. Recall that an aesthetic experience is something that supposedly arises when a perceiver focuses exclusively on the structural elements of a musical work. In the aesthetic view, a truly musical experience serves no practical purpose. An aesthetic experience is (and must be) intrinsic, immediate, disinterested, self-sufficient, and distanced. Any meanings, functions, or experiences not directly related to a work's structural patterns are deemed incidental, irrelevant, referential, or nonmusical.[59]

This praxial philosophy argues the opposite: Musical experiences are not rightly conceived of (or engaged in) as aesthetic experiences.[60] In the first place, musical experiences are neither impractical nor self-sufficient. Musical experiences are valuable in practical terms. Music makers and listeners achieve self-growth, self-knowledge, and enjoyment in the constructive actions of musicing and listening. What could be more practical to human beings than bringing order to consciousness, achieving self-knowledge, and maintaining the motivation to seek further growth through the cultural actions of musicing and listening?

Consider, also, that in the processes of performing and improvising, music makers must necessarily concern themselves with acting intelligently in relation to standards and traditions of musical practice. Again, what could be more "interested," purpose-full, and inclusive of pragmatic concerns than the thought-full actions of artistic music making?

Second, whereas aesthetic educators believe that musical experiences result from immediate, disinterested, aesthetic perception,[61] this praxial philosophy holds the contrary. Musical experiences depend on culturally and contextually determined understandings, both tacit and verbal. The deep absorption and personal integration that musicers and listeners tend to experience while musicing and/or listening result from cognizing musical performances in relation to personal and practice-specific understandings and beliefs. Musical experiences only seem immediate. In fact, context-dependent forms of thinking and knowing arbitrate all human interactions with the physical events we call musical works.

Third, musical experiences always include a variety of considerations because musicianship and musical works (even works of pure instrumental music) are multidimensional social constructions. The experiences we identify as musical experiences depend on the musical artistry of human agents. Thus musical experiences always include the social realities of particular kinds of musicers and listeners to greater and lesser degrees.

Furthermore (as I detail in the next three chapters), musical works can be expressive of many kinds of meanings, including moral, didactic, iconic, political, religious, or personal meanings. Indeed, the works of many musical practices are often linked to matters of communication, entertainment, ritual, and personal and community validation. The fact that conventional music education philosophy deems these functions and meanings nonaesthetic is of no consequence; they are still *musical*. In short, musical experiences are far richer and more complex than past philosophy allows or understands. Wayne Bowman concurs: "Musical meanings are negotiated, not absorbed; constructed, not given; appropriated, not bestowed. The processes and experiences we call musical, then, never reside in a hermetically-insular 'aesthetic' realm, but are part of our lived, social reality."[62]

While self-growth, self-knowledge, and musical enjoyment may be called the primary values of musicing and listening, the musical expression and evocation of various kinds of meanings (cultural, religious, moral) must also be counted as important cognitive and cultural values of musicing and listening. (In Chapter 6 I explain the reasons why and how this is so.) Suffice it to say that the continuation and enhancement of self-growth, self-knowledge, musical flow, and self-esteem depend on musicers' and listeners' becoming fully cognizant of the several dimensions of information that musical sound patterns evince.

In sum, musical experiences are not impractical, purposeless, disinterested, or intrinsic or the one-dimensional outcomes of perceiving aesthetic qualities. And musical experiences are not "experience for the sake of experience."[63] People may well and rightly continue to describe musical experiences as beautiful and moving. But a truly musical experience is not aesthetic in its nature or value, as conventional music education philosophy maintains.

Whereas the aesthetic concept of music and music education separates musical experiences from everyday life by placing them in the rarified and purposeless realm of disinterested perception, this praxial philosophy urges the opposite view. The concern of the present discussion is to reconnect musicing, listening, and musical experiences with the core of what it means to be human. That MUSIC is eminently beneficial for (and, therefore, of practical value to) the individual human self does not diminish the significance of musicing, listening, and musical works. On the contrary, it heightens the significance of musical practices and musical works for each self and for human society as a whole.

There is no such thing, then, as *the* musical experience, because the contents of consciousness differ from person to person. In addition, the kinds of information presented by the audible patterns of music differ from practice to practice, and different musicers and listeners in the same practice bring different levels of knowledge and interpretation to the same musical works. Thus, all we can say in general about musical experiences is the following:

1. A musical experience results from a matching relationship between a specific kind of musicianship and a specific kind of musical challenge.
2. The fundamental values of musical experiences are self-growth, self-knowledge, and enjoyment.
3. During musical experiences, musicers and listeners often experience focused concentration and deep absorption.
4. In the process of musicing and/or listening knowledgeably, no other motivations are needed to sustain attention and effort apart from the experiences of enjoyment and integration that arise from one's goal-directed musical actions (overt and covert).

In the present view, then, musical experiences are a subset of that larger class of experiences that Csikszentmihalyi variously calls flow experiences, optimal experiences, or autotelic experiences.[64] Musical experiences share certain basic characteristics in common with the flow experiences that arise in other domains, including sports and games and other artistic pursuits. But musical experiences are unique because musicing and music listening involve challenges and thought processes that are entirely different from those required for any other endeavor. Indeed, we must not overlook the centrality of artistically and culturally produced sound to everything musical; historied sound is the sine qua non of MUSIC.

In other words, the *conditions* of musical flow experiences are specific to musicing and music listening. Accordingly, the conscious contents of musical experiences—their cognitive and affective qualities, the way they feel while they last, their short- and long-term effects—differ significantly from other forms of experience, including other kinds of artistic experience.

Because the unique characteristics of musical experiences and music education are often overlooked (especially in broad discussions of "arts education"), let me highlight several basic features of auditory transactions. According to Stephen Handel, there is a profound difference between listening and looking: "Listening is centripetal; it pulls you into the world. Looking is centrifugal; it separates you from the world."[65] This is so, says David Burrows, because vision tends to distance us from the objects and events that it isolates, fixes, and distributes in space.[66] The cognitive consequence of looking for something is a sense of the world as things out there: separate, distanced, unambiguous, durable objects.

In contrast, audition tends to foster intimacy with the world by subordinating details of shape, size, and distance to inward experiences of continuously unfolding events and multi-directional energy. As Handel notes, whereas "looking makes each of us a focused observer, listening makes each of us a surrounded participant."[67] Bowman agrees: "if visual experience is of things out-there, sonorous experience is of events in-here."[68] Accordingly, sound has enormous potential to soothe or startle, calm or unnerve, exhilarate or insult, inform or confuse. The connective power of sound is underscored by the fact that our social relatedness depends crucially on sounding out and listening for each other's intentions and meanings in the sonic inflections, timbres, dynamics, accents, and inflections of speech.

Sonic awareness is not static but temporal and, therefore, full of ambiguity. Audition is moment-by-moment renewal and, therefore, "phenomenally processual and disembodied."[69] The result is that "we see the world as a noun and hear it as a verb."[70] Burrows continues: "Sight draws me out, sound finds me here. And sound goes beyond touch, which respects the perimeter of my skin, and beyond its degree of intimacy in seeming to be going on within me as much as around me."[71]

The continuous presence and flux of the audible world penetrates consciousness to such an extent that people often feel positively or negatively enveloped in, infused with, or invaded by sonic energy. Don Ihde offers a positive example:

> If I hear Beethoven's Ninth Symphony in an acoustically excellent auditorium, I suddenly find myself *immersed* in sound which *surrounds* me. The music is even so *penetrating* that my whole body reverberates, and I may find myself absorbed to such a degree that the usual distinction between the sense of inner and outer is virtually obliterated. The auditory field surrounds the listener, and surroundability is an essential feature of the field-shape of sound.[72]

Bowman concludes that listening is a "truly distinctive mode of construing and constructing the world. It captures and reflects aspects of the world and our place in it that nothing else can."[73]

These fundamental links between human beings and aural information are not surprising when we consider the research that suggests the auditory powers of the human fetus are already considerable before birth and that the sounds of the mother's body and voice together with the music and speech of her culture penetrate the womb and the nascent consciousness of the fetus (see Chapter 4). Perhaps the fetal brain forms in relation to the sounds of its culture. At the very least, the last stages of fetal development are most likely imbued with auditory information that the fetus cognizes to some degree. On the basis of these thoughts, I make bold to suggest that sound (including musical sound) has few if any rivals for the attention and cognition of the human fetus. If so, then we may have grounds for bolder conclusions: that music, our "first art," is one of the essential connectives between ourselves and our world. Indeed, if memes turn brains into minds, and if excellent works of music are among the most complex memes that humans produce, then the multidimensional nature of musical sound has enormous importance for the ordering and development of consciousness even before birth.

The keys to understanding the uniqueness and power of musical experiences and music education include the following: an awareness of the contextual nature of musicing and musical sounds as artistic-social-cultural actions, properties, and cognitive challenges; the contextual dependency of music cognition; and the unequaled phenomenology of auditory experiences as events that seem to enter us—"becoming in that process not so much something we have as something we are."[74]

In sum, the nature and quality of self-growth, self-knowledge, and flow as experienced in musicing and music listening are unique to the practice of MUSIC overall and to the specific practices in which different kinds of musicing, listening, and musical challenges arise. Thus, music making, music listening, and the involvements that result from these particular forms of action are distinctive sources of self-growth, self-knowledge, flow, and self-esteem.

11. Three Fundamental Concepts

We are now in a position to summarize this philosophy's central concepts of (a) MUSIC, (b) musical experience, and (c) the values and aims of music education.

a. MUSIC is an open concept: it eludes precise rules of definition because there is no fixed set of properties that hold for all musical practices.[75] Although several features seem constant across the majority of Musics (including the presence of musicers, listeners, musicing, listening, and audible musical achievements), and although we have proposed that most if not all instances of musicianship involve several common categories of knowing, we can never eliminate the possibility of an unforeseen feature or category arising that might cause us to modify these proposals. Moreover, the features and categories we have identified are filled in differently from practice to practice.

The implausibility of producing a strict definition (or a closed concept) of MUSIC is reinforced by the fact that music (in the sense of audible musical achievements or works) is historically and contextually determined. Thus, what any given practice counts as musical sounds or works of musical sound cannot be counted as the one true nature of music as such. In short, music is also an open concept.

The purpose of these remarks is to stress that the following concept of MUSIC is not intended as a fixed and final definition. It is put forth as an open or working concept that (I believe) can be modified to accommodate future possibilities without losing its basic identity. This concept attempts to clarify the idea of MUSIC to the degree that it allows and, in so doing, to show its relation to such associated matters as musical values, actions, and sounds.

MUSIC is the diverse human practice of overtly and covertly constructing aural-temporal patterns for the primary (but not necessarily the exclusive) values of enjoyment, self-growth, and self-knowledge. These values arise when musicianship is sufficient to balance or match the cognitive challenges involved in making and/ or listening for aural patterns regarded significantly, but never exclusively, as audible designs.

This praxial concept of MUSIC has four major aspects.

1. MUSIC is a human endeavor. It is people who make and listen for musical works in deliberate and culturally patterned ways. Musical practices, musical works, and the musicianship they depend on for their existence are social-cultural constructions.

2. MUSIC is never a matter of musical works alone, and musical works are never a matter of formal elements, auditory designs, or sound patterns alone. A significant level of attention to the structural designs of syntactic and nonsyntactic musical patterns (such as melody, rhythm, and timbre) is always a fundamental part of music listening, but only a part. This is so because while musical design elements constitute the distinguishing dimension of musical achievements (instrumental and vocal), musical works are multifold constructions that always include at least four and often as many as six interrelated dimensions of musical information (see Chapters 4, 6, and 8).

3. The phrase "to balance or match the cognitive challenges involved in making and/or listening for aural patterns" in this concept of MUSIC is meant to include related actions such as moving, dancing, and worshiping that people may engage in as part of, or in addition to, musicing and listening.

4. This concept of MUSIC acknowledges that musical sounds can be made for a variety of purposes and functions across cultures. For example, as accompaniments to celebrations and dances; as vehicles for communicating beliefs and values; or as invocations to gods. What this philosophy proposes, however, is that underlying or within these purposes and functions are the fundamental values of musicing and listening as unique sources of enjoyment and, whether participants understand it formally, self-growth, and constructive knowledge.

b. *Musical experiences tend to be characterized by intense absorption and involvement in the actions of musicing and/or listening. Musicers and listeners may also obtain a sense of personal wholeness, integration, and self-growth during (and/or following) their active engagement in musicing and/or listening.*

Note, again, that the qualitative contents of musical experiences depend on two main conditions: musical challenges and musicianship, both of which are multidimensional and social-cultural in nature. Musicianship (which includes listenership) is the key to self-growth and self-knowledge and their affective concomitants: enjoyment, flow, absorption, and/or a sense of control, wholeness, integration, differentiation, and self-esteem.

c. *The primary values of music education are the primary values of MUSIC: self-growth, self-knowledge, and optimal experience. Music education is a unique and major source of one of the most important kinds of knowledge human beings can attain: self-knowledge.*

The aims of music education, and the primary goals of every music teaching-learning situation, are to enable students to achieve self-growth, self-knowledge, and musical enjoyment by educating their musicianship in balanced relation to musical challenges within selected musical practices. It follows from this that musicianship is also a unique and major source of self-esteem.

In this praxial view, a music education curriculum-as-practicum is both a means and an end. It is the means for students to develop the musicianship they require to achieve the values of MUSIC outside school and after schooling is over. In addition, a music curriculum-as-practicum ought to be organized and carried out in ways that enable learners to realize the values of self-growth, self-knowledge, and optimal experience in the *present*.

Stated in broader terms, music education is not merely desirable but *essential* to the full development of every student because the primary values of MUSIC and music education overlap the essential life values that most individuals and societies pursue for the good of each and all: personal growth, differentiation, complexity, enjoyment, self-esteem, and happiness. The welfare of a society depends on the ability of its citizens to pursue and achieve these values regularly. The quality of individual and community life depends on providing people with the knowings and the opportunities they require to make a life as well as a living. (I elaborate on this position in Chapter 12.)

From this perspective, the means and results of educating students to make and listen for music well are simultaneously personal, social, and cultural. They are also political. To the Greeks, the word *politics* meant whatever involved people in human concerns beyond their own individual needs. The development of musicianship allows people to participate constructively in the generation, expression, and impression of complex memes that can imbue their everyday lives, and the lives of others, with meaning and purpose. The development of musicianship benefits self and other.

Accordingly, a school that denies children a sustained and systematic music education curriculum is not simply incomplete; it imperils the quality of students' present and future lives by denying them the cognitive keys to a unique and major source of fundamental human life values. If a society wishes to invest in a basic education for every child, then public schooling must center on the domains of thinking and knowing that are accessible, achievable, and applicable to all. MUSIC is one of these basic cognitive domains.

I explain several additional values of MUSIC and music education in the next four chapters. What needs attention now is the popular claim that music education is a valuable means of improving students' academic achievement scores. Indeed, teachers' anecdotal reports often imply strong links between school retention rates, student morale, and scholastic achievement scores on the one hand, and the presence of challenging school music programs on the other.[76]

As I view the evidence, the findings of music education researchers, developmental psychologists, and cognitive scientists support several conclusions. First, studies of the relationships between music instruction and academic achievement are relatively few in number and fraught with procedural weaknesses.[77] This is still a fledgling area of research. Not surprisingly, the results are contradictory. Some studies suggest that students who do well in music tend to have higher academic achievement scores that nonmusic students; others deny it. In any event, positive correlations are not explanations of causation.

Second, it seems clear that consciousness consists of a number of discrete intelligences or cognitive modules that follow their own developmental paths.[78] The cognitive operations involved in each domain (such as language, mathematics, and music) are essentially domain-specific. Thus, says Gardner, "music deserves to be considered as an autonomous intellectual realm."[79] If so, then it would be surprising to find intimate cognitive relationships between musical thinking and the distinctly nonmusical thought processes that ground propositional subjects such as mathematics, spelling, history, and reading.[80]

While there is no doubt that competent music making and listening involve several categories of thinking that occur in other subject domains (including critical reflection, formal thinking, and creative generation), the contents, contexts, standards, goals, and outcomes of these categories differ fundamentally from subject to subject. Thus attempts to link specific cognitive components of musical thinking with those of other domains are essentially spurious.

However, because our various cognitive modules and processes are parts of consciousness as a whole, there may be interactions among these modules and processes at a more general level of cognition. As Gardner suggests, there are "higher level" cognitive capacities such as "the intelligence of the self," analogic thinking, personal wisdom, and supervisory knowing (or general common sense) that seem to exist both within and beyond discrete intelligence modules.[81] Perhaps a systematic music education contributes to the development of these broader capacities which, in turn, interact with or transfer to other domains.

Indeed, if there is a significant relationship between the development of musicianship and academic achievement, I conclude that it most likely lies in the primary values of music education. As I noted earlier in this chapter, self-growth, self-knowledge, optimal experience, and their concomitants do not simply improve human experience in the moment. They make an essential contribution to the order, differentiation, and complexity of the self and, therefore, to one's overall quality of life: "people who are often in flow have higher self-esteem than those who experience flow rarely."[82] Accordingly, says Csikszentmihalyi, "[t]eenagers who report more flow tend to be happier, and they develop academic talents further than teens who are in flow less often."[83]

It follows that the most effective way to achieve any adjunct benefits of music education is to concentrate on the primary aims of music teaching and learning. Attempts to divert music education from its primary musical aims in the hope of advancing or integrating specific academic skills will only block the development of musicianship and, therefore, negate the possibility of achieving any results that may transfer across domains.

12. Implications for Music Education

The ideas in this chapter suggest several principles of music teaching and learning that can be added to the principles explained in Chapters 3 and 4.

• *Relationships between musical challenges and musicianship.* The two conditions necessary for self-growth and musical enjoyment can relate to each other in several ways. The diagram in Figure 5.3 adapts Csikszentmihalyi's original model of flow[84] and pictures four ways that musical challenges and musicianship can relate to each other. The letter S in the diagram represents our fictional music student, Sara.

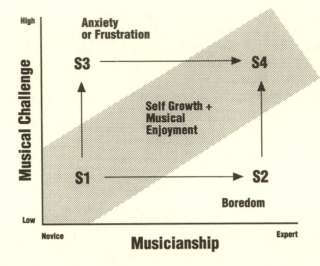

FIGURE 5.3. Varied Relationships Between Musicianship and Musical Challenges

Point S^1 in the diagram indicates that Sara enjoys her music making and listening because the level of musical challenge (vertical axis) set by her teacher (a musical work to perform, improvise, compose, arrange, conduct, or listen for) matches Sara's beginning level of musicianship (horizontal axis). In other words, musical enjoyment and self-knowledge can be attained even at the earliest stages of musical learning.

At the same time, Sara's enjoyment at S^1 will not last long. As Csikszentmihalyi's model explains, one of two things is likely to happen as Sara's musicianship develops. Either Sara will become bored with the continuing lack of challenge (S^2) or, anticipating an imbalance between her new level of musicianship and the possibility of increasing challenges ahead, Sara will become anxious or frustrated (S^3).

Given the prime tendency of consciousness to achieve order, Sara will be motivated to overcome her boredom or frustration by rebalancing the relationship between her musicianship and specific musical challenges. To do so from the point of boredom (S^2), Sara must undertake a higher level of musical challenge. This could mean either returning to a previous musical challenge to find new goals or moving on to more advanced projects with new musical goals in mind. Either way, Csikszentmihalyi's model of flow suggests that this new balancing of musicianship and musical challenge will bring order to consciousness, restore enjoyment, and place Sara back in the channel of enjoyment and self-growth (S^4).

If Sara is anxious about whether her musicianship will be enough to meet new musical demands (S^3), Sara and her teacher have two ways to go. They can either increase Sara's musicianship (and move to S^4), or they can lower the level of challenge and move Sara back to S^1. But in reality, moving back to S^1 is not a viable solution. For enjoyment and self-growth do not result from the partial deployment of musicianship or the continuous success of meeting less than demanding challenges.

Of course, as music teachers well know, some students who arrive at points S^2 or S^3 may give up altogether. Some students may not buy into the challenge-knowledge relationship as it manifests itself in the musical context. There are two related reasons for this. First, each person is an individual self. Human beings are not billiard balls. People do not simply react to objective conditions; they select, target, and interpret opportunities in relation to their individual values, goals, needs, contexts, genes, and memes. Accordingly, there will always be a few students who find MUSIC (all musical practice and all forms of musicing and listening) incongruent with their personal values and goals. In other words, people differ in their desires and abilities to give attention to certain kinds of information, including the ideas, feelings, situations, and associations that arise in making and listening for the musical works of different practices.[85]

A second reason that some students may not invest in musicing or listening has to do with a topic we will examine in Chapter 8: the cultural and ideological meanings involved in musicing, listening, and musical works. Because musical practices and musical works are social constructions, musical works delineate cultural beliefs and values. Some students may find it difficult to make or listen for the music of some musical practices (or music cultures) because of their knowledge and beliefs (or lack thereof) and the negative cognitive emotions that arise from their beliefs.

Let us return to the situation of Sara. Notice that points S^1 and S^4 in the diagram both lie in the flow channel of self-growth and enjoyment. What is the difference between these two points? Csikszentmihalyi explains that because the flow experience at S^4 requires a higher level of know-how to meet a higher level of challenge, S^4 is more complex than S^1. Of course, once Sara reaches the S^4 level, then the whole cycle begins again if the musical domain into which Sara is being inducted offers progressively increasing musical projects and progressive levels of musicianship. Most musical practices are dynamic practices. Csikszentmihalyi explains the significance of this dynamism:

> It is this dynamic feature that explains why flow activities lead to growth and discovery. One cannot enjoy doing the same thing at the same level for long. We grow either bored or frustrated; and then the desire to enjoy ourselves again pushes us to stretch our skills, or to discover new opportunities for using them.[86]

• *Musical values and the quest for excellent musicianship.* Self-growth, self-knowledge, flow, and self-esteem do not result from setting and meeting trivial goals. The primary values of musicing and listening result from the continuous investment of musicianship in musical problem solving that spirals upward in complexity in relation to recognized criteria and traditions of musical practice. In realistic terms, then, the aims of music education will not be accomplished if teachers merely entertain their students or if students merely dabble in ersatz sound-producing activities. Self-knowledge and enjoyment arise from the extension of one's powers of consciousness, from significant and knowledgeable effort. What this means for music teaching and learning is that the values of MUSIC result from learning to make and listen for musical works well—from the deliberate and sustained pursuit of musical competency, proficiency, and expertise. To pursue musical excellence is to pursue self-growth, constructive knowledge, and enjoyment.

• *Centering*. Music educators are professional practitioners who know how to balance their students' growing musicianship with appropriate musical challenges. Music educators know how to develop the musicianship of students like Sara in ways that keep them centered in the channel of self-growth and musical enjoyment. From this we see that the professional expertise of the music educator involves several kinds of knowing (tacit and verbal), including the following: knowing how to diagnose, coach, critique, and correct a student's musical thinking-in-action; knowing when (and when not) to interrupt musicing and listening for verbal reflections; knowing how to reduce temporary problems that impede musical problem solving; and knowing how to encourage students' ongoing efforts when they experience temporary boredom or frustration. Implicit in a music educator's expertise is the ability to center students in the musical flow channel by adjusting musical problems and challenges, directing students' attention to new goals, and providing constructive feedback in relation to recognized ideals and demands of musical artistry.

• *Standards and traditions*. The goals of musicing and listening are not always perfectly clear. For example, while the importance of good intonation in the accurate performance of a blues melody is not difficult to grasp, the problems involved in learning how to improvise a blues melody in relation to the traditions of urban blues or country blues are not as easy to find. The reason for this is that learning to perform or improvise musically requires the development of several situated forms of knowing. These knowings require musical problem solving in relation to authentic blues works and close approximations of real blues practices.

Students require coaching in setting musical goals according to practice-specific traditions and standards. Students also require practice in recognizing when, why, and how they are meeting their musical goals. Unless students learn how to gauge feedback in relation to norms and benchmarks of musical practice, they will not experience self-growth and musical enjoyment.

• *Modeling*. Knowing how to provide appropriate feedback to students rests on knowing how to model and how to explain why and how students' actions are musically intelligent, or not. A teacher's efforts to model and to explain musical standards enables students to learn the dispositions, strategic judgments, musical criteria, and problem-finding abilities they require to achieve the values of music education.

• *Depth*. Music education programs ought to favor musical depth over musical breadth. If self-growth and musical enjoyment depend on learning how to meet increasingly complex musical challenges, then enabling all students to achieve self-growth and enjoyment (now and in the future) depends on developing the depth of their musicianship by moving students from beginning levels to competent, proficient, and expert levels of musicianship through progressive musical problem solving, problem finding, and problem reduction. Caring deeply about one's students (all music students) means enabling and promoting their efforts to fashion the key to lifelong musical enjoyment: musicianship.

This does not mean that music education programs should concentrate on teaching and learning one musical practice. Since MUSIC is a diverse human practice, then MUSIC is inherently multicultural. MUSIC consists in many musical practices, or music cultures. Accordingly, music educators have a fundamental responsibility to induct children into a variety of musical practices during the long-term time period of a music program. Yet this responsibility must be carefully weighed against the necessity of developing students' musicianship deeply enough that they can attain the fundamental life values of music making and listening.

To conclude, if we conceive music education as the systematic development of musicianship in balanced relation to progressive musical challenges, then music education programs will provide the optimum conditions for realizing the values and aims of music education. What this means, in turn, is that students will come to view the development of musicianship as a specific kind of process that they are capable of pursuing, learning, and enjoying. In this process, students will also learn firsthand why and how MUSIC is a valued global practice.

Questions for Discussion and Review

1. Summarize the strategy employed in this chapter to develop a position on the values of musicing, listening, and musical works.

2. Explain the concept of memes. Summarize the role of genes and memes in the development of consciousness.

3. Summarize the central functions of consciousness. Explain the relationship between incoming information and the nature of the self. In what sense is the self circular and dynamic?

4. Several thinkers identify a central tendency of human consciousness that can be stated in several overlapping ways. State this tendency in at least four ways.

5. Explain the differences between pleasure and enjoyment. In addition to enjoyment, what other terms do scholars use to name the positive affect that accompanies self-growth?

6. What conditions are required to achieve self-growth? In what sense can the self be said to grow when people engage in endeavors that meet these conditions?

7. Summarize the relationships between self-growth, self-knowledge, (or constructive knowledge), and self-esteem.

8. In addition to enjoyment, what other features are characteristic of self-growth experiences?

9. This chapter's concept of consciousness identifies several basic human tendencies. Summarize these tendencies. Explain how these tendencies relate to the human values of (1) music making and (2) music listening.

10. This chapter proposes that musical experiences are not rightly thought of as aesthetic experiences. Explain why you agree or disagree.

11. What distinguishes musical experiences from other sorts of flow experiences?

12. Summarize this chapter's concepts of (a) MUSIC (b) musical experiences, and (c) the primary values of music education.

13. Is it possible for novice musicers and listeners to achieve the fundamental values of musicing and listening? How so? What ideas help to explain the fact that some students refuse to invest themselves in music?

14. Explain the relationships between the primary values of music education and (1) striving for musical excellence; (2) centering; (3) depth.

Supplementary Sources

Mihalyi Csikszentmihalyi and Isabella Csikszentmihalyi, eds. *Optimal Experience: Psychological Studies of Flow in Consciousness.* Cambridge: Cambridge University Press, 1988. Chapters 1 and 2 offer an introduction to the flow concept and its significance for human psychology. Chapters 15 through 22 provide empirical studies of self-growth and flow, as well as reflections on these studies.

Mihalyi Csikszentmihalyi. *Flow: The Psychology of Optimal Experience.* New York: Harper and Row, 1990. An accessible and clearly documented explanation of Csikszentmihalyi's concepts of consciousness and enjoyment.

David J. Elliott. "When I Sing: The Nature and Value of Choral Music Education." *Choral Journal* 33, no. 8 (March 1993): 11–17. A choral perspective on several concepts detailed in this chapter.

David J. Elliott. "Music as Knowledge." *Journal of Aesthetic Education* 25, no. 3 (Fall 1991): 21–40. A synthesis of several themes presented in Chapters 2 to 5 of the present book.

Daniel C. Dennett. "Memes and the Exploitation of Imagination." *Journal of Aesthetics and Art Criticism* 48, no. 2 (Spring 1990): 127–35. A succinct explanation of the meme theme.

Mihalyi Csikszentmihalyi. *The Evolving Self: A Psychology for the Third Millennium.* New York: HarperCollins, 1993. Chapter 5, "Memes *Versus* Genes," examines more issues involved in these topics. Chapter 7, "Evolution and Flow," relates the concepts of self-growth and enjoyment to broader societal concerns.

6

Musical Works

Listening for musical performances involves thinking and knowing in relation to several simultaneous dimensions of musical information. Thus, musical works may be conceived as thought generators—as intentionally constructed challenges to our powers of consciousness.

In Chapter 4 I introduced three dimensions of musical information that are part of every musical work: (1) the musical performance-interpretation dimension, (2) the musical design dimension, and (3) the practice-specific dimension of shared musical standards and traditions. In this chapter I explain why some musical works may involve additional dimensions.

1. Form-Content Relationships

In discussions of musical works, the terms *form* and *content* refer to the ways in which musical patterns are organized (or formed) in relation to each other (*intra*-musically), in relation to other musical works (*inter*musically), and in relation to other human interests.

Several factors predict that music makers around the world will organize musical works in more than one way. The first factor is the human tendency to make values of necessities: the tendency to emphasize, extend, or elaborate common needs, actions, and occurrences. This tendency suggests that in addition to purely musical sound patterns, the sounds of everyday existence (e.g., speaking sounds, working sounds) will likely become part of the content of some musical works. The second factor is the wide range of things people can do with sounds inter-musically, intramusically, and in relation to all other human interests. This factor suggests that musicians will sometimes link musical patterns to a variety of cultural and personal concerns, including religious, moral, technological, practical, political, and historical ideas or events. The next factor involves the related human tendencies to pursue enjoyment and self-knowledge. These tendencies predict that musicians will often push the limits of composing, improvising, or performing in terms of the complexity of musical designs and the combination of musical designs with other kinds of content. The fourth factor is the variable intensities of human interests. This factor suggests that musical works around the globe will vary greatly in the extent to which they emphasize syntactic patterns, nonsyntactic patterns, musical-social relationships, and various combinations of these.

The realities of musical practices and products worldwide seem to confirm the legitimacy of these predictions. In the first place, human beings do tend to emphasize, extend, and elaborate human necessities and actions in various musical ways. For example, humans tend to superimpose rhythmic patterns on such regular sound patterns as those that arise from breathing, walking, playing, and working.[1] Such occurrences provide the ingredients for the deliberate making of musical works (1) to accompany work and play, (2) to recall meanings associated with the original impetus for rhythmicizing work and play, and (3) to perform and listen for as rhythmic patterns in themselves.

Humans also tend to extend and develop the acoustic features of voices. For example, we apprehend meanings from the rise and fall of pitch in human expressions of happiness and sadness and from the division of speaking sounds into phrases and sentences. In short, the sounds of human utterances, such as laughing, crying, sighing, and speaking, provide both the impetus and the ingredients for the deliberate making of music (1) to assist or vary spoken communication, (2) to help people recall or dramatize messages to each other, and (3) to be listened for as auditory patterns in themselves.

Implicit in this range of steps is a process of gradual objectification. Sparshott explains that just as ordinary running becomes more elaborated when taken up as part of football or hockey, the syntactic and nonsyntactic patterns of some musical works may be heard as elaborations of intensified human speech and movement.[2] Similarly, consider how the weeping and wailing sounds of grief might gradually become musical patterns imitative of the sounds of grief, or musical patterns that are culturally symbolic of grief, or musical forms (a lament, a dirge, a requiem mass) reminiscent of (but not directly felt as) grief.

In fact, there are many examples of musical works across practices and cultures that include such meanings as part of their syntactic and nonsyntactic designs. For example, some musicians create musical works that illustrate, depict, narrate, describe, stylize, symbolize, or characterize meanings associated with the original intent of spoken messages. In addition, many (if not most) vocal and choral works dramatize the sounds of speech to be expressive of specific human emotions or to invite listeners to empathize with such expressions. Similarly, composers often link musical sounds to special events or people in their lives, much as spoken language links subjects to predicates. (Music is not a language, but it is speechlike in this way.)

We begin to see how musical works may include several kinds of content, ranging from the most obvious conventional references (such as vocalized stories and song texts) to the musical depiction and characterization of people, places, and things to the most subtle musical expressions of specific human emotions.

We use the term *expressional* music for works in which syntactic and nonsyntactic musical patterns seem to evince the characteristics of human emotions. The term *representational* music is used for works that include the musical description, depiction, narration, or characterization of ideas, events, or other human interests.

It is also unsurprising to find musical practices aimed at making works of music to be listened to primarily for their syntactic and nonsyntactic designs. Indeed, there are many instances of music in many cultures that stand as examples of the heights to which humans can rise in composing, performing, or improvising complex intramusical relationships. In many Western practices, for example, composing is often directed toward the design of instrumental works that sustain and repay the musical thinking of listeners primarily (but not exclusively) because of the intricacies of their structural patterns. Peter Kivy refers to such works as "pure" music, or "music alone."[3] Other writers use the terms abstract music, formal music, design-based music, or absolute music. I suggest we use the term *design-based* music to refer to musical works that seem especially concerned with syntactic and nonsyntactic relationships. Examples include Bach's *Well-Tempered Clavier*, Schoenberg's Woodwind Quintet, John Coltrane's improvisation on *Giant Steps*, Hindemith's *Chamber Music I*, Ellen Taaffe Zwilich's *Symphony No. 1*, Duke Ellington's *Echoes of Harlem*, and examples of modern Balinese *kebyar*, Korean *kayagŭm sanjo*, and traditional Ottoman *peshrev* and *samā'ī*.

This discussion suggests three broad and flexible categories of musical form-content relationships: (1) design-based music, (2) representational music, and (3) expressional music.

These three categories are, of course, merely handy ways of thinking about the complexities of musical works. They are heuristic devices; while some works may fit precisely within these categories, many will not. Indeed, many instrumental, vocal, choral, and operatic works cut across all three categories. I suggest, for example, that many esteemed works of the Western "classical" tradition, including Elgar's *Enigma Variations*, Berlioz's *Symphonie fantastique*, Monteverdi's *Orfeo*, and Brahms's *Ein deutsches Requiem* are simultaneously representational, expressional, and yet centrally concerned with matters of syntactic and nonsyntactic musical design. So too with the sacred songs of the Australian Pitjantjara peoples, and many examples of jazz and Indian classical music. Viewed as heuristic devices, then, these three categories simply provide us with a useful way of organizing our thoughts about the natures and values of musical works.

2. Design-Based Works

Since all musical works consist in syntactic and nonsyntactic musical sound designs of some sort, and since I have already discussed (in Chapters 3, 4, and 5) the natures and values of making and listening for musical sound patterns, please read this section as an extension of (or as a footnote to) these previous discussions.

Thinkers have pondered the significance of pure instrumental music for centuries. How can musical sound patterns—sounds with no apparent relationship to anything but themselves—give rise to enjoyable experiences? Briefly, this philosophy argues that musical performances of instrumental compositions (or improvisations) are, in fact, multidimensional cognitive challenges. To the extent that a listener's practice-specific musicianship enables him or her to cognize the several dimensions of musical information presented in a work of instrumental music, that listener will tend to experience musical enjoyment, or flow. But there is more we need to say now (and in Chapter 8) by way of clarification.

In his book *Music Alone,* Peter Kivy explains that some seventeenth- and eighteenth-century philosophers conceived the sounds of instrumental music as physical stimulants.[4] Musical patterns were believed to penetrate directly through the ears to the soul to induce pleasure. Closely tied to this idea was the notion that instrumental music stimulates in the sense of arousing sadness, happiness, and other specific emotions. Clearly, however, stimulant theories rest on several false assumptions, the main one being that pieces of music are autonomous objects that listeners merely pick up im-mediately (without mediating acts of cognition) and ingest like wine or aspirins.

Later, and as an alternative to noncognitive stimulant theories, referential theories attempted to make a place for cognition in a listener's experience of instrumental music. From at least the time of Arthur Schopenhauer (1788–1860) to the present, referential theories have attempted to explain people's enjoyment of design-based works by suggesting that musical sounds contain some sort of hidden message, deep narrative, moral lesson, disguised analogy, or "program" that listeners supposedly detect intuitively. But clearly, referential theories want their cake and eat it, too. On one hand, they claim that the sounds of pure instrumental music are just that: pure, absolute, nonreferential (aesthetic) patterns. On the other hand, they claim that music is valuable because listeners find hidden references in musical patterns (including, says MEAE, insight into and symbolic representations of the "life of feeling").

Stimulant theories and referential theories do not understand that listening for the auditory patterns of instrumental music involves thinking, knowing, and believing in relation to a complex array of culture-specific intramusical and intermusical details. Earlier thinking fails to explain the significance of instrumental music because it overlooks the cognitive complexity (and, therefore, the cognitive challenge) of instrumental music listening. In terms of intramusical connections, early theories fail to appreciate the intricate ways in which syntactic and nonsyntactic patterns can challenge our human abilities to construct relationships among sounds-in-time. For example, the apparently simple melodic pattern C–G–E sounded over a C_7 chord in F major becomes intelligible to Western listeners if (and only if) they know how to cognize this pattern in relation to other horizontal and vertical sound patterns. If listeners possess the culture- and practice-specific listening know-how, then the relationships among and between syntactic and nonsyntactic musical patterns in F major are heard as internally coherent. Composers and improvisors of instrumental music construct musical patterns that make sense intramusically in virtue of the rules and strategies available in given musical practices and styles. Again, by musical practices and styles we do not mean only Western musical practices. With important modifications, what has just been said about the complexity of intramusical relationships in Western tonal music applies also to Indian *raga,* Arab *māqam,* Iranian *radif,* and Sardinian *launeddas.*

Consider, next, that the cognitive demands of listening for performances of intramusical designs increase dramatically with the flexibility and ambiguity of tonal systems. For example, in addition to sounding the pattern C–G–E over a C_I chord, the rules of Western harmony also allow musicers to exploit the potential of this pattern in different ways in the same key by sounding C–G–E over an $Fmaj_7$, Dm_7, or Am_7 chord.

There is an analogy we can use to draw these ideas together. Whether we focus on instrumental works in particular, or the design dimension of works of music in general, intramusical relationships establish a kind of mini-world of aural-cultural relationships through which listeners make a mindful journey.[5] The rules governing the syntactic and nonsyntactic relationships of a particular practice and musical work create the borders of each mini-world and mark the routes that listeners travel (well or poorly) depending on their musicianship. The journey itself (the listening experience) is more or less adventurous, more or less controlled, more or less enjoyable depending on how well listeners can mind where they are going in the musical design context of a given work.

Listeners, like travelers, may have a sense of their journey in different ways. Given a new work in a familiar style, expert listeners will know tacitly and verbally where they are, where they have been, and where they are likely to be going next at most points in their journey. Intelligent music listening involves anticipating, hypothesizing, imagining, believing, and knowing what will and will not come next during the journey of a given music-listening experience. At best, novice listeners will have a vague sense of where they are, just as an innocent traveler might sense he is somewhere in upper New York State instead of southern Quebec. Competent listeners will have a firm sense of where they are and where they might go next.

A listener's thought-full experience of a beautifully designed Western musical "journey" (e.g., Beethoven's *Grosse Fuge*, op. 133) seems to transport the listener into another world because consciousness is fully engaged in the knowledgeable and constructive act of music listening. During musical experiences, "me" tends to become background while "I" becomes foreground.[6] The self is fully functioning but not aware of itself. To a knowledgeable listener, the process of listening for an artistic performance of a musical composition has an exquisite kind of integrity. This integrity is due to the artistic and cultural specificity of the musical knowledge such listening invites and demands. This knowledge-in-action separates musical listening from the randomness of everyday life because it provides a bounded field of musical information that human consciousness takes as coherent and significant.

Additionally, it is important to keep in mind that, during the process of cognizing intramusical relationships, knowledgeable listeners also cognize the ways that musical artists interpret and perform musical works. In doing so, listeners can make intermusical comparisons—comparisons between the performance they are listening for now and past performances of the same work or of similar works in the same style and practice. In addition, because artistically generated instrumental compositions, arrangements, performances, and improvisations are the outcomes of artistically situated thinking and knowing, the musical patterns of instrumental music always evince particular musical traditions that, in turn, "locate" musical works stylistically and culturally.

There is considerable controversy among scholars about whether the term *meaning* applies to the relationships among syntactic and nonsyntactic musical patterns. Peter Kivy maintains, for example, that intramusical relationships do not ''mean'' anything in the ordinary sense that words are said to mean.[7] The relationships among musical sound patterns do not ''mean'' in the literal sense (or in the metaphorical sense) that one musical pattern implies, points to, or means another musical pattern. Kivy grants that this may be a useful way of talking about the relations among and between musical patterns. But it is misleading all the same. For to claim that musical patterns mean something always disappoints us by failing to explain exactly what it is that musical patterns refer to in the common sense that speech sounds mean something.

On the other hand, there can be no doubt that intramusical relationships establish specific fields of musical information that invite listeners to use their practice-specific musical knowings to anticipate, infer, and predict what may be coming in the immediate and more distant future. Moreover, most intramusical designs have an implicit logic and coherence because their sonic materials are already musical (pre-organized sounds-as-tones and timbres) before music makers organize them into works of music based on practice-specific rules and strategies.

Thus, Kivy's view of meaning may be too severe. For meaning does not necessarily imply reference in the obvious sense that words and sentences refer or designate. There are many shades to the concept of meaning. For example, as Jean-Jacques Nattiez and Robert Austerlitz argue,[8] *meaning* can and does apply to the kind of situation in which knowledge is required to predict what will follow musically from what is presently known and understood in the moment. In technical terms, Austerlitz suggests that the meaning intramusical patterns convey ''is basically deictic, cataphoric, in the sense that it is *prediction*.''[9]

We might also argue that the syntactic and nonsyntactic patterns of musical works have meaning to the extent that they have practical consequences. For example, intramusical patterns can be said to have meaning if and when musicers and listeners experience enjoyment in making and listening for intramusical patterns. People respond publicly and privately to musical sound patterns because musical works provide opportunities for people to deploy their musical thinking-in-action and thereby achieve musical flow experiences. In this view, the syntactic and nonsyntactic patterns that make up the design dimension of musical works are meaningful because they are significant; they challenge our conscious powers of listening-for. The sounds themselves do not have meaning in the sense that words stand for a specific idea. Instead, self-growth and musical enjoyment arise from a listener's conscious generation and comprehension of *relations* among successive and simultaneous musical events in awareness of practice-specific rules of musical organization.

Furthermore, an important part of the meaning of listening for live musical performances lies in the occasions themselves. For example, cognizing the artistic musical patterns of live instrumental performances often includes *witnessing* the efforts of musicers who are intent upon stretching the limits of current listening practices, or introducing new forms of musical sound organization, or finding ''new meaning'' in well-known works, or solving formal musical problems. When people make music, they *mean* to accomplish things or produce effects. Thus, intramusical sound patterns mean in the sense that the expression and impression of these patterns challenge and move people in ways they understand (nonverbally and verbally). The ethnomusicologist Timothy Rice elaborates:

> [T]he acts of creating, performing, and appreciating music are not simply exercises in pure form or pure production. The creating of music always involves an act of appropriation and interpretation of traditional procedures and images. These images and procedures are historically meaningful, socially meaningful, and individually meaningful. . . . Music receives its meaning through unending interpretations by individuals in the world. That world, the world in which music has meaning, is our world: the world in which music from the past, or from another culture, is borrowed, reconstructed, listened to, and performed. It receives its meaning in the world in which new works and performances are created through appropriation, distillation, and recombination of elements of tradition. Music's meanings are not limited to those that the original creators assigned to it in the past, or in another culture. . . . Music is given new meanings in each new world in which it is appropriated, recorded, taught, and performed. As long as time passes, the accretion of possible meanings continues and is, in principle, unending. The fact that music . . . can be interpreted in widely divergent ways by different people should not lead us to conclude that music has no meaning, but, on the contrary, that it is capable of absorbing and reflecting a surfeit of meanings.[10]

There is more to say about the meaning of musical works and the cognitive-affective nature of musical experiences. What has been developed to this point represents this book's main thrust, but not its complete explanation. More will be added in Chapter 8. To conclude this section, I suggest that an artistic performance of an instrumental composition (or an instrumental improvisation) is analogous to an onion rather than to an apple. There is no core message to be found. Instead, there are layers of relationships for listeners to construct among and between (1) performance-interpretation details, (2) intramusical design details, and (3) the practice-specific standards and traditions evinced in the sounds that form dimensions (1) and (2). To listen for a verbal message, a connected visual image, or a narrative program in the sounds of instrumental music is to mistake an onion for an apple. There is no central seed of literal meaning located at the core of design-based works. Accordingly, what is indescribable in our experience of an instrumental work is not the performance or the composition involved. We have all sorts of ways of describing the artistic, intramusical, and intermusical relationships we cognize in a work of instrumental music. What is ineffable is the complex process of thinking-in-action we call music listening and the exhilarating experience of flow that arises from the match between our musicianship and the cognitive challenges posed by the intramusical and intermusical relationships of the musical work we are covertly constructing in time.

3. Expressional Music

The topic of musical expression brings two issues into head-on collision. On one hand, it is an established fact that people everywhere talk about music being happy, sad, irritable, and so on. Many listeners talk as if they actually hear identifiable emotions in pieces and passages of music. Not only small children and naive adults say such things; knowledgeable composers, performers, conductors, critics, educators, theorists, and musicologists also apply emotive descriptions to musical works. It is safe to say, then, that there is an established tradition of attributing expressive emotional properties to music, including works of instrumental music.

On the other hand, musical purists (or "absolutists") claim that specific emotions cannot exist in music and play no role in our musical enjoyment. To Eduard Hanslick, one of the most influential music critics and philosophers of the nineteenth century, musical works were incapable of being expressive of specific emotions: "[T]he representation of a specific feeling or emotional state is not at all among the characteristic powers of music. . . . [M]usic is incapable of expressing definite feelings."[11]

But as Peter Kivy notes,[12] even Hanslick is inconsistent on the issue of musical expression. Compare Hanslick's statement with the following excerpt from his concert review of Schubert's "Unfinished" Symphony, an example of design-based music if there ever was one.

> [A]fter the few introductory measures, clarinet and oboe in unison begin their gentle cantilena above the calm murmur of the violins. . . . The whole movement is a melodic stream so crystal clear . . . that one can see every pebble on the bottom. And everywhere the same warmth, the same bright, life-giving sunshine!
>
> The Andante develops more broadly. A few odd hints here and there of complaint or irritation are interwoven in a cantilena otherwise full of heartiness and quiet happiness; their effect is that of musical thunder clouds rather than of dangerous clouds of passion.[13]

For Hanslick (the supreme absolutist), Schubert's instrumental music is clearly not a matter of musical sound patterns alone; Hanslick is impressed by the musical expressions of emotion in this work.

Yet the obvious problem with Hanslick's description of this music as calm, warm, irritable, and happy lies in the fact that sounds are inanimate things. Human beings can feel irritable or happy, but sounds cannot. In short, there is no logical fit between musical sounds and actual feelings.

What explains the historic tendency to attribute emotional qualities to musical patterns? There are several theories. The most common idea is that some musical works sound sad (or happy, or whatever) because they arouse an actual feeling of sadness in listeners. This theory, called the arousal theory of musical expression, is implausible for two reasons. First, it makes no sense that people would deliberately listen to *Tristan und Isolde* in order to be plunged into despair or anguish. If musical listening were such an emotional roller coaster ride, then most audience members would be rendered helpless on the floor. But this is not what happens. Listeners are not masochists. People do not usually listen for music in order to experience actual feelings of anguish, despair, sadness, or happiness. Instead, knowledgeable listeners tend to *enjoy* listening to *Tristan und Isolde*.

Second, and contrary to what arousal theories imply, musical sounds are not stimulants, and listening is not a passive process like digestion. Sounds do not arouse specific emotions the way a tablet changes heartburn to relief. Recall our earlier discussion of cognitive emotions (see Chapter 3). Emotions are not simple physiological reactions; they usually result from our cognitive evaluations of people, places, and things. Emotions, says Kivy, are

> concept-laden modes of attention and attitude that cannot logically exist in the absence of appropriate objects and attendant circumstances; and even when they are neurotic or pathological (or unconscious), this is so. We are not just angry, or frightened, or sad: we are angry *at* someone, frightened *by* something, sad *about* some state of affairs. Having these emotions involves believing as well as feeling.[14]

While music listening often seems to move people in the sense that listeners experience an exhilarating sense of flow, or enjoyment, musical patterns do not usually cause listeners to feel sad, frightened, or angry. This is so because there is nothing in musical patterns for listeners to feel sad, frightened, or angry about. There may be occasions when a listener's idiosyncratic cognition of a particular piece or passage of music reminds that listener of something in his or her personal history that causes her to feel real sadness, or another emotion. She is not sad about the musical patterns themselves; she is sad about the personal memory or association brought to mind while she is listening. In any event, idiosyncratic associations do not provide a firm foundation for a reasonable explanation of musical expression.

Another common view holds that a piece or passage of music "sounds sad" because the composer was sad when he or she composed it. This implies that composers must wait to feel grief before they can compose a lament, a requiem, or a funeral march. This suggestion is illogical, not to mention impractical. Composers do not need to experience specific emotional states to compose emotionally expressive music. If requested, I will compose a recognizably bittersweet melody or an upbeat march. My only problem as a composer will be how to compose musically (in relation to existing practices of melody writing and march writing), not how to feel bittersweet or upbeat myself.

In a related vein, some people suggest that the "sad sound" of a piece or passage of music results from the sad feelings of the performers who perform it. But if performers felt all the emotions attributed to themselves and their music, they would be unable to sit or stand up straight, let alone perform artistically.

4. A Concept of Musical Expression

I have implied that listeners would be able to distinguish the bittersweet or upbeat qualities of my melody or march regardless of whether I was bittersweet and upbeat when I composed them. They do this by identifying the characteristics of the musical patterns themselves. How do we know when a friend is sad? We see and hear our friend's sadness in the way he walks, talks, or looks; we notice the way his words and actions evince his sadness.

To recognize the musical expression of specific emotions is to do exactly that: to recognize.[15] As Peter Kivy and Francis Sparshott explain,[16] music "sounds sad" not because it arouses sadness in us but because we apprehend or cognize something in the musical patterns themselves that is *expressive of* sadness. This process of thoughtful interpretation and apprehension parallels the ways in which people regularly apprehend emotional expressiveness in the qualities of human speech and human behaviors.

For example, people use sounds to express themselves in all sorts of ways. People weep, wail, whistle, whimper, whine, sigh, sob, snivel, and scream. Listeners recognize certain qualities in these sounds as expressions of what people are thinking and feeling. In addition, people express their thoughts and feelings in their actions. Observers recognize certain features of human actions as expressive of people's thinking and feeling. It should not be surprising, then, that music makers imitate, develop, and enhance human expressions of emotions in musical sound patterns. It is even less surprising that music listeners should apprehend these affinities when the following points are taken into account.

First, the sounds of speech contain not only words but intonations. Intonation, says Stephen Handel, is "the melody of language. It is the combination of changes in frequency (pitch), duration, loudness, tempo, voice register, and timbre."[17] Intonation, says D. L. Bolinger, is "the melodic line of speech, the rising and falling of the 'fundamental' or the singing pitch of the voice."[18] Vocal intonations affect the meaning of the words conveyed by spoken languages. Indeed, part of the ambiguity of English lies in its use of intonation to indicate the way words are to be taken. And many other languages use inflections to communicate ideas as well as attitudes. Of course, communication can take place without intonation, as written language clearly shows. But even when we read silently we often add or follow inflections the author has embedded in the text. In short, vocal intonations affect what we communicate in spoken language. Intonations reveal meanings, emotions, and attitudes. Compare the emotional-attitudinal differences between the sound of resignation in this first expression

all
↘ right,

and the sounds of brash exuberance in this second expression:

rrrrright !!!!!
↗
Alllllllll

Extensive research has been carried out on the communication of emotions in speech. The process is extraordinarily complex. The human nervous system controls muscle actions and tensions that, in turn, affect breathing, air pressure, the size of the vocal tract, and the position of the vocal fold. These factors, in turn, affect the fundamental frequency of the voice and its resonant frequencies. Understandably, then, there is no one-to-one relationship between a specific physical feature or sound attribute and our comprehension of an emotional quality. Still, the outcomes of these interlocking influences are emotional tone qualities that listeners are remarkably adept at picking out.[19]

The same holds for music listening. Vocal (and choral) music can be (and often is) cognized as sounding expressive of emotions because of its affinities with the expressive qualities of human speech. We listen for identifiable emotional qualities (e.g., happiness, disappointment, sadness) in the way singers perform texts. And we do so in the same way that we listen for such qualities in the sounds of impassioned speech. Indeed, the Swedish voice scientist (and singer) Johan Sundberg[20] has long maintained that the acoustic characteristics of emotion in singing seem to be the same as those in emotional speaking. In sum, the close resemblances between emotional speech and singing explain one way in which vocal music can be expressive of identifiable emotions. Vocal music, says Kivy, is an "emotive icon."[21] Sparshott elaborates:

> [T]he difference between saying and singing is like the difference between saying and whispering or shouting, only much more subtle. It [singing] conveys what you feel or want others to feel about what you are saying, your attitude to it (or the attitude you wish to evoke to it), or how you want it to be taken (ironically, quizzically, seriously); it is an elaborate form of using a special tone of voice.
>
> The music of song, then, conveys not so much what the text means as what one means by the text or the way one means it. It does not say this, but shows it; and the word conventionally used for this kind of showing is "expression."[22]

Just as listeners can apprehend expressions of emotion in the sounds of speech and vocal music, listeners can also apprehend resemblances between the intonations of speech and the syntactic and nonsyntactic patterns of instrumental music. For example, instrumental melodies are often expressive of identifiable emotions due to their affinities with the patterns of human utterance. This is particularly obvious in the instrumental music of many operas and oratorios, in many instrumental jazz solos and, of course, in instrumental accompaniments that are expressive of the emotional qualities conveyed by a sung text.

But the similarities between emotional speech and instrumental patterns explain only part of what listeners cognize in the sounds of instrumental music. What other resemblances might exist? Consider this. People everywhere make music to accompany dancing. This suggests that dance music can be taken, in part, as expressive of what it feels like to be waltzing, "swinging," ragging, or "just doin' the twist." In other words, human speech is only one of many expressive human actions that musical sound patterns can resemble, as Nelson Goodman points out: "[T]he forms and feelings of music are by no means all confined to sound; many patterns and emotions, shapes, contrasts, rhymes and rhythms are common to the auditory and the visual and often to the tactual and the kinesthetic as well."[23]

As Peter Kivy details in *The Corded Shell* (1980), there are many correlations between musical patterns and the patterns of expressive human gestures and movements. As a result, says Kivy, a specific piece or passage of music may be listened for and heard as "a 'sound map' of the human body under the influence of a particular emotion."[24] Of course, these analogous relations vary widely from the most obvious to the most subtle. Kivy offers an example.

> The most obvious analogue to bodily movement in music is, of course, rhythm. And it is an embarrassing commonplace, but nonetheless true, that in all sorts of ways, the rhythmic movement of the human body in all kinds of emotive expressions is

mirrored by and recognized in music. To state the most common of the common-places: *of course* funeral marches are slow and measured, as sadness slows and measures our expression of it; *of course* rapid rhythmic pulses in music are sugges-tive of rapid behavior under the influence of lighter emotions; *of course* jagged and halting rhythms have their direct analogue in human expressive behavior.[25]

More subtly, listeners may hear resemblances between the physical sound fea-tures of instrumental music and the contours and patterns of expressive human actions. Let me explain this proposal by summarizing part of Kivy's argument.[26]

Many people tend to see the shape of a "weeping" willow tree as if it were sorrowful-looking—as if it were expressive of sorrow, or sadness. This is not be-cause the tree feels sad. Instead, we come to know informally (through experience) what sorrowful or unhappy people tend to look like in our culture. Among other things, sorrowful people tend not to smile broadly, or laugh easily, or walk tall. People in sorrow tend to walk slowly, with lowered heads and shoulders, as if carrying a heavy burden. True, not all sorrowful people in all cultures do such things, but many do. We learn to "read" such looks and gestures; we know them tacitly and verbally. It is not surprising, then, that people might tend to see the contours of weeping willow trees as expressive of sadness.[27] The natural features of weeping willow trees come to be seen as expressive of sorrow, melancholy, and other "sad" conditions.

These ideas accord with our earlier discussion of memes and their role in the development of human consciousness (see Chapter 5). I suggest that cultural ex-pressions of emotion also count as memes. That is, the ways in which different cultures decide to see things and hear things as expressive of a particular emotion become part of the information that shapes consciousness (individual and collec-tive) in a culture. Cultural expressions of emotion are memes that are collectively developed and passed on in a culture's ways of speaking, mourning, worshiping, celebrating, and moving and in a culture's ways of musicing and listening.

On one level, then, listeners learn to recognize expressions of emotion in mu-sical patterns because specific musical features resemble other cultural expressions of emotion. Some syntactic and nonsyntactic musical patterns have characteristics that are sufficiently like other human expressions of emotion that listeners cognize them as such.[28] Listeners learn to hear that musical patterns are expressive, which is very close to saying that listeners come to know and believe that certain patterns are expressive of certain emotions. For example, says Kivy,[29] Westerners may hear the contour and pacing of a slowly descending chromatic line as structurally anal-ogous to and therefore expressive of melancholy or, more generally, of sadness. Kivy goes on to suggest that the emotional quality of melancholy is an objective property of this descending chromatic line, just as a cheerful emotional quality belongs to or is a natural part of the color we call canary yellow.[30]

Although I agree with many of Kivy's thoughts on musical expression, I dis-agree with this last point for several reasons. First, Kivy's comparison of canary yellow and a descending chromatic melody is untenable. Yellow is a natural aes-thetic quality of some birds and flowers and most bananas. In contrast, descending chromatic melodies are human-made, artistic constructions. Melodies are made of specially organized sounds that are already musical in character before composers and performers come along. Cognizing yellow requires little knowledge; cognizing descending chromatic patterns in Western musical works requires a significant amount of culture-specific musical understanding. In addition, people are not born knowing that yellow is innately cheerful (if it is). And people are not born knowing that certain kinds of melodies are expressive of melancholy or happiness. One must learn these things informally and formally.

Indeed, musical expressions of emotion occur within specific musical-cultural contexts. Our ability to hear an expression of melancholy in a slowly descending chromatic line is contingent upon hearing these sounds as tones-in-a-system. The expressiveness of a musical pattern may therefore be thought of as a musical figure (expressive pattern) against a musical ground (e.g., the Western tonal system, or the North Indian system of *raga*s). To hear the expressive musical figure, a listener must first be familiar with the musical ground in which the figure is embedded and in relation to which it reveals itself. At the very least, a listener must have an informal understanding of the practice-specific principles underlying a particular musical system to grasp examples of musical expressiveness. In addition, to cognize a musical pattern as expressive of an emotion based on resemblance, a listener must be tacitly or verbally familiar with the vocal customs and gesture customs that musical patterns resemble.

These reflections bring us to another aspect of musical expression. What people know as "their music" is usually an outcome of long traditions of music making and listening. This suggests that when listeners call music "sad" they do so, in part, because they have come to know musical sadness when they hear it. Certain musical patterns and contextual cues become associated with musically conventional expressions of sadness. Sparshott calls this *"expressiveness by convention."*[31] Musical patterns sound sad to listeners in a given culture because the musicers and listeners in that culture have developed specific conventions of making and listening to sounds over time that, to them, sound like the sounds a sad person might sing or play to express that sadness or the sounds that people would want to hear on the occasion of a funeral.[32] In other words, people tend to transfer the emotion words deemed suitable in particular circumstances (a wedding, a funeral) to musical patterns used in these circumstances.

In addition, musicers and listeners often associate specific syntactic and non-syntactic patterns with identifiable emotions. Consider, for example, how some Western composers have combined the timbres and textures of trombones with melodic patterns that are expressive of sombre dignity, deep foreboding, jovial good humor, and romantic love. Such musical expressions of emotion are as real as the musical conventions that inform the composition, orchestration, and performance of trombone passages in such works as Mozart's *Zauberflöte,* Bartok's *Concerto for Orchestra,* Dvořák's Symphony No. 5 ("From the New World"), Ravel's *Boléro,* and Tommy Dorsey's *I'm Getting Sentimental Over You.*

Let me tie these ideas together. The thinking of several philosophers suggests that musical patterns can be expressive of human emotions because vocal music can and does partake of the inherent emotional qualities of the human voice and because musical patterns can and do bear resemblances to expressive human gestures. Moreover, humans have a tendency to invest the looks of things and the sounds of things (animate and inanimate) with emotional qualities: "[W]e tend to 'read' music emotively where it gives us the opportunity to 'read' it as animate."[33] Furthermore, we learn to make and apprehend musical expressions of emotion by means of musical conventions and associations.

I suggest that an important *cognitive value* of musicing and listening inheres in the human use of musical patterns for expressive purposes. Musical patterns give us the artistic means to extend the range of our expressive powers beyond those we find naturally and ordinarily.

5. Identifying Expressive Musical Properties

Admittedly, there are no proofs that can establish the presence of musical expressions of emotion with absolute certainty. There are no clear rules for deciding the specific emotion that a musical passage may be expressive of. But just as there is often agreement among Westerners that the contour of a weeping willow tree is more likely to be seen as expressive of sadness than of happiness, there are widespread cultural and musical conventions by which listeners come to understand the emotions that a particular piece or passage of music may be expressive of. This understanding is part of the informal and impressionistic knowledge that becomes proceduralized in the musicing and listening of people who are inducted into specific musical practices. Educated listeners within practices and cultures tend to agree that certain musical patterns are expressive of identifiable emotions, although they may not always agree on gradations of a certain quality (e.g., sad in the sense of being melancholy? bittersweet? depressing?).

In other words, says Sparshott, while there may not be a formal method or a standardized set of rules for deciding exactly what emotion a piece or passage of music is expressive of, "the claim that interpretability requires rules is indefensible."[34] Kivy agrees: "[T]he failure to show that music is a 'language' (which it isn't) is not necessarily a failure to show that music is expressive of particular, identifiable human emotions."[35]

It follows that although an instrumental work like Schubert's "Unfinished" Symphony involves a complex network of successive and simultaneous musical designs to listen for, some of these artistic musical qualities are also expressive of emotions. These musical expressions of emotion present *one more dimension of musical interest and challenge to cognize in an artistic performance* of the "Unfinished" Symphony.

This is not to say that the "Unfinished" Symphony is "about" happiness, warmth, or sadness.[36] Instead, some of its musical patterns are expressive of sadness and, therefore, only metaphorically (not actually) sad. And just because this work includes such expressiveness does not mean that we should make up a story to correlate with instances of emotionally expressive musical patterns. We should not.

If and when they are present, musical expressions of emotion are there to be cognized as one more dimension of the multidimensional cognitive challenge we call a musical work. As music educators, part of our task is to examine whether expressive musical qualities are operative in the works we select for music teaching and learning. There is no rule or formula. For example, a great deal of Romantic symphonic music, many popular songs, a host of lieder, and most operas include musical expressions of emotion that beg to be listened for and understood. In addition, some music will be expressive of broad affective patterns (e.g., tension and release) in the way that Susanne Langer's theory suggests (see Chapter 2).[37] (Perhaps it is clearer now why I argue that Langer's theory mistakes one aspect of the expressional dimension of musical works for the nature and value of MUSIC overall). On the other hand, many instrumental works (such as Bach's "Goldberg" Variations) are not recognizably expressive of any identifiable emotions. Finally, some works may be cognized as expressive in a nonspecific sense: "expressive without being expressive of anything in particular."[38]

6. Representational Music

Representational works involve the use of syntactic and nonsyntactic musical parameters to describe, depict, narrate, characterize, refer to, or otherwise re-present people, places, ideas, events, and other aspects of our world.

There are several actual and possible ways to create representational music. One of the most common ways is exemplified in program music. This involves ordering or unifying a work by linking musical patterns to an underlying narrative. The most obvious form of this strategy is to coordinate the narration of a story with accompanying musical patterns that have been specially designed and timed to underscore events in the narrative. Examples include Prokofiev's *Peter and the Wolf,* Copland's *Lincoln Portrait,* and Persichetti's *Fables.*

Alternatively, a composer may associate a specific musical pattern (e.g., a melodic motive) with a character in an opera, an idea in a vocal or choral text, or an event in a film. Once such links are made, the meaning and significance of the "loaded" musical pattern may be modified through variation or combination with other motifs or texts, or undermined by its placement in subsequent dramatic or musical contexts. There are endless ways of linking musical events with other kinds of events to foreshadow, propel, inhibit, comment upon, or resolve dramatic actions.

Third, and more subtly, a narrative may be implicit in the structure of a musical work in the same way that the pillars of a building are hidden from view but essential to its shape and strength. Examples include Liszt's *Faust Symphony,* Messiaen's *Quartet for the End of Time,* Ellington's *Black, Brown, and Beige,* and Joan Tower's *Sequoia.*

Fourth, it is not uncommon for particular musical forms to become conventional references. Consider the musical differences that distinguish funeral marches, wedding marches, military marches, and convocation marches. Consider, also, how a particular musical practice may be linked to a stipulated set of feelings (e.g., Indian *raga*s). The listenables of whole musical practices are often cognized as embodying a particular social group's way of life, as in Scottish folk songs or Cape Breton fiddle music. Such references may be promulgated by the practitioners of the musical practices themselves or by listeners who infer some relationship between themselves and their music.[39]

Fifth, composers and arrangers often set vocal texts or accompany dances in ways that depict, parallel, punctuate, exaggerate, or contradict what the words or movements intend or present. In these cases, musical sounds, words, or movements form a referential loop.

Sixth, musical representations and references are not limited to people, places, and things. Composers and improvisors often take musical patterns from one musical work and reference them in another work through direct quotation, variation, or development. Recall, for example, how Berlioz uses the *Dies irae* chant in the Witches' Sabbath of his *Symphonie fantastique*. More generally, jazz artists often infuse their improvisations with melodic phrases borrowed from other works. These musical footnotes not only make sense within the musical designs of jazz improvisations but often give rise to humor and reflection in knowledgeable jazz listeners.

I was present one hot August night at a remote jazz club in the woods of northern Wisconsin. The jazz saxophonist Richie Cole was the guest artist with a local rhythm section that was well below Cole's expert level of musicianship. After many gallant efforts to make music with his local colleagues, Cole improvised a brilliant solo on *All the Things You Are* that included several melodic quotes from well-known jazz standards. To this listener, Cole's musical footnotes provided a witty musical commentary on his artistic plight. For among the melodies Cole referenced in his improvisation were the following: *Don't Blame Me, I Can't Get Started, I Got it Bad, What Am I Gonna Do?, Why Don't You Do Right?* and *Bewitched, Bothered, and Bewildered*.

In summary, the main question regarding representational works of music is not whether to listen for the ways and means of musical reference in these works, only *how*. In the praxial view taken in this book, the musicianship required to make and to listen for representational music intelligently includes a deep understanding of the specific links that exist between particular musical patterns and what they re-present. Leonard B. Meyer endorses this position in a study of musical form-content relationships:

> The specification of the phenomenon being represented is by no means a trivial matter. Despite the appealing "purity" of formalism, a title or program that denotes a particular phenomenon is, in my view, just as much an attribute of a composition as are the pitches, durations, and other relationships notated in the score. The significance of a composition depends on the interactions among a set of stimuli (the sounding music), a competent listener, and a cultural context (including what we know about a composition). Knowledge of what is being represented changes the significance of the composition not only because such knowledge affects human experience, but because by directing attention to particular features of a pattern, such knowledge influences our understanding and response to what is presented.[40]

7. Musical Description and Characterization

Consider Beethoven's "Pastoral" Symphony, Honegger's *Pacific 231,* and Handel's *Israel in Egypt*. Is it correct to say that what we hear in these works are the *actual* sounds of (respectively) a cuckoo, a train, and buzzing flies? No. Performances of these compositions do not include either the original sounds of these things or even prerecorded aural copies. Instead, listeners are presented with musical renditions of a cuckoo's song, train sounds, and buzzing flies. As Peter Kivy and Jenefer Robinson both point out, listeners recognize these sounds because they sound enough like the everyday sounds they represent that we need no other clues to understand the intended references.[41] The trains we hear in Honegger's *Pacific 231,* Duke Ellington's *Daybreak Express,* and Villa Lobos's *Little Train of Caipira* are made of entirely musical patterns. This holds for most musical depictions and descriptions.

Of course, some representational works include the actual sounds of everyday events for listeners to cognize (or re-cognize) and enjoy. But even when music makers use everyday sounds, the larger musical settings of which they are part cause us to listen for these sounds as elements in an artistic construction. Accordingly, we listen for these sounds under a different set of knowings than we would if we encountered them in their natural settings.

Jenefer Robinson suggests that when music makers represent ordinary sounds and events in musical works, they are not merely depicting or denoting things outside the music itself (as thunder might denote a storm).[42] Instead, they are "representing" in the much richer and cognitively challenging sense of musically describing and characterizing. Just as Van Gogh's *Sunflower* offers viewers neither a real flower nor a simple representation of a flower but an artist's visual conception of a sunflower, representational works of music offer listeners musical conceptions of subjects, objects, and events.

Here is another *cognitive value* of musicing and listening. When a musical work describes or characterizes something, it is delineating some aspect of our world in a new and interesting *musical* way.[43] By portraying, characterizing, and contextualizing aspects of our world in musical sounds, music makers offer listeners alternative artistic conceptions of the world. Taking this point one more step, consider that just as novels, films, and paintings often portray the same subject in alternate ways, different musicians often characterize the same subject in alternate ways. For example, compare George Gershwin's *Summertime,* Vivaldi's summer concerto from the *Four Seasons,* and Debussy's *Prélude à l'après-midi d'un faune.* We neither see nor read what summer is like in these works, nor are we told what a particular summer is like. Instead, each work includes and offers a different musical characterization of summer.

How do music makers and musical works present listeners with the kinds of information they need to realize musical characterizations? Jenefer Robinson offers a plausible answer.[44] She suggests that a piece or passage of descriptive music functions like a predicate in a sentence.

Robinson explains that, when paired with an identified subject of some sort, a descriptive piece of music forms something similar to (but not identical with) a verbal statement. A cue of some sort—a title, program, text, lyric, or film scene—serves to link a piece or passage of descriptive music to a subject. For example, the titles or programs of *La Mer, Fingal's Cave, Till Eulenspiegel,* and *Prélude à l'après-midi d'un faune* function as cues to advise listeners what musical subject-predicate pairings to make. These cues inform us that the musical patterns we hear can be taken as characterizations of the subject indicated by the cue. In *Till Eu-lenspiegel,* the "Till theme" characterizes Till as a mischief maker; the title and program of this composition tell us that the expressive qualities we hear in the music (the mocking, mischievous quality of the Till theme) are to be attributed to Till. In this work, listeners are presented with a character sketch of a subject analogous to a painter's portrait. Similarly, Schubert's *Gretchen am Spinnrad* characterizes both the dreary sound of the spinning wheel and Gretchen's continuous grief. Extending this strategy, we see how a composer might also decide to link a subject with a musical description that surprises us or contradicts the impression we have of a person, place, or thing.

Within the representational subcategory of descriptive music there is a wide range of possibilities. At one end of the continuum we find descriptive works like Duke Ellington's *Daybreak Express.* There is no doubt that this composition is Ellington's musical portrait of a train ride. Knowledgeable listeners know and believe that what they hear is a "musical train" moving slowly out of the station, accelerating, cruising along, and slowing down at its destination. Ellington's title only confirms the subject we cognize and enjoy. But such clear examples of musical illustration are rare.[45] As we move toward the other end of the continuum we find that most examples of descriptive music do not illustrate or depict clearly identifiable subjects. Instead, their musical patterns embody expressive qualities that listeners connect with a subject because clues or directions (including titles, texts, and programs) suggest what linkages to make and when to make them. Such works, says Robinson, are more accurately said to characterize rather than represent because they contain no subject that we can actually hear in the music.[46]

In *Till Eulenspiegel,* a musical theme with a mischievous quality is linked to a character named Till by means of a program. We do not hear a person in this work the way we hear a musical train ride in *Daybreak Express.* Thus, between the poles of the descriptive continuum we find a host of works that describe and/or characterize subjects, objects, and events in a variety of ways. And just as expressional music extends the bounds of what humans can ordinarily convey, representational music extends our possibilities of describing, depicting, illustrating, characterizing—and, therefore, of understanding—important aspects of our world.

Of course, almost any piece or passage of music is vulnerable to "descriptive misuse" because any piece of music can be enlisted to characterize one subject or another. For example, if a film director synchronizes a passionate love scene with the second movement of Brahms's Fourth Symphony, then the director is partaking of the established musical practice of linking ordinary subjects with musical predicates. But such an arbitrary pairing does not qualify the second movement of Brahms's Fourth Symphony as descriptive music.[47]

It is easy to understand how novice listeners might arrive at the erroneous conclusion that all music everywhere is "about" some identifiable subject. In addition to long-established practices of musical representation across cultures, the penchant of television, film, and video producers to make precisely timed links between musical patterns and visual images only reinforces the false impression held by many that all music everywhere is representational, referential, or descriptive. A predictable overreaction to this situation is to claim wrongly (as absolutists

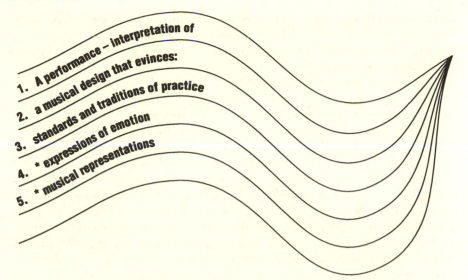

1. A performance – interpretation of
2. a musical design that evinces:
3. standards and traditions of practice
4. * expressions of emotion
5. * musical representations

FIGURE 6.1. A Musical Work: Five Dimensions. The asterisks in the fourth and fifth dimensions indicate that some (but not all) musical works are applicable.

claim) that all music everywhere must be listened to aesthetically—as sound patterns alone. Neither extreme is reasonable.

8. Implications for Music Education

In preparing and planning to teach, music educators need to keep in mind that musical works are *multidimensional* challenges. As a result, *there is no one way to listen for all music everywhere.* Instead, *different musical works present different dimensions and combinations of musical dimensions to listen for.* In addition, different musical practices around the world have different ways of organizing musical designs, musical expressions of emotion, and musical representations.

To develop their musicianship, music students need to learn what there is to make and listen for in musical works of various kinds and in the musical works of various practices and cultures. Otherwise, many opportunities for self-growth and musical enjoyment will be lost. Until students become aware of what they might find by deeper listening, they have no way of knowing what they may be missing. A major part of our task as music educators is to know the musical works we intend to teach through and through, in all their musical dimensions.

The diagram in Figure 6.1 summarizes what musical works can demand of musicers and listeners alike. This philosophy proposes that every musical work involves at least four and often as many as six simultaneous and interrelated dimensions of musical information. To this point in the book I have discussed five of these six dimensions. I review each dimension briefly now.

1. Listening is always a matter of listening for a performance of one kind or

another: either a performance of a composition (or a remembered work) or an improvisation. All the other dimensions of a musical work are made determinate in the actions of musical performing. (Chapter 7 probes the concepts of performance and improvisation.)

2. Each and every musical performance involves a composed or improvised musical design consisting of syntactic and nonsyntactic musical parameters. Listeners actively construct the relations among and between the patterns of the musical design dimension as interpreted and expressed by musical performers.

3. Every heard performance or improvisation evinces the stipulations and standards of a particular musical practice (however old or new that practice might be). While cognizing a performance of a musical design, knowledgeable listeners know whether music makers are meeting or departing from relevant musical norms and traditions. A regular aspect of knowledgeable listening involves situating and evaluating musical works in relation to previous performances of the same work or similar works in the same practice. Musical traditions and criteria are inherent in the artistic qualities of musical sound patterns and in the artistic ways that music makers perform, improvise, compose, arrange, and/or conduct musical works.

4. As this chapter has explained, the musical designs and performances of some (but not all) musical works evince musical expressions of emotion. An essential task of music teaching and learning is to develop student musicianship in regard to musical expressiveness. This is a fundamental aspect of artistic problem solving that music students must engage in actively and learn to carry out. Kivy agrees: "[M]usical expressiveness is such an integral part of our musical culture and experience that it is almost impossible to imagine full musical competence in the absence of the ability to make the basic emotive distinctions in music."[48]

Teaching for musical expressiveness proceeds in several related ways: by deliberately selecting works that contain musical expressions of emotion; by targeting students' attention to instances of musical expression; by presenting students with interpretive problems of musical expression to solve artistically in performance projects, composition projects, or arranging projects; by providing models of expressive music making for students on a regular basis; by comparing and contrasting recorded examples of expressive and nonexpressive musicing; and by offering formal knowledge about specific instances of musical expression.

Emotive descriptions of musical works have an important role to play in music teaching and learning. When it is reasonable to infer from the musical (textual and/or contextual) information one is cognizing that the patterns of a musical work are expressive of emotions, it is appropriate to use emotion words and emotional analogies to focus students' attention on the expressive features of syntactic and nonsyntactic musical patterns. Just as formal medical terminology is unable to render everything a patient may experience or want to know about his health, a strictly formal approach to musical analysis is usually insufficient to capture all the dimensions of a musical work, especially the expressional dimension.

This is not a recommendation to assign emotive descriptions to all music everywhere. There are intellectually reasonable ways of knowing when musical patterns are expressive of emotions. This knowing is chiefly a matter of knowing the traditions and standards of the musical practice to which a given work belongs. In sum, making and listening for musical expressions of emotion are eminently musical things to do, depending on the specific practice and piece of music involved.

5. The musical designs and performances of some (but not all) musical works include musical representations of various aspects of our world. Yet another important task of music education is to make students aware of the many actual and possible ways that musical patterns can represent and refer to various kinds of subjects while emphasizing that only *some* musical works are representational. By carefully selecting works that include musical representations of various kinds, and by drawing students' attention to examples of musical representation in the music they are learning to make and listen for, teachers can enable learners to think intelligently with regard to this dimension of musical meaning.

The most important way of educating students' musicianship in this area is to present students with problems of musical representation to solve in performance, composition, improvisation, arranging, and conducting projects. During such projects, teachers can introduce representational descriptions of musical patterns and relevant background knowledge parenthetically (e.g., historical information, political information). Representational descriptions enable learners to discern those aspects of musical patterns that are simultaneously artistic qualities of a work and musical representations of referenced subjects or meaningful references to other musical works. Formal background knowledge is often necessary to help students understand the links between particular musical patterns and what these patterns are intended to represent.

I emphasize again that this praxial philosophy is not claiming that all music is representational. It is not even claiming that a work of music that includes a representational dimension of information should be listened to primarily for instances of musical description, characterization, and so on. This philosophy is proposing that there are widespread practices of making listenables that combine musical and extramusical material and that it is musically intelligent to listen for musical representations in conjunction with listening for the other relevant dimensions of such works.

Just as music teachers and learners should not assign emotive descriptions to all music everywhere, teachers and learners should not assign representational descriptions to all music everywhere. There are logical ways of knowing when musical representation is operative in a given work. This knowing is chiefly a matter of knowing the traditions and standards of the practice of which a given listenable is a piece. For example, knowing the traditions and standards of nineteenth century Romantic music includes knowing why and how the musical representation and glorification of natural phenomena (such as storms and country scenes) was important to composers, audiences, and performers of the time.[49]

It is possible to listen exclusively for the musical design dimension of Mussorgsky's *Great Gate of Kiev*. And it is possible to enjoy such listening without attending to or knowing the relationships between the musical patterns of this work and the painting these musical patterns represent. But the praxial philosophy put forward by this book suggests that to do so would be to misunderstand the full nature and value of Mussorgsky's composition and its proper performance. Indeed, we cannot fully understand how to interpret and perform a representational work (or the musical expressions of emotion it may also contain) without knowing what the work is intended to be descriptive and/or expressive of.

I suggest that it is because our powers of consciousness are so powerful and flexible that there is no prohibition on listening simultaneously and/or sequentially for the several dimensions of musical information that musical works can (and often do) present for our cognition. The full challenge of musicing and listening and, therefore, the full enjoyment of musicing and listening comes from thinking-in-action in relation to the various combinations of these dimensions when they are present together in the temporal events of a musical performance. We relish what we construct (overtly and covertly) and therefore understand to be the combined effect of the interpretive, formal, traditional, expressional, and representational dimensions of a work when these are brought together in an artistic musical performance. An essential part of our enjoyment of works that integrate these dimensions is the way in which music is being made of many human interests simultaneously, including matters of artistry, design, creativity, tradition, emotion, narration, characterization, culture, ideology, and community.

Questions for Discussion and Review

1. Across cultures, musical works tend to exhibit a wide variety of form-content relationships? Do you agree? If so, what factors might help to explain this variety?

2. Explain the terms *expressional* music, *representational* music, and *design-based* music. What does it mean to say that these categories are heuristic devices?

3. Chapter 4 suggests that all musical works involve the cognition of three basic dimensions of musical information. Name these three dimensions. Chapter 6 argues that, in addition to these three dimensions, some musical works may involve musical expressions of emotions and/or musical representations of various kinds. But perhaps you disagree? Indeed, some writers claim that musical sound patterns cannot be expressive of emotions. Explain your position on musical expression. Explain why you agree or disagree with this statement: "Musical sounds cannot represent or characterize anything 'outside' themselves."

4. Using the titles suggested in this chapter, listen for one example of expressional music, representational music, and design-based music (with attention to the three, four, or five dimensions of musical information involved in each work). Next, locate, listen for, and reflect on the differences between two contrasting performances of each of the three works you selected. Next, select any three recordings you wish and (using diagram 6.1 as a reminder) listen for the presence (or absence) of the various dimensions of musical information discussed to this point in the book.

5. Identify three musical works that seem to combine a strong emphasis on formal musical design with musical expressions of emotion and musical representation.

6. Explain the weaknesses of the old stimulant and referential theories of instrumental music.

7. Do you believe that the intramusical sound patterns of instrumental works can have meaning? Why?

8. Chapter 4 offers an explanation of the cognitive processes involved in listening for the sound patterns of musical works conceived as artistic or historical properties. Chapter 5 offers a grounding explanation of the human significance of listening for the sound patterns of musical works. This chapter has just offered thoughts on the additional dimensions of meaning that different kinds of music can require us to listen for. Review and reflect on these explanations. Briefly explain to yourself, or others, why knowledgeable musicers and listeners might experience enjoyment or flow while listening for (say) a Chicago Symphony performance of Schubert's "Unfinished" Symphony, Whitney Houston's performance of "Savin' All My Love," or Joan Tower's *Sequoia.*

9. Explain three educational implications of the philosophical proposals in this chapter.

Supplementary Sources

Peter Kivy. *Music Alone: Philosophical Reflections on the Purely Musical Experience.* Ithaca, N.Y.: Cornell University Press, 1990. An illuminating discussion of design-based works.

Ismay Barwell. "How Does Art Express Emotion?" *Journal of Aesthetics and Art Criticism* 44, no. 2 (Winter 1986): 175–81. A well-argued view of artistic expression.

Peter Kivy. *The Corded Shell: Reflections on Musical Expression.* Princeton, N.J.: Princeton University Press, 1980. An essential source for anyone interested in the topic of musical expression.

Doreen Rao. *ACDA on Location, Vol. 1: The Children's Choir.* Lawton, Okla.: The American Choral Directors Association, Educational Videotape Series, 1988. This videotape includes an example of how musical expressions of emotion can be taught and learned in relation to interpreting and performing Bach's *Duet from Cantata No. 15.*

Jenefer Robinson. "Music as a Representational Art." In *What is Music? An Introduction to the Philosophy of Music,* ed. Philip A. Alperson, pp. 167–92. New York: Haven Publications, 1987. A detailed and illuminating discussion of musical representation.

Francis E. Sparshott. "Portraits in Music—A Case Study: Elgar's 'Enigma' Variations." In *The Interpretation of Music: Philosophical Essays,* ed. Michael

Krausz, pp. 231–45. Oxford: Clarendon Press, 1993. An analysis of the many strategies that one composer uses to musically represent, characterize, and narrate.

Peter Kivy. *Sound and Semblance: Reflections on Musical Representation.* Princeton, N.J.: Princeton University Press, 1984. Another insightful concept of musical representation.

Leonard B. Meyer. *Style and Music: Theory, History, and Ideology.* Philadelphia: University of Pennsylvania Press, 1989. Meyer offers examples and explanations of musical representation in Romantic music.

7

Musicing in Context

Thus far the philosophy put forth in this book has proposed that MUSIC is a diverse human practice and that musical practices pivot on musicianship. Musicianship is directed toward the practical end of constructing musical works overtly and covertly. Musical works are multidimensional artistic-social constructions. Musicers/listeners can achieve self-growth, constructive knowledge, and optimal experience when their musicianship matches the challenges presented by a given musical work (or musical "thought-generator"). And because the dominant forms of knowing that constitute musicianship are essentially nonverbal and situational, the development of musicianship is intimately related to the authenticity of the musical situations in which it is taught, learned, and used; that is, musical action and musical context work together to coproduce musical understanding.[1]

Because it displays these several characteristics in combination, MUSIC is a highly social and situated form of human practice. But there are additional characterstics that need examination. Indeed, a fuller understanding of the contextual nature of MUSIC, MUSICIANSHIP, and MUSICAL WORKS is essential to a fuller understanding of the nature and values of music education.

In this chapter I revisit musicing to examine the interdependencies among and between composing, performing, conducting, improvising, and arranging.

1. Composing in Context

The musicianship of every musical practice is learned through interactions with musically significant "others": with teachers and, in a more distanced way, with the community of practitioners who have established, maintained, and advanced the musical domain a novice wishes to learn. When the musicianship of a practice is complex, a variety of people become involved in the teaching-learning enterprise, both directly and indirectly. Even a person who is largely self-taught inevitably makes use of past and present practitioners directly (through personal advice) and indirectly (through books, concerts, recordings, and videotapes). Alasdair Mac-

Intyre sums the significance of these observations: "To enter into a practice is to enter into a relationship not only with its contemporary practitioners, but also with those who have preceded us in the practice, particularly those whose achievements extended the reach of the practice to its present point. It is thus the achievement, and . . . [even more certainly] the authority, of a tradition which I then confront and from which I have to learn."[2]

Let us apply these thoughts to composing. Whenever individuals begin to compose, they are never acting "alone." Their composing is always "situated" and social in the following ways. First, the musicianship required to compose particular kinds of music develops in relation to the thinking of other composers and performers, past and present, who have immersed themselves in the achievements and the authority (or the standards and traditions) of particular compositional practices. As Nicholas Wolterstorff reminds us, composers, like all musical practitioners, take up their ways of composing at a certain point in the history of musical practices and in a certain place.[3] One learns to compose by being inducted into culture-based and practice-centered ways of musical thinking that particular groups of musical practitioners maintain, refine, and embody in landmark compositions.

Second, composing is highly contextual in that composers do not generate and select musical ideas in abstraction. Composers do not simply "compose." They compose particular forms of music: songs, film scores, fanfares, preludes, laments, dance suites, string quartets, symphonies, marches, overtures, operas, requiems, sonatas, concertos, cantatas. In doing so, composers depend on established models and criteria of compositional practice that they decide to follow, adjust, redevelop, or transcend.

Third, among the most important guidelines that composers use to channel and evaluate their composing are performance practices.[4] Composers necessarily think about the instruments or voices they compose for, about the music makers who will perform their compositions, and (often) about when and where their compositions will be performed. In fact, composers frequently compose for individual soloists, ensembles, or occasions. Accordingly, there is an important conversational relationship between composers, performers, and conductors, because composers usually want their works to be interpreted and performed well (according to precise individual and contextual criteria). Composers must therefore learn how to communicate their intentions to performers indirectly (through scores and written instructions) and directly (in person).

It follows from this that musical scores not only stipulate sounds, they also stipulate (or, at least, guide) the actions of performers and conductors. In other words, *performance practices are constituent elements of musical works* because composers take matters of performance into account when they generate their compositions. As Wolterstorff explains, "it is a mistake to think of musical works as 'consisting' entirely of sounds—even to think of them as 'consisting' of sounds *heard* in a certain way. They consist as well of actions. Music is not just an art of sounds but *an art of sounds and actions.*"[5]

These thoughts bring us back to a central theme of this praxial philosophy: that the nature and identity of musical compositions depend on interlocking social relationships.[6] Thus (and again), musical works are not autonomous aesthetic objects.

Everything about a heard musical performance is artistic, from the nature of its auditory materials and compositional procedures to its conventions of musical expression and representation to its artistic practices of musical interpretation and presentation. Unless composers deliberately include "found sounds" (as in musique concrète), even the material means of compositions (e.g., scale tones) are the result of generations of theoretical and practical development.

In addition to the dialogical relationship between composers and performers, composers carry on an equally important (albeit a more distanced) relationship with their potential listeners. For composers usually make basic assumptions about the listening abilities and/or preferences of their future audiences and, therefore, take account of their listeners (directly or indirectly) before or during the process of composing. For example (and most fundamentally), composers do not usually invent new musical materials each time they compose a new work. Except for aleatoric practices, most composers begin with the predetermined musical sounds of their music cultures (e.g., tones-for-us, timbres-for-us). In this way, listening procedures inform composers' decisions and actions.[7]

Also, since composers usually listen for their unfolding compositions in their aural imaginations or "live" as they generate and select musical ideas, they often anticipate whether their compositions will meet or depart from the current listening practices of their audiences. Some composers (like Milton Babbitt) tend to compose for extremely sophisticated listeners. Others (like Philip Glass and Steve Reich) make some of their works rather easy to listen for. (The same "challenge continuum" of music-listening opportunities seems to hold in most practices, including jazz, rock, and pop.) Even composers who force changes in traditional listening procedures are usually aware of the problems (aural, cultural, and commercial) that their works will present to listeners. As a result, they often provide help. For example, many "new music" performances include preperformance lectures by composers, conductors, and performers in which audiences receive formal musical analyses, contextual clues, historical and creative insights, graphic listening guides, and/or other cues to help them listen intelligently for new works.

In all these ways, there is a give-and-take or interresponsive exchange between composers and their real or imagined audiences and, often, a tension between old ways of listening and new ways of composing. And whether composers decide to match or stretch conventional ways of listening within a given practice, such decisions imply that they have taken their listeners into account. Here again, the form and content of compositions can be seen to reflect cultural and social relationships.

No matter how individually produced or nonutilitarian they may seem, all works of music incorporate social and practical realities. Musical works are inherently communal constructions; they are expressive of the social and cultural practices through which, and in relation to which, composers compose at different times and places. Wolterstorff concurs:

> Composers do not lock themselves in with sounds. Social practices are embodied in their works, at some points even to the extent of being constitutive of the identity of those works. They contribute to the 'why' of those works, to their rationale. The rationality of a work of art is neither purely interior to the work nor purely interior to the artist; not even its identity is.[8]

2. Performing in Context

Just as composers require knowledge of how performing and listening are carried out by the people for whom they compose, performers require knowledge of composing and listening practices. This is so because performing involves much more than merely producing the notes of a score. It is useful to compare what a performer does with what a speaker does. Thomas Carson Mark has developed this comparison elsewhere.[9] I shall borrow several of Mark's ideas to anchor the following discussion.

Suppose I am playing tennis with a friend called Terry. After winning the third of three straight sets, Terry runs to the net and asks triumphantly: "David, do you give up now?" I utter these immortal words in reply: "I have not yet begun to fight!"

What have I actually done? First (and besides losing badly at tennis), I have quoted John Paul Jones. Quoting has two aspects: (1) producing another person's precise words and (2) deliberately intending that one's own words coincide with another person's words. It is the deliberate intention to repeat someone else's precise words, says Mark, that makes an utterance a quotation rather than merely a statement or an accident.

Second, in deciding to reply to Terry with the words, "I have not yet begun to fight!" (instead of simply saying "Yes" or "No"), I am not merely quoting John Paul Jones. I am using his precise words to *assert* something. I want my partner to understand that I will not surrender as easily as she might think. In other words, says Mark, for a quotation to be an assertion, a speaker must deliberately intend that his quotation be understood as making some sort of pertinent point.

Quoting and asserting have important parallels in musical performing. For example, when we say that a pianist is performing Bach's "English" Suite No. 2 in A minor, what we mean in part is that the performer is producing the precise sounds indicated in the score and deliberately intending that the sounds he makes are the sounds that Bach stipulated. To this extent, what a musical performer does is analogous to what a speaker does when he utters a quotation. Similarly, when Claudio Abbado conducts the Berlin Philharmonic in a performance of Schubert's "Unfinished" Symphony, what he is doing in part is coordinating the orchestra's production of the precise sounds indicated in Schubert's score and ensuring that the sounds the orchestra makes are those that Schubert intended.

But there is obviously more to musical performing than this. The "more" lies in Mark's distinction between quoting something and asserting it. To qualify as a performance, a performer or conductor must not merely quote what a composer has indicated. He or she must also assert it in the sense that a speaker intends a quotation to be thoroughly understood by his listeners. Mark explains:

> As is the case of assertion in language, the principal requirement for assertion [in musical performance] is intentional. . . . [I]n music, the performer intends that the sounds he produces will be taken as having cogency, as articulating how things musically are. . . . The intention of a performer—the intention that makes his production of sounds a performance—is that his listeners will take the sounds produced to have this authority, this claim to attention which is analogous to the claim made on our belief by sentences that purport to be true.[10]

In other words, quoting John Paul Jones to assert a point demands that I first understand what Jones means and that I interpret his words correctly. Merely repeating words that one does not understand does not count as an assertion or an interpretation.

Performing a musical work is analogous to quoting someone else's words in order to assert something.[11] A performer performs a musical composition in order to express his or her personal *understanding* of that composition. A musical performance is not simply an audible reproduction of what a score indicates. Performing is not the aural equivalent of making a photocopy of an original painting or print; if it were, then any competent production of a score would count as much as any other. But this is not so in musical reality. One of the most enjoyable aspects of truly musical listening is listening for a special artist's (and/or a specific ensemble's) *interpretation* of a given composition. The quality of a musical interpretation conveys the level of musical understanding—the *musicianship*—possessed by the performers involved. This is what we mean when we say that MUSIC is a performing art.

In summary, performing is not a matter of actualizing musical works for people who cannot hear scores in their heads. A performance projects a musician's understanding of the several dimensions of a given composition into a definite context so that the performance itself is open to the consideration and criticism of knowledgeable listeners.

3. Musical Interpretation

Success in musical performing depends on understanding *all* relevant dimensions of a given composition. As well as knowing how to produce and perform its syntactic and nonsyntactic patterns in relation to pertinent standards and traditions of practice, performers must understand whether a composition is expressional and/or representational. If either (or both) of these dimensions is present, performers must decide how these dimensions relate to the composition as a whole. Performers must also decide the relative importance of different aspects of a composition at different points in its temporal unfolding. Actualizing these understandings in a performance amounts to plotting and instantiating an elaborate cognitive map of intramusical, intermusical, and contextual relationships.

But there is more. In the actions of performing, performers convey their understanding of a composition in relation to (a) what the composer must/could/should have intended, (b) what past performers must/could/should have intended, (c) what they believe their audience would expect or enjoy hearing emphasized in a composition, or (d) some combination of the above.

These ideas explain why contrasting interpretations of the same composition might be not only possible but equally legitimate. Like a spotlight shone at different angles on the same sculpture, different interpretations may reveal (or hide) different aspects of a composition's design and, if present, different details of musical expression and musical representation. Second, performers and conductors may decide to rethink the intentions or directions of a composer or the traditional ways of interpreting compositions in a practice, especially when these ways are ambiguous. Third, performers and conductors may "restore" works in keeping with what they understand to be the original standards and conventions of performing and listening in a given practice. In short, most (but not all) compositions and practices offer a range of possibilities for the expression of both individual and established musical beliefs. A score, says Sparshott, "does not command but merely specifies and thus provides opportunities."[12]

Let me restate these points from another perspective. Performing is not a matter of re-creating a composer's written intentions as obediently as possible. For what a composer hears in his or her musical imagination and commits to paper is not a real performance. As a result, what a composer writes in a score is not the final word. In a real performance, decisions are being made and completed (successfully or not) such that every detail of the performance is determinate. In contrast, a composer's imaginary hearing (or "audiation") of his own work requires no such concrete decision making. In other words, an imagined performance of a composition is indeterminate. This explains why it is possible for a performer (or a conductor) to perform a work in a way that is better than, or different from (but still compatible with), the performance a composer originally intended, imagined, or expected. This also explains why it is reasonable to say that expert performers may be the most knowledgeable when it comes to knowing what a musical score really intends. For it is only in the artistic performance of a musical composition that everything the composer conceived is actually decided.[13]

Peter Kivy maintains that an artistic musical performance of a composition is the "ultimate nonverbal description of the work."[14] I agree. And I also suggest that a truly excellent performance of a musical composition can be taken as a full nonverbal explanation of what an artistic performer considers to be all the important relations and values in a composition. Alan Goldman puts it this way: "[A] performance . . . instantiates, exemplifies, or implicitly conveys the performer's interpretation. What it exemplifies or implicitly conveys is an explanation of the work and its elements, one that reflects the performer's view of the values inherent in the piece."[15]

Our enjoyment of performing and listening for musical performances derives, in major part, from the richness of the performance-interpretation process. When the criteria of a practice encourage performers to develop and project competing interpretations of compositions, the possibilities for achieving self-growth and enjoyment increase because there is an inherent dynamism in the practice. Interpretive options give performers and listeners more and more musical challenges to find, solve, and express. Accordingly, interpretive options invite, encourage, and demand the dynamic growth of musicianship.

We can tie these thoughts together in the following way. A musical performance (in the Western tradition, at least), always involves not one but two works of musical artistry. For example, when the pianist Ivo Pogorelich performs Bach's "English" Suite No. 2 in A minor we cognize (1) the multidimensional work that is Bach's "English" Suite No. 2 in A minor that includes (2) the *musicianship* of Pogorelich (the knowledgeable actions of the artist-pianist Pogorelich that project his individual understanding of Bach's "English" Suite No. 2).

Let me make the same point in relation to music teaching and learning. When Sara participates in an excellent performance of an arrangement of "Pie Jesu" from Fauré's *Requiem*[16] with her class choir, she is not merely producing or re-producing notes on a page. Sara and her classmates are responsible for two achievements: their performance of the multidimensional work stipulated by the notated score of Fauré's "Pie Jesu," and their working understanding of "Pie Jesu," that is, the choir's knowledgeable interpretation of Fauré's composition. The students' knowledgeable actions of singing "Pie Jesu" musically (in accord with relevant demands and traditions of practice) instantiate their musicianship in a way that is far richer and more complete than any verbal test of their musical understanding.

4. Obligations and Ethics

Musical performing frequently involves a basic ethical dilemma. On one hand, knowledgeable audiences usually expect performers to exercise their musical individuality within the bounds set by a musical score. On the other hand, to be inducted into a musical practice is to develop a sense of responsibility toward the artistic conventions of that practice. This sense of obligation includes the disposition (supervisory knowledge) to be faithful to a musical score or (in oral/aural traditions) to be faithful to a remembered performance. Thus, says Morris Grossman, performing involves an important tension between constraint and freedom that amounts to a "double obligation."[17]

In reality, competent, proficient, and expert performers do not simply follow a score. They decide what a composition wants and needs in relation to its several dimensions. They produce "draft" performances of a composition in rehearsals and practice sessions that they subsequently refine, redo, reaffirm, and rethink. On the basis of these kinds of "re-searching" performers decide what to provide. Performing engages people in making decisions about their artistic obligations to a composition (and its practice) and the procedures they intend to follow to fulfill their obligations.

The ambiguities of scores make this interpretive-ethical decision-making process even more challenging. For example, whereas the syntactic relationships in a notated melody are usually precise (but not always exact), dynamics, tempos, timbres, and articulations are more relative. Similarly, some features (such as swing eighth notes, cadenzas, and ornaments) may be indicated vaguely by a composer, or not at all. In addition, composers do not always (or usually) supply conductors and performers with clearly written guidelines for interpreting the overall shape and pacing of musical transition sections and climaxes. Furthermore, whereas some composers and musical communities encourage interpretive freedom and spontaneity, others do not.[18]

To various degrees, then, an ethical contract comes into play when someone undertakes to interpret a musical composition. Our actions in musical performing parallel our actions in moral affairs. As with all ethical situations, there is a self-other obligation.[19] A score offers an opportunity to create an individual statement through interpretation. Yet a score is a kind of authority. Accordingly, says Grossman, each and every musical performance of a score is "a continuation of a search, not the presentation of a settled discovery."[20]

Even when musical practices do not rely on notated scores, performance obligations still exist. In most instances of jazz, African drumming, and Persian instrumental music a performer's musicianship includes a formal or informal sense of responsibility to a tradition of improvising that demands and celebrates original variations on well known themes or patterns. In oral/aural practices, a performer's obligations are not to a score or a composer but to what a previous performer has done, to a recording, or to what a community wants to hear done again. For example, in the musical practices we collectively call rock music a recorded performance can be a much stricter master than a score. The reason for this is that a remembered performance is much more precise than a score.[21] Scores allow freedoms that remembered performances do not. Thus, rock musicians often go to expensive lengths to duplicate the details of their recordings in live performances. If they fail, their fans often become upset. Part of the reason is that rock music listeners (and music listeners in general) often assume (knowingly and unknowingly) that there is an unspoken musical obligation on the part of their favorite performers to sound identical with their recordings or to prove that they can meet the standards of performance they have already set for themselves on recordings.

On some occasions, musical obligations and ethics are difficult to separate from moral obligations and ethics. For example, Sir Georg Solti's long-standing refusal to conduct in Hungary while his homeland remained under Communist domination demonstrates the intersection of musical and moral decision making. Contrast Solti's sense of artistic-social-ethical responsibility with Herbert von Karajan's decision to continue conducting and recording in Germany under Hitler's Third Reich. Do such decisions influence how we listen for the musical interpretations and performances of different artists? I believe they do. Why, how, when, where, and whether we listen for musical performances depends on our knowings and beliefs— musical, moral, social, and cultural. (This point is developed in more detail in Chapter 8.)

In a related vein, Morris Grossman characterizes the pianist Glenn Gould's celebrated decision to withdraw from live performing in favor of the recording studio as a kind of ''moralistic statement'' about musical obligation and artistic integrity. Gould questioned the very idea of ''live performance'' (especially its characteristic elements of risk and display), which he viewed as compromising the ideals of music making.[22]

In summary, performing involves various kinds of responsibilities and ethics. Teaching and learning musicianship include teaching and learning different kinds of musical obligations and ethics as they apply in different musical communities. Of course, our decisions about such matters do not always follow neatly. But this is not surprising. For the self-other dialogue that we find at the center of music making is continuous with all other forms of ethical existence.[23]

5. Improvising in Context

Musical improvising is common across many musical times and practices. For example, improvising was central to early Greek musical performances; it has an important role in many Baroque, Classical, and avant-garde works; and it figures prominently in several African, Indian, Persian, and Asian musical practices. In addition, of course, improvisation is synonymous with the essence of most jazz practices.

But what does musical improvising actually involve? Some writers assume that improvising is a kind of performing that occurs spontaneously in the sense of singing or playing without musical notation. Others use the word *improvising* to mean a kind of composing on the spot.

While there is some truth in these common notions, they both rest on oversimplified ideas of composing and performing. Composing and performing are not mutually exclusive but interdependent. Composers often perform what they compose either before, after, or in the process of notating their ideas. And performers sometimes engage in such composition-like tasks as generating and notating cadenzas, ornamenting melodies, realizing figured bass parts, and "comping" jazz accompaniments from chord symbols.

Overall, as Philip Alperson suggests, musical improvising involves both performing and composing.[24] Improvising is a form of musicing in which one or more people spontaneously and simultaneously (1) compose, (2) interpret, and (3) perform a musical work.[25] What distinguishes an improvisation from a performance is the human effort to compose in real time. The composing aspect of improvising varies with the musical practice in question. It can include everything from spontaneously varying or embellishing given rhythms and melodies while performing, to developing complex and extended variations on musical themes to creating entirely new works. During a musical improvisation, "it is as if the improviser's audience gains privileged access to the composer's mind at the moment of musical creation."[26]

To clarify how spontaneity figures in improvising, consider one of the most revered improvisations in the history of jazz: John Coltrane's improvisation on *Giant Steps*.[27] The originality, complexity, and speed of Coltrane's music making is astonishing. It is important to realize, however, that this is not spontaneous music making in the sense of thoughtless, unpremeditated, unstudied, or unconscious activity. It is the opposite. Coltrane's solo is thoughtful, premeditated, studied, and conscious. What Coltrane achieves in *Giant Steps* is firmly rooted in Western tonal music generally and the bebop jazz tradition specifically. Moreover, to musically think-in-action at such a rapid tempo, Coltrane had to develop an extraordinarily high level of musicianship. Indeed, as part of his musical preparation and practice, Coltrane reproduced and studied the improvisations of his predecessors in great detail. He worked hard at his ability to produce complex melodic patterns over rapid chord changes.[28] Coltrane not only understood complex harmonic theory (formal musical knowledge); more important, he learned how to think harmonically in action (procedural musical knowledge). In sum, although Coltrane did not know (and could not say) precisely what he would compose and perform on the spot, he knew everything he needed to know in advance of creating this brilliant improvisation "spontaneously."

Of course, the challenge to compose in real time adds an extra degree of risk (and interest) to the usual music performance situation.[29] An improviser is in a more precarious position than a composer or performer because improvisations unfold without second chances to correct, edit, or polish musical ideas.

The educational implications are clear. First, the teaching and learning of improvisation ought to include both performing and composing. For if improvising is essentially concerned with generating, evaluating, selecting, and remembering musical patterns in the rapid passing of real time, it makes sense that student improvisers would benefit from opportunities to engage in these same processes in the more deliberate and forgiving tempo of compositional-notational time. Second, the process of composing a musical work in real time is as important to listen for as the structural patterns an improviser actually works out in real time. Third, listening for an improvisation often includes comprehending the contributions of other musicians who work behind an improviser as he or she improvises. Listening for an improvisation should not focus exclusively on what is being composed on the spot or on how it is being performed but on both. Our listening must include a relational understanding (informal, impressionistic, and supervisory knowledge) of the special situational artistry of improvising. As Alperson says, we must consider "what has proven to be possible within the demands and constraints of improvisatory musical activity, the creation of a musical work as it is being performed."[30]

6. Arranging in Context

Arranging is an umbrella term for several kinds of musical effort: editing, transcribing, harmonizing, orchestrating, re-composing. All such efforts are essentially concerned with tailoring a precomposed or preperformed work for particular performers or settings by adding to it, taking away from it, enhancing it, recasting it, or rethinking it entirely.

Arrangers must have a deep working understanding of musical practices. For even in the relatively straightforward task of transcribing an orchestral composition for a wind ensemble, an arranger must know a great deal. He or she must know how performing, improvising, composing, conducting, and listening relate within the musical contexts represented by both the original work and the "new" work he is arranging.

Depending on practices and circumstances, arranging may involve a considerable amount of original composing (e.g., introductions, countermelodies, transition sections). In the case of Broadway musicals, for example, arrangers (sometimes called "orchestrators") frequently complete full scores from little more than a composer's original sketch of melody lines, lyrics, and chord symbols. Such well-known arrangers as Robert Russell Bennett, Billy Byers, Philip J. Lang, Ralph Burns, Michael Starobin, and Jonathan Tunick are highly respected for their ability to put the orchestral "flesh" on skeletal scores. But they are also renowned for their ability to give musical expression to the emotional and representational dimensions of lyrics and librettos. For example, the music critic Laurie Winer applauds Jonathan Tunick's ability to "get under the number and express the unsaid" in one of the many musicals Tunick has arranged for Stephen Sondheim:

> In "No More," from Mr. Sondheim's "Into the Woods," . . . Mr. Tunick takes a very
> dark and nuanced moment—a man coveting death after his wife has died—and under-

scores it with a light, hopeful sound that delicately prefigures the solace and emotional reawakening the character will find in the next number, "No One is Alone."[31]

In a related vein, performers, conductors, record producers, and others often ask arrangers (like jewelers) to create brilliant settings for rather ordinary materials. Quincy Jones and Nelson Riddle are two among many arrangers who have succeeded in transforming ordinary singers and songs into "hits" through exquisite arrangements that highlight musical strengths and hide musical weaknesses.

Examined from a broader perspective, arrangers and arrangements can be seen to fulfill an essential function in musical practices by making compositions and experiences available that would otherwise remain unavailable (or inaccessible) to students, amateur musicians, and professional performers alike.

Aaron Copland's *Fanfare for the Common Man* (for brass and percussion) is a musical challenge that non-brass performers can know only as listeners. Or so it seems. But a professional saxophone sextet called the Nuclear Saxes refused to accept this limitation. Because they admired Copland's composition so much, they commissioned an arrangement of his *Fanfare* to perform themselves.

Is this an odd thing to do? Perhaps. But consider two points. First, a musically intelligent arrangement can expose facets of an original work that might otherwise go unnoticed by performers and listeners alike, much in the way an intelligent interpretation can highlight otherwise unnoticed dimensions of a composition. Second, the opportunity to participate in performing a work like *Fanfare for the Common Man* offers music makers something deeply related to the social, ethical, and communal nature of many musical practices. This "something" was expressed well by one member of the Nuclear Saxes in a radio interview following the group's live performance: "We love Copland's music; we just had to perform it. Although our performance is not precisely what he had in mind, we view our arrangement as a tribute to Mr. Copland's artistry."[32]

I suggest that an essential part of the self-growth, enjoyment, self-knowledge, and self-esteem that many people experience in music making arises from connecting with significant musicians (especially, perhaps, composers) whom we honor in performing, conducting, and arranging their music well.

Of course, arranging (arrangers and arrangements) are also extremely important to the professional practice of music education. For teachers and students need excellent musical works to perform and study. Yet students are often unable to perform compositions in their original forms. Enter the arranger who provides specially adapted versions of excellent musical works for the teaching-learning context.

Unfortunately, not all arrangers (and music publishers) are as competent and musically ethical as they ought to be. Accordingly, music educators must often ask important questions of themselves and others as they select music for their curricula. For example: "Is this transcription (edition/arrangement) of a Baroque (bebop, Balinese, Beethoven) work true to (or authentic in relation to) the standards, traditions, and intentions of the musical practice to which it belongs?" Music teachers may well (and properly) decide to engage their students in asking and answering these same questions.

I hasten to add, however, that problems of musical authenticity are not matters that can or must be settled definitively. The educational values of such problem-solving episodes lie in the reflective processes themselves. In addressing issues of musical authenticity, teachers and learners need to consider how a given arrangement relates to: (1) a performance of the original composition (or rendition) by the actual practitioners of the practice in question; (2) the original instruments and/or text used by those practitioners; (3) the audience of listeners for whom the music is usually performed; and (4) the setting in which such a performance usually takes place. Indeed, as I have emphasized in this book, any given piece of music is exactly that: one piece of a much larger whole—a musical practice.

Learning to interpret and perform musical arrangements presents teachers and students with important opportunities to compare and contrast original works with adaptations in ways that can broaden and deepen musicianship. When we engage in debating the musical authenticity and quality of arrangements we thrust ourselves into the web of musical-social relations that constitute the very essence of musical practices. We are obliged to think in relation to the intentions, principles, traditions, and boundaries of a distinct community of music makers. (In Chapter 9 I pursue the qualitative issues of music good and great.)

Arranging is a valuable form of musicing that teachers and students should plan to engage in systematically from time to time. The many issues of authenticity and artistry connected with producing an arrangement immerse students in the musicianship—including the principles, values, and beliefs—of musical practices in immediate and productive ways. At the same time, arranging projects provides significant relief from the central problem involved in composing: the challenge of generating and selecting completely original musical ideas. At the very least, arranging projects are a logical and engaging way of enhancing students' ongoing performance efforts and preparing the way for future composing projects.

7. Implications for Music Education

This chapter has suggested that all forms of musicing are mutually reinforcing and interdependent from a social, artistic, ethical, and educational point of view. But because the curricular time allotted to music does not always permit the teaching and learning of all forms of music making, decisions must be made about which forms of musicing to emphasize.

• *The centrality of performing and improvising.* The arguments in this chapter bolster the previous contention (explained in Chapters 3 and 4) that performing and improvising (when improvising is germane to a practice) ought to be the foundational and primary forms of music making taught and learned in music education programs. Arranging, composing, and conducting (when germane) should also be included systematically as time permits.

MUSIC is a performing art. The intended outcome or work in the performing arts is not a self-sufficient object (like a painting, novel, or sculpture) but rather a performance. As I explained in Chapter 4, musical works are *performances,* physical events that are intentionally generated by the knowledgeable actions (overt and covert) of interrelated human agents (composers, arrangers, performers, improvisers, conductors) to be intentionally conceived as such by other knowledgeable agents (musicers and/or listeners). Musical works involve intermediate agents (e.g., singers, instrumentalists, and conductors) who contribute substantively and artistically to the events that listeners cognize as musical performances.[33] This is why we say that it is only in an artistic performance of a musical composition that everything a composer conceives and intends is decided. Only in a musical performance do all the dimensions of a composition, rendition, or improvisation come together in a determinate way. And this is why a musical performance is the most complete nonverbal description of a musical work and of a music maker's understanding of that work.

For all these reasons, making music through performing and improvising takes learners to the heart of musical practices, and improvising links students to performing and composing in practical and musical-social ways. The same holds for conducting when this form of musicing is pertinent to a practice. Composing is also an important way of developing musicianship and immersing students in musical practices. But unless or until students come to know the essential nature of musical works as performances, composing should not be the primary way of developing musicianship. Instead (and time permitting), I suggest that composing is a reasonable and important supplement to the development of students' musicianship through performing and improvising (both of which demand keen listenership).

The emphasis in this book on musical performing, improvising, composing, arranging, and conducting receives additional support from Israel Scheffler's dictum that *making* ought to be central in all domains of education. For if a student knows how to make something well, says Scheffler, he or she understands it.[34] Scheffler argues that the process of learning to make a mathematical proof, a scientific experiment, a philosophical argument, or a musical performance is essential to a student's understanding of the products of such efforts.[35] Engaging in the process of making, says Scheffler, "allows us to relate process and product, to understand them in connection with one another and so to learn something valuable about action in general."[36] A student's involvement in making develops his or her ability to shift concentration back and forth between the process of making as something worthwhile in its own right (as an end in itself) and the outcome of his efforts.

To give attention to how things are done—to qualities of action, to traditions and standards of practice, to one's actions as a performance—is to modify one's viewpoint and understanding. Students so informed expand their sense of responsibility and the locus of their energy. The subject at hand—mathematics, chemistry, gymnastics, music—is no longer a disembodied collection of verbal concepts to accumulate, or a course to be taken, or a "thing" to be consumed. It is a process to be lived. Learning to make music well is what makes the difference between simply having (accumulating, collecting) and *being* (doing, achieving, enjoying). Scheffler decries the mentality that separates product from process in education.

To view past works—whether of art, or science, or architecture, or music, or literature, or mathematics, or history, or religion, or philosophy—as given and unique objects rather than incarnations of process is to close off the traditions of effort from which they emerged. It is to bring these traditions to a full stop. . . . *To value such traditions requires an emphasis on process. Conversely, the strength of our emphasis on process is a measure of the values our education embodies.* Appreciating the underlying process does not, by any means, exhaust the possibilities of understanding. But the understanding it does provide is a ground for further creativity in thought and action.[37]

• *Listenership is rooted in musicianship.* Implicit in these thoughts is another familiar theme of this philosophy: that intelligent music listening depends on learning how to make music well. To understand MUSIC and the nature of musical works requires knowledge of music as a "performative presence."[38] The ideal listener for a given performance is the music maker who has achieved a proficient level of musicianship with respect to the musical practice of which a performance is a piece.

This theme is not original to the present book. It has been echoed in the writings of several philosophers down the centuries. Recall Gilbert Ryle's remarks in *The Concept of Mind.*

A person who cannot play chess can still watch a game of chess. He sees the moves being made as clearly as does his neighbor who knows the game. But the spectator who does not know the game cannot do what his neighbor does—appreciate the stupidity or cleverness of the players. What is the difference between merely witnessing a performance and understanding what is witnessed? . . . [39]

Understanding is a part of knowing how. The knowledge that is required for understanding intelligent performances of a specific kind is some degree of competence in performances of that kind. The competent critic of prose-style, experimental technique, or embroidery, must at least know how to write, experiment or sew. . . . [T]he one necessary condition is that he has some mastery of the art or procedure, examples of which he is to appraise. . . . [40]

[T]he capacity to appreciate a performance is one in type with the capacity to execute it . . .[41]

John Dewey made a similar argument. In his *Art as Experience* (1934), Dewey affirms that what holds for the education of the music maker holds also for the education of the music listener. Dewey maintains that in contrast to someone who is merely able to do something, the knowledge of the person who really knows how to do something renders his or her cognition of a given situation "more acute and intense and incorporates into it meanings that give it depth."[42] But, says Dewey, "precisely similar considerations hold from the side of the perceiver."[43] To really know what to listen for in musical performances requires readiness on the part of the listener's cognitive action abilities.[44] Dewey explains:

A skilled surgeon is the one who appreciates the artistry of another surgeon's performance; he [or she] follows it sympathetically, though not overtly, in his [or her] own body. The one who knows something about the relation of the movements of the piano-player to the production of the music from the piano will hear something the mere layman does not perceive—just as the expert performer "fingers" music while engaged in reading a score.[45]

The developmental psychologist Nancy Thomas elaborates this theme in relation to schooling:

> That music is a live performance art sets it apart from most other kinds of school learning. Several important implications for studying students' music involvement follow from this characteristic. First, a student's accomplishment is most crucially revealed in the *doing,* in present and prescribed time, not in problem solutions, written assignments, or passed examinations. This is not to say that learning to listen is unimportant or that music training does not have attached to it an extensive body of knowledge that is testable in the conventional sense, but "making music" is the essential activity. [Thomas cites the ethnomusicologist John Blacking:] "Music is available for use and exists only in performance." Ultimate literacy, even for the good listener, is best grounded in the experience of making music oneself.[46]

In fact, Aristotle laid the foundation for these praxial views centuries ago in his *Politics:*

> And now we have to determine the question which has been already raised, whether children should be themselves taught to sing and play or not. Clearly there is a considerable difference made in the character by the actual practice of the art. It is difficult, if not impossible, for those who do not perform to be good judges of the performance of others. . . . We conclude then that they [children] should be taught music in such a way as to become not only critics but performers.[47]

Aristotle goes on to emphasize that whereas active participation in music making from childhood is crucial to the subsequent development of musical judgment, practical wisdom, and theoretical knowledge, exposure to music through passive listening results in little or no learning and quickly declines into mere entertainment. What teaches us about "right action," says Aristotle, is active engagement in productive music making.[48]

This praxial philosophy of music education maintains that *all* music students ought to be taught in essentially the same way: as reflective musical practitioners engaged in music making in general and musical performing in particular. Artistic music listening ought to be taught and learned in conjunction with artistic music making.

One of the most unfortunate legacies of the MEAE philosophy is the way its weakly grounded theoretic assumptions have encouraged a practical split in some school systems between listening-based general music programs and performance programs. This split runs contrary to what MUSIC is, what musicianship is, and what music invites and demands of music listeners. Listening-centered general music programs negate the artistic, performative, and musical-social nature of musical works. Having students learn to be quiet and develop so-called psychical distance while consuming recorded sounds may please aesthetic educators, but it is the antithesis of what musical understanding involves and what MUSIC education ought to be.

Imagine a general music classroom in which children sit listening to recordings aesthetically by following a call chart[49] listing dabs of formal knowledge (e.g., short phrases, drums punctuate). What do you see? Silent children! A music curriculum centered on recordings and absolutist "aesthetic" call charts is an effective way to silence music students.

Recordings and listening charts of various kinds deserve an important place in the education of all music students, providing that they serve to supplement students' active, goal-directed music making and guide students toward the multidimensional nature of musical works. But conventional listening-based general music curricula built around recordings, verbal concepts, and "activities" fail to meet these basic conditions. The MEAE philosophy conceives music students as consumers (or customers) in training for a world of industrial commodity and exchange through the purchase of recorded "collectables." Although recordings provide easy access to and limitless repetitions of all forms of music, these positive features have negative consequences for music students when teachers employ recordings improperly. For there is an important sense in which music recordings are the aural equivalent of photocopies; music recordings are mass produced reproductions. When music educators permit recorded music to overwhelm or replace genuine music making in the general music curriculum, the individuality of music students and musical works is devalued. Recorded music has enormous potential to eradicate musical origination and originality. Contrast the aesthetic emphasis on *having* with this book's praxial emphasis on *being* in the actions of music making. The consumption emphasis of MEAE separates process and product. It splits musicing and listening apart. It rips musical works out of their performative contexts and decontextualizes them through an attitude of "immaculate perception."

Jacques Attali captures the upshot of listening-based general music programs in his discussion of recordings: "Musical consumption leads to a sameness of the individual consumers. One consumes in order to resemble and no longer to . . . distinguish oneself. . . . [T]he record bought and/or listened to anesthetizes a part of the body."[50]

• *Musicianship is social and situational.* There is an important sense in which musicianship, like all forms of robust knowledge, is a kind of instrument or tool.[51] The musicianship we deploy in the actions of singing and playing is a tool for achieving the life goals of self-growth, self-knowledge, flow, and self-esteem. But learning how to use this tool appropriately occurs only when it is engaged for authentic purposes in realistic situations: in relation to the working beliefs and values of the practices in which the tool has been developed and refined.

This tool comparison highlights an important distinction between the mere acquisition of formal knowledge about musical works and the development of useful, robust musicianship. Students can acquire musicianship and learn how to use it only through progressive musical problem solving in genuine musical practice situations. Authentic musical problem solving requires immersion in the belief system of the music culture in which the tool is used. As Brown, Collins, and Duguid maintain:

> People who use tools actively rather than just acquire them . . . build an increasingly rich implicit understanding [informal knowledge and impressionistic knowledge] of the world in which they use the tools and of the tools themselves. The understanding, both of the world and of the tool, continually changes as a result of their interaction.

> Learning and acting are interestingly indistinct, learning being a continuous, life-long process resulting from acting in situations.[52]

As I explain in Chapter 10, this praxial philosophy recommends that all music education curricula (including general music curricula) be organized and carried out comprehensively—in terms of musical practices and artistic musical actions—not narrowly in terms of verbal concepts about autonomous works. For it is always the musical community or practice that determines the nature and appropriate use of musical understanding.

Suppose, for example, that a singer employs his musicianship as a tool to achieve an artistic performance of a composition. His musicianship is an instrument for musical expression, self-growth, and enjoyment. But when he encounters a new composition from another musical practice, his musicianship must be expanded. The tool he is using—his musically knowledgeable singing voice—is the same tool, but he now puts it to work in ways that reflect the standards and strategies of a different musical practice and a different community of practitioners. Brown, Collins, and Duguid elaborate this point with a clear-cut comparison: "[C]arpenters and cabinet makers use chisels differently. Because tools and the way they are used reflect the particular accumulated insights of communities, it is not possible to use a tool appropriately without understanding the community or culture [or music culture] in which it is used."[53]

As I have noted, conventional music curricula often organize teaching episodes in terms of verbal concepts about musical elements and ersatz activities. This is especially true of many listening-based general music texts. But while conventional curricula may have a surface plausibility, they are nonartistic and acontextual in essence. Hence, they fail to provide the necessary conditions for the development of procedural, informal, impressionistic, and supervisory musical knowings. To learn to use a tool as a reflective practitioner uses it, a music student, like an *apprentice* (from *apprehendere:* "to learn, grasp, or apprehend"), must be *inducted* into a practice and its culture: "in a significant way, learning is . . . a process of enculturation."[54]

By designing learning situations based on realistic and engaging musical challenges and projects and by working (in a coaching-directing mode) with students in a class chorus, a class instrumental or vocal chamber group (a class arranging workshop, and so on), music educators develop students' musicianship appropriately and effectively in situ (or contextually). What Brown, Collins, and Duguid rightly observe about education in general is especially true of praxial performance-based music education programs.

> Given the chance to observe and practice in situ the behavior of members of a culture, people pick up relevant jargon, imitate behavior, and gradually start to act in accordance with its norms. These cultural practices are often recondite and extremely complex. Nonetheless, given the opportunity to observe and practice them, people adopt them with great success. Students, for instance, can quickly get an implicit sense of what is . . . legitimate or illegitimate behavior in a particular activity. The ease and success with which people do this (as opposed to the intricacy of describing what it entails) belies the immense importance of the process and obscures the fact

that what they pick up is a product of the ambient culture rather than of explicit teaching.[55]

Teachers in many subject domains are beginning to realize a key educational tenet that excellent performance-oriented music educators have always understood: that learning to speak and write (and learning to be a physician, lawyer, architect, teacher, or artist) is essentially a matter of apprehending the actions and belief systems developed by distinct communities or cultures of practice. In other words, people learn effectively by becoming apprentices in particular domains of effort. And the apprentice-type contexts in which people learn the right actions (or tools) of a practice are, very often, informal but richly informative.

I expand on these ideas in terms of music curriculum making in Chapters 10 and 11. At this juncture, a brief example suffices to highlight several key aspects of music teaching and learning. (Please reread the following section once or twice and substitute different situations and examples for the one offered here.)

• *Musicing and music education in context.* Suppose I am a secondary school music teacher and jazz is one of the several practices into which I have decided to induct my students. Suppose that at one point in this induction process I decide to bring my students' musicianship into balance with a musical challenge called *Basie—Straight Ahead.*[56]

In preparing to teach this work, I remind myself that *Basie—Straight Ahead* is but one piece of a larger whole. The whole of which this work is a part is the blues-rooted, four-beat, Southwest "swing" practice of which Count Basie was an acknowledged master. As my students and I interact while working to interpret and perform Sammy Nestico's *Basie—Straight Ahead,* I view them as entering into a particular jazz practice. I am not merely attempting to help my students learn notes, play an instrument, or play a piece. I seek to develop their musicianship, which includes their knowledge of the music culture or the musical whole: the Southwest, four-beat, swing practice. This practice, in turn, is related to yet distinct from other swing practices (e.g., Eastern two-beat swing) and jazz practices in general (e.g., bebop and cool). In short, *Basie—Straight Ahead* offers an opportunity to learn a musical practice by learning an excellent piece of this practice.

In teaching this work, I also keep in mind that *Basie—Straight Ahead* is a multidimensional challenge. Learning how to interpret, perform, and listen for this musical work involves learning how to relate the musical design of *Basie—Straight Ahead* to the traditions and standards of Southwest jazz swing practice, as well as any musical expressions of emotion and/or musical representations in this work (if these last two dimensions are present). In fact, while it is reasonable to claim that *Basie—Straight Ahead* involves musical expressions of emotions, it does not involve musical representations.

Developing the musicianship of learners in this example means activating and integrating their practice-specific musical knowings: procedural, formal, informal, impressionistic, and supervisory. The process proceeds by *gradually* finding and solving *increasingly* challenging musical problems within *Basie—Straight Ahead.* Indeed, a common tendency among students (and some teachers) is to leave a work too early, to move on as soon as students produce accurate pitches and rhythms. As I have explained, however, the accurate production of stipulated patterns in a score is only one part of what musical performances (and musicianship) actually involve. A basic tenet of this praxial philosophy is to make a "full-course meal" of each and every musical work one selects for music teaching and learning by returning to it systematically, and at regular intervals, to balance students' growing musicianship with the increasing levels of challenge one finds in that work. Indeed, excellent musical works usually sustain musical problem finding and solving over long periods of time. Thus, even a few carefully selected and fully performed works will go a long way toward developing students' musical understanding.

Of course, a necessary part of teaching and learning the practice exemplified by *Basie—Straight Ahead* involves helping learners reduce such problems as reading syncopated rhythms, playing melodic and harmonic patterns in tune, and improvising on chord changes. Experienced music educators develop a variety of efficient ways to reduce such problems in parenthetical relationship to the central process of musical problem solving.

As well as selecting viable musical challenges and establishing realistic music-making situations, inducting learners into musical practices demands that teachers continuously *contextualize* musical works. In fact, the desire to satisfy the criteria and obligations implicit in an authentic work like *Basie—Straight Ahead* tends to fuel students' interests in knowing more about the savvy, legends, lore, heroes, and traditions of the practice concerned. The parenthetical use of related recordings, videos, historical readings, computer software, and live performances by other school and professional musicians are the most common means of contextualizing musical challenges.

Since MUSIC is a diverse human practice, ways and means should be found to deepen students' musicianship while broadening it in relation to several musical domains. In relation to the example of *Basie—Straight Ahead,* it would make sense for my student instrumentalists to move back and forth across several related practices, including dixieland, bebop, cool, and South African "township" jazz, as well as more distantly related practices, such as Classical, Romantic, and avant-garde wind music. In all this, artistic music listening can and must be developed in relation to the musical works students are learning to interpret and perform competently, proficiently, and expertly.

Of course, all the above suggestions apply equally (but in appropriately altered details) to singing in a class and school choir, or playing in a class string ensemble, guitar ensemble, wind ensemble, brass ensemble, African drumming ensemble, and so on.

• *Musical values revisited.* Self-growth, constructive knowledge, flow, and self-esteem are what the philosopher Alasdair MacIntyre calls the "internal goods" of musical practices.[57] These "goods" are specific to, and can be obtained only by, participating actively and productively in musical practices. Anyone who does not possess the musicianship to participate in a musical community is not a competent judge of its internal goods. Three points follow from MacIntyre's concept of human practices and their internal goods.

First, the level of competency, proficiency, or artistry a student achieves is also an internal good of music making. For musicianship is something that belongs to the individual music maker: "I am this person who can do this thing well."[58] Learning how to meet musical challenges provides music students with knowledge about their actions (their quality and effects) and, therefore, a clear awareness of who they are.[59] The results of one's actions, and the changes one's actions make in musical materials, contexts, and audiences, provide feedback about the self and the relation of that musical self to others.

But while musicianship is an individual achievement, it is also socially determined. For a student's level of musical achievement is always relative to the achievements of past and present music makers. Let us suppose, for example, that Tim Pani's musical education is centered on his class choir and his school chorus. Suppose Tim is inducted into several choral practices (e.g., Baroque, jazz, Romantic, Renaissance, pop, Zulu choral singing, avant-garde choral music) through learning to perform a variety of choral compositions, including works by Bach, Handel, Ella Fitzgerald, Schubert, Praetorius, and R. Murray Schafer.[60] In this context, what Tim achieves is related to (1) past and present children in his class and school chorus, (2) past and present children's choruses-at-large, and (3) past and present choral singers-at-large. These musical-individual-social relationships make up part of the broad social context of Tim's developing musicianship. And this context grows from (and is shaped by) Tim's progress from one point to another along a path that moves toward, and past, landmark musical achievements.[61]

From this perspective, to enter and take up a musical practice is to be inducted into a music culture, or a musical world. The musical world as a whole, and each mini-world (the jazz choral world, the Baroque world, and so on), rests on musical-social traditions and standards that provide students with knowledge about who they are and what they can do in relation to themselves, to each other, and to past others.

Students who learn to make music according to the artistic criteria of a musical practice, and who thereby participate in the maintenance and progress of that practice, gain yet another "internal good." They achieve what MacIntyre calls "a certain kind of life."[62] Sparshott's term is *Lebensform:* a "form of life."[63] By entering into and learning musical practices—by living a part of one's life as a music maker—a student (child through adult) gains a valued way of being in the world: he or she gains the unique value of living out a greater or lesser part of her life as a maker-of-Musics.[64]

Moreover, when teachers induct children into music cultures as active, reflective practitioners, they not only speed children toward developing a certain kind of life in music; they also create the necessary conditions for the sustained development of self-esteem. As I explained in Chapter 5, higher overall levels of self-esteem do not result from the simple addition of isolated flow experiences. Instead, self-esteem is intimately related to involving one's self more and more deeply and continuously in the opportunities and complexities of a particular domain of practice and of a certain way of life: in "a system of meanings that gives purpose to one's being."[65]

In this view, knowing that one is gradually entering into or participating in a musical kind of life is an intangible but important part of a person's "life themes."[66] People (including many politicians and school principals) who do not possess the musicianship to participate in musical practices cannot fully understand or pass judgment on these values. The internal goods of musical practices are available only to those who take part productively in the situational knowledge formed around and for artistic music making and listening.[67]

In the process of striving to become musical, students inevitably influence, and are influenced by, their social-musical relationships with others. Our example of Tim's musical-educational situation is typical. The classroom chorus to which Tim belongs does not function in isolation. It is linked to the larger children's choral movement that has grown by leaps and bounds in the United States, Canada, the United Kingdom, Scandinavia, and other parts of the world since the 1970s.[68] Taken together, this network of school and community children's choirs forms a vast musical family that embraces thousands of students from Helsinki to Chicago, Hong Kong to Cape Town, Toronto to London, Vancouver to Sydney, and all stops in between. The most outstanding programs serve as models for music teachers and music students in schools and communities everywhere. (This is partly what Csikszentmihalyi means when he suggests that the feedback provided by our social environments is among the most effective kind of feedback in the development of self-knowledge.[69])

Children's choral singing links directly to real-world practices of amateur and professional choral singing of many kinds. In all these ways, classroom, school, and community children's choirs provide natural musical contexts that enable children to achieve a certain kind of life in which self-growth, constructive knowledge, enjoyment, musical competency, and a continuous quest for musical excellence are the norm. Of course, the same holds for many well taught string and wind instrumental programs, guitar programs, and so on.

Mention of "excellence" brings me to the last point in this chapter. It is difficult to distinguish the *pursuit* of musical competency and excellence from the internal goods of self-growth, self-knowledge, flow, and self-esteem. Aristotle explains why: "[E]njoyment supervenes upon successful activity in such a way that the activity achieved and enjoyed are one and the same state."[70] In other words, *striving* for musical competency, proficiency, and excellence through the progressive development of musicianship is not elitist. It is both an essential condition and a natural concomitant of self-growth and optimal experience. Stated another way, the opportunity to develop and excel musically is a basic right of each self and, therefore, of all children everywhere.

In conclusion, music making is a viable educational end for all students. Music making is not secondary to music listening in music education. Music making and music listening are interdependent. More fundamentally, music making is something worth doing for the sake of the self, and others. The internal values of musicing are not abstractions. Through the progressive development of musicianship, all students can achieve self-growth, constructive knowledge, enjoyment, and self-esteem in a musical way of life.

Questions for Discussion and Review

1. Summarize the social and practical relationships between (a) composing and performing, and (b) composing and listening.

2. Do you agree that "all works of music incorporate social and practical realities" to some degree? Why?

3. Some people assume that performing means producing the sounds notated in a score. Explain why you agree or disagree.

4. Suppose a musicologist discovers a lost score in Beethoven's handwriting titled Symphony No. 10. Suppose the New York Philharmonic invites you to conduct the world premiere of Beethoven's composition. What factors will you consider in preparing and rehearsing your interpretation of this work?

5. Explain why music performing often involves ethical obligations and dilemmas.

6. Explain three main differences between performing and improvising. Explain three main differences between listening for a live improvisation and listening for a previously recorded performance of a composition.

7. What kinds of musicing does the term *arranging* include? Explain why arranging is both an artistic and a social enterprise. How does the topic of musical authenticity relate to arranging? To what extent are arrangers and arrangements important to music educators?

8. Although all music students should have opportunities to develop their musicianship through all forms of musicing, this chapter proposes that performing and improvising ought to be the main forms of musical endeavor in music education. What reasons support this view?

9. Explain why the development of listenership depends on learning how to perform music competently.

10. Explain the musical and educational weaknesses of listening-centered general music programs.

11. In what ways is musicianship a kind of tool. Explain what it means to induct music students into musical practices.

12. "To achieve the primary values of music education, music curricula must treat all children as reflective musical practitioners." Explain the reasoning behind this statement.

Supplementary Sources

Israel Scheffler. "Making and Understanding." In *Proceedings of the Forty-Third Annual Meeting of the Philosophy of Education Society,* ed. B. Arnstine and

D. Arnstine, pp. 65–78. Normal: Illinois State University Press, 1988. An analysis of doing and making in education.

Nicholas Wolterstorff. "The Work of Making a Work of Music." In *What is Music? An Introduction to the Philosophy of Music,* ed. Philip A. Alperson, pp. 103–29. New York: Haven Publications, 1987. An analysis of composing as an artistic-social endeavor.

Thomas Carson Mark. "Philosophy of Piano Playing: Reflections on the Concept of Performance." *Philosophy and Phenomenological Research* 41 (1981): 299–324. Mark makes many important distinctions at several levels of the musical interpretation-performance process.

Peter Kivy. "Live Performers and Dead Composers: On the Ethics of Musical Interpretation." In *The Fine Art of Repetition: Essays in the Philosophy of Music,* ed. Peter Kivy, pp. 95–116. Cambridge: Cambridge University Press, 1993. Kivy argues that composers' intentions ought to have a major role in performers' interpretations of scores.

Randall R. Dipert. *Artifacts, Art Works, and Agency.* Philadelphia: Temple University Press, 1993. Chapter 11, "Performance Art Works," offers a penetrating analysis of the concept of performance.

Philip A. Alperson. "On Musical Improvisation." *Journal of Aesthetics and Art Criticism* 43, no. 1 (Fall 1984): 17–29. Alperson examines the concept of improvisation from several perspectives.

Jeff Pressing. "Improvisation: Methods and Models." In *Generative Processes in Music: The Psychology of Performance, Improvisation and Composition,* ed. John Sloboda, pp. 129–78. Oxford: Clarendon Press, 1987. A detailed psychological analysis of the improvisational process.

8

Music Listening in Context

The philosophy propounded in this book has proposed that intelligent music listening consists in deliberate acts of informed thinking in relation to performed or improvised patterns of musical design that, in turn, evince histories and norms of musical practice. In addition, and depending on the musical work and practice involved, intelligent music listening may also involve the cognition of musical expressions of emotion and/or musical representations.

In this chapter I propose that since all forms of musicing are inherently artistic-social-cultural endeavors, and since musical works are social-cultural constructions, and since listeners live in specific times and places, music listening also involves the cognition of cultural-ideological information. Put another way, musical works both constitute and are constituted by culture-specific beliefs and values (tacit and verbal).

The idea that music listening and musical works are inseparable from social realities is not original to this book. Plato's concern for the ethical aspects of musical practices is a strong precedent. In our own time, studies of music from the perspectives of ethnomusicology, anthropology, sociology, feminism, semiotics, and analytic philosophy have brought us to a deeper understanding of the ways in which culture and ideology mediate music making and music listening.

1. Orientation

In the aesthetic view, "good" music is that which rises above the nitty-gritty of everyday life; good music transcends its own time and place. All music ought to be listened to aesthetically to ensure that the presented form will be responded to in and of itself and not as any kind of "generalized, communicated information."[1] Reimer articulates the aesthetic doctrine: "[T]he better the work of art, the more it transcends its time of creation and is relevant to human experience in general. . . . The notion that art works should be regarded as "an expression of their time"

... misses the point of art's value except for the most superficial works, which really are little more than 'an expression of their time.' ''[2]

The corollary of such thinking is that so-called ethnic, popular, and/or commercial Musics are inherently social, cultural, and ideological and, therefore, of lesser musical worth than so-called serious, autonomous, or high-art music.

The praxial philosophy of music education offered in this book recommends the opposite view. Music making, and the works that musicers make, are among the most fundamental ways in which human beings express and impress cultural values and beliefs. MUSIC as a diverse human practice is central to the constitution of cultural and individual identities. A fundamental part of the challenge, enjoyment, and human significance of musicing and music listening concerns the cultural-ideological nature of these forms of action and the cultural-ideological information that musical works convey.

The next three sections of this chapter offer several basic arguments and selected musical examples in support of this view. I emphasize "basic" and "selected" because a detailed study of the relationships among musicing, listening, culture, and ideology across musical practices is beyond the scope of any one book (let alone one chapter). My intent is only to develop this book's previous points about the situational nature of MUSIC by explaining in slightly more detail why and how musicing, listening, and musical works are imbued with cultural and ideological information. (I shall leave it to you, the reader, to extend the ideas in this chapter to other musical examples that I cannot make space for here. For suggestions, see the Supplementary Sources section at the end of this chapter that lists several studies of the relations among musicing, listening, culture, and ideology within specific musical practices.) In preparation, let me offer a brief summary of two important concepts that also deserve book-length studies of their own: culture and ideology.

Culture is a term that various fields of inquiry apply in various ways.[3] In addition to its use in biology and physical development, the term *culture* is often used by sociologists and anthropologists in the process-sense to mean a people's ongoing way of life, including the language, customs, and preferences of a particular social group. In this sense, most (if not all) people are "cultured" because everyone belongs to, or is inducted into, some human society.

Culture in the ethnographic or product-sense refers to a body of tangible achievements (e.g., poems, paintings, musical works) that people tend to categorize in various ways (e.g., "high culture" or "low culture"). In this view, a "cultured" person is one who is knowledgeable about certain cultural products.

A combination of these definitions yields a more plausible concept of culture. To survive in a given time and place, a group of people must adapt to and modify their physical, social, and metaphysical environments. In this "situated" sense, the culture of a social group is its shared program for adapting, living, and growing in a particular time and place. Culture is generated by the interplay between a group's beliefs about its physical and social circumstances and the forms of knowledge it develops and preserves to meet its needs. Hence, culture is not something that people have but something that people make.

By the term *ideology* I mean a set of beliefs and values that is held tacitly and/

or verbally by members of a culture. An ideology, says Meyer, is "a complex network of interrelated beliefs and attitudes consciously or unconsciously held by the members of some culture or subculture."[4]

2. Culture and Ideology Influence Music

The instrumental compositions of J. S. Bach are traditionally assumed to be prime examples of pure, formal, or abstract music, or "sounds alone." Popular wisdom has it that compositions like Bach's Fifth "Brandenburg" Concerto not only transcend their own time and place, they transcend all times and places. In this view, Bach's music is universal. As if to prove the claim, the 1977 Voyager space probe blasted aloft with selected recordings of Bach's music on board. As one eminent NASA scientist quipped: "We would have sent the complete works of J. S. Bach, but that would have been bragging."

There is no denying that the brilliant compositional designs of Bach's instrumental music are a central part of the challenge these works present to knowledgeable listeners and, therefore, a central part of our enjoyment of these works. At the same time, it seems unreasonable to claim that musical design (or pure form) is all there is to listen for in Bach's instrumental compositions. In addition to what we have already suggested about the performance-interpretation dimension and the practice-specific traditions evinced in Bach's Baroque masterpieces, the musicologist Susan McClary emphasizes that Bach's music is "indelibly marked with the concerns and conventional social constructs of his time and place."[5]

How so? Consider the first movement of Bach's Fifth "Brandenburg" Concerto. On the surface, this concerto grosso is a straightforward matter of musical design. The development of this design is propelled by exchanges between the ensemble and the soloists. But as McClary argues, the interactions between the soloists and the ensemble in this movement are not only a formal musical device, they are metaphorical. The ensemble is stable while the soloists are the instruments of individual musical expression. McClary places the concerto grosso structure in wider perspective:

> The fact that this genre developed in the early eighteenth century is not surprising, given that it so systematically addresses the tensions between the dynamic individual and stable society—surely one of the most important issues of the increasingly prominent middle class. By contrast, the medium favored by the sixteenth century was equal-voiced polyphony in which the harmony of the whole was very carefully regulated. The seventeenth century saw the emergence of solo genres (sonata, cantata, opera) that celebrate individuality, virtuosity, dissonance, and extravagant dynamic motion.[6]

The solo-ensemble interactions in the first movement of Bach's composition are metaphorical, says McClary, to the extent that they offer a musical analogue of "the interactions between individual and society."[7] This structured musical interchange incorporates an essential theme of Bach's time and place: the tension between the desires of the individual as a member of the new middle class and the need for social harmony. The musical structure gives musical form and expression to a basic social contradiction in the prevailing ideology of Bach's time: the desire for social tranquility and individual freedom.[8]

Some readers may object that McClary overemphasizes the social-cultural nature of Bach's music. Others will argue correctly that Bach left nothing in the way of personal reflections about his motivations or intentions that would confirm or deny McClary's interpretation.[9] Does this lack of certain evidence mean that we should retreat to the safety of a purely formal, asocial concept of Bach's music? No.

The musicologist and Bach scholar Christoph Wolff maintains that an understanding of the artistic, social, and cultural circumstances of Bach's production is of great importance for an understanding of his music and that many of these circumstances are well known.[10] For example, musicians occupied an inferior status in the hierarchy of Baroque society. Performing and composing were considered forms of service that musicians most often carried out under the considerable restrictions of city, church, and court employers. As one whose musicianship was deeply rooted in the guild tradition of his musical family, Bach understood all facets of his trade, including the restrictions of his social position and the necessity of balancing his desire for artistic independence with the economic realities of his dependence on a variety of employers.

Wolff emphasizes that Bach worked hard throughout his career to shift this balance in favor of his musical independence.[11] In virtue of his extraordinary artistry, intelligence, and political savvy, Bach was able to use all the possibilities that each appointment offered him to achieve "an astonishing personal latitude" despite his obligations and subordinate status.[12] Accordingly, says Wolff, Bach cannot be considered typical of his age: "It is part of the unusual quality of his music that it stands as the expression of a strongly willed and, for the first half of the eighteenth century, atypical artistic personality."[13] In fact, toward the end of his life Bach's circumstances closely resembled the nineteenth-century ideal of the independent artist.[14]

It seems reasonable to conclude that Bach was very familiar with the social dichotomy that McClary believes is embodied in the first movement of the Fifth "Brandenburg" Concerto. Moreover, Bach learned the concerto style from careful studies of Vivaldi's compositional processes which combined a new concern for musical thinking with an important dialectic of two very different premises: musical simplicity (purity and correctness) and complexity (sophistication and elaboration).[15] This dialectic is also reasonably construed as structure *versus* freedom.

The first movement of this concerto is not only the longest and most complex of all the "Brandenburg" movements. Here, for the first time in the history of the genre, the harpsichord is elevated from its standard accompaniment role to that of a soloist with an exceptional solo cadenza added. There can be no doubt that Bach, as this work's composer and first harpsichord soloist, understood both the musical and the social significance of this artistic decision.

At the very least, then, this movement provided Bach with an opportunity to reaffirm his virtuosity within the musical hierarchy of the court and/or, as Malcolm

Boyd suggests, to display the new harpsichord that his patron Prince Leopold had purchased for the Cöthen *Kapelle* in 1719.[16] Although we cannot know for certain whether Bach intended to create a musical metaphor, the fact that this brilliant and socially aware musician did not work in relation to the aesthetic notion of autonomous works makes the possibility plausible.

Acknowledging the cultural-ideological aspects of this work does not reduce or contaminate the musical greatness of Bach's achievement. On the contrary, the cultural-ideological dimension is one of several musical dimensions (one of several layers of musically generated information) that make up the rich musical challenge we call the Fifth "Brandenburg" Concerto. This concerto is not literally "about" Bach's society. There is no core message or story to decode. Instead, and more subtly, the musical form of this work evinces its social-cultural time and place of composition. Such information is one part of what an informed listener knows and constructs and, therefore, one part of what an informed listener can enjoy.

Indeed, an essential part of the musicianship required to make, listen for, and enjoy Bach's music is knowledge (procedural, formal, informal, and impressionistic) of the artistic-cultural syntheses and nuances that Bach achieves in his compositions. The same holds doubly for Bach's choral works. For example, in his sacred vocal compositions (including the *Saint John Passion* and the *Saint Matthew Passion*), Bach's texts function as both musical design elements (for example, the timbral use of consonants and vowels) and direct means of communicating the cultural beliefs and values of his time and place.

A second example of the influence of culture and ideology on musicing and listening is found in Romantic musical practices. In *Style and Music* (1989), Leonard B. Meyer explains how the beliefs underlying the ideology of Romanticism "were translated into and influenced the musical choices made by nineteenth-century composers."[17]

At root, Romanticism was a revolt against European social privilege based on birth and inheritance. It arose in opposition to traditional societal rules that kept a small class of aristocrats politically and economically superior to everyone else. As we mentioned in our discussion of aesthetics in Chapter 2, the traditional European concern for wealth and privilege by inheritance was replaced in the nineteenth century by an emphasis on individual freedom and equality, on the inherent values of things (apart from their backgrounds or contexts), and on naturalness in all its forms. In short, Romanticism celebrated the egalitarian, the acontextual, and the natural.

Several conventions of nineteenth-century musical design, musical expression, and musical characterization manifest these values. For example, whereas the metaphor of musical form in the Classical period had been language (notions of musical phrases, sentences, and so on), the Romantic metaphor was organic form:[18] the continuous, natural flowering of coherent musical units from motivic seeds.[19] In opposition to and in personal conflict with the purist principles of the aesthetic concept, many Romantic composers produced musical representations of nature and "the sublime" through the continuous unfolding of musical ideas.[20]

As Meyer explains, however, in order to unify large organic forms and to make it easier for nineteenth-century audiences to remember musical patterns over long time spans, many nineteenth-century composers invented striking musical ideas that emphasized such nonsyntactic parameters as timbre, texture, and dynamics. (Consider the highly memorable beginnings of Schubert's "Unfinished" Symphony, Berlioz's *Symphonie fantastique*, and Debussy's *Prélude à l'après-midi d'un faune*.) In addition, because the listening abilities of the new nineteenth-century audiences were less sophisticated than those of the smaller court audiences of the Classical era, Romantic composers tended to compensate by relying more and more on nonsyntactic parameters.[21] Why? Because musical designs that unfold in terms of louder/softer, brighter/darker, thicker/thinner, faster/slower, and higher/lower (for example, Ravel's *Boléro*) are much easier for listeners to follow than musical designs that depend on subtle melodic and harmonic developments. Moreover, the exploitation of nonsyntactic musical parameters offered Romantic composers many ways to develop musical characterizations of natural phenomena (such as storms and pastoral scenes) and musical expressions of human passions (e.g., rage, struggle, grief, sexual longing).

Wagner's "Transfiguration" (or "Liebestod") from *Tristan und Isolde* is a prime example of the influence of Romantic ideology on musical structure.[22] Not only do Wagner's melodic sequences and ambiguous harmonies evince the Romantic values of natural, organic development, but the overall rise and fall of these musical patterns in terms of the nonsyntactic parameters of pace, articulation, dynamics, and orchestration offer a clearly metaphorical description of Isolde's death and the reunion of the lovers.

Recall, next, that the decline of the aristocracy in the nineteenth century meant a decline in noble and ecclesiastical patronage. As a result, the private court orchestras and ensembles of the old nobility became things of the past.[23] The new egalitarian age and the growth of an affluent upper middle class resulted in increased audiences for concerts and opera. Larger audiences meant larger concert halls and opera houses. These circumstances encouraged the development of greater orchestral forces to fill these halls with sound. Larger orchestral forces led, in turn, to new compositional opportunities (such as extended instrumental ranges and more varied orchestral timbres and textures).[24]

In all these ways, the culture and ideology of nineteenth-century Europe influenced the compositional decision making of many Romantic composers.[25] Meyer summarizes the relationship between compositional means, musical patterns, and the ideology of Romanticism: "[I]t seems reasonable to argue that such means were chosen and similar patterns were replicated not only because they were consonant with the values of Romanticism and its elite adherents, but because the resulting music could be appreciated by the less sophisticated members of the audience—in short, because such music was egalitarian."[26]

Although it is possible to listen for and enjoy several dimensions of Romantic compositions and performances without knowledge of their cultural-ideological dimensions, to do so is to miss a significant aspect of what Romantic musical practices involve, demand, and reward. More practically still, to achieve artistic musical performances of many Romantic compositions requires an understanding of the ideological beliefs and conflicts reflected in and delineated by such works.

The Dagomba drumming of Ghana (discussed in Chapter 3) offers a third example of the social and situational nature of musicing, listening, and musical works. Dagomba music making reflects the values of African traditional wisdom by encouraging social interaction and musical participation in a way that informs people about social values. To elaborate on this view, I draw, again, from the work of John Miller Chernoff.[27]

The rhythmic form and vitality of Dagomba drumming depends on the way the drummers select rhythms that complement, "pressure," and alter other rhythms.[28] But in an African musical event, the music being made is not the responsibility of the drummers alone. A drummer's decisions are informed by the way the Dagomba community of listeners-as-dancers move their feet and bodies. In other words, the Dagomba community is an integral part of Dagomba musicing and the musical works and experiences that result. Through its moving and dancing, the community contributes to the several layers of rhythmic activity performed and improvised by the drummers. This is possible because the overall rhythmic fabric is always open to contributions by drummers, listeners, or dancers. Although Dagomba drumming may sound like a dense and unintelligible stream of rhythms to uneducated listeners, the music is actually an arrangement of gaps. The Dagomba musicers and dancers contribute individual rhythms in the gaps much the same as they might contribute to an ongoing social conversation: thoughtfully and respectfully. The moving and dancing of the audience is essential in bringing the musicing, the musical sounds, and the artistic-social context together.[29] The best dancers add rhythms that are not already present in the overall texture. In these ways, the audience contributes to the wholeness and success of the musical-social situation. Through the mutual participation of musicers and listeners, the musical occasion becomes "sweet."[30]

The musicianship that guides a drummer's timing of rhythmic changes is yet another example of socially embedded or situated knowledge. Cultural beliefs and values inform a drummer's musical thinking-in-action. The Dagomba drummer, says Chernoff, "demonstrates his involvement with the social situation in a dramatic gesture that will play upon the minds and bodies of his fellow performers and his audience. . . . In the control of his changes, the drummer directs the movement of the whole occasion."[31]

It is a small step from these ideas to the larger understanding that "music-making in Africa is above all an occasion for the demonstration of character."[32] For in addition to exemplifying a concern for rich musical design (both improvised and pre-organized), the polymetric musical forms of Dagomba drumming demonstrate a concern for balancing individual needs with the plurality of concerns that make up the social fabric of the Dagomba community.[33] Musical actions result in musical performances that are personal performances in both the ethical and the moral sense. One's musicing reveals one's sense of musical and social ethics. Through their participation in music making, the Dagomba people transform the musical situation into a concern for character and community. One person, like one rhythm, means nothing without the others. And the many ways a person contributes to a musical situation is parallel to the many ways a person views a social situation. In social life, as in musical life, Dagomba drummers and dancers tend to regard their participation "as an effort to *contribute* because they believe that involvement will lead to caring and that a participant will find a way to complement a situation."[34]

3. Culture, Ideology, and Listening

I have just offered three examples to illustrate the proposal that, to greater and lesser degrees, compositional designs and musical performances are influenced by and reflective of their cultural-ideological contexts. (Additional examples follow in a moment.) But the same proposal holds from the other direction. That is, and to greater and lesser degrees, music listening always involves cognizing musical expressions of culture-specific information (including cultural beliefs and values). Meyer agrees: "Influence is not, of course, a one-way street, running only, say, from politics to ideology to music. It runs the other way as well. . . . [T]here is little doubt that music has often confirmed beliefs and attitudes, acting as a reinforcing influence."[35]

How can it be argued that listeners apprehend confirmations (or negations) of their cultural beliefs and affiliations in musical patterns? As I have suggested, the answer lies in the influence of culture (memes) on the nature, development, and functioning of human consciousness (including the nature, development, and functioning of auditory cognition).

Recall from Chapter 4 that human auditory processing is highly dependent upon the context in which it operates. Listening, like all forms of thinking and knowing, is profoundly situated. We use every bit of information at our disposal to make sense of what we hear. It seems reasonable to suggest, therefore, that in the process of cognizing musical works, listeners "place" or contextualize musical sound patterns by drawing upon all the cues and knowledge (both tacit and verbal) at their disposal. Listening as covert knowing-in-action involves assimilating culture-specific and practice-specific musical patterns to a web of culturally determined beliefs, values, and concepts, or *memes*. As an active, constructive process, music listening includes constructing a kind of cultural profile of the musical sounds we are cognizing. In the words of Lucy Green, musical listeners assess the "delineated meanings" that musical works manifest or reflect.[36]

In "slow motion," I suggest that the process of constructing and assessing the cultural profile of a musical work is analogous to diagnosing a problem by asking and answering a series of questions, including the following:

- Have I heard musical patterns like these before?

- To what culture and musical practice do these patterns belong?

- Are these sounds tones-for-me?

- What cultural-ideological values are embodied in the musical patterns of this work?

- Do these beliefs and values match my own (conflict with my own, stretch my own)?

Unfortunately, words are the only means I have of outlining this musical-cultural profiling process. As the reader now understands, however, listening as thinking-in-action and knowing-in-action does not require that we talk to ourselves about how we are actually accomplishing our music-listening procedures. Of course, we can reflect verbally on our listening processes to some degree, and we often do. But, in general, I suggest that our cultural analyses of musical sound patterns is most often tacit. Such assessing is but one of several streams of processing that human consciousness carries out in parallel and distributed fashion during the overall act of music listening.

My proposal, more specifically, is that a listener's covert construction of musical patterns includes the construction of cultural meanings on the basis of learned conventions. Recall (from Chapter 6) that one way music listeners seem to cognize musical expressions of emotion is by learning to associate certain features of musical patterns (e.g., melodic contour or rhythmic vitality) with specific emotions by convention. In Chapter 6 I explained that a piece or passage of music may sound sad to listeners in a given culture because the musicers and listeners in that culture have developed and adopted certain musical conventions over time which, to them, sound like the sounds a sad person might sing or play to express sadness or the sounds people want to hear on the occasion of a funeral.[37] The process is essentially a matter of transferring the emotions associated with particular circumstances and occasions to the pieces and passages of music heard in these circumstances.

What I am suggesting now is that listeners also learn how to apprehend cultural information in, and attribute cultural meanings to, musical patterns and musical works by convention. Listeners come to hear musical patterns as tones-for-them—as musical patterns expressive of their social affiliations, homelands, beliefs, values, cultural convictions, and ideals. Hence a fundamental aspect of musical enjoyment for many listeners is the match that occurs between individual cultural-ideological beliefs or values and individually cognized musical expressions of these beliefs or values. This matching of knowledge and musical challenge not only results in self-knowledge and enjoyment but tends to place or locate listeners in definite contexts of social-cultural communities.

Here is another value of MUSIC as a multifarious human practice: the socially determined and shared ways of thinking we call musicing and listening tend to link self and other in community.[38]

This book's proposal that listeners actively contextualize musical patterns may not be accepted by all researchers in music cognition. For in the absence of an overall model of human consciousness, and in line with the old aesthetic concept of disinterested perception, studies of music cognition often suggest that music listening is limited to aural processing alone. But as I have attempted to argue here, human consciousness is more layered, more distributed, and more situated in nature than many conventional notions of music cognition tend to acknowledge.

Of course, advocates of the MEAE philosophy will also resist this book's cultural view of music listening on the basis of their conviction that all music everywhere must be listened to in one way: purely, or acontextually—for aesthetic qualities alone, free of all other references and associations. What aesthetic educators overlook, however, is that musical sounds are culture-based artistic constructions, not aesthetic qualities. There is nothing natural or autonomous about the sounds of Beethoven, Bartok, or bebop. The material means of these works are the result of centuries of artistic and musical-theoretical development.

Furthermore, MEAE's notion of aesthetic listening is, itself, a cultural construction. To perceive music aesthetically is, in fact, to adopt a socially embedded ideology of music and listening that owes its implausible tenets to a small group of dead, white, European male thinkers. What could be more cultural, ideological, referential, or external than an eighteenth-century theory that instructs all people everywhere to listen to music in exclusive relation to absolutist concepts? As Susan McClary emphasizes, to listen for Beethoven's "Eroica" Symphony through a theoretical grid derived from dubious abstract reflection is a far greater imposition of external reference than listening for musical expressions of emotion or cultural-musical conventions.[39]

4. Further Examples of Cultural-Ideological Influences

Through the combination of words and characteristic musical patterns, rock musicians give expression to ideologies that, in turn, confirm the beliefs and values of certain listeners. As Simon Frith says, rock music is popular not only because it is expressive of certain value systems but because rock music tends to shape the beliefs of its listeners about what popularity means.[40]

For example, rock music practices are largely concerned with the composition and performance of heterosexual love songs. Rock songs often give voice to particular ways of interpreting and managing beliefs and emotions that are fundamental to young people in particular.[41] Rock songs often involve lyrics, musical expressions of emotion, and musical characterizations of people and events that combine to project a kind of communal common sense (an ideology) about how and what to feel in certain circumstances, how to voice one's thoughts and emotions, and how other people live with the joys and sorrows of relationships. The musical patterns of these songs are invariably expressive of specific emotions (e.g., sadness, happiness, frustration, anxiety) that, in turn, either support or undercut the ideas stated directly or metaphorically in the lyrics of these songs.

It is interesting to consider the extent to which contemporary pop and rock music practices adopt the structural strategies of several nineteenth-century Romantic composers, especially the Romantic tendency to exploit the nonsyntactic parameters of timbre, articulation, and dynamics. For just as it is easier to identify the rise of a crescendo than the harmonic underpinnings of a melody, it is easier to detect and remember the distinctive timbre of a particular singer's voice, or the characteristic sound of a group, than a complex harmonic progression. The fact that nonsyntactic musical patterns are rather easy to identify and remember, and that musicians can easily make these parameters expressive of certain values and beliefs by convention, explains in part how rock songs are able to grab and hold the attention of many listeners.

In addition, what rock songs share in common with musical works from many other times and places, including nineteenth-century Romantic works, is a tendency to develop musical expressions of human physicality that invite listeners to experience their own physicality and sexuality in various and often new ways. McClary offers the following example.

> [T]o say that one hears sexual longing in the *Tristan* prelude is not to introduce irrelevant "subjective" data into the discussion. Surely that is the point of the opera, and we are missing the point if we fail to understand that. The process by which Wagner's music accomplishes this is not at all mystical. In part, his music draws on his own (excessively documented) experiences in the sexual realm, and we as listeners perceive longing in his music likewise because we are human beings with bodies who have experienced similar feelings firsthand. . . . Wagner's music relies heavily on the traditional semiotics of desire available in the musical styles he inherited, and listeners understand his music in part because they too have learned the codes (the minor sixths demanding resolution, the agony of the tritone, the expectation that a dominant-seventh chord will proceed to its tonic, and so on) upon which his metaphors depend.[42]

Of course, both the experiences selected for representation by music makers and the musical conventions they develop to represent these experiences are not universal but culture-specific. McClary continues:

> The explosion of rock 'n' roll in the mid-1950s brought a vocabulary of physical gestures to white middle-class kids that parents and authorities quite rightly perceived as subversive of hegemonic bourgeois values. Sheltered Northern adolescents picked up on the dance rhythms of the Southern honky-tonk and black R & B, and their notions of sexuality—their perceptions of their own most intimate dimensions of experience—split off irrevocably from those of their parents.[43]

Another illustration of the way in which musical works can delineate cultural values and beliefs lies in the way rock music producers and performers deliberately link specific voice types with specific value systems. Consider, for example, that the lyrics of many hard rock songs are aggressive expressions of male supremacy.[44] Accordingly, the vocal timbre of many male rock singers is typical of what many North American audiences might consider "macho": a low, raw, constricted, rasping voice. In this case, a musical parameter (vocal timbre) is used to be expressive of dominance, pain, anger, or frustration in conjunction with particular vocal texts.

The flip side of male-dominated hard rock is soft rock, or Top 40 pop. Depending on the target audience and the narrative content of the lyrics, the sentimental love ballads of soft rock, pop, and much country and western music are usually performed by singers with particular vocal timbres, or by singers who can modify their vocal timbres to fit the shifting emotional expressions of love song lyrics. For instance, it seems fair to suggest that the pop/country singer Anne Murray speaks to the working woman and housewife about male-female relationships in a typically warm and nurturing vocal timbre. In contrast, Madonna often uses an innocent little-girl voice in ironic fashion to impersonate the older and wiser woman-as-seductress.[45] As McClary points out, what Madonna's mass audience of young women understands (which male music critics often overlook) is Madonna's sly potshots at female stereotypes. More broadly, says McClary, Madonna's singing is linked to a long history of narrative vocal music that places emphasis on female expressions of both the spiritual and the erotic in the traditions of Bessie Smith, Billie Holiday, and Aretha Franklin, among others.[46]

5. Love, Hate, and Other Musical Matters

Recognition of the cultural-ideological dimension of music listening and musical works helps to unlock several related issues of musical preference and music education.

On the surface, the tendency to love or hate different kinds of music is a curious matter. How is it that people develop a deep sense of attachment or aversion to inanimate sounds?

Part of the answer, of course, is that musical works are not autonomous aesthetic objects but socially constructed, socially embedded, and socially mediated constructions. Accordingly, it seems plausible to suggest that among the consequences of cognizing musical patterns and their delineated meanings are cognitive emotions (positive and/or negative) about whether the cultural conventions of a given work (say, a piece of country and western music) matches a listener's cultural beliefs and values.

In other words, musical preferences rest on cognitive appraisals of several related musical dimensions: namely, the interpretation-performance dimension; the musical design dimension; the dimension of practice-specific traditions and standards; the cultural-ideological dimension; and, in some works, the expressional and representational dimensions. I suggest that personal appraisals of the cultural-ideological dimension are especially powerful in listeners' preference decisions. Listeners are easily drawn or repelled by delineated musical meanings—by the cluster of associations they apprehend in, or attribute to, particular kinds of musical patterns.[47] (Again, by "cognitive appraisals" I do not necessarily mean verbal appraisals. Indeed, musical preferences are often tacit and impressionistic.)

Accordingly, when a music student says, "I know what I like," what he or she actually means is, "I like what I know." And what young listeners often know best (or hold the most assumptions about) is neither musical design nor artistic interpretation but the cultural-ideological dimension of particular musical works. In more elaborate terms, then, "I know what I like" most often means "I prefer musical works that I believe to be (and therefore hear as) consistent with my cultural-ideological values, affiliations, and beliefs."

In fact, listeners often construct cultural-ideological profiles and beliefs about certain pieces (or whole musical practices) before they even begin to listen. Music educators are familiar with this phenomenon. I call it the "listening ahead" or the "already listening" phenomenon. The most obvious form it takes is a cognitive emotion that grips music students (positively or negatively) the moment they interpret a cue of some sort, such as the advertising jacket of a CD, the title of a work, the mention of a composer's name, the venue of a live performance, or the look of a performer.

The commercial side of musical production is vitally concerned with delineating the cultural-ideological meanings of different musical genres through carefully co-ordinated images. The advertising that wraps recordings is a good example.[48] Glance around your local music store. Reflect on the links that record producers make between the images on CD jackets and the recorded music waiting inside the wrapper. To many listeners, a photo of the maestro Sir Georg Solti in a tuxedo on the outside of a recording of Wagner overtures delineates the recorded music inside the wrapper by attaching Solti's classic, wealthy, establishment look (and other cultural-ideological values attached to this look) to the so-called serious music inside the wrapper.

Delineated musical meanings are easily manipulated. Consider Nigel Kennedy, a young British violin virtuoso. Kennedy succeeded in making Vivaldi's *Four Seasons* a best-seller among his teenage followers by altering the cultural values that teenage listeners most often attribute to the sounds of "classical" music. Kennedy dresses like a rock musician, produces fast-paced rock video versions of his classical performances, stages the look of the symphony orchestras that participate in his concerts, and so on. These strategies often persuade young listeners to suspend their collective disbelief in classical works long enough to begin listening for the sounds of this music as tones-for-them.

A reverse example of this process occurred decades ago when the Boston Pops Orchestra recorded an instrumental medley of songs by a (then) controversial rock band called the Beatles. Whereas the traditional Boston Pops audience of the time might have assessed the authentic sounds of the Beatles as delineating socially unacceptable values, the BPO's symphonic orchestrations of these same tunes, imbued with the values of nineteenth-century Romanticism, tended to be heard as delineating socially acceptable values. In this case, music arranging was engaged in and functioned effectively as a musical and social homogenization process.

In summary, a basic part of music listening involves cognizing musical patterns in relation to socially determined beliefs. In the process, listeners assess music as delineating a particular belief/value system with which they then do or do not empathize.

What is important for music educators to keep in mind is that because this cultural profiling aspect of music listening is a matter of thinking and knowing, the outcomes of this process (like the outcomes of all forms of thinking and knowing) can be reasonable or unreasonable, superficial or profound, incisive or not. Listening for the cultural-ideological dimension of musical works is something most children learn to do at a novice or beginning level without formal instruction. Unfortunately, what children pick up about music listening (like the knowledge they pick up about history, geography, health, or people from unfamiliar cultures) is frequently biased, or just plain wrong. So, when a student dismisses a whole musical practice by saying something like "I hate Bach," he is not demonstrating the presence or absence of musical "taste." He is asserting a belief about musical works of a particular kind. This belief rests, in turn, on the presence or absence of knowledge about particular musical works and the musical practices of which they are part. And the knowings and beliefs that anchor such sweeping statements usually relate to one musical dimension in particular: the cultural-ideological dimension.

Fortunately, knowledge and belief systems are susceptible to illumination through education. Put another way, music educators need not be concerned with changing bad musical taste into good musical taste, because musical works are not equivalent to pizzas or chocolates. Musical works, musical experiences, and musical preferences result from knowledgeable acts of cognitive construction, not taste buds, gastric juices, or some sort of innate sensitivity. In short, the real issues of concern are students' beliefs and the cognitive emotions that musical beliefs generate. Music educators can exert a positive influence on the beliefs and knowings that anchor students' musical appraisals, preferences, and cognitive emotions by developing students' musicianship—that multidimensional form of knowledge that includes knowing how to listen intelligently for the relationships among (a) musicing and musical works and (b) cultural-ideological influences.

6. Music as Culture

Given the two-way relationship between musical practices and cultural influences, it is not surprising that different societies and different groups within societies tend to identify themselves with particular kinds of music. As I have explained, and as the ethnomusicologist Bruno Nettl also observes, musicing and musical works are powerful ways of capturing and delineating the character of a culture.[49] In many Western countries, for example, different teenage subcultures tend to develop and adopt certain musical practices to constitute and proclaim their cultural-ideological beliefs and values. They wear their chosen musical sounds like a bold team badge or a T-shirt slogan. Some people even live out the beliefs and values delineated by the sounds of their music. To some country and western music fans, for example, country music is a way of life that includes a preference for particular kinds of clothes, cars, speech patterns, sports, social rituals, and personalities.

Nettl underscores the extent to which human beings use music to separate themselves from others by pointing out that in some societies people guard their musical secrets from inquisitive outsiders; in others, musical works are considered to be owned by individuals, clans, or tribes.[50] Contrary to popular legend, then, not all musicians relish the opportunity to share their musical traditions. The reason is clear. A people's music is not only something they make; a people's music is something they *are*. Thus, to share the music of one's culture with others is to risk that outsiders will not understand and respect one's self. Accordingly, music practices are often highly inclusive and exclusive at the very same time.

These ideas serve to negate the popular assumptions that certain kinds of music are universal, or that music is an international language. Aside from the fact that musical sound patterns do not constitute a language, there is no one style of musical sound patterns that all humans immediately understand and prefer. Indeed, most people do not understand or enjoy all the Musics made within their own national borders, let alone the musical works of all cultures and practices everywhere. Kivy agrees and elaborates the basic point that MUSIC, MUSICIANSHIP, and MUSICAL WORKS are culture-specific and practice-centered.

Not only is music not "international," it is not even "national": witness the fact that many highly trained musical people find Bach unintelligible, while they listen with pleasure [i.e., enjoyment] and understanding to the complex polyphony, intricate rhythmic structure, and variation techniques of jazz while their equally musical counterparts dote on the intricate canonic writing of the *Goldberg Variations* and find jazz a buzzing, blooming confusion.

The only lesson to be learnt from this is that music no more appeals directly to the uneducated senses than does literature to the uneducated mind. To appreciate even a folk song or a Strauss waltz, let alone the *Goldberg Variations* or a Josquin motet, we have to know a whole lot of things, as we do if we are to appreciate *Faust* or *The Magic Mountain*. And to appreciate them *fully* requires not merely what I shall call subliminal knowing [or informal and impressionistic knowing], but knowing in the full-blooded conscious sense as well [or formal knowledge], as I must know about politics in Germany prior to the First World War to fully appreciate *The Magic Mountain,* or philosophy in Germany in the late eighteenth century to fully appreciate *Faust*.[51]

I suggest that if we combine these ideas with the themes of Chapter 7, we arrive at the larger conclusion that musical practices may also be rightly conceived as music cultures.[52] For a musical practice is a little social system, or a mini-world. MUSIC, overall, is a universe of mini-worlds (e.g., the jazz world, the world of choral music), each of which is organized around indigenous knowings, beliefs, values, goals, and standards toward the production of certain kinds of musical works for a particular group of listeners. Furthermore, each music culture is linked in a two-way relationship to its surrounding cultural context such that the beliefs, values, and so on that constitute a music culture are constantly being practiced, refined, and modified in relation to larger cultural concerns. Viewed from this perspective, the musical works that grow from musical practices are inseparable from their roots—their underlying network of beliefs and values.

The concept of music cultures drives home a key principle of the philosophy of this book: that the education of musicianship and the achievement of self-growth, constructive knowledge, and musical enjoyment will not occur if music teachers and learners approach music narrowly (or aesthetically), as a collection of autonomous pieces. To develop full musical understanding and appreciation, we need to re-mind ourselves and others that MUSIC is a diverse artistic-social-cultural practice. As Wolterstorff insists, "we shall have to renounce our myopic focus on works of art and look at the social practices of art. . . . [W]e shall have to look at the interplay between works, practices, and participants in the practices."[53] At the same time (and not surprisingly), one of the most important benefits of a more comprehensive concept of music is a more complete understanding of the nature and significance of musical works.

7. A Multidimensional View of Musical Works

Having considered several relationships between MUSIC and culture-ideological influences, this book's multidimensional view of music listening and musical works

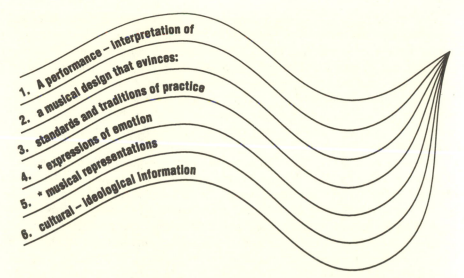

1. A performance – interpretation of

2. a musical design that evinces:

3. standards and traditions of practice

4. * expressions of emotion

5. * musical representations

6. cultural – ideological information

FIGURE 8.1. A Musical Work: Six Dimensions. The asterisks in the fourth and fifth dimension indicate that some (but not all) musical works are applicable.

is essentially complete. As pictured in the diagram in Figure 8.1, this philosophy suggests that listening intelligently for musical works involves the knowledgeable, covert construction of at least four, and often as many as six, interrelated dimensions of musical meaning, or information. In this view, dimensions one, two, three, and six are involved in our cognition of all musical works; dimension four (musical expressions of emotion) and dimension five (musical representations) are marked with asterisks because these dimensions may or may not be present for our cognition in any given work. I review these dimensions briefly now.

1. *Performance-interpretation.* Works of music are physical events of a special kind. Musical works are performances: physical events that are intentionally generated by the knowledgeable actions (overt and covert) of human agents (or musicers) to be intentionally conceived as such by other knowledgeable agents (musicers and/or listeners). Thus, music listening is always a matter of listening for a performance-interpretation of some kind: either a performance-interpretation of a written composition (or a remembered work) or an improvisation. All the other dimensions of a musical work are made determinate in the actions and events of a musical performance.

2. *Musical design.* Every musical work involves a composed or improvised musical design consisting of syntactic and nonsyntactic musical parameters. The syntactic parameters of musical design include melody, harmony, and rhythm. The nonsyntactic parameters of musical design include timbre, texture, tempo, articulation, and dynamics. Listeners covertly construct the relationships among and between the patterns of the musical design dimension as interpreted and performed by music makers.

Syntactic and nonsyntactic musical patterns are artistic qualities. This is so because the auditory materials of musical works are not just any old sounds but sounds organized by means of practice-specific histories and principles. Music makers do not invent the materials of music each time they compose, improvise, perform, arrange, or conduct. In most cases, music makers begin with a delimited set of materials (pitches, timbres, durations, and intensities) that are already artistic because they have been preselected and preorganized in relation to specific systems of pitch organization, rhythmic organization, and so on. In short, the basic design materials of musical works are inherently musical before musicians begin to organize and present them.

3. *Traditions and standards of practice.* Melodic, harmonic, rhythmic, timbral, textural, and formal musical designs embody their musical style-context affiliations. This holds doubly for vocal/choral works. In addition, every aspect of a heard musical work results from an individual or collective interpretation and performance of a musical design, or an improvised design. Thus, every auditory aspect of a musical work is inexorably tied to some artistic-musical-historical tradition. In other words, the successive and simultaneous sound patterns of a musical work not only relate intramusically (to each other), they also relate intermusically by manifesting stylistic features in common with other works in the same musical domain of effort.

4. *Musical expressions of emotion.* The musical designs and performances of some (but not all) musical works are rightly cognized as being expressive of specific emotions and/or musical expressions of such broad affective patterns as tension and release or conflict and resolution. Making and listening for musical expressions of emotion are eminently musical things to do, depending on the musical practice and work involved.

5. *Musical representations.* The musical designs and performances of some (but not all) musical works include musical representations of various aspects of our world. Indeed (as explained in Chapter 6), there are various and widespread means of making listenables that combine musical and extramusical materials.

6. *Cultural-ideological information.* In this chapter I have argued that musical works both constitute and are constituted by cultural knowings, beliefs, and values. This is so because (1) all forms of musicing are inherently artistic-social-cultural endeavors, (2) musical works are social-cultural constructions, and (3) musicers and listeners live in particular places and time periods. In short, music listening and musical works always involve some degree of cultural-ideological information. At the very least, and because syntactic and nonsyntactic musical patterns evince their practice-style affiliations, musical works delineate their broader historical and cultural links (e.g., their times and places of composition).

I suggest that the multidimensional concept of musical works I have just summarized is sufficiently comprehensive and flexible to accommodate the works of many (if not most) musical practices. At the same time, I am the first to admit that there may be musical works past, present, and future that involve additional dimensions not accounted for here. In other words, this philosophy's multidimensional concept of musical works is an open concept. Its six categories are heuristic devices. For the reasons explained in the last several chapters, I contend that if music teachers and music students keep in mind that there is no one way to listen for all music everywhere, and if this "map" of musical works is used as an adaptable guide, then students are more likely than not to experience a fuller measure of the human values that musicing and listening involve.

8. On the Ontology of Musical Works

In Chapter 2 I explained why it was necessary to overhaul the conventional notion of musical works. This overhaul is concluded. We have confronted the assumptions of the nineteenth-century work-concept of music as an ideal object and replaced it with a concept of musical achievements as individually cognized audible performances of various kinds. Also, we have replaced the one-dimensional aesthetic notion of music as sound patterns alone with a multilayered model of works based on a range of flexible dimensions. In doing so, the main questions of the ontology of music—What kinds of things are musical works? and Wherein lies the essential being of musical works?—have been addressed. It only remains to tie several key points together.

First, although sounds constitute the material reality of musical works, sounds do not constitute the essence, or being, of musical works. Musical works are not simply sonic structures; they involve musical actions and artistically designed sound patterns. As I have already noted, musical sounds also have intermusical meanings because of their embeddedness in traditions of musical performing, improvising, composing, arranging, and conducting.

Second, musical works are not equivalent to compositions. For a composer's intentions become determinate only in a performance of his or her composition. Besides, it is quite possible to have musical works without compositions (as when a musician improvises or performs on the basis of a remembered performance).

Third, although a written score stipulates many features of a composed work and therefore guarantees its basic identity across times and places, the being of a composed work is not the same as a musical score because scores are seen and not heard.

Fourth, a musical work is not purely in the mind of the listener because many people have a shared understanding of such works as Brahms's Symphony No. 1 in C minor and because many people continue to know and learn this work well past the time of its first performance (and long after Brahms's death).

Fifth, it is unlikely that the essence of musical works lies in a special relationship between musical sounds and time. True, it is often assumed that music is "the art of time" or that the time spans in which musical patterns unfold are ontologically different from ordinary time. Susanne Langer, for example, claims that the primary apparition of music is "virtual time": "Music makes time audible, and its form and continuity sensible."[54] (Alperson has already disputed these claims at length elsewhere.[55]) Suffice it to say (as I have explained in Chapter 5) that one of the chief characteristics of musical flow experiences is that musicers and listeners often become so absorbed in musicing and listening that they tend to lose track of ordinary clock time. We seem to enter another dimension where time passes either more quickly or more slowly than normal. But although this characteristic of flow is typical of musical experiences, it is not unique to musical experiences. As Alperson suggests:

> The emergence of a quality of temporality in the perception of musical forms is no more or less an illusion or more or less actual than the emergence of a sense of transcience in the perception of other phenomena which unfold in time. . . . The truth of the matter seems to be that the temporal dimension of musical experience is *not* fundamentally different from that of any other sort of temporal experience.[56]

What we can say, in sum, is that a musical work is neither all "out there" nor all "in the mind." A musical work is something that listeners experience through their conscious efforts to covertly construct performed musical sound patterns that are contextually qualified by their artistic and cultural circumstances of composition, interpretation, and audition.

Taking a cue from Jean-Jacques Nattiez,[57] I suggest that an essential part of the being of a musical work is the way intramusical and intermusical meanings are presented together for the interpretation of musicers and listeners in definite situations. If there is an essential being of musical works, it lies in the way we cognize musical sounds as combinations of intramusical, intermusical, and cultural-ideological meanings. Musical works are, in short, multi-layered thought generators.

One last point in relation to the above: It follows from everything in this book that music makers and musical works can and do communicate. I hasten to add, however, that by *communicate* I do not simply mean the sending of unambiguous messages. True, the texts of all sorts of vocal and choral works may be correctly viewed as examples of direct verbal communication. But the concept of communication (from *communicare,* "to impart or make common") includes more than simple message sending and far more than verbal information. Communication also involves having a causal influence on, or making some sort of difference in, a person or situation. (Reflect back, now, to parallel points on musical meaning in Chapter 6.)

Indeed, and in addition to the formulation and reception of unambiguous verbal messages, humans also communicate with and understand each other through shared actions, gestures, and emotional expressions and all sorts of culture-specific memes that contain no propositional content. This is possible because humans often consider what other humans may be thinking, doing, and intending in relation to social norms and conventions. In doing so, many sorts of inferences and meanings are imparted, conveyed, and understood.

Thus, and if we take account of (1) the several strata of information that musical works can evince, and (2) the ontology of musical works, and (3) the contextual nature of music listening, then it seems right to conclude that (in the presence of a knowledgeable listener) musical works can and do communicate in several ways, including the following: by being expressive of artistic-cultural traditions and values; by being expressive of emotions; by conveying musical representations and characterizations of people, places, and things; by manifesting cultural values (as tones-for-us); by providing the necessary conditions for self-growth and flow (thereby exerting a causal influence on individuals and communities); and by conveying personal interpretations of valued (or meaningful) musical works conceived as memes.

Indeed, musical works also count as memes. (Recall from Chapter 5 that a meme is any enduring form of information produced by intentional human action.) Musical works-memes impart their musical-cultural forms of information among and between generations of musicers and listeners through intentional acts of musicing and listening.[58]

9. Summary of the Music-Affect Relationship

I presented this book's main explanation of how music making and listening give rise to profoundly enjoyable experiences in Chapters 5 and 6. I now revisit and refine this explanation with the themes of this chapter in mind.

The philosophy of this book holds that music listening is a matter of deploying one's conscious powers of attention, awareness, and memory to construct covertly musical patterns and the several layers of musical information embodied in musical patterns. The enjoyment, absorption, and self-transcendence humans tend to experience while cognizing musical works arises when (and because) there is a match or balance between their current level of musical understanding and the cognitive challenges that a heard musical performance presents to their conscious powers (i.e., details of performance-interpretation, design, musical expression, representation, and cultural-ideological meanings).

In this view, the significance of musicing, listening, and musical works does not lie in the arousal of musical affect (or musical enjoyment) alone. The human significance of musicing, listening, and musical works lies in the *thought-full* processes required to meet the challenges presented to human consciousness by musical works and the actions of musicing and listening. Enjoyment or flow is the affective consequence of, the affective accompaniment to, and the prime motivation for the thoughtful actions of musicing and listening. Human beings possess tacit and verbal knowledge, concepts, and beliefs about everything in their lives. Our feelings are about people, events, and circumstances; affect is directed at things. It is because people develop and hold beliefs and knowledge about the several dimensions of musical works that people can be emotionally moved while listening.

The psychological researcher Richard Lazarus provides further support for this view of affect and the music-affect relationship.

> Cognitive activity is a necessary precondition of emotion because to experience an emotion, people must comprehend—whether in the form of a primitive evaluation perception or a highly differentiated symbolic process—that their well-being is implicated in a transaction, for better or worse. A creature that is oblivious to the significance of what is happening for its well-being does not react with an emotion.[59]

In fact, says Lazarus, cognition is both a necessary and a sufficient condition for affect of any kind: "*Sufficient* means that thoughts are capable of producing emotions; *necessary* means that emotions cannot occur without some kind of thought.''[60] The key phrase, of course, is ''some kind of thought.'' Indeed, as emphasized many times in this book, thinking is not one-dimensional. Thinking takes many forms. The cognitive operations and appraisals underlying emotional experiences are usually nonverbal. They are implicit in the actions we take. Although it is sometimes possible to verbalize the cognitive appraisals that underpin emotional experiences after the facts of their occurrence, our cognitive appraisals are usually implicit in the act of feeling a particular emotion.

Let me put a human face on these ideas. If seventeen-year-old Clara Nette enjoys (is moved to enjoyment) in the covert actions of cognizing the sounds of Brahms's Symphony No. 1 in C minor, it is because she possesses sufficient musicianship to cognize many aspects of the musical information that a performance of this composition presents. One of the most basic beliefs underlying Clara's cognitive-affective experience of this symphony is her belief that these sounds are music in the sense of tones-for-her. Clara has come to know that she has a social/cultural affiliation with these historied sounds. On the basis of this knowledge, Clara also believes and understands that the Chicago Symphony's performance of this composition is highly artistic, musically excellent, or ''beautiful.'' As a proficient listener, Clara knows (believes) that the structural design of these syntactic and nonsyntactic musical patterns is highly original and significant in relation to the standards and traditions of the Romantic musical practice of which Brahms was an acknowledged master. These musical patterns are concrete things about which Clara holds knowledge and beliefs. The intensity of her enjoyment grows as she listens for the musical expressions of emotion that she understands to be part of the artistic musical design and performance of this work. Clara also knows that this work is an example of Romantic music and, therefore, an embodiment of Romantic values and beliefs.

In all of this, Clara's actions of thinking, knowing, believing, and understanding are directed toward (are focused upon) something very specific indeed: the Claudio Abbado/Chicago Symphony performance/interpretation of a nineteenth-century European symphonic composition by Johannes Brahms. There is much in these musical sounds to hold knowings and beliefs about. Accordingly, there is much in these sounds to be moved about. As a result of the musicianship she has acquired by making and listening for the music of several different music cultures, Clara is also moved in similar (but not identical) ways when she listens for Duke Ellington's *Daybreak Express,* Stravinsky's *Rite of Spring,* Toru Takemitsu's *Water Music,* Handel's *Water Music,* and the *kete* drumming of the Asante people.

Then again, not all acts of music listening move Clara in the positive sense. Some musical works are what she understands and believes to be musically thoughtless (i.e., trite, unoriginal, insignificant) in terms of their design, their performance, or their musical expressiveness. In addition, there are whole musical practices that delineate cultural values that Clara believes (cognizes and, therefore, ''feels'') to be at odds with her own. In the case of rap music, for example, Clara hears *As Nasty as They Want to Be* (by 2 Live Crew) as alien to her values and beliefs. Tim Pani hears *Nasty* in the same way, yet he enjoys and participates in the rap of the group Public Enemy because he understands (or believes) that this style of rap is congruent with his cultural values.

More broadly, the works of many music cultures worldwide remain opaque to Clara because she does not yet possess the practice-specific forms of thinking and knowing (procedural, formal, informal, impressionistic, and supervisory) that are necessary for her to construct the various patterns and dimensions of these listenables.

Because there are several levels of information to cognize in musical works, there are many things to know, learn, discover, relish, and, therefore, to enjoy (or feel enjoyment about). Many people possess tacit beliefs and understandings (however deep or shallow) about the several dimensions of various works, including what they believe particular works delineate in terms of cultural beliefs and values. If a listener understands that a certain work has a conventional emotional significance (e.g., a lament), then her understanding matches this aspect of the overall musical challenge presented by the lament. Similarly, when a listener knows (or suspects) that the melody she is listening for is expressive of sadness, her enjoyment may include being moved by her cognition of this musical expression of emotion. Recall from Chapter 6 that when listeners hear a musical expression of happiness or sadness, they do not usually experience actual happiness or sadness. Instead, listeners enjoy apprehending (or understanding) the way a musical expression of sadness is achieved by a composer or performer. Listeners do not hear sadness in musical patterns; rather, listeners hear *that* musical patterns are expressive. Clearly, an affective musical experience involves a complex web of beliefs, knowings, and dispositions that are unique to each musicer and listener.[61]

Unlike many human pursuits that can order consciousness and bring enjoyment (such as tennis or mountain climbing), the artistic-cultural constructions we call musical works tend to engage people's beliefs about deeply important matters: about culturally shared expressions of emotion, culture-specific traditions of artistry, community values, or musical characterizations of socially shared events, personalities, or issues. Intentionally designed expressions of emotion are not present in the features of tennis games or mountains. Tennis and mountain climbing are enjoyable pursuits for many people. But they are not enjoyable primarily because they involve the cognitive construction of complex artistic patterns, artistically generated expressions of emotion, artistically codified characterizations of events, or artistically generated expressions of cultural values.

I have just said that musical affective experiences are unique to each individual. Yet one of the remarkable features of live concert performances is the way musical events set up a kind of magnetic field that brings people of different musical understandings and backgrounds together.[62] Each listener, like each member in a conversation, participates in the occasion differently and leaves with a unique cognitive-affective experience. Yet each shares the same occasion. There is something obvious yet inexplicable in this musical-social phenomenon. Nevertheless, says Sparshott,

> the inexplicability is not disturbing because it is the basic condition of human social existence: strangers from different backgrounds understand and misunderstand each other, and we cannot articulate or hope to unravel this fact because it comprises the entire substance of our knowledge of social reality and is therefore not to be reduced to anything simpler (and therefore less substantial).[63]

In summary, the emotional nature of musical experiences is essentially a matter of positive affect: enjoyment, deep satisfaction, or flow. Musical enjoyment arises when there is a balance between a listener's current level of musicianship and the cognitive challenges presented by a given musical work. Stated another way, musical affect arises in listeners when they know how to listen for, solve, or cognize the challenges in a musical work; when they know they are cognizing a musical work successfully; and/or when their musical expectations (in various musical dimensions) are being largely fulfilled.

I hasten to add, however, that knowledgeable listeners may also be surprised, delighted, or disappointed about something unexpected in a work that is otherwise familiar to them stylistically. To this limited extent, Leonard B. Meyer's early theory of musical affect[64] is probably correct (see Chapter 2). That is, *within* the continuously positive feeling of enjoyment or flow that arises from the balance between a listener's musicianship and a given musical challenge, a listener may (and likely will) encounter unfamiliar twists and turns in musical patterns that cause temporary confusions or frustrations of his or her musical expectations.

Clearly, the generally positive affect of musical flow cannot be explained by Meyer's theory of continuous musical frustration. Instead (and again), musical flow results from having a sufficient level of the necessary practice-specific musicianship to process enough of the multidimensional information presented by a given work that one's musical expectations are frequently fulfilled and one's consequent self-knowledge is this: "I am this person who is *meeting* this musical challenge as a music-maker and/or music-listener."

10. Implications for Music Education

If music listening and musical works are culturally informed and informative, what is the most appropriate way to develop students' understandings of them? My answer is: by teaching students to meet significant musical challenges in teaching-learning situations that are close approximations of real music cultures.

• *Learning by induction.* Musical practices are little social systems, or music worlds. Teaching students to make and listen for music with an understanding of the relationships between musical works and cultural influences requires music teachers to engage their students in the interplay of beliefs, actions, and outcomes at the core of music cultures. The educational process is one of inducting students into the way of life of a music culture; of engaging students in a living encounter with the knowings, beliefs, and values of a Music. As Israel Scheffler emphasizes, a culture (and the expressive products of a culture) remain opaque until understood as the embodiment of beliefs, plans, and actions—as the outcome of "intelligent action in the pursuit of purpose."[65]

The active, praxial approach to the development of musicianship and musical-cultural understandings has a practical advantage. Recall that many students tend to "listen ahead" for delineated musical meanings. Hence, many students tend to turn off at the first hint that an upcoming musical work is incongruent with their cultural affiliations and beliefs. A music curriculum centered on recordings is sufficiently decontextualized and passive that students' surplus attention shifts easily away from musical matters toward their own self-ish concerns. An effective way to increase students' attention to and awareness of the cultural-ideological dimension of musical works is to confront students with musically productive problems of performing, improvising, composing, arranging, and/or conducting. Such active, artistic-cultural problem finding and solving obliges students to "live" a music culture's ways of thinking, believing, and valuing; immerse themselves in the meanings of a music culture's sounds as tones-for-them; and reflect critically on their personal responses to a music culture.

A music curriculum centered on artistic music making also enables learners to develop the supervisory knowledge they need to understand and listen for the works of a music culture as embodiments of situated thinking, knowing, and believing. Active music making, and the kind of artistic listening that fuels music making, encourages students to connect the fruits of a music culture (its musical works) with the culture-specific roots of these fruits. The full nature and enjoyment of listening lies in a full awareness of the socially and historically determined ways of thinking that mediate the making of musical works in a given practice.

• *Music education is multicultural in essence.* The themes of this chapter have prepared the way for a central tenet of this philosophy that can be stated as follows. If MUSIC consists in a diversity of music cultures, then MUSIC is inherently multicultural. And if MUSIC is inherently multicultural, then music education ought to be multicultural in essence.

When I suggest that music education ought to be multicultural, I mean more than that music curricula ought to engage students in a reasonable range of musical practices. For multiculturalism involves more than diversity.

As a descriptive term, *multicultural* refers to the coexistence of unlike social groups in a common social system.[66] In this sense, the term simply means culturally diverse, or pluralistic. But *multicultural* also has an evaluative sense. It connotes a social ideal; a policy of support for exchange among different social groups to enrich all while respecting and preserving the integrity of each. This explains how a nation (or a community of any kind) may be culturally diverse but still not qualify as a multicultural nation. That is to say, while a nation may contain many different cultures, it may not enact equal legal, educational, and economic opportunity for all groups.

Following Richard Pratte,[67] I suggest that the term *multicultural* is most appropriately applied to a community that meets three criteria: (1) it must exhibit cultural diversity in the sense of including a number of different cultures (be they political, racial, ethnic, religious, economic, or age-based); (2) these coexisting microcultures must approximate equal political, economic, and educational opportunity; and (3) there must be a public policy commitment to the values of multiculturalism as a basis for a viable system of social organization.[68]

In this view, the United States, like other Western nations (including Canada, Australia, and the United Kingdom), may be seen to consist of a shared core culture (a macroculture) as well as many smaller subcultures (or microcultures). Micro-cultures come in a variety of forms. In addition to ethnicity-based cultures, there are institutional (school, university) and corporate cultures, age-based cultures (such as teen cultures), gender-based cultures, and religion-centered cultures.

Macrocultures and microcultures are not static but fluid. The shared concepts and beliefs of a macroculture (e.g., a shared belief in democracy and equality of opportunity) are interpreted and taken up differently within microcultures. As often happens, microcultures hold beliefs that are more or less alien to their related (or dominant) macroculture, and these differences in beliefs and values form the bases for misunderstandings among cultures.

If we combine the concept of music cultures with these ideas, we arrive at a useful way of thinking about music education in global and local contexts. Con-sidered from a musical perspective, the United States, like other Western nations, is culturally diverse. That is, the United States consists of a shared core of related music cultures (a musical macroculture of largely Western European practices) as well as several musical microcultures. The shared concepts and beliefs of the mu-sical macroculture are mediated by (as well as interpreted and taken up differently within) numerous musical subcultures. These microcultures frequently depend on beliefs and principles that are more or less alien to their dominant musical macro-culture.

But while MUSIC is inherently multicultural, and while the United States, Can-ada, the United Kingdom, and many other countries are musically pluralistic, many music teachers in these countries take the opposite view (knowingly and unknow-ingly). That is, many school music programs seem to limit students to one or two Western classical practices, or one or two jazz or pop practices. Thus, students not only fail to learn that MUSIC is a diverse human practice, they fail to understand that MUSIC is a diverse national, regional, and local practice.

If we accept the problem, how do we develop a solution? Music educators cannot possibly teach all music cultures to all students everywhere. Still, there are reasonable and practical steps teachers can take toward teaching and learning MUSIC (as opposed to one or two Musics), providing that other main principles of this praxial philosophy are also put into practice.

Suppose, for example, that a class of eleven-year-old children is organized as a choral practicum. Suppose the students' musicianship is being developed and contextualized as they learn to interpret, perform, and listen for Bach's *Duet from Cantata No. 9*, the Russian folk song *Good Night,* the gospel song *I'm Goin' Up A-Yonder,* and a jazz samba called *The Boston Trot*.[69] And suppose the music educator involved in teaching this practicum supplements the students' productive efforts with appropriate recordings and occasional projects in composing and con-ducting. If so, then the children involved are being inducted into four distinct but related music cultures: Baroque choral music, Russian folk music, African-American gospel singing, and Latin jazz. As the students learn to interpret and perform these works artistically (in awareness of all relevant dimensions of musical meaning), and as they learn to link each work to its relevant music culture, the children's musicianship becomes progressively more differentiated and integrated.

Now let us suppose that the teacher enriches his or her curriculum-as-practicum by introducing just one more unfamiliar music culture (e.g., Zulu choral singing). In doing so, the teacher takes another major step toward promoting the students' understanding of MUSIC as a diverse human practice. As the teacher enables his or her students to interpret and perform the Zulu song *Siyahamba*[70] authentically— with full awareness of all this song's dimensions of meaning (including the original text, the authentic movements used by the Zulu singers, and genuine African drumming patterns)—the music educator begins to induct the students into a new music culture. By revisiting and developing students' musicianship in relation to all these works, and by introducing other related and unrelated works over time, the teacher can continue musical induction and immersion so that the students' musicianship continues to deepen and broaden.

Reflect back now on the meanings of *multicultural*. What I argued in this chapter and this book is that a proper understanding of music leads to the conclusion that music education is (or should be) concerned with MUSIC as a diverse, multicultural practice. What this means is that a music educator who is genuinely concerned with teaching and learning MUSIC is also engaged in a unique and major form of humanistic education.

In the process of inducting learners into unfamiliar musical practices, music teachers link the primary values of music education to the broader goals of humanistic education. Venturing forth to live the artistic and cultural-ideological meanings of an unfamiliar music culture provides students with an important growth opportunity that only active musical risk taking can provide: the opportunity to know one's self (musical and otherwise) and the relationship of one's self to others. Musical risk taking (and the temporary disorientation that may follow) activates self-examination and the personal reconstruction of one's relationships, assumptions, and preferences. Such musical-cultural confrontations enable students to develop the disposition to consider that what may seem natural, common, and universal to them is not. Harold Osborne puts it this way: "The best and perhaps the only sure way of bringing to light and revivifying . . . [our] fossilized assumptions, and of destroying their powers to cramp and confine, is by subjecting ourselves to the shock of contact with a very alien tradition."[71]

If it is accurate to say that music education functions as culture as much as it functions in relation to culture, then induction into unfamiliar music cultures offers something few other forms of education can provide. A truly multicultural MUSIC curriculum connects the individual self with the personhood of other musicers and audiences in other times and places. And the effectiveness of music in this regard resides in its essential nature as praxis: as thinking-in-action. A MUSIC curriculum centered on the praxial teaching and learning of a reasonable range of music cultures (over a time span of months and years) offers students the opportunity to achieve a central goal of humanistic education: self-understanding through "other-understanding."

Thomas Regelski expresses several of these same themes another way:

> Art generally, and especially a time art such as music, gives us our only glimpse of how life is experienced in and through the minds of other intelligent and sentient Beings. Thus we can stress its importance as a mode of knowing without dictating

or debating in the abstract what is to be or should be known in the way of the
"content" of this or that culture. . . . [T]he key will be to emphasize the "humans
Being" that we can glimpse, understand, share and profit from only through musical
praxis—intensely intentional involvement.[72]

• *Selecting musical practices.* In general, insufficient care is given to selecting
musical practices for music teaching and learning. Many music teachers have a
tendency to decontextualize music education from the outset by thinking narrowly
in terms of a given verbal concept or piece, with too little concern for the musical
whole, the musical practice of which each piece is a part.

If this is so, then music teachers have good reasons to ask: How shall we go
about selecting musical practices for music teaching and learning? Are some musical practices better than others? Does it make sense to select musical practices
on the basis of students' cultural traditions? And once a practice is selected, how
does one determine the musical merit of individual works within a given practice?

It is not uncommon to find people who believe strongly that all Western European classical practices are inherently superior to rock, pop, or avant-garde practices. Others want to claim that folk music is inherently natural and honest, while
rap is inherently bad music.

What can we make of such talk? Suppose we attempt to decide which is "best"
among three different Musics: a Schubert song, a piece of urban blues, and a work
of *karnataka sangeeta* (South Indian classical music). To decide which is the best
musical practice we would have to base our judgments on (1) the values and
standards of one of these three practices, on (2) the standards of a completely
unrelated musical practice, on (3) the standards of no musical practice whatever.

The first option, of course, is ethnocentric. The second option is nonsensical.
And the third option is unmusical by definition. In sum, no musical practice or
music culture is innately better than any other. Musicing and its outcomes are
always practice-specific. Just as it is illogical to debate whether apples are better
than oranges, it is also illogical to debate whether a Schubert song is better than a
blues, or a piece of *karnataka sangeeta*. There is no best Music compared across
different musical practices. (As Chapter 9 explains, however, there are reasonable
ways of deciding the merits of different musical works within the same musical
practice). The ethnomusicologists Mark Slobin and Jeff Todd Titon agree:

> Each music-culture is a particular adaptation to particular circumstances. Ideas about
> music, social organization, repertoires, and music's material culture vary from one
> music-culture to the next, but it would be foolish to say that any one music-culture
> was "better" than another. Why? Because such a judgment is based on criteria from
> inside a single music-culture. To call another music-culture's music "primitive"
> imposes one's own standards on a group that does not recognize them.[73]

But while no one Music is innately superior to any other, some musical practices may be educationally more appropriate than others. In other words, music
education occurs not in a vacuum but in relation to a variety of constraints—
practical, social, cultural, ideological, and political. Chief among these is the practical problem of curricular time. There is simply not enough time to teach all the
world's Musics to all children. Thus, difficult choices must be made. I suggest
several guidelines for making such choices.

First, the musical practices we select for music teaching and learning at the outset of a child's musical education ought to make the most of the tacit dimensions of musicianship—procedural, informal, impressionistic, and supervisory musical knowings—that children begin to develop themselves through early musicing and listening in their own cultural contexts. It is essential for self-growth and enjoyment that learners achieve a match between their novice level of musicianship and the first musical challenges they meet in music education curricula. Put another way, in deciding which practices to teach first, teachers ought to take account of a student's musical memosphere. For the musical knowings that infants and young children achieve on their own amount to a bridge between young brains and young musical minds.

Second, achieving the primary values and aims of music education depends on the continuous deepening of musicianship in balanced relation to increasingly demanding musical works. Self-growth, constructive knowledge, and musical enjoyment arise through engagements with progressively more challenging musical goals. Moreover, as Sparshott reminds us, people for whom the music of their own culture is all the music there is "can live into that music as people of broader culture cannot; their musical world is a cultural entity that belongs to them and to which they belong."[74] This sense of musical belonging (a practice-specific way of musical life) is something to be cherished. In short, musical breadth is not necessarily a virtue.

Accordingly (as noted in Chapter 5), when time and resources are limited, this praxial philosophy supports an emphasis on musical depth over breadth. Our central responsibility (to deepen students' musicianship) indicates that music education curricula ought to build on a foundation of several closely related musical practices that spiral upward in the demands they make on students' growing musicianship. Once established, music curricula may then move out toward more unfamiliar cultures.

Indeed (and paradoxically), because MUSIC is a diverse human practice, and because induction into unfamiliar musical practices links the values of music education with the values of humanistic education, music teachers ought to make an important place in their curricula for music cultures that are more distantly related[75] to the culture-specific forms of musicianship that children develop early in the context of their culture. Thus, and in addition to the obvious criteria of students' interests, the availability of authentic repertoire, and a teacher's knowledge and/or disposition to learn new practices over time, it also makes sense to use the musical variety of one's own local region or nation as a launching pad to the teaching of more "distant" Musics.

For example, several Australian delegates to a conference of Asian Pacific music educators suggested that a reasonable music curriculum for their national situation might include five broadly based practices reflective of Australia's musical pluralism: Australian aboriginal practices, Asian music practices, Pacific practices, historic and contemporary Western European practices, and Australian folk (or "crossover") cultures.

Implicit in this example is a key tenet of multiculturalism and another important criterion for selecting among musical practices: recognition. Personal and cultural recognition are essential to the growth and education of the self. As the philosopher

Charles Taylor points out, recognition is closely tied to self-identity.[76] Students' identities include a personal awareness of who they are, "of their fundamental defining characteristics as a human being."[77] Taylor argues that the development of personal identity rests on the deliberate and accurate recognition (or affirmation) of people's cultural beliefs and values. When recognition is withheld or dishonest, the consequences can be grave:

> [A] person or a group of people can suffer real damage, real distortion, if the people or society around them mirror back to them a confining or demeaning or contemptible picture of themselves. Nonrecognition or misrecognition can inflict harm, can be a form of oppression, imprisoning someone in a false, distorted, and reduced mode of being.[78]

I suggested earlier in this chapter (following Nettl) that people tend to identify themselves with particular Music(s) and that a people's Music is, very often, something they are. If so, then recognizing the traditional music cultures of one's students and one's community may contribute significantly to self-identity. As Taylor emphasizes: "Due recognition is not just a courtesy we owe to people. It is a vital human need."[79]

A musical practice is not something that operates autonomously in a culture; it constitutes and is constituted by culture and ideology. Similarly, music education is not something that operates autonomously in a culture; it also functions powerfully as culture.

Questions for Discussion and Review

1. Explain three ways in which a composer's decisions about musical form and content can be influenced by his or her social and cultural circumstances.

2. Explain three ways in which a performer's interpretative decisions about a composition can be influenced by his or her social and cultural circumstances.

3. "Listeners can apprehend confirmations (or negations) of their cultural beliefs and affiliations in musical patterns." Summarize the reasoning that supports this proposal. Explain why you agree or disagree.

4. Summarize the essential ideas conveyed by each of the following terms: culture, ideology, macroculture, microculture, multicultural.

5. Select one pop, rock, and country and western recording. Using Figure 8.1 as a guide, listen to your selections for the presence (or absence) of the various dimensions of musical information discussed to this point in the book. Describe how the composers, arrangers, and/or performers of your selections combine musical patterns and lyrics to delineate cultural-ideological beliefs and values. Repeat this process with selected operas, Broadway musicals, madrigals, cantatas, and so on.

6. This chapter suggests that musical taste is essentially a matter of musical and cultural beliefs. Do you agree? Why?

7. Does it makes sense to say that musicing, listening, and musical works involve communication? Why?

8. The MEAE philosophy conceives musical works as aesthetic objects. This book's praxial philosophy takes an entirely different view. Compare and contrast these two philosophies in regard to the nature of musical works.

9. There is little doubt that musicing and music listening often give rise to positive affect, or flow. Drawing on the relevant discussions in Chapters 5 through 8 of this book, summarize this philosophy's explanation of the music-affect relationship.

10. Explain several ways in which music educators can develop students' understanding of the cultural-ideological nature of musicing, listening, and musical works.

11. Explain why and how "MUSIC is multicultural in essence." What criteria can be used to select musical practices for music teaching and learning? Explain the relationships between MUSIC education, humanistic education, and the enhancement of self-identity and self-esteem.

Supplementary Sources

Christopher Page. *Discarding Images: Reflections on Music and Culture in Medieval France*. Oxford: Clarendon Press, 1993. Page examines the links between musical practices and the social-culture nature of medieval France.

Peter Kivy. *Osmin's Rage: Philosophical Reflections on Opera, Drama, and Text*. Princeton, N.J.: Princeton University Press, 1988. Chapter 11, "Opera as Music," explains how philosophy and psychology influenced the development of European operatic practices, especially opera seria.

Lydia Goehr. *The Imaginary Museum of Musical Works: An Essay in the Philosophy of Music*. Oxford: Clarendon Press, 1992. Chapters 5 and 6 explain how the historical-cultural notions of serious music, musical works, and musical meaning emerged in eighteenth-century Europe and influenced Classical and Romantic practices.

Michael W. Harris. *The Rise of Gospel Blues: The Music of Thomas Andrew Dorsey in the Urban Church*. New York: Oxford University Press, 1992. Harris examines the relations among musicing, listening, religion, culture, and ideology in the evolution and practice of gospel blues.

Timothy W. Ryback. *Rock Around the Bloc: A History of Rock Music in Eastern Europe and the Soviet Union, 1954–1988*. New York: Oxford University Press,

1990. Ryback documents the interactions between rock music practices and polit-ical-cultural currents in the former Soviet Union.

Danker Schaareman, ed. *Balinese Music in Context*. Frankfurt: Amadeus Ver-lag, 1992. Thirteen scholars discuss the complex interrelationships between music and the socio-cultural patterns of Bali.

Richard Leppert and Susan McClary, eds. *Music and Society: The Politics of Composition, Performance and Reception*. Cambridge: Cambridge University Press, 1987. This collection of essays offers many examples of the cultural-ideological nature of musicing, listening, and musical works.

Lucy Green. *Music on Deaf Ears: Musical Meaning, Ideology, Education*. Man-chester: Manchester University Press, 1988. A stimulating study of the socially embedded nature of music.

Philip A. Alperson. " 'Musical Time' and Music as an 'Art of Time'." *Journal of Aesthetics and Art Criticism* 38, no. 4 (Summer 1980): 407–17. Alperson chal-lenges the claim that music has a special status in relation to time.

David J. Elliott. "Key Concepts in Multicultural Music Education." *Interna-tional Journal of Music Education* 13 (Summer 1989): 11–18. A probe of the philosophical and curricular assumptions involved in multicultural music education.

Wayne Bowman. "The Problem of Aesthetics and Multiculturalism in Music Education." *Canadian Music Educator* 34, no. 5 (May 1993): 23–30. Bowman considers music education in our "post-aesthetic," multicultural era.

9

Musical Creativity in Context

To many people, music making is synonymous with creating and creativity. But the richness of musical works causes us to wonder whether it is possible to educate music students toward creative musical achievements. Perhaps musical creativity is only for geniuses. Then again, perhaps every instance of music making is creative because every music maker is a unique individual.

This chapter has two goals. The first is to explain what creativity is. The second is to develop guidelines for teaching students how to achieve creative musical results. In this chapter I argue that music educators can enable and promote musical creativity, because developing students' musical creativity overlaps and extends the process of developing students' musicianship.

1. The Concept of Creativity

In the domain of music, as in chemistry, dance, mathematics, visual art, and poetry, there are specific terms for the kinds of making that go on. In poetry, we speak of writing or composing a poem. In dance, we speak of dancing or choreographing. In chemistry and mathematics, we speak of theorizing, problem solving, or experimenting. In visual art, people talk about drawing, sketching, painting, and sculpting. In music, we speak of composing, improvising, arranging, performing, and conducting. Thus, Beethoven was a composer who composed many musical compositions, including the "Eroica" Symphony, and *Fidelio*. What more needs to be said? Why substitute the word *creating* for the word *composing?* Why use the terms *creation* or *creative achievement* for the more specific terms *musical composition, symphony,* or *opera?* Wynton Marsalis is a performer who improvises brilliantly. Again, what more needs to be said? Why call his improvising *creating?*

To answer these questions, I begin by offering the personal observation that I do not know how to draw very well. Accordingly, if I step up to a school blackboard and say, "Look, I am drawing," you will most likely reply, "Yes, so I see." But if I also say, "Look, I am creating," would you automatically agree? Some people would answer, "Yes, David is creating because he is a unique human being and this fact alone qualifies his drawing as creating." In this view, every instance of drawing, writing, talking, breathing, or looking counts as creating simply because it is individually controlled, or human-made. Is this what we mean when we talk about Beethoven's creating the "Eroica"? I think not. In Beethoven-type situations, we seem to use the word *creating* in relation to a tangible product or achievement of some kind that knowledgeable people value or cherish for one reason or another.

If so, this begins to explain why my actions at the blackboard are rightly called drawing but not creating. Drawing, dancing, and composing involve identifiable human actions that we can pick out from the vast array of human actions as easily as we can identify examples of deep-sea fishing or water skiing. But examples of creating cannot be picked out as easily, because to identify an instance of creating or creative achievement requires that we judge the *merit* of something that someone has done or made.[1] In other words, people create *by means of* drawing, composing, dancing, or experimenting. Whether we call these forms of action creating or creative depends on the quality of what gets done. Creating is a particular kind of making or doing that results in tangible products or achievements that people deem valuable, useful, or exceptional in some regard.

In this view, the words *creator, creating, creative, creation,* and *creativity* form a family unit. Creative people, as David Perkins points out, "are people who often produce creative results. . . . The idea of a creative outcome or product is the conceptual center; all the other words in the family get their meanings from it."[2]

To reiterate, although creativity involves (1) making something and (2) something that is made, it is the tangible outcome or product that has priority in determinations of creativity. *Creative* is a congratulatory term that singles out a concrete accomplishment that knowledgeable people judge to be especially important in relation to a specific context of doing and making.

But while most people seem to have little trouble agreeing that Beethoven's "Eroica," Alexander Graham Bell's telephone, and Rembrandt's *Night Watch* are examples of creative achievement, many people seem to have difficulty saying why. Indeed, how do we decide whether something deserves to be called creative?

2. Originality and Significance

People often associate the word *creative* with the new, the unique, the innovative, the divergent, the imaginative, and the original. This seems right as far as it goes. In relation to what other musicians knew in Beethoven's time and place, Beethoven's "Eroica" was surely original in the sense of un-usual, un-familiar, or extraordinary. But originality is only part of the story. That is, originality is a necessary condition for calling something creative, but it is not sufficient. For when we focus exclusively on a product's foreground of unfamiliar features, we overlook the product's background of familiar features, including its links with past achievements. In other words, without some relationship to other accomplishments—without the context or background of past achievements—new productions would merely be bizarre, not original.

To call something original is to acknowledge that it is simultaneously similar to, yet different from, its relevant ancestors. For example, to call a new overture for wind ensemble original is to connect it with other things of a similar kind, namely, other overtures for wind ensemble that have come before, and out of which this extraordinary, unusual, or original overture has been developed. An original overture is embedded in a definite tradition of composing and performing. At the same time, it departs from this tradition in some way. Of course, the degree of departure may vary from work to work. But some link to previous achievements in a history of practice is a necessary condition for deciding to call something original.

These perspectives cause us to reconsider popular associations between creativity and novelty. Extraordinary achievements are not called creative because they are solitary in type or character. It would be difficult to imagine something truly novel in the sense of something completely unrelated to what we already know, unless it was brought from Mars. In such a case, it would be called strange, weird, or alien, but not creative. Beethoven's "Eroica" is highly original, not novel. The "Eroica" is a symphony that combines musical strategies and exhibits musical features that were both familiar and unfamiliar in Beethoven's musical time and place.

Said differently, Beethoven's "Eroica" (his third symphony) stands on the shoulders of previous musical works that Beethoven's predecessors and colleagues composed or that Beethoven himself composed. As explained in Chapter 7, compositional practices are ongoing social practices. When a composer begins to compose, he or she is not acting alone. Whatever music gets done is connected to a network of direct and indirect musical, social, and cultural achievements and relationships. People who achieve creative results inevitably stand on the shoulders of past and present doers and makers in their domain. The "head and shoulders" view of musical creativity in Figure 9.1 is meant to emphasize the musical interdependence of music makers and creative musical achievements past and present.

The praxial concept of creativity that I am developing receives added support from several studies of creativity, including independent studies by Perkins and Csikszentmihalyi. Perkins recommends we take the long view of creativity to remind ourselves that knowledge and continuous effort in a specific domain of practice are the main sources of creative achievement.[3] After twenty-five years of investigating the nature of creativity, Csikszentmihalyi draws the same conclusion:

> We cannot study creativity by isolating individuals and their works from the social and historical milieu in which their actions are carried out. This is because what we call creative is never the result of individual action alone; it is the product of three main shaping forces; a set of social institutions, or *field,* that selects from the variations produced by individuals those that are worth preserving; a stable cultural *domain* that will preserve and transmit the selected new ideas or forms to the following generations; and finally the *individual,* who brings about some change in the domain, a change that the field will consider to be creative.[4]

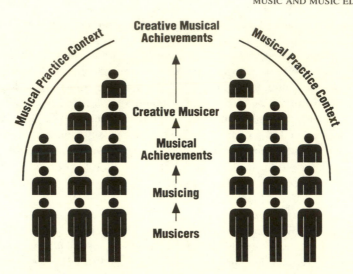

FIGURE 9.1. Musical Creativity: A Head-and-Shoulders View

Notice the emphasis that Perkins and Csikszentmihalyi place on the role of the practical context, domain, or field in creative achievement. Implicit in this emphasis is another essential characteristic of creative achievements: They are highly significant in relation to other achievements within their field or domain. To count as creative, a product or accomplishment must not only exemplify originality, it must make a notable contribution within a domain of effort.

Suppose, for example, that I design and produce a new type of car. My car is not only beautiful, it is original. My car combines the best of past and present technology. There is only one problem: My car has no room for a driver. Is my car creative? No. It is merely bizarre.

Beethoven's "Eroica" is rightly considered a creative musical achievement because it is both original and significant in relation to its relevant domain of musical practice. When a musical composition does not depart radically from a musical tradition, our judgments about its musical originality and importance are not especially difficult, providing we know the musical practice involved. The task of judging involves comparing the originality and significance of the new composition's several relevant dimensions (design, expression, representation, and so on) to previous compositions in the same practice. Again, without a field or domain of practice, a composer could not begin to make something that might qualify as original and significant, and a critic could not begin to judge its musical merit.

Of course, some musical achievements are more extra-ordinary than others. Consider several of Debussy's works, especially *Pélleas and Mélisande, Nocturnes,* and *Prélude à l'après-midi d'un faune.* Debussy's highly original approach to composing derived partly from his desire (or deliberate plan) to seek out musical opportunities in the music of other cultures, partly from the cultural influences of late Romanticism (see Chapter 8) and partly from his interest in (or strategy) of developing musical parallels to the works of the impressionist painters and poets of his time. Part of what the knowledgeable musicer and listener values in Debussy's compositions is their unusual inventiveness. Although Debussy was thoroughly familiar with Western European classical traditions, he did not work within these traditions as much as he reinvented them by employing new concepts of scale organization, orchestration, form, and melody. Debussy modified the practice-specific rules and strategies of Classical and Romantic composing (and listening) that he inherited from his musical predecessors. As a result, Debussy expanded the horizons of composing, performing, and listening and paved the way for the musical innovations of many twentieth-century composers. Several of Debussy's compositions were highly original in relation to the works of other composers of his time and place, but his best compositions were also highly significant. They played an important role in modifying Western musical practices and in preparing the way for new compositional strategies.

In radically different but equally important ways, the operas of Monteverdi, the twelve-tone compositions of Schoenberg, the jazz improvisations of Charlie Parker, and the songs of Stephen Sondheim parallel Debussy's brand of musically original and meaningful achievement. Yet even these more discontinuous examples of creativity can be seen to connect with the factors and conditions that spawned them. Sharon Bailin reiterates the reasons: "The novel element [in a creative achievement] arises in the context of an enterprise that has a history and is part of a tradition; and the tradition has a direction, goals, and meaning in light of which the innovation can be understood."[5]

In the domain of MUSIC, then, the words *creative* and *creating* apply to achievements of musical composing, improvising, and arranging that are original and significant within the context of a particular musical practice, including instances of musicing that depart in highly original and important ways from existing traditions. In this view, the criteria of originality and significance (and, therefore, of musical creativity) are not elusive. They are objective to a considerable degree.

But what can we say about the relationship between musical creativity and musical performing? I have deliberately avoided the question until now to highlight several separate but related points. The literature of music education often makes a rigid distinction between performing and creating. There is a widespread assumption in our profession that (1) performing cannot be creative, only re-creative, and (2) composing and improvising are always, and automatically, creative. Both assumptions are false for several reasons.

First, as I explained in Chapter 7, only in a performance do the intentions of a composer and the dimensions of his or her composition become determinate. I argued, also, that musical compositions are usually open to a wide range of legitimate but contrasting interpretations. Accordingly, performing and conducting can result in highly original and significant musical achievements; performing and conducting can be (but are not always) creative.

To decide this point for yourself, compare and contrast rival interpretations-performances of the same composition. You will often hear why and how some performances are pedantic, unoriginal, and insignificant, whereas others are astonishingly fresh, original, and insightful.

Examples abound. Consider two different recorded performances of *The Planets* by Gustav Holst.[6] On one hand, Charles Dutoit and the Montreal Symphony Orchestra achieve a remarkably well balanced, carefully paced, expressive, and atmospheric performance of this composition. Dutoit's interpretation brings out all the relevant dimensions of this work. Not so, I believe, with Andrew Davis and the Toronto Symphony. The balance among the sections of the Davis/TSO interpretation is dull and uneven. Davis often rushes the tempos. These interpretive weaknesses negate the work's musical expressions of emotion and prevent the TSO from achieving the dramatic climaxes that give the Dutoit/MSO performance its excitement. Accordingly, I consider the Dutoit/MSO performance highly creative, whereas the Davis/TSO performance is competent. (Perhaps you disagree? If so, then we should listen again and debate our views. After all, comparing, contrasting, and debating the merits of different performances are natural concomitants of music-listening practices. Such critical reflections add to musicianship and, therefore, enjoyment.)

While every form of music making can be creative, not all instances of composing, arranging, improvising, performing, and conducting are automatically creative because they involve "arts" of musical sound. Like all forms of thinking and knowing, music making can be done well or badly, creatively or uncreatively. Just because I compose a song does not mean I am creative or that my composing counts as creating. What shall we say if my song has a trite melody, incorrect harmonies, and too much rhythmic variety? I have merely composed a bad song. Nothing more, nothing less. Needless to say, it is easy to find many good examples of bad improvising, incompetent conducting, and poor arranging.

The educational implications of this discussion are mainly three. First, it is quite possible for children who achieve proficient levels of musicianship to achieve creative musical results in their performing, improvising, composing, arranging, and conducting. Indeed, and because of musical music educators, there are many situations in many school and community music education programs where students in choirs, wind ensembles, jazz combos, and composition classes do achieve original and significant interpretations, improvisations, and compositions in relation to relevant traditions and norms of musical practice. (More on the *what* and *how* of teaching musical creativity in a moment.)

The second implication of my discussion concerns music listening. As part of their effort to place recordings and aesthetic listening at the center of the general music curriculum (and displace authentic music making), advocates of MEAE hype the nature of listening with the claim that when a person is listening to the aesthetic elements of music in a concentrated way, "he is, in a real sense, creating along with the music."[7]

But the claim is false. Music listening is clearly central to any form of music making that achieves creative results, and a proficient level of listenership is crucial to creative musical achievement. As I explained in Chapter 4 of this book, there can be no doubt that proficient music listening is a highly complex form of cognition. But when someone listens for a musical performance as an audience member, his or her covert act of listening does not count as creating. For music listening, by itself, produces no tangible musical achievement that others can witness and judge as competent, let alone original or significant. Can a critic's musical criticism be creative? Possibly. But this is a different matter. For in music criticism there is a tangible product to witness: a written criticism (which is a literary achievement, not a musical achievement) that follows after knowledgeable listening to a musical effort.

Third, there is a tendency in our field (especially popular in the 1970s) to equate musical creativity with any effort to make aleatoric music, electronic music, computer generated works, free-form improvisations, or "soundscapes." The assumption underlying this tendency is that if children attempt to make music in relation to the principles and standards of contemporary musical practices, they are automatically being creative.

But no musical practice is inherently more creative than another. Just because students bang pots and pans freely, or record and edit the sounds of a dripping tap, or sing R. Murray Schafer's *Epitaph for Moonlight*[8] does not necessarily mean they are producing creative musical results. Whether their musicing is creative depends on the musical originality and significance of their achievements.

3. Spontaneous Originality

An important distinction between creativity and spontaneous originality serves to support and elaborate these arguments.

What is spontaneous originality? Young children often respond to their environments in uninhibited and unusual ways. Most youngsters burst with observations and ideas that are original by adult standards. Hence, adults (especially proud parents) are quick to assume that all children are naturally creative. Does this make sense? I think not. What young children often do with finger paint, crayons, or pots and pans may seem creative to many adults because it is unconventional in relation to conventional adult behavior.[9] But whether adult spontaneity is deemed creative or simply bizarre depends on adult standards of conduct. In other words, what many adults deem creative in the things young children produce is more likely a matter of spontaneous originality and this, in turn, is largely a matter of innocence, or lack of knowledge. Spontaneous originality usually has no relationship to recognized domains of practice except, perhaps, in a naive, exploratory way. (Consider that many music education research efforts that claim to be investigating, testing, or measuring musical creativity may actually be concerned with spontaneous originality.)

Spontaneous originality ought to be treasured and nurtured in children. It may play a role in later creative achievement. But overall, there is no lack of young children who exhibit spontaneous originality while exploring sounds, words, clay, or finger paint. And there is no lack of adults who act spontaneously. But there is an important shortage that should concern all educators everywhere: a shortage of children and adults who succeed in achieving original and consequential results within important domains of practice.

The distinction between creativity and spontaneous originality alerts us to the fact that people who engage in creative efforts are not merely reacting spontaneously to their environment or responding to their emotions like puppets on a string.

And they are not playing in the sense of dabbling in undirected activities. Instead, creative efforts are characteristically concerned with achieving particular kinds of results. Creative efforts are *intentional*. A creative performance or improvisation may seem like child's play to an uneducated observer. But the term *child's play* misrepresents the informed and goal-directed nature of the effort.

This is not to say that creative people do not enjoy what they are doing. On the contrary, when people are working at the edge of their abilities in order to achieve original and significant outcomes (to meet a challenge of some kind), flow is not only the reward but also the motivation for persisting in such demanding efforts.

Moreover, to say that creating is a matter of intentional, goal-directed effort is not to say that creative people know exactly what they are going to achieve before they begin or that they can state their intentions explicitly. For example, a composer is not likely to say, "I am now going to compose a creative song." Instead, a composer works at composing a song until he or she meets (or fails to achieve) the intended result. The composing process is goal-directed, whether the details of the musical goal are known clearly or vaguely at the outset. And whether someone deserves to be called creative or just a mediocre songwriter depends on the relationship between the song he composes and the relevant criteria and traditions of songwriting by which we judge the originality and significance of his song.

Again, it is important to emphasize that a creative achievement is a tangible accomplishment that knowledgeable people consider original and significant within a definite domain of practice. The sounds my three-year-old nephew makes while banging the piano in the parlor may be original and notable to him and, perhaps, to his adoring grandmother. But these evaluations do not make his sounds musical, let alone creative.

Some readers may object that I am being too grumpy or harsh. Some readers will insist that all children are creative. I suggest, instead, that while all children may be original, not all children are musically creative just because they have a pulse or just because they produce self-made sounds.

The importance of distinguishing between spontaneous originality and creativity has nothing to do with being harsh and everything to do with caring deeply about the development of children's musicianship, self-growth, enjoyment, and musical creativity. For the more we can clarify what musical creativity involves, the more effectively we can enable and promote our students' efforts to achieve creative musical results. When a music teacher decides that everything counts as creative—that all activities and sounds by the children in his or her class qualify as creative musical achievements—then that teacher cheats those students by removing the two basic conditions necessary for self-knowledge and musical enjoyment: a musical challenge and the musicianship needed to meet the challenge. In a situation where everything counts, nothing counts, and the concepts of musical challenges, musicianship, and creative achievement evaporate. Notice, also, that when a teacher declares that everything his or her students do is automatically creative, then there is nothing more to do and the teacher is instantly free to teach nothing at all.

To hit musical targets, we must set musical targets. To develop musical creativity, music educators must be honest with students about what counts as musical and what counts as musically creative in relation to past and present attainments in musical practices.

4. Creative Personality and Creative Process

Some writers attribute creative achievements to special "mental stuff" that creative people supposedly share in common. This notion rests on two false assumptions. The first one is that creativity is a special mental capacity (like general intelligence) that some people have and others do not. The second assumption is that the kind of thinking that creative people do is a trick form of thinking unrelated to any known form of cognition. These assumptions combine to persuade many people that creative achievement is possible only for gods, geniuses, or people with enough wealth to purchase the latest creative snake oil (e.g., creative thinking techniques, creativity exercises, "sensitivity training").

The weaknesses of these assumptions are well understood by philosophers and cognitive scientists. In the first place, the notion that we can explain the creativity of an achievement by reference to some special mental capacity is based on a logical fallacy.[10] For it does not follow that if someone achieves a creative result, then he or she is automatically the owner of some special mental capacity called creativity. Suppose, for example, that we located a creativity center in the brain of someone like the composer Philip Glass. Even if we could detail precisely what exists in the Glass brain and explain how it works, these findings would not be the general traits of creative people. They would be the specific traits of one composer who composes specific things like *Music in Twelve Parts, Einstein on the Beach,* and *Satyagraha.* At best, a successful analysis of Philip Glass's brain would tell us only how to reproduce *Music in Twelve Parts* and *Satyagraha* and other things that Glass himself has made. And since Glass has already produced these works, this is not what we need to know.

More broadly, a creative achievement, which is unpredictable in essence, cannot be predicted or tested for in any meaningful way. To suggest that creativity resides somewhere in consciousness like a benign tumor or that there is such a thing as the creative personality, is to suggest that anyone having such things will in fact produce creative products. But if this were true, then creativity would be a matter of everyday prediction and guarantee and, therefore, no longer creative.

Underlying the belief that creativity depends on a trick form of cognition or a special kind of illumination process is another false assumption: that creating is essentially passive. In this view, creative people work under the control of special urges, flashes of insight, special feelings, or a muse. Early research in creativity was largely devoted to the search for a secret illumination process, or "the creative process." In contrast, cognitive scientists today tend to hold that what goes on in consciousness during the making of creative products involves the same kinds of cognitive strategies we use to solve everyday problems, including metaphorical, analogical, and lateral forms of thinking.[11] Perkins puts it this way:

The ordinary acts of recognition that warn us away from open manholes can, in the right situation, warn us away from pitfalls in problem solving. Acts of recollection that tell us where we last used the pen with the blue cap can, in different circumstances, give us a word of poetry. Such resources are not what makes people creative, but they are what does much of the work of creating.[12]

The roots of ordinary thought (including comparing, contrasting, remembering, inferring, and rule following) also root the kind of thinking that yields creative achievements. And the cognitive appraisals that give rise to emotions in daily life also give rise to affective experiences (including enjoyment) that occur while people are working toward creative outcomes. So, while feelings (and impressionistic musical knowledge) play a role in musical creating, they do not play the dominant role that Romantic theorists maintain.

Contrast this praxial perspective on creativity with the aesthetic view. According to MEAE, the criterion for deeming something creative lies not in a product but in a special process. An achievement is creative, says Reimer, if its creator conforms to a process of exploring and discovering feeling in communion with the aesthetic qualities of a medium.[13] The aesthetic concern is that nothing be allowed to contaminate the subjectivity of creating by interrupting the maker's developing feelings and the developing independence of the maker's chosen medium. In fact, says Reimer, if an artist gets in the way of his feelings by trying to regulate his creating with conscious intent or by trying to achieve something external to the the needs of his developing feelings, "he has violated his art and thereby corrupted it."[14]

In opposition to aesthetic notions, both logic and a wealth of empirical research suggest that creative achievement is not linked to isolable creative abilities, nor is creativity a matter of feelings that are different in kind from those that accompany human thinking of all kinds. Just as there is no such thing as athleticity in the sense of specifically athletic abilities that make a person a great tennis player, there is no such thing as creativity in the sense of specifically creative abilities, sensitivities, or feelings.[15] While creating seems to make use of several kinds of thought patterns, there is no such thing as "*the* creative process." Instead, says Perkins, the cognitive processes involved in producing creative results "can be understood as exceptional versions of familiar mental operations."[16]

5. Foundations of Creative Achievement

If creative achievements are not the result of something called *the* creative personality or *the* creativity capacity or *the* set of creative abilities, what factors enable and promote creativity? In the domain of MUSIC, the answer is: that multidimensional form of knowledge called MUSICIANSHIP.

A proficient or expert level of knowledge in a field both enables and promotes creativity. This theme is echoed in many contemporary philosophical and psychological studies of creativity.[17] Expertise makes it possible for a person to generate and select ideas that have promise for creative achievement.[18] In the actions of composing, arranging, improvising, performing, and conducting, music makers *generate* and *select* musical ideas in terms of syntactic and nonsyntactic rules and strategies, of expressive musical conventions, and/or representational strategies.

Bereiter and Scardamalia suggest that music-making projects may be thought of as large problem-solving efforts that include a whole series of subproblems. Unlike a math problem, however, the overall problem of (say) composing a concerto is not fully specified until the project itself is actually finished, or near completion, because new ideas and solutions alter the relationships among previous and future solutions in a domino effect. It is relatively easy to analyze how the component parts of a composition or improvisation fit together after musical actions are finished. But this is impossible to see in advance because the subproblems and subgoals that need to be solved and met at the outset are emergent: They reveal themselves only in the actions of music making. As Perkins suggests, efforts to achieve creative results require makers to continuously narrow possibilities by adding constraints.[19] For example, every melodic phrase a composer or improviser generates and selects functions as a constraint by influencing the generation and selection of the next melodic phrase. Each choice reduces future choices and, at the same time, activates one's thinking in regard to future choices.

This helps explain why creating does not usually follow a linear path from the identification of a musical project or problem to its solution. Creating is like trying to hit a moving target; new goals and problems are constantly arising in the course of challenging projects. We do not usually know ahead of completion precisely what the intermediate steps or the final outcome of our efforts will be. Instead, the music maker deploys and organizes his or her musicianship by means of what Perkins calls "plans."[20] The term *plans* refers to the working patterns a person follows in rehearsing, composing, and arranging, and all other kinds of musicing. Plans are part of the supervisory and informal knowledge components of musicianship and include self-management strategies, musical imagination processes, and analogical thinking habits.[21] Plans promote both the generation and the selection of promising musical ideas. As Perkins notes, Beethoven's sketchbook was a kind of plan.[22] It was a means Beethoven used to develop, organize, retain, edit, and refine the musical ideas he generated through his extraordinary musicianship. Beethoven did not simply "have" great musical ideas. He worked very hard and often to generate and select new musical themes and designs. And he did so according to his judgments of which musical ideas had the most potential or promise for artistic and creative musical expression within his musical practice.

Another key to creative achievement, then, is problem finding. A proficient level of musicianship not only makes it possible to generate and select musical possibilities, it also alerts us to problems and opportunities that hold the promise of musical significance. Bereiter and Scardamalia suggest that what a proficient practitioner knows how to do includes knowing how to recognize the creative promise of situations that arise in the actions of striving toward creative achievements.[23] Stated differently, the musicianship of creative musicians includes a kind of creative musical "promise detector."

Suppose, for example, that Clara decides to compose a short jazz flute duet in bebop style. Given her proficient level of musicianship in jazz practices, Clara should have little difficulty in generating and selecting a number of melodic ideas and fitting them together harmonically, given time and the guidance of her teacher. Clara should also be able to tell whether her musical ideas are trite, derivative, or original in relation to examples of bebop tunes and arrangements she already knows. But deciding which of her ideas holds the most promise for composing an original duet is a very different matter. Musical creativity pivots on making decisions and predictions about the musical potential or promise of one's musical choices, goals, and subgoals.

Learning to identify and predict musical promise has parallels in many other domains, including learning to read or learning to play a sport. For example, a reader can treat every phrase in a book as equally important. Alternatively, he or she can make predictions about which sentences are most important in the narrative. Similarly, a hockey player skating toward an opposing goalie can treat every moment with the puck as an equal opportunity to score. Alternatively, he or she can look for specific cues in the movements of the goalie that predict the best time and place for him to shoot the puck. Of course, there are no guarantees in making judgments about creative promise. Even people with long histories of creative achievement make choices that do not always fulfill their initial promise.

Students learn to predict and select for musical promise by attempting to find and solve authentic music-making problems that are just beyond their current levels of musicianship. In other words, the process involved in developing one's musicianship from a novice to an expert level is the same process required to develop a "creative musical promise detector." The process is motivated and directed by targeting one's attention toward increasingly challenging musical problems. This upward spiral of difficulty requires learners to set new goals that, in turn, demand higher levels of musicianship. Taking progressively larger steps by setting increasingly challenging goals is what obliges students to deploy and develop their judgments of musical promise.

True, taking larger steps involves risks, because teachers and learners may sometimes fail or become frustrated. But consider this. While small, safe increases in the difficulty of musical works or projects increase musicianship, self-knowledge, and enjoyment, small steps do not increase the likelihood of creative musical achievement, because safe increases in musical complexity do not take students far enough beyond their present levels of musicianship to require judgments of musical promise.

Implicit in this last point is another important educational principle. Enabling and promoting creativity includes helping students to acquire a learning-to-be-creative disposition.[24] Creative achievement requires that one be continuously on the look out for promising musical ideas and plans. This positive, inquiring mindset is another aspect of supervisory musical knowledge. It develops when students are guided and encouraged to reflect in, on, and about the originality, significance, and creative promise of the musical ideas they are generating and selecting. A learning-to-be-creative disposition helps to counteract students' fear of tackling musical projects that are beyond their current level of musicianship. It also helps to neutralize the impatient tendency students often have to "listen ahead" and then write off musical works prematurely on the basis of snap judgments. To the creatively disposed music student, everything is potential grist for the mill of creative music making. Learning to be on the prowl for musical ideas, with an inquiring musical mind-set, encourages students to approach musical works artistically—as models, examples, and lessons in artistic musical achievement, not as autonomous idols of worship.

Music teachers may sometimes misjudge the educational potential of a musical challenge. This may cause some learners to succeed too easily, or not at all, and therefore become musically bored or frustrated. But if music educators never risk setting progressive challenges for their students, music students will have no opportunities to develop the promise detectors they need for creative achievement.

Then again, a practical dilemma of teaching for musical creativity lies in the fact that teachers and students must succeed in meeting their musical goals on a regular basis. Repeated failures do not spawn musicianship, creative achievement, or flow. Here is another reason why music educators require proficient musicianship themselves. Teachers who have achieved creative musical results themselves possess what unmusical teachers do not: creative musical promise detectors. Music teachers who possess a high level of subject-matter knowledge (musicianship) help to ensure the creative development and success of their students because they know where and how to coach their students' efforts to produce creative interpretations, improvisations, and compositions.

In sum, there is little point in trying to promote musical creativity without developing students' musicianship. Musical creativity and musicianship are mutually interdependent and interactive. This does not mean that it is impossible for music students to produce creative musical results until they become experts. Musicianship and musical creativity can and should be developed concurrently. That is, learners who become creative do so because they are regularly required to strive for creative results in the normal course of their musical learning. This is how students' musical promise detectors develop: in concurrent (not consecutive) relation to the development of their musical understanding.

6. Creativity and Imagination

The terms *creativity* and *imagination* are not synonymous. As I explained briefly in Chapters 3 and 4, musical imagination is one aspect of the musicianship a person needs for artistic and creative musical achievement. I now elaborate on this view by revisiting the concept of imagination.

The original meaning of *imagination,* and the first sense we need to consider, refers to envisaging sights and sounds like those we already experience in reality.[25] *Imagining* in this sense includes such covert acts as picturing a far-off place in the mind's eye ("Imagine lying on a Florida beach"), or seeming to hear the doorbell ringing when it really isn't ("I just imagined it!"), or deliberately imagining the sound of a doorbell in one's mind ("Can you imagine a doorbell ringing?").

We might also speak of someone "imagining ghosts" while sitting alone in a dark basement. This sense of *imagining* overlaps with hallucinating, but not dreaming. (The dreams one has while asleep are not imaginings, they are very real to the dreamer.) On the other hand, if a young girl dreams of playing first base for the New York Yankees, then this sense of *dream* might overlap with the first sense of imagining.

Imagining also refers to the ability to envisage actual things or to alter mental images of actual things as a means of solving problems. In this sense, imagining is an important form of nonverbal thinking.[26] Imagination is not a place in the brain; it is another form of covert thinking-in-action. And a person can develop this way of thinking in visual and auditory images. (Again, see Chapters 3 and 4.)

Another sense of imagination refers to the ability to formulate possible things or events that do not yet exist in any concrete form. Sparshott explains this sense of imagination in the following way: "[A]s perception is to the real, so imagination is to the unreal and the possible."[27] Forming images and linking images in the absence of actual events and objects is not merely duplicating the look or sound of something in one's mind, it's a matter of generating and selecting as yet unseen or unheard possibilities.

Imagining can play an important role in musicing and musical creating in several ways. First, when composers and performers have a mental image of a "dark" clarinet tone, they are imagining in the first sense. They have a nonverbal concept (an aural image) of a sound that exists in reality and that they may or may not be able to detail in words. Second, a composer might imagine how a melody will actually sound when scored in alternate ways or how a symphonic movement might sound when some features are emphasized instead of others. Third, musicers might envisage new possibilities by composing, performing, improvising, or conducting in their mind's ear. In this sense, says Sparshott, musicing is an "art of imagination"[28] because music makers envisage new musical possibilities that they know how (and learn how) to realize (or make concrete) in actual sounds.

A person can learn to be musically imaginative in any of these ways. Most often, however, being musically imaginative refers to the process of generating and selecting as yet unsounded musical patterns and designs in one's mind as part of creating a real musical outcome. (In contrast, to be fanciful, whimsical, or "off the wall" is to be imaginative in the sense of envisaging things that may be interesting, but not particularly worthwhile. Imagine that!).[29]

These distinctions help us understand why some people tend to confuse imagining with creating. As I have shown, however, the ideas are distinct. For although I may be able to imagine musical possibilities in my mind's ear, I must also know how to make my musical imaginings into concrete sounds to achieve creative musical results.

In sum, musical imagining is one part of musicianship and, therefore, part of what is required to achieve creative musical results. Musical imagining ought to be developed in its several forms because "inner hearing" is an important aspect of musical thinking-in-action.

7. Creativity in Review

Just as intelligence is considered not one-dimensional but multidimensional, so cognitive scientists no longer speak of individuals as "having creativity" or "being creative'' in any general sense. Intelligence, cognition, knowledge, creativity—all of these are context-specific, or domain-specific. People who achieve creative results do so within specific domains of practice.[30] Looked at head-on, then, the creative person is recognizable as a person who has a high level of practice-specific knowledge and the ability to use this expertise to produce original and significant outcomes in relation to the standards and traditions of a domain. Hence, we speak of creative scientists, and creative architects, creative managers, and creative music makers.

The key to musical creativity lies in the education of a multidimensional form of working understanding called musicianship. Indeed, and again, musicianship is educable. And what about the role of musical intelligence? A high degree of innate musical intelligence may enable a person to become musically creative. But there is no clear evidence that any innate potency promotes musical creativity. That is, says Perkins, "the more intelligent one is, the more one can be, but still may not be, creative."[31] A potency (for example, perfect pitch) may equip a person for making music well, but it does not predict (let alone guarantee) creative musical results. Potencies do not make a person creative; they simply allow the person to be creative if other factors support and encourage it.[32] The most important of these factors is musicianship (which always includes listenership).

Contrary to myth, then, creative products do not arise by accident, or by spontaneous insight, or as a result of unconscious processes. Accidents and so on may be involved in creating, but they are not central or unique to creating.[33] Creative achievements result from know-how, from ideas generated and selected by deliberate choice, by plans continuously altered, by commitments to goals, and by judgments of creative promise. In all of this there is repeated undoing and redoing. Subgoals and subproblems become temporary ends in progress toward a final end product.

A number of studies suggest that the motive force that initiates and drives creative achievement is a desire to search out gaps in what is already known, to advance the way things are done in a practice, or to go beyond what is already understood or accepted.[34] That creativity should be strongly linked to going above and beyond one's current level of ability is exactly what our earlier discussion of musical values suggested (see Chapter 5). That is, the desire to achieve creative results is one with the human drive to differentiate and integrate consciousness by seeking more and more complex challenges. Self-growth, self-knowledge, flow, and self-esteem are the motivations and the payoffs of striving for creative musical results.

I suggest, then, that if creative people share any characteristic in common, it may be the tendency toward self-growth. Several studies suggest that creative individuals have strong inclinations to be self-reliant, independent-minded, self-confident, and self-critical.[35] In addition, the desire to stretch one's self may also promote creative achievement by functioning as a filter or guide in generating, selecting, and judging the creative promise of ideas and solutions.[36]

Clearly, modern thinking does not support the Romantic "explore-and-discover" notion of creating advanced by past music education philosophy.[37] Music makers are not rightly compared to solitary adventurers traveling alone in virgin territory full of chance and accident. A creative musical achievement is neither the

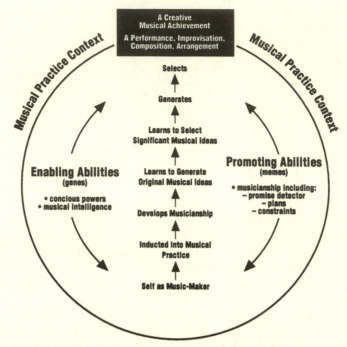

FIGURE 9.2. Musical Creativity in Context

chance discovery of an innocent explorer nor the outcome of an emotional pup-
peteer pulling the strings of a vulnerable musicer-puppet.[38] Musical creating occurs
in the context of well-known histories of effort and achievement. There is wide
agreement among researchers that creating within a specific domain or practice is
a deliberate enterprise that takes time and has many variable phases.[39] A creative
performance, composition, arrangement, or improvisation is the tangible result of
effort expended, expertise deployed, promises realized, and enjoyment felt. Figure
9.2 offers a visual summary of these themes.

8. Music Good and Great

Judging the merit of music making and musical works is a regular feature of music
teaching and learning. Teachers must decide which musical works are best for their
students to perform, listen for, and improvise. On another level, students' self-
growth and enjoyment depend importantly on the feedback we provide about the
quality of their daily music making. But how do we make such judgments? What
considerations are involved? What shall we listen for?

Taken together, the philosophy espoused in this book implies several guidelines
for evaluating musical works. Before explaining and applying these guidelines, let
me review a few obvious points about musical evaluation.

Music teachers, like critics and audiences in general, are concerned with the ongoing pursuit and attainment of musical excellence and creativity, not with deciding the best performances or compositions of all time. As Stephen Davies suggests, the evaluation of musical works aims at a comparative ranking as better or worse, not "best" versus "everything else."[40] Davies continues: "The evaluation of musical works aims to identify those works which are worth knowing and which reward renewed acquaintance, and there is no problem in allowing that many works (and types of works) might so qualify."[41]

This point underlines something I noted in Chapter 8: No musical domain is innately better than any other. Musicing and its outcomes are always practice-specific. Just as it is illogical to debate whether oranges are innately better than apples, it is illogical to debate whether Schubert songs are inherently better than examples of *karnataka sangeeta*. When we talk about the evaluation of music, we are talking about evaluations of works within musical practices, not evaluations of works across different musical practices. Even when we limit ourselves to within-practice evaluations, the point is not to decide the best single piece in that practice (say, the best Romantic symphony ever composed). Musical evaluations are aimed at deciding the comparative excellence of works considered in relation to their relevant traditions. Accordingly, there is little use for the simplistic notion of good and bad music.

Thinking in terms of music education, the sequence of concern is the following: (1) Decide the musical practices you intend to teach, then (2) evaluate the excellence of works within the practice you intend to teach. With these thoughts in mind, let us now consider what guidelines we might follow.

Musical works are the products of musical thinking. To evaluate a musical work is to judge the thoughtful achievement of a music maker and, therefore, his or her level of musicianship. In other words, an excellent musical work will necessarily exhibit a high level of musical thinking, or artistry. In addition, a truly excellent musical work will be creative; it will be original and consequential in relation to similar works within in the same musical domain.

More specifically, evaluating a musical work requires us to judge its artistry and creativity in relation to each and all its relevant dimensions: its design dimension, its cultural-ideological dimension, and, if present, its expressional and representational dimensions. In addition, evaluations are always influenced by the artistry and creativity of the performance-interpretation dimension of a heard musical work. Thus, and because musical works are multidimensional constructions, every work is legitimately evaluated from a number of related perspectives. For example, it is quite possible for a work of film music to be artistically excellent in terms of its syntactic and nonsyntactic parameters, yet weak and unoriginal in the way it characterizes dramatic events in the film. Then again, it is very possible for a composition to be better than the first or second performances it receives. All these matters are (or should be) part of our judgments of musical works.

Implicit in this view is the belief that proper musical evaluations should involve far more than the snap judgments that many music critics pass off on the public as critical musical reviews. A truly critical musical evaluation involves a full appreciation of a work in the several senses I have described—a fully informed consideration of a work's full range of dimensions.

Let me tie this discussion together with one example. Gunther Schuller (a jazz authority by anyone's standards) considers Duke Ellington's *Daybreak Express* "astonishing"—a "superior example of Ellington musical composition."[42] What grounds does Schuller have for his enthusiastic evaluation?

Suppose we have just listened carefully and knowledgeably for Ellington's recorded performance of *Daybreak Express* (1933) two or more times.[43] On this basis,[44] I submit that the compositional design of this work is not only musically expert, its syntactic and nonsyntactic patterns are highly original and significant when compared to similar "big-band" jazz compositions of Ellington's musical time and place.

As I explained in Chapter 6, *Daybreak Express* is also a prime example of representational music. As suggested by the title, the form of this piece is intimately related to its subject matter: a train ride. Is this representational factor relevant to our judgments of musical artistry and creativity in this case? I believe it is. Musical representation is an important dimension of many musical works from many music cultures. (In contrast, the acontextual MEAE philosophy takes the opposite view: "We cannot judge music as good or bad artistically on the basis of functional or referential components."[45]) In the case of *Daybreak Express,* we can and must make Ellington's musical representation of a train ride an important consideration in our judgment of this work's excellence, just as we must judge the representational dimensions of most film music and a great deal of vocal and choral music. Furthermore, this is what Ellington's title promises to deliver. Thus, the excellence of Ellington's composition depends, to a considerable extent, on whether his musical representation of a train ride is derivative or original in relation to other descriptive jazz compositions.

Indeed, at the time Ellington composed this work, there was already a long history of musical representation in jazz. This tradition included many nostalgic references to and representations of train sounds in blues and other African-American musical practices reaching back well into the nineteenth century.[46] Included in this tradition are such compositions as Scott Joplin's *Crush Collision March* and Wesley Wallace's *No. 29.*

Considered in this context, *Daybreak Express* is a highly creative musical representation of what it promises. Schuller agrees: "*Daybreak Express* was a landmark not only as a technical performance tour de force but as a stunning lesson in the capacity of the jazz medium to equal or better anything that was being done in classical program music—and in Ellington's case with an orchestra of only fourteen!"[47]

In addition to the originality and significance of its musical design dimension and musical representations, this work has many syntactic and nonsyntactic patterns (melody, rhythm) that combine to convey musical expressions of exuberance, playfulness, and frivolity.

But what shall we say about the cultural-ideological dimension of this work? Does this dimension have a place in our evaluation? I believe it does. *Daybreak Express* is one of many examples of Ellington's strong interest in musical representation and his efforts to link his artistry with African-American culture. Ellington's many jazz "tone-poems" depend on musical representations of visual, literary, and historical themes to solve the formal problems inherent in organizing long jazz compositions (a musical problem Ellington worked long and hard to solve[48]). A prime example is Ellington's orchestral suite *Black, Brown and Beige* (1943), which Ellington himself described as "a tone-parallel to the history of the American Negro."[49] I suggest that knowledgeable jazz listeners during Ellington's time understood and valued the intermusical and musical-cultural relationships evinced by Ellington's works. Our own awareness of these factors enables us to understand why and how this work involves an important dimension of musical-cultural information and why informed listeners during the 1930s might have listened enjoyably to *Daybreak Express* on several levels. As Schuller notes, Ellington's musical train ride can also be heard as a musical celebration. For it was recorded shortly after the Ellington band completed a path-breaking tour of theaters in the southern United States—one of the first African-American bands to do so.

Of course, it is very possible to perform and listen for this work without understanding its cultural-ideological dimension and its relationship to the practice-specific traditions of 1930s American jazz. But to do so would be to overlook and "under-hear" something significant. For Ellington and his fellow musicians lived at a particular time and place in the history of the American macroculture and made their music in relation to its unique values.

Generalizing from this example, I suggest that these kinds of understandings are an important part of what music students need to learn while learning how to make musical works of various types and practices. These kinds of knowings are best introduced in context while students are attempting to make music artistically and creatively. Also, and because music teachers are involved in music *education*, it is reasonable for us to include educational criteria in our evaluations of musical works. For example, there is no disputing the fact that *Daybreak Express* is a highly artistic and creative work. But for educational purposes, other considerations come into play: Is Ellington's composition appropriate for my students to perform or listen for at this point in the development of their musicianship? If not, why not? If so, why? As well as deciding artistic and creative merit, then, music educators must also consider the educational "rightness" or appropriateness of individual works.

I suggest that a great musical work is one that people with high levels of musicianship consider a landmark achievement within a musical tradition. A great work is one that is exceptionally original and consequential in relation to particular criteria of musical practice. Sparshott supports this view when he suggests that determining musical greatness requires a unified musical tradition such that the history of a musical practice is susceptible to being influenced by the production of such a work.[50] What it also means, says Sparshott, is that performing or listening for a great musical work not only yields profound enjoyment to people with a high level of musicianship but inspires admiration and respect in such listeners.[51] A great work exhibits musicianship and musical creativity to a degree that even most experts will never achieve. Sparshott sums the point: "A great work is one of which we are convinced that no being such as ourselves could ever break through to the level at which such achievements are possible. There really is great music because we are often right about that."[52]

9. Implications for Music Education

The ideas in this chapter imply several principles for the development of musical creativity. First, enabling and promoting musical creativity depends on enabling and promoting musicianship. Thus, developing musical creativity involves all the same principles of music teaching and learning that I have tried to explain to this point in the book: engaging students in authentic musical problems and projects, targeting their surplus attention, setting up progressive problem solving and problem finding situations, and so on. Students also require opportunities to develop creative musical promise detectors in relation to challenges that exceed their current levels of understanding.

Second, the development of musical creativity requires a receptive environment that encourages risk taking and the constructive evaluation of students' efforts to achieve creative results.

Third, we ought to highlight musical "opportunity finding" by involving students in formulating (rather than just carrying out) worthwhile musical projects. By "formulating" projects I mean encouraging students to research and select innovative musical works to perform on their own or in their ensembles; generate multiple approaches to interpretive, improvisational, and/or compositional problems; plan innovative interpretations; generate plans and sketches of musical arrangements; and edit given compositions or arrangements.

Fourth, students should be encouraged to evaluate performances and compositions for their excellence and creativity in all relevant dimensions. In this way, students can develop musical values that will promote their ability to select musical possibilities that have the most creative promise.

Fifth, music education for musical creativity requires sustained periods of time for students to generate, select, rework, and edit their performances, improvisations, interpretations, compositions, or arrangements.

Sixth, we need to avoid undermining our students' motivation and enjoyment by gushing, hovering, or taking over while they work at producing creative musical results. Guiding students toward artistic and creative achievement seems to call for a music teacher-as-coach, adviser, and informed critic, not teacher as proud mother, stern father, or know-it-all big brother.

These principles may be both descriptive and causative of musical creativity. That is, if we step back and imagine the kind of music students that these principles describe, we see music students who participate actively in music making and listening; enjoy developing their musicianship; strive for musical excellence; evaluate musical performances and compositions critically; demonstrate a positive "learning-to-be-creative" disposition; and feel comfortable taking musical risks and testing their judgments of creative musical promise.

Before concluding this chapter, I need to expose a set of implications that lie hidden in the argument that musicing, listening, and musical creativity depend on musicianship. Knowing how to make music well (and knowing how to listen artistically) is neither a gift nor a talent in the sense of an innate ability that some infants are born with and others are not. This needs saying out loud because many people in our society have a special interest in perpetuating the romantic myth of "music-as-talent."

I do not deny that some people may be born with a predisposition to aural stimuli and that some infants may have extraordinary attentional capacities, auditory memory capacities, and knowledge-building capacities. But even extraordinary powers of consciousness and a high level of musical intelligence will not promote the development of musicianship or musical creativity. Proficient music making and creative musical achievement depend on genes *and* memes, on our innate capacities of consciousness and on an acquired form of situated knowledge called musicianship. Musicianship is not an accident of birth. It is not something that some people are born with and others are not. Excluding the presence of congenital deficiencies, every person has the conscious powers necessary to make music and to listen for music competently, if not proficiently. Hence, all children deserve the opportunity to develop musicianship for their own self-growth, self-knowledge, and enjoyment and, quite possibly, for the enjoyment of future audiences who encounter the music making of those among our students who may continue to make music as amateurs or professionals after leaving school.

Although musicianship is a form of knowledge that is applicable to and achievable by the majority of children, some teachers and administrators base their decisions about music curricula on the false assumption that music making is possible and appropriate only for special students; namely, the so-called talented. This assumption taps into a widely shared mind-set in the West that resists any suggestion that musical ability may be a form of intelligence or knowledge. Even scholars, scientists, and well-educated musicians prefer to talk in vague, romantic terms about the talent involved in all instances of music making, while ignoring all the evidence that musicing and listening are cognitive through and through. As Howard Gardner reminds us, the decision to label music a talent instead of an intelligence or a form of knowledge is a matter of cultural beliefs and values, not cognition.[53]

Unfortunately for children, our society's irrational tendency to label music a talent instead of a form of knowledge is politically and financially convenient for many politicians and administrators. Perpetuating the myth of music-as-talent is an effective way to marginalize music and music education in the school curriculum and, therefore, in the lives of most children. To call something a talent is to put it beyond the reach of most mortals. The unexamined association between music and talent causes parents, administrators, and the general public to assume, wrongly, that music is inaccessible, unachievable, and, therefore, an inappropriate or unnecessary subject for the majority of school children. In this way, the talent notion serves a political purpose; it saves public education a great deal of money that would otherwise have to be spent hiring qualified music teachers to teach all children music in the same way that all children are expected to be taught math or reading.

In other words, North American culture (in particular) promotes a hierarchy of school subjects in which literacy and numeracy are deemed matters of intelligence or knowledge because they pivot on verbal thinking and knowing and (perhaps) because business, labor, and political leaders want to promote math, science, and other scholastic subjects that serve the needs of their economic concerns. Indeed, math, science, and English are rarely considered talents but are seen as basic ways of thinking that are accessible, achievable, and applicable to all children.

In sum, the notion of music-as-talent is an effective way of keeping music and music education on the periphery, out of the way of "basic" subjects. The justifications are political and ideological, not rational.

Let me drive these points home with a three-part parallel. No one is born literate. Instead, people are born with the conscious capacities of attention, awareness, and memory that enable them to learn how to think linguistically—to read and write one or more languages competently, if not proficiently. Literacy is achieved through teaching and learning; it is neither a gift nor a talent. True, some people seem to have high levels of linguistic intelligence and high levels of interest in learning to read and write well. These factors may enable such people to develop literacy more deeply and broadly than others. Nevertheless, the vast majority of people have sufficient linguistic intelligence to achieve at least a competent level of literacy through systematic programs of reading and writing education.

No one is born numerate. Instead, people are born with the conscious capacities of attention, awareness, and memory that enable them to learn how to think mathematically—to add, subtract, and divide competently, if not proficiently. Numeracy is achieved through teaching and learning; it is neither a gift nor a talent. True, some people seem to have high levels of mathematical intelligence and high levels of interest in learning to do mathematics well. These factors may enable such people to develop mathematicity more deeply and broadly than others. Nevertheless, the vast majority of people have sufficient mathematical intelligence to attain at least a competent level of numeracy or mathematicity through systematic programs of mathematics education.

No one is born musical. Instead, people are born with the capacities of attention, awareness, and memory that enable them to learn to think musically—to make music and listen for music competently, if not proficiently. Musicianship is achieved through music teaching and learning; it is neither a gift nor a talent. True, some people seem to have high levels of musical intelligence and high levels of interest in learning to make and listen for music well. These factors may enable such people to develop musicianship and musical creativity more deeply and broadly than others. Nevertheless, the vast majority of people have sufficient musical intelligence to achieve at least a competent level of musicianship through systematic programs of music education.

Not everyone who is taught how to read and write can become a Shakespeare or a Robert Frost. But schools still attempt to teach all students to read and write well. Not everyone who is taught math can become an Albert Einstein. But schools still attempt to teach everyone to do math well. Not everyone who is taught music can become (or is expected to become) a Mozart or a Jessye Norman. Nevertheless, all schools should attempt to teach all students to make and listen for music well. For the values inherent in knowing how to make and listen for music intelligently are central to making a life; self-growth, self-knowledge, self-esteem, creative achievement, humanistic and cultural empathy, and enjoyment are central life goals and life values in all human cultures. If these life values are not among the basics of human *being,* nothing else is. Part of our task is to educate parents, colleagues, administrators, and members of the public about what MUSIC is and what it takes to make music well. The artistic, creative, and enjoyable futures of our young people—and the growth of their *selves*—depend on it.

Questions for Discussion and Review

1. Are all human actions creative? If so, why? If not, explain how (or when) to decide whether an action of making or doing also counts as creating.

2. What does it mean to call a product or achievement original? Is it important to consider a product's contextual significance in judging its creative merit? Why?

3. In what ways do creative music makers stand on the shoulders of other musicers past and present?

4. Is a person automatically creative because he or she composes a musical work? Why? Some writers claim that performing can only be "re-creative," not creative. Explain your viewpoint.

5. Select and listen for two contrasting performances-interpretations of the same musical work. Keeping the multidimensional nature of musical works in mind (see Figure 8.1), decide whether one or both of your selected performances count as creative.

6. This chapter contends that while music listening is highly cognitive and constructive, music listening by itself is not a matter of creating. Explain the reasons why you agree or disagree with this view.

7. Distinguish between creativity and spontaneous originality.

8. Does it make sense to claim that creativity is a special mental capacity or emotional sensitivity that a few people are born with and all others are not? Why? Is it likely that feelings direct and control musical creativity? Why?

9. The praxial philosophy argued in this book maintains that musicianship is the key to developing musical creativity. Discuss the reasons underlying this view. What new kinds of knowing does this chapter add to the dimensions of musicianship explained in previous chapters?

10. Distinguish between musical creativity and musical imagination. Explain three ways in which musical imagining can contribute to musical creativity.

11. Summarize the criteria involved in determining the artistic excellence and creativity of a musical work. Apply these criteria to a recorded improvisation of your choice.

12. Explain the importance of a "receptive environment," constructive feedback, and opportunity finding in the education of musical creativity. Outline three other important conditions for the education of musicianship and musical creativity.

Supplementary Sources

D. N. Perkins. *The Mind's Best Work*. Cambridge, Mass.: Harvard University Press, 1981. An engaging and incisive discussion of creativity.

Carl Bereiter and Marlene Scardamalia. *Surpassing Ourselves: An Inquiry into the Nature and Implications of Expertise*. La Salle, Ill.: Open Court Publishing, 1993. Chapter 5, "Creative Expertise," supports and expands upon several concepts explained in this chapter.

Sharon Bailin. *Achieving Extraordinary Ends: An Essay on Creativity*. Boston: Kluwer Academic Publishers, 1988. Bailin places skill, in the sense of know-how, at the center of creative achievement.

V. A. Howard. *Learning By All Means: Lessons From the Arts*. New York: Peter Lang, 1992. Chapter 3, "Expression as Hands On Construction," explains why creative expression depends on directed, disciplined effort.

Robert J. Sternberg, ed. *The Nature of Creativity: Contemporary Psychological Perspectives*. New York: Cambridge University Press, 1988. This collection of essays examines many aspects of creativity from many viewpoints.

D. N. Perkins. "Creativity and the Quest for Mechanism." In *The Psychology of Human Thought,* ed. Robert J. Sternberg and Edward E. Smith, pp. 309–36. New York: Cambridge University Press, 1988. An analysis of the relationships between cognition and creativity.

III

MUSIC TEACHING AND LEARNING

10

Music Education and Curriculum

Music Matters has attempted to develop a philosophy that explains the nature and significance of music education. In the process, this book has also attempted to outline several basic principles of music teaching and learning.

The next main question is this: How can music educators organize music programs in ways that are congruent with the nature and values of MUSIC as a diverse human practice?

Implicit in this praxial philosophy is a distinctive concept of curriculum for music teaching and learning. Chapters 10 and 11 make this concept explicit. To anticipate, the central theme of these next two chapters is that *all* music education programs (general music programs and otherwise) ought to be organized and taught as reflective musical practicums.[1] Of course, the precise details of each music curriculum-as-practicum will differ according to local circumstances. Nevertheless, this philosophy holds that achieving the values and aims of music education depends on designing, maintaining, and operating music teaching-learning situations in relation to several connected principles encapsulated by the term *reflective musical practicum.*

The second half of this chapter explains why the practicum concept of curriculum is congruent with the nature and significance of MUSIC and, more broadly, with the thrust of contemporary research in curriculum development and developmental psychology. The discussion then proceeds to detail the nature of the reflective musical practicum.

To prepare the way for this discussion, in the first half of this chapter I scrutinize several common beliefs about the nature of curriculum and curriculum making. Since MUSIC is distinctly different from scholastic subjects, it would be imprudent to assume from the outset that the curriculum-making procedures commonly used in science, history, or mathematics education are automatically appropriate for music education. Indeed, as I argue, many conventional ideas about curriculum making are problematic for (if not inimical to) teaching and learning in general and music education in particular. Thus, and for the sake of MUSIC education, it is imperative that we probe curriculum doctrine and rethink the concept of curriculum development from the ground up.

1. The Concept of Curriculum

Curriculum derives from the Latin word *currere* ("to run"). In ancient times, curriculum meant several things, including a running, a race, a course to be followed, a race course, and a career. Cicero extended these early senses of curriculum to include the time frame in which events occur and the things people select to fill their time.[2] Indeed, the kinds of things one might ask about the course of a race (e.g., "How long is it?," "What obstacles does it present?") extend naturally to the kinds of questions one might ask about the course of a person's education (e.g., "How long does it take?," "What should it contain?"[3]).

For most of the last two thousand years, *curriculum* has been synonymous with *content*. The main question asked by educators in ancient, medieval, and early modern times was "What information should be taught?" Once decided, educators then asked, "What is the best way to organize this content?" The answers to questions of how to teach were largely taken for granted. The prevailing assumption about teaching and learning was that students learned content in one way: through a teacher's lectures. This idea began to change in the eighteenth century. By 1900, *how* began to overtake *what* as the central curriculum concern.[4] Kieran Egan explains the consequences of this shift: "The emphasis on the question *how,* as distinct from *what,* led to focusing on the individual learner as an important variable. Thus individual differences, in styles of learning, ability to learn, developmental stages, interests, socioeconomic background, and so on, had to be taken into account before one could begin to specify *what* the curriculum should contain."[5]

Today, *curriculum* is defined in many ways, depending on which aspects of the teaching-learning process a curriculum theorist decides to emphasize. To some, curriculum still means a course of study. But to most theorists, curriculum is a much more elaborate (or multidimensional) phenomenon, because the *what* of education cannot be realistically decided apart from the *why* and the *who* and because matters of *when* and *how* inevitably circle around to teachers' decisions about *why, who,* and *what.*

The following excerpts from well-known texts sample the range of thinking about the nature of curriculum.

A curriculum is a plan for learning. . . . (Taba, 1962[6])

[Curriculum is:] All the experiences a learner has under the guidance of the school. (Foshay and Beilin, 1969[7])

[Curriculum is:] The planned and guided learning experiences and intended learning outcomes, formulated through the systematic reconstruction of knowledge and experience, under the auspices of the school, for the learner's continuous and willful growth in personal-social competence. (Tanner and Tanner, 1975[8])

[C]urriculum is an explicitly and implicitly intentional set of interactions designed to facilitate learning and development and to impose meaning on experience. The explicit intentions usually are expressed in the written curricula and in courses of study; the implicit intentions are found in the "hidden curriculum," by which we mean the roles and norms that underlie interactions in the school. (Miller and Seller, 1985[9])

Many (if not most) books on education consider curriculum as consisting of experiences or the activities that engender these experiences. But this usage confuses curriculum with instruction. A more precise view of curriculum—and the common understanding of curriculum among laypeople—is that it is what is taught in school or what is intended to be learned. (Posner and Rudnitsky, 1986[10])

[Curriculum is:] The total set of stimuli deliberately brought to bear during a designated time period, with the intention of nurturing or producing student learning. (Robinson, Ross, and White, 1985[11])

In theory, then, there are several different concepts of curriculum from which to choose. But this is not the case in practice. We can summarize the reason for this in the following way. Until lately, the field of curriculum has been analogous to a situation in which a group of car designers (curriculum theorists) agree in principle that cars (curricula) can and should take a variety of forms, depending on their intended uses. Unfortunately, these designers have then proceeded to make all cars the same for everyone according to one car-making procedure.

Since the 1950s, one curriculum-making procedure has monopolized the thinking of scholars and teachers alike. It is called technical-rational curriculum making,[12] or the Tyler rationale (after its author, Ralph Tyler). The Tylerian procedure has dominated curriculum development to the point that it has become synonymous with curriculum itself.[13]

2. Conventional Curriculum Making

Tyler maintains that curriculum making should follow a four-step, linear process: (1) state the objectives (or ends) of learning in specific terms; (2) select learning activities (or means) in relation to one's objectives; (3) organize learning activities in relation to objectives; and (4) develop means of evaluation in relation to one's objectives. In this view, it is essential that objectives "describe or illustrate the kind of behavior the student is expected to acquire so that one could recognize such behavior if he saw it."[14] Tyler also recommends that curriculum designers select a type of organizing element (e.g., behaviors or verbal concepts) to sequence teaching and learning. Tyler's aim was to offer a highly rationalized or scientific way of designing curricula to meet the overall purpose of education, that is, to bring about "significant changes in the student's patterns of behavior."[15]

Following the publication of Tyler's *Basic Principles of Curriculum and Instruction* (1949), curriculum development intensified and expanded. At the same time, and throughout the post-Sputnik curriculum reform movement of the 1960s and 1970s, curriculum theorists became consumed with reverence for science in general and behavioral psychology in particular. Because Tyler's simple, linear procedure fit the simple, mechanistic notions of behavioral psychology, curriculum theorists quickly revamped Tyler's four-step procedure in behaviorist terms.[16] Curriculum making was reduced to specifying vast numbers of atomistic behavioral objectives in fastidious verbal detail.[17] Some curriculum theorists still advocate behavioral versions of the Tylerian approach.

A softer variation on Tyler's scheme emerged in the 1960s. Instead of beginning with behavioral objectives, some curriculum theorists began stating objectives in terms of verbal concepts about the structure of their subject domains, or disciplines. The structure-of-disciplines approach to curriculum making (advocated by Jerome Bruner, Philip Phenix, and others) was based on the assumption that every subject has a foundational pattern of verbal concepts that, when understood by teachers and students, enables all other aspects of that subject domain to fall into place. This idea had two other implications: (1) curricula ought to be sequenced according to verbal concepts about a subject's inherent structure, and (2) subject-matter experts (not teachers) should take responsibility for deciding the structure of each subject and stating instructional objectives for teachers and students to follow.

Separately, and in combination, the Tylerian concept and the structure-of-disciplines approach resulted in a steady stream of "teacher-proof" curricula that continues to flow to the present day. The majority of educational theory texts, government curriculum guides, and commercial subject curricula published in North America since the 1950s are behavioral and/or verbal concept variations on Tyler's objectives-based approach.

The same holds in music education. Behavioral versions of the Tylerian model have been widely produced and adopted by music education theorists.[18] The use of behavioral objectives has influenced music education profoundly. In consequence, as Abeles, Hoffer, and Klotman point out, a large number of state and local school districts provide lists of behavioral objectives as guides for music programs, despite some backlash among music teachers.[19] In addition, many music curricula combine variations on Tyler's formula with the structure-of-disciplines approach. Examples of the latter include general music texts based on the aesthetic philosophy (including Reimer's *Silver Burdett Music* [20]) that organize lessons and units in terms of verbal concepts about the so-called elements, processes, and styles of musical works.

In summary, many music education theorists in the past have been persuaded that the technical-rational procedures traditionally used in scholastic curriculum making are entirely appropriate for music curriculum development. Moreover, says Reimer, to become a "basic" subject, music must become a "genuine" curriculum by conforming to "the principles of curriculum development guiding all basic subjects."[21]

3. Against Conventional Curriculum Making

On the surface, the objectives-based approach is persuasive. Teaching is an intentional activity. Teachers and learners require direction. An objective is intentional. It directs teachers to future outcomes. And it does so in a highly determinate way.

In the jargon of curriculum theory, the term *objective* usually indicates an exceedingly specific level of intention (or target) compared to a moderately definite *goal*, or a broad *aim*. In addition, Tyler suggests a plausible way of deciding specific objectives by determining student, community, and subject-matter characteristics. Moreover, Tyler's linear approach is comforting in the way it cuts through the everyday complexities of teaching and learning. In technical-rational fashion, Tyler-type curricula follow a simple, one-way path from theory (ends) to practice (means).

All this makes sense as far as it goes. But it does not go very far. A number of philosophers and curriculum theorists, including Joseph Schwab, Lawrence Stenhouse, Wilfred Carr, Stephen Kemmis, F. Michael Connelly, and Shirley Grundy, offer compelling arguments against the Tyler doctrine and the mentality of technical rationality that underlies its many variations. From the standpoint of music education, there are four main problems with conventional curriculum making.

First, technical-rational curricula rest on a mechanistic concept of teaching. The teacher is viewed as someone who solves well-formed problems (ends) by applying "scientific" theories of teaching and learning (means).[22] The underlying assumption is that educational ends and means are separate and that knowing is different from doing. In this view, teaching is a matter of "interpreting" a prepackaged script and then delivering the product (a curriculum) to consumers (students) as efficiently as possible. (What we need, says Reimer, is "expert applications of a solid curriculum."[23]) Teachers are viewed as educational retailers who "sell" the received wisdom of subject matter specialists to students by means of step-by-step scripts. This belief in means-ends solutions through scientific research is what Jurgen Habermas originally called "technical rationality."[24]

Second, the prime motivation of curricula organized around behaviors and verbal concepts is control. The chief means of control is objectives. Notice the root association of this word with *objects*. Conventional curriculum making conceives of the learning environment as an object to be managed from afar by preprogramming the "behaviors" of students and teachers.[25] Requiring teachers to compose ultra-specific objectives and implement step-by-step lesson plans is an effective way to "manage" teaching toward a simplistic end point: a change in a learner's behavior.[26] The goal is not knowledge, nor growth, nor enjoyment, but the achievement of reductionistic objectives.

Michael Apple's description of an objectives-based (and "teacher-proof") science curriculum applies equally to many general music texts past and present: "The material specifies all of the goals. It includes everything a teacher 'needs' to teach, has the pedagogical steps a teacher must take to reach these goals already built in, and has the evaluation mechanisms built into it as well.... Not only does it prespecify nearly all a teacher should know, say, and do, but it often lays out the appropriate student responses as well."[27]

Conventional curriculum making conceives of a curriculum as something outside the teacher, outside the learner, and outside the learning environment. Objectives-based curricula transform teachers into managers whose main task is to control classroom behavior while students receive the teacher's interpretation of an expert's wisdom. As teachers surrender curriculum making to technical-rational procedures, teaching is reduced to acting out scripts and managing information. The ultimate effect of technical-rational curricula is to deprofessionalize teachers.

Third, conventional curriculum making assumes, falsely, that all knowledge in all fields can be reduced to some kind of verbal description. The task of the teacher is to subdivide the content of his or her subject into verbal concepts and/or verbally specified behaviors. Why does technical rationality place a premium on verbal specification? Why do objectives-based curricula fail to distinguish among various kinds of thinking and knowing? They do so because technical rationality is hopelessly dualistic. Traditional curriculum theory tends to assume that the mind is "mental" (and therefore intelligent) and that the body is physical (and therefore dumb). In this view, subject domains that pivot on procedural knowledge (including music, dance, and physical education) are not taken seriously unless (or until) they become "genuine" curricula. As we now understand, becoming a "genuine" curriculum means negating the procedural essence of music, dance, and athletics by reducing these knowledge domains to simplistic verbal objectives and concepts.[28]

Many general music texts look "educational" in the pseudo-scientific sense that their organization is linear and propositional. In the process of hopping from concept to concept across pieces and styles, however, these curricula negate what is most needed to develop musicianship: continuous and active immersion in meeting significant musical challenges in the contexts of authentic music cultures. In their zeal to control students and teachers by specifying everything in words, conventional curriculum makers fracture music programs into ersatz activities that have little relation to what musical artists and artistic music listeners actually do. Teachers and students are reduced to chasing isolated objectives and identifying structural fragments in recorded examples that curriculum developers have selected to "illustrate" verbal concepts about "aesthetic qualities." The resultant teaching-learning situation is musically phony; it is "school music" in the most contrived sense of the term.

Traditional curriculum making is oblivious to a fundamental reality of MUSIC and MUSIC education: that the procedural essence of musicianship is epistemologically prior to verbal conceptualization.[29] Brown, Collins, and Duguid explain the problem this way: "Teaching methods often try to impart abstract concepts as fixed, well-defined, independent entities that can be explored in prototypical examples and textbook exercises. But such exemplification cannot provide the important insights into either the culture or the authentic activities of members of that culture that learners need."[30]

These thoughts bring us to the fourth failure of conventional curriculum making: the structure-of-disciplines notion. Recall that the "disciplines" notion assumes that all subject domains have an inherent structure that can be identified, broken down, specified, and organized in relation to verbal concepts. During the 1970s and 1980s, aesthetic educators adopted the structure-of-disciplines model wholly and uncritically and applied it vigorously to general music curriculum development.[31] Many general music teachers continue to assume that the most appropriate way to organize lessons and units is to use verbal concepts about "elements, processes, and styles" of musical works. Indeed, Reimer still maintains that "concepts *about* music" are "the best tools we have for creating manageable curricula."[32]

As the curriculum scholars and historians Daniel Tanner and Laurel Tanner emphasize,[33] mainstream curriculum theorists discarded these assumptions in the mid-1970s after early advocates (including Bruner himself) acknowledged serious mistakes in the disciplines notion and retreated from the idea.[34]

First, the pivotal claim of the structure-of-disciplines approach rests on a false assumption. For there is little evidence that any subject has an inherent structure. As the curriculum scholar William Schubert notes, apart from a few basics, even experts in mathematics and science education have failed to agree on what constitutes the structure of their disciplines.[35] The philosopher Clive Beck puts the problem in perspective: "[T]here is no such thing as the logical structure of a subject. A subject, like a barn, has many structures at once. Different experts are aware of different fundamental principles and have different mental processes for conjuring up principles and concepts and for bringing them to bear on problems. They even use different principles to solve the same problems. There is no one set of topics and no one order in which topics should come to mind. In learning, the most we should be concerned with is to have a . . . working understanding."[36]

It is not the case that MUSIC reduces to a collection of objects that can be neatly broken down and packaged in terms of verbal concepts about their formal structures. MUSIC is a human practice, and all musical practices depend on a form of knowledge called musicianship that is procedural in essence. One dimension of musicianship is propositional. And while verbal concepts (and other types of formal knowledge) about musical design properties are useful in parenthetical relation to artistic musicing and listening, their use as curriculum organizers misrepresents the nature and significance of MUSIC. As I have argued in earlier chapters, concepts about structural design elements are not the core knowledge of MUSIC. And learning to perceive and react to so-called aesthetic qualities does not begin to address the nature of music listenership, let alone musicianship. In sum, the MEAE assumption that the structure of music (all music everywhere) is equivalent to the formal elements of musical works (in the nineteenth-century aesthetic sense) is hopelessly simplistic and ethnocentric.

Interestingly, Keith Swanwick also opposes the use of verbal concepts as curriculum organizers. For one thing, says Swanwick, verbal concepts about the formal properties of musical works encourage teachers to substitute verbal generalizations for musical experiences.[37] For another, "they only pick up fragments of the total experience." Swanwick continues:

> A danger with "concepts" is that we tend to work from them and to them, looking for music which exemplifies their characteristics. This can diminish whatever prospect there may be for musical encounters in classrooms, as though music was merely an illustration of something else. So I might choose to rehearse a song because it demonstrated the concept of "changing meter," whereas the only good reasons for choosing anything are that it has musical potential . . . and is within the vocal and emotional range of the students.[38]

There is yet another problem. The structure-of-disciplines idea derives from a primary concern for scientific disciplines. As Arthur Efland points out,[39] a scientific discipline conceives its content as an object of inquiry, as something outside the learner that he or she tries to understand through verbal thinking. Thus, and not surprisingly, when the scientific structure-of-disciplines approach is applied to music education curricula, the educational emphasis shifts (wrongly) from active participation in artistic music making to the passive consumption of preformed objects. As Tanner and Tanner point out, one of the most unfortunate legacies of the structure-of-disciplines idea was that it led teachers in many fields (including music education) to imitate math and science educators in their search for *the* structure of their discipline. As a result, emphasis was given to "abstracting puristic concepts and neglecting . . . performance in such areas as music."[40]

Indeed, since the 1970s, aesthetic educators have labored to shift general music curricula away from authentic music making and toward record-centered listening programs and "multi-arts" curricula on the false assumption that performing is inadequate as the primary mode of musical involvement for general music students.[41] I have already argued that past music education philosophy fails to understand the nature and significance of music making (especially performing) and that performing and improvising deserve a central place in all music education curricula.

What needs attention now is yet another fallacious claim of MEAE: that "the arts" can and should be integrated (or taught together). Indeed, the multi-arts idea is invalid. It takes several flawed assumptions to the extreme. Thus, and not surprisingly, the multi-arts idea has also taken music education to the brink of extinction in many school systems.

Politically speaking, it makes sense for music teachers to join with colleagues in the other performing and nonperforming arts to gain support for artistic endeavors in public schooling. Musically speaking, it is true that many musical practices worldwide combine music and dance, music and poetry, or music and drama. In these cases, the relationships between music making and dance, poetry, and drama are an important part of what specific practices and works present for our understanding and enjoyment. These relationships are part of the cultural-ideological dimension of listening and listenables. Accordingly, to learn how to make and listen for musical works that involve other artistic practices requires reference to the whole web of beliefs, concepts, traditions, and standards that explain how certain musicers and listeners understand the contribution that other performing and nonperforming arts make to their music cultures.

For example, in music cultures where music and dance are intimately related, musicianship, self-growth, and enjoyment depend on going more and more deeply into the music-dance relationship. All such learning and teaching is *situated:* to learn the musicianship of a musical practice that involves other artistic processes and products (e.g., Dagomba drumming and dancing), a music student must enter into that music culture by making the music of that community.

What I have just outlined is very different from the notion variously called multi-arts education, integrated arts, teaching-the-arts-together, general arts, combined arts, or Aesthetic Education. The assumption underlying the latter is that different arts (painting, music, dance, poetry) can and should be taught together.

This assumption is not only philosophically invalid, it is practically and politically counterproductive.

First, multi-arts approaches rest on the claims of the eighteenth-century aesthetic concept that each performing and nonperforming art is essentially a collection of autonomous objects. By focusing on the aesthetic qualities of these objects (e.g., paintings, poems), students are supposed to improve something called "aesthetic sensitivity" and gain insight into "feeling." I have already explained the logical failures of these basic claims (see Chapter 2). It is only necessary to point out now that multi-arts approaches extend all the theoretical mistakes and misconceptions of the aesthetic ideology to all other artistic endeavors.

Second, merely becoming aware of the elements of one kind of artistic product will not give an understanding of other kinds of artistic outcomes, let alone an understanding of other artistic practices. For each performing and nonperforming art is a specific kind of human practice that rests upon an independent form of situated thinking and knowing. Hence, each kind of artistic knowing needs to be taught and learned in its own context through active involvement in artistic making. Musicianship, for example, involves an entirely different kind of cognition than the knowing required to understand visual art, dance, or poetry. Learning to notice the qualities of visual textures in paintings will not advance one's ability to compose, improvise, or listen for musical textures anymore than learning to watch hockey will help a person understand cricket. The development of musicianship depends on inducting children into musical practices and on targeting their conscious powers on progressively more subtle aspects and dimensions of musical works. Neither condition is present when the attention of learners is being directed to nonmusical matters such as balance and focus in painting or gesture in dance. True, it is possible for a music maker to rethink musically ideas originally presented in other arts or to incorporate these ideas in his music making. But to do so first requires musicianship.

Consider, also, that Aesthetic Education rests on another questionable assumption. It assumes the existence of a general capacity called *aesthetic sensitivity* that supposedly improves with awareness of the "aesthetic elements" of things: visual art, sunsets, flowers, forests, musical sounds, bird songs, or whatever. But as David Best explains:

> the notion [of aesthetic sensitivity] seems to be of a faculty which can be developed in any of these ways, rather as a muscle may be developed by various forms of exercise.
>
> The conception only needs to be spelled out as explicitly as this to be revealed as absurd. For . . . it could surely never be seriously supposed that increasing a child's awareness of the aesthetic quality of a gymnast will ipso facto increase his (her) capacity for the appreciation of poetry or music, or that to develop an understanding of one art-form will necessarily give an understanding of others.[42]

Indeed, it is highly doubtful that there is any such general capacity as aesthetic sensitivity. Multiple intelligence theories and contemporary studies of creativity argue against the possibility. In short, to understand and enjoy music requires a specific kind of situated cognition that will not develop from the study of elements or issues across different kinds of artistic practices. For these contexts are, by definition, not musical.

Politically and practically speaking, to perpetuate the false notion that music is being taught and learned in the context of multi-arts classes is to hasten the demise of school music programs. For as soon as administrators suppose that music is being taught and learned along with all the other arts, or that something called aesthetic sensitivity exists and can be developed by teaching any art whatever, then music educators will become dispensable and music education will be removed from the program. In fact, many directors and supervisors of music education have been replaced with "fine art" consultants, many school music teachers have been replaced with "interdisciplinary arts" teachers, and numerous music education programs have been replaced by multi-arts courses. True, some music education theorists advocate general arts classes only as additions to "single-arts learnings." But this slight compromise does not alter the logical failures of the idea, let alone its negative results.

Fortunately, Aesthetic Education has been successfully resisted by many more teachers and administrators. Stanley Madeja, one of the original leaders of the Aesthetic Education Program, admits that his efforts to introduce multi-arts programs during the 1970s encountered great resistance from teachers, especially those educated as music specialists and visual art specialists.[43] Moreover, Madeja found that many school administrators were unwilling to implement multi-arts programs because of the "tremendous support base from parents for a performance-oriented music program or a studio-based art program within their schools."[44]

Madeja implies that multi-arts programs failed to take hold in American schools partly because of the misunderstandings of teachers, parents, and administrators.[45] In Madeja's view, educators and parents failed to understand that teaching the arts together during the formative years of elementary school is "more palatable and conceptually sound than the individual-discipline-oriented curriculum in the schools."[46]

I suggest the opposite. I suggest that many music educators, administrators, students, and parents grasped a key idea (informally and formally) that many educational theorists still fail to understand: that musicianship (and the knowledge involved in every other kind of artistic pursuit) is domain-specific. Thus, multi-arts approaches are philosophically, artistically, developmentally, and practically unsound. The same holds for the use of verbal concepts and behavioral objectives as means of organizing music curricula. I shall propose an alternative to past notions in a moment. Before doing so, however, there is one more related aspect of this topic to consider.

4. Teachers and Curriculum Making

One important finding of studies of teacher decision making and planning is that expert teachers tend *not* to use the objectives-based model of curriculum planning that is most often taught during pre-service teacher education.[47] The same holds for curriculum development teams. "In fact," say Walker and Soltis, "many curriculum groups never stated objectives at all; and those that did generally did so near the end of their work, as a way of expressing their purpose to teachers, rather than at the beginning, as the fundamental starting point of their work."[48]

John Dewey anticipated these findings decades ago when he emphasized that educational objectives are not the prespecifications of learning, but rather, the outcomes of teaching-learning interactions.[49] Objectives emerge in and achieve specification only during teaching-learning transactions. Teachers are not mind readers. We cannot anticipate precisely how our students' thinking and knowing will fit with their previous thinking and knowing. Some learning (perhaps a great deal) is not fully acquired or integrated until some time after it is introduced.

Research on teaching also suggests that teachers' informal mental preparations tend to be far more complex and important to their professional practices than written plans.[50] To prepare, many teachers seem to engage in a reflective conversation with themselves and others about a wide range of variables, including subject matter knowledge, resources and materials, students' abilities, lesson aims and goals, teaching strategies, and evaluation procedures. In other words, a teacher's decisions about the *why, what,* and *how* of teaching and learning cannot be realistically separated from questions of *who, when,* and *where.* Accordingly, preparation and planning processes are idiosyncratic; there is no predominant way of preparing and planning for teaching-learning situations.[51]

These reflections highlight several other characteristics of teaching that conventional curriculum making either negates or misses altogether. Most important, perhaps, technical rationality fails to appreciate that teaching is a matter of intentional thinking-in-action. As Allen Pearson says in *The Teacher,* "when someone is teaching, he or she has the purpose, goal or intention of getting someone to learn something."[52] What characterizes professional teaching is the centrality of thoughtful actions directed toward bringing about learning. This intention not only distinguishes the actions of teaching from other kinds of action, it also creates specific kinds of "intentional situations."[53] Put another way, because teaching occurs not in isolation but in relation to students, a teacher's knowledge-in-action is what gives meaning to the teaching-learning situation. Indeed, a teacher's intentional actions depend fundamentally (though not exclusively) on his or her subject matter knowledge. (I say "not exclusively" because the fluid and unpredictable qualities of teaching situations invariably modify a teacher's intentions and knowings-in-action in one way or another.)

What we realize, then, is that *teaching expertise is fundamentally procedural and situational.* The dynamics of the teaching-learning situation inform a teacher's actions as much as a teacher's actions shape the teaching-learning situation. Conventional concepts of curriculum fail to understand that many of the key problems teachers must solve do not reveal themselves before a lesson begins. Teaching is fuzzy this way. In many circumstances, teachers must find and frame teaching-learning problems during their interactions with students. This helps to explain why it is very possible to have a great deal of formal knowledge about education, and ultra-specific lesson scripts, and still not be able to teach well, let alone expertly.

To possess teaching expertise is to possess a working understanding of teaching-learning situations. The word *working* emphasizes the practical, situated, and improvisatory nature of teaching. From this perspective, expert teaching is much closer to improvising over "changes"[54] than rendering an accurate reading of a score (a step-by-step lesson plan). Teachers "trade" feedback with students in a kind of call-response pattern characteristic of jazz improvising. An expert music teacher, like an excellent improviser, deals with moment-to-moment problems and opportunities on the fly. These problems and opportunities are both musical and educational in nature. The professional music educator is well prepared to solve musical and educational problems in action because he or she possesses two complementary forms of expertise: musicianship and educatorship.

Musicianship is the subject matter knowledge one must possess to be a professional music educator. A teacher cannot form the intention for students to learn something if he or she has no knowledge or beliefs about what students should learn. The greater a teacher's musicianship, the more he or she can enable and promote the musicianship and the musical creativity of music students. The music educator's educational expertise is highly tuned to the nature of musical practices, musical works, musical values, and music students.

Educatorship is another kind of working understanding. It is not a skill, nor a habit, nor a knack, nor a science, nor a collection of facts about educational psychology or philosophy. Educatorship is the flexible, situated knowledge that allows one to think-in-action in relation to students' needs, subject matter criteria, community needs, and the professional standards that apply to each of these. Professional teaching standards exhibit themselves in a teacher's judgments about the kinds of knowing that are most appropriate or desirable for students to learn and the kinds of teaching strategies that are most appropriate to use in helping students develop these knowings. Music teachers are not merely intermediaries in an educational delivery system. They are reflective practitioners who can think-in-action and know-in-action in relation to highly complex and fluid teaching-learning situations.

Unfortunately, there will always be those who claim to be music educators but who lack the subject matter knowledge (musicianship) to warrant their claim. To accommodate (or justify) their lack of musicianship, musically uneducated teachers frequently reduce music teaching and learning to little more than verbal memory work, bogus "activities," or spurious "appreciation lessons" designed to entertain and placate students. Also not surprisingly, there will always be publishers who (knowingly and unknowingly) contribute to unmusical education by producing teacher-proof curricula designed not to educate music students but to prop up unqualified teachers. Attempts to reform music education through glossy, teacher-proof curricula doom music students and the future of music education by aiding and abetting such unmusical teaching.

These remonstrations are not news. The Music Educators National Conference has made its own position clear on these matters on several occasions, especially with respect to the staffing of general music programs at the elementary school level. It should be clear why the praxial philosophy proposed in this book endorses the following:

> [T]he Music Educators National Conference takes the following position: . . . that satisfactory instructional leadership can best be provided by specialists. A specialist

may be defined as a skilled teacher whose preparation includes substantial work in music leading to those competencies that have been suggested by the MENC Commission on Teacher Education. This would include the person who has a music education degree as well as one who may have a strong minor or second major in music.[55]

Perhaps we should say, then, that the most important long-term goal of the music education profession is not only music for every child, but more accurately, *musical* teachers for children everywhere.

Expert teachers in many domains of education, including mathematics and reading,[56] are now recognizing what expert music educators have long understood: that there is a basic lack of fit between conventional ideas of curriculum making and the realities of teaching and learning. Conventional curriculum making errs in placing too much emphasis on the verbal specification of teaching plans and too little emphasis on the procedural and situational nature of teaching. An increasing number of contemporary curriculum theorists are beginning to acknowledge the cyclical and interactive nature of teaching and learning. For the most part, however, little has changed in the curriculum-making procedures of most subject domains (including music education) for several decades. Most efforts in curriculum making continue to perpetuate the acontextual, impersonal, and dualistic notions of technical rationality and the structure-of-disciplines. Accordingly, there are good reasons to believe that conventional curriculum making is problematic for (if not hostile to) the essential nature of music, education, and the processes of preparing and planning for music teaching and learning.

5. An Alternative Concept of Curriculum Making

Music educators require a systematic way of bringing order to the plurality of problems that swirl around music teaching and learning while maintaining a flexible, personal, and situational stance. But if conventional notions of curriculum development are problematic, how can we approach the process in ways that are more in tune with the nature and values of music, teaching, and music education?

Since the 1970s, several scholars and teachers have proposed alternatives. One of these, called practical curriculum inquiry,[57] has its roots in the writings of pragmatic philosophers such as Charles Pierce, George Herbert Mead, and John Dewey and educational scholars such as William H. Kilpatrick, Joseph Schwab, and William Reid.

How does practical curriculum making differ from conventional procedures? Recall that older theory directs teachers either to follow or to develop curricula by looking outside themselves and their situations. Teachers have been instructed (or obliged) to follow a universal set of inflexible, step-by-step procedures. In contrast, advocates of practical curriculum inquiry urge teachers to look to themselves and their own teaching circumstances. As Joseph Schwab suggests, decisions in matters of curriculum, like decisions in matters of job choice and spouse choice, involve a variety of factors related to particular people, places, and things.[58] These decisions call for back-and-forth reflection and deliberation, but they do not require the application of universal and linear theories of curriculum determination any more than spouse choice requires a universal, step-by-step theory of spouse determination.

Practical curriculum making holds that the most important solutions to curriculum problems will not be found in highly specific written plans or the abstract conjuring of curriculum theorists. Solutions will be found, instead, in the professional reflections and judgments of individual teachers engaged in specific teaching-learning situations. Practical curriculum making holds that the best curricula arise when teachers focus on their own circumstances, rather than on the generic scripts of theorists and publishers who tend to see similarities across teaching situations that cannot be grouped together defensibly in reality. The interests of practical curriculum making lie in shifting away from the technical-rational notion of teachers as curriculum retailers or interpreters to teachers as reflective practitioners; away from the specification of acontextual objectives to the organization of situated knowledge; away from highly specific verbal concepts and scripts to situated preparations and plans; and away from measurement and testing to assessment and evaluation. In sum, and in opposition to curriculum doctrine, practical curriculum making places the teacher-as-reflective-practitioner at the center of curriculum development.

6. Curriculum Commonplaces

A useful approach to organizing and resolving the problems of curriculum making begins with Aristotle's *Topica*.[59] Aristotle suggested that when people encounter a problem that involves a number of considerations and competing views, it is useful to develop a set of flexible topics or categories that describe the problem realistically while making allowances for competing ideas. In line with this approach, it seems reasonable to suggest that virtually all teaching-learning situations involve a basic set of variables, topics, or "curriculum commonplaces." Joseph Schwab was one of the first to posit the idea of curriculum commonplaces as a curriculum-making strategy.[60] The following list expands Schwab's original set of commonplaces.

- Aims
- Knowledge
- Learners
- Teaching-learning processes
- Teacher(s)
- Evaluation
- Learning context

These factors are "commonplaces" in the sense that they appear in all teaching-learning situations and in all discussions of curriculum making. We cannot escape them. A comprehensive curriculum must resolve the problems presented by each commonplace and by the interactions that occur between and among them. (Of course, if teachers or curriculum development teams have good reasons to add to or subtract from this set, they should do so.)

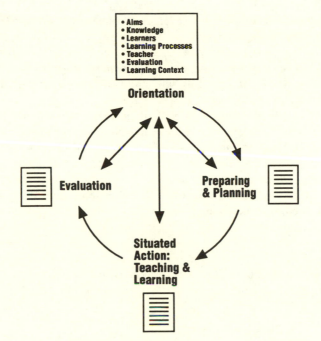

FIGURE 10.1. Music Curriculum Making: A Four-Stage View

Curriculum commonplaces are open categories; they remain empty until filled in by each teacher's beliefs, understandings, intentions, and actions. In other words, there are as many different ways to conceptualize these commonplaces as there are philosophies, theories of educational psychology, or ideologies.

What a teacher believes and does in relation to the commonplaces before, during, and after each teaching-learning episode shapes the educational experiences of learners in a specific teaching-learning situation. One word for "specific teaching-learning situation" is *curriculum*. Following Connelly and Clandinin, I propose that a curriculum, at root, is something that teachers and learners experience in particular situations as a result of the interactions between and among curriculum commonplaces.[61]

7. Music Curriculum Making

When combined with the concept of curriculum commonplaces, the above themes suggest a systematic yet context-sensitive approach to music curriculum development. The diagram in Figure 10.1 summarizes this book's approach to music curriculum making.

As pictured in Figure 10.1, the curriculum-making procedure involves moving from general curricular decisions to specific decisions-in-action (and back again) in a four-stage process. Each stage involves making curricular decisions by reflecting back and forth about the same seven commonplaces as an overlapping set of concerns. In this view, curriculum making is interactive (not linear), context-dependent (not abstract), and flexible (not rule-bound). Practical curriculum making has a realistic quality to it because each stage requires teachers to make decisions about the same set of concerns they will ultimately encounter and decide in the teaching-learning situation itself.

More specifically, the curriculum-making process suggested here takes the following form. Music educators (or music curriculum teams): (1) orient themselves to the music teaching-learning situation; (2) prepare and plan music teaching and learning in relation to their orientations and their individual teaching situations; (3) teach by thinking-in-action in relation to their orientations, preparations, plans, and the contextual demands of their own teaching situations; and (4) evaluate the first three stages of curriculum making.

8. Four Stages of Curriculum Making

Stage One: Orientation

Developing a music education curriculum begins by developing critically reasoned perspectives on each of the seven curriculum commonplaces and their interrelations. This requires teachers (or curriculum development teams) to think critically and comprehensively about the nature and values of music and music education. In other words, laying the foundations of a music curriculum involves cycling back and forth between one's philosophy of music education and the questions raised by each commonplace. In addition, other relevant sources can and should be consulted as needed (e.g., child development research, educational psychology) to supplement one's philosophical position on each commonplace. Among the questions to be answered in the orientation stage are the following.

- What are the aims of music education?
- What do these aims mean in relation to the knowings that music involves?
- What is the nature of the knowledge I am trying to teach?
- What teaching-learning processes are involved in developing this knowledge?
- How should I think about my role as a music educator?
- How should I conceive the roles and responsibilities of music students?
- What means of assessment and evaluation shall I use?
- What is the most appropriate teaching-learning context for music education?

As music educators clarify their views on each of the curriculum commonplaces, an image of the teaching-learning context begins to form. (Indeed, imagining the music curriculum-in-action is an important and legitimate part of decision making in the first stages of music curriculum development.) The process is analogous to the way the big picture begins to emerge as the pieces of a puzzle gradually fit together. The decisions made in the orientation stage sum to an overall concept of the music curriculum-in-action.

Stage Two: Preparation and Planning

This stage requires curriculum makers to apply the conclusions of Stage One to their own circumstances. The goal of this stage is to make concrete decisions for short-term and long-term teaching and learning. Once again, the task involves decision making in relation to the entire set of commonplaces. Aims need to be translated into short-term and long-term goals, and decisions must be made about the musical knowledge to be learned by specific students in specific situations.

Making decisions at this stage of curriculum making involves both preparing and planning. Preparation seeks a general framework for future action and expects diverse responses, surprises, and shifting objectives-in-action. It also recognizes the undesirability and impossibility of trying to nail down every uncertainty in advance. "Preparation," says Robert Yinger, "leans toward participation and responsiveness."[62]

Preparing for teaching tends to be more general and nonverbal than planning. Teachers prepare by forming mental images of themselves operating in future teaching-learning situations, sketching personal narratives of their impending interactions with students, mentally rehearsing specific teaching strategies, and making lists of materials and resources.

Planning, in contrast, is more formal. The focus of planning is on constraint; it tends to pull us back from future teaching-learning situations; whereas preparation tends to draw us toward them.[63] Planning seeks to defend against uncertainty by stipulating actions and outcomes in words.[64] Accordingly, plans often provide confidence and security for novice teachers. Writing or reading lesson plans in advance of teaching episodes can help some teachers establish priorities and feel organized. By writing things down, some teachers may also feel more committed to making sure that what is written will be covered in a week, a month, or a year.

In the end, however, ultra-specific verbal plans or scripts run contrary to the nature and value of teaching. Highly detailed plans are neither necessary nor sufficient for excellent teaching. Teaching is a reflective practice; excellent teaching is evidenced by the educational effectiveness of a teacher's actions, interactions, and transactions with students. In terms of an earlier comparison, a written plan is to teaching as chord changes are to a jazz improviser. Requiring teachers to write ultra-specific behavioral objectives and lesson scripts is analogous to demanding that jazz improvisers explain every detail of their impending improvisations in words before they begin to perform. The demand is unreasonable. In essence (and in the end), teaching (like improvising) is a matter of artistic knowing-in-action, not mechanical reproduction. Like improvisers, music educators engaged in specific teaching-learning situations exhibit their musical and educational expertise in relation to highly complex contexts that have their own tempos, rhythms, designs, and expressions of emotion.

In the present view, a music educator's professional plans (short-term and long-term) for music teaching and learning need only summarize the essential features of each commonplace (goals, knowledge, learning processes) at a moderate level of written detail. Moment-to-moment instructional objectives arise *in* the actions

of teaching and learning. The transactions and interactions of teaching and learning
are far richer and more complex than words can ever capture. Of course, if a teacher
finds it helpful to write excessively detailed plans, then he or she should do so;
then again, some teachers may find it more useful to write a summary lesson plan
after their teaching-learning episodes are complete. In this way, a teacher may grow
and plan by reflecting *on* his or her thinking-in-action after the fact. Such self-
reflections can often serve to register the wisdom of one's decisions and actions
for future reference and revision.

In practice, some teachers may have no choice but to produce extremely detailed curriculum documents (called *political* curricula) for principals, headmasters,
superintendents, or school boards who want "proof" that "education" will occur
(or has taken place) at a given time. Clearly, the assumption that a written plan
will provide such guarantees is false. Indeed, lesson plans are neither guarantees
nor binding contracts where students are concerned. Hence, teachers will ultimately
be guided by what they think, know, and decide *during* their interactions with
students.

In sum, it is essential to remind ourselves what preparing and planning are
meant to get us ready for. To Robert Yinger, the most appropriate image of teaching
comes from the root sense of the word itself: "to show, or to demonstrate."[65] This
helps us place our professional energy where it belongs: not on written plans but
on designing particular kinds of teaching-learning contexts in which particular
kinds of actions, transactions, and interactions can take place productively and
enjoyably. This is what one-dimensional, linear plans cannot capture or enable.

Stage Three: Teaching and Learning

We said that a curriculum, at heart, is something that teachers and students experience together in particular teaching-learning situations. Accordingly (and obviously), the teaching-learning stage is the most important stage of the
curriculum-making process; it is where the commonplaces interact as human
entities.

Put another way, it is because individual teachers and students put their personal
stamps on the educational aims, subject matter knowledge, teaching processes,
learning processes, and assessment procedures (and so on) that teaching, learning,
and curricula are highly fluid and unpredictable. The decisions that teachers make
in the first two stages of curriculum making can and do determine the nature and
values of the teaching-learning stage in fundamental ways. In the end, however,
an excellent curriculum is an excellent *teacher* interacting with students in educationally sound ways.

Stage Four: Evaluation

In the early part of this century, curriculum evaluation concentrated on measuring
student achievement in relation to highly specific objectives. When students failed

to achieve the intended objectives, the fault was assumed to lie with the students, not with the curriculum. This narrow notion of curriculum evaluation is still alive today. Many curriculum evaluation procedures still depend on standardized test scores alone. These data are used to compare the achievement of students across different locations and situations, with each situation controlled as much as possible.

In contrast to this acontextual view of curriculum evaluation, many curriculum theorists recommend more holistic and humanistic approaches.[66] Educators are urged to view curriculum evaluation as a means of improving and renewing the teaching-learning process by taking all the curriculum commonplaces into consideration. This is the view of curriculum evaluation I endorse and that I explain later in Chapter 11.

9. The Praxial Music Curriculum

It is time to connect this book's philosophy of music education with each of the stages of curriculum making outlined above. In doing so, I hope to explain more definitely what this philosophy means for the practical realities of music teaching and learning. The next and last section of this chapter focuses on the orientation stage. With this foundation in place, Chapter 11 continues by explaining (in general terms) what this praxial philosophy means for short- and long-term preparation and planning, music teaching and learning, and music curriculum evaluation.

10. Stage One: A Praxial Orientation

By "filling" each of the commonplaces with the central tenets of this philosophy, we arrive at a praxial orientation to (or rationale for) the music education curriculum. The upshot of this orientation is an overall concept of the music curriculum-in-action.

In addressing each of the seven commonplaces, I offer a tight summary of this book's key proposals and draw upon supporting arguments from the literature of developmental psychology and curriculum theory to enhance my main proposals.

• *Aims.* Self-growth, self-knowledge, and flow are the central values of MUSIC and, therefore, the central aims of music education. These values and aims are also the primary and practical *goals* of each and every teaching episode. They are accessible, achievable, and applicable to all students, providing that musical knowledge is developed progressively and in balanced relation to authentic musical challenges. To the extent that these aims and goals are achieved, music education will most likely contribute to the development of students' self-esteem and self-identity.

• *Knowledge.* What knowledge is most worth learning by *all* music students? This philosophy's answer is clear: *musicianship*. Musicianship is the key to achieving the values, aims, and goals of music education. Musicianship, which includes listenership, is a rich form of procedural knowledge that draws upon four other kinds of musical knowing in surrounding and supporting ways. Musicianship is context-sensitive, or situated: that is, the precise nature and content of musicianship differs from musical practice to practice, and musicianship develops through progressive musical problem solving in teaching-learning environments designed as close likenesses of real music cultures.

Although verbal concepts contribute to the development of musicianship, formal musical knowledge is secondary to procedural knowledge in music education. Howard Gardner supports this view when he argues that in a domain such as music, formal knowledge (or "talk" about music) is "an ancillary form of knowledge, not to be taken as a substitute for 'thinking' and 'problem solving' in the medium itself."[67] Although most children are capable of grasping considerable amounts of formal knowledge about musicing and listening, formal knowledge should not be acquired without integral relationship to students' active and authentic music making. The special kind of nonverbal knowing-in-action required for artistic music making is easily overwhelmed by the emphasis schooling tends to place on verbal knowledge. In short, music education programs must not become just one more situation for the development of verbal knowing-that.[68] Gardner agrees: "[I]t is my belief that artistic forms of knowledge and expression are less sequential, more holistic and organic, than other forms of knowing, . . . and that to attempt to fragment them and to break them into separate concepts or subdisciplines is especially risky."[69]

• *Learners.* Musicianship is not something given by nature to some children and not to others. Musicianship is a form of thinking and knowing that is educable and applicable to all. Accordingly, all music students ought to be taught in the same essential way: as reflective musical practitioners, or musical apprentices. Put another way, the best music curriculum for the best music students is the best curriculum for all music students: a music curriculum based on artistic musicing and listening through performing and improvising in particular, and composing, arranging, and conducting whenever these are possible and relevant. Gardner concurs with the thrust of this position: "[I]n the arts, production ought to lie at the center of any artistic experience. Understanding involves a mastery of the productive practices in a domain or discipline, coupled with the capacity to adopt different stances toward the work, among them the stances of audience member, critic, performer, and maker."[70]

Because all music education programs share the same aims, all music education programs ought to provide the same basic conditions for achieving these aims: (1) genuine musical challenges and (2) the musicianship to meet these challenges through competent, proficient, and artistic music making. What will differ between and among music education programs across grade levels and school regions is not the essential content of the music curriculum (musicianship) but the kinds and levels of musical challenges inherent in the curriculum materials chosen for (and, perhaps, with the cooperation of) one's own students. In addition, music programs will differ in the kinds of music-making media (e.g., wind instruments, voices, string instruments, electronic instruments) chosen for (or with) one's students.

This praxial view of music students holds across early, middle, and secondary school programs. In agreement with Gardner's views, I believe that the early school years are a time when ''youngsters are capable of mastering techniques and styles; of learning more difficult approaches . . . ; and of becoming involved in apprentice-type relations, where they can acquire various kinds of skill and lore in a more natural kind of setting.''[71] This window of music teaching and learning opportunities must not be lost or sacrificed for the sake of listening to recorded music or acquiring formal knowledge. To the extent that historical data, ersatz activities, or recordings come to dominate the music curriculum, the development of musicianship in the young music maker will be nipped in the bud.[72]

The same applies to students at the middle school and secondary school levels. Just because older students may have more facility with verbal concepts does not mean that general music programs at the middle, junior high, and secondary level should shift their focus from music making to historical, theoretical, or listening-based ''appreciation'' programs. A continuing emphasis on reflective musical practice through active music making is still more desirable at these ages than a scholastic approach or a listening-centered approach based on recordings. Tanner and Tanner agree:

> [J]ustification for the separation between appreciating and creating smacks of the medieval dualism of mind and matter, thought and action—a dualism that runs counter to human development and experience. . . . [W]hen performance is deprecated in favor of appreciation, it is doubtful that adolescents will gain the level of appreciation expected. For they are denied the opportunity of concretely engaging in the act of doing, or making, or creating. Such separation would appear to mitigate against appreciation as a function of general education.[73]

While acknowledging that older students can benefit from purely historical and analytical studies, Gardner emphasizes that *''these topics are less crucial for most students than the possibility of continuing active involvement in the arts as reflective practitioners.* There will be time enough in university, and beyond, for these more 'distanced' forms of artistic appreciation to become dominant.''[74]

• *Learning processes.* Music education is not only concerned with developing musicianship and musical creativity in the present. An essential part of our task is to teach students how to continue developing their musicianship in the future. This philosophy has suggested that the process of developing musicianship is a particular kind of learning process that students can both engage in and learn how to employ themselves. I have argued that the growth of musical understanding depends fundamentally on progressive musical problem solving, problem finding, and musical problem reduction. These processes require that students learn how to target their surplus attention on more and more subtle aspects of the musical challenges they are attempting to meet. Achieving proficient and expert levels of musicianship also involves learning to reflect critically on the creative musical promise of the musical ideas one generates and selects.

Implicit in all these processes is the broader requirement that all music students be engaged in rich and challenging music-making projects in classroom situations that are deliberately organized as close parallels to true musical practices. In this kind of authentic, action-based learning environment, procedural, formal, informal, impressionistic, and supervisory musical knowings can be developed most naturally through performing, improvising, and conducting and, if time allows, composing and arranging. (In the many cases where moving is an integral part of musicing or listening, movement ought to receive an appropriate emphasis.)

Unfortunately, while composing has received considerable curricular attention since the 1970s, student projects in arranging and conducting have been largely overlooked. Both forms of musicing deserve more attention from researchers and teachers alike. For one thing, while arranging involves many of the same kinds of thinking and knowing as composing, the positive constraints of working within the pre-established boundaries of given works makes arranging more realistic than composing for many students and teachers. Arranging also offers a natural and logical bridge to the considerable challenges involved in generating and selecting the musical ideas required to produce original compositions. Gardner reinforces these principles from a developmental perspective: ''[S]tudents learn effectively when they are engaged by rich and meaningful projects; when their artistic learning is anchored in artistic production; when there is an easy commerce among the various forms of knowing . . . ; and when students have ample opportunity to reflect on their progress.''[75]

• *The Teacher*. The music educator's professional knowledge is diagrammed in Figure 10.2.

Musicianship and educatorship are interdependent; one without the other is insufficient. To teach music effectively, a teacher must possess, embody, and exemplify musicianship. This is how children develop musicianship themselves—not through telling, but through their actions, transactions, and interactions with musically proficient and expert teachers; ''it is imperative to have a cadre of teachers who themselves 'embody' the knowledge that they are expected to teach.''[76]

The second major aspect of a music teacher's expertise is what I have already referred to as educatorship. Excellent teaching is evidence of a distinct form of procedural knowledge that, in turn, draws upon several other kinds of educational knowledge, including formal, informal, impressionistic, and supervisory *educational* knowledge.

Formal educational knowledge includes such familiar areas of scholarship as music education philosophy, educational psychology, curriculum theory, and child development theory. Teaching and learning are sufficiently complex that formal knowledge must be consulted at various times during one's advancement as a music teacher. Verbal concepts about education can influence, guide, shape, and refine a teacher's intentions before, during, and after teaching-learning episodes. By itself, however, theoretical knowledge about teaching and learning is inert. This knowledge ought to be viewed critically, as a continuously growing and changing source of suggestions for improving the reliability of one's thinking-in-action as a teacher.

Informal educational knowledge represents what the expert music educator takes to be obvious about teaching a specific group of students at various points in their musical development. The most important source of informal educational knowledge is active problem solving in authentic teaching-learning situations. (Hence the importance of practice teaching and viable pre-service field experiences.) Of course, informal educational knowledge may also develop to some extent from one's personal modifications of textbook knowledge about various aspects of

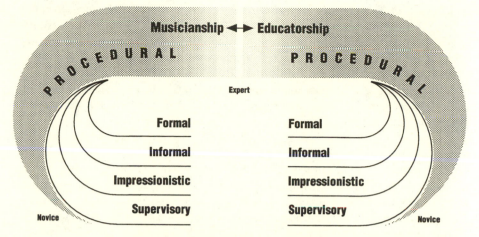

FIGURE 10.2. The Professional Music Educator

teaching and learning. But in the real world of music teaching, music educators must know how to make moment-to-moment predictions, judgments, and decisions in action.

In addition to possessing formal and informal educational knowledge, expert music teachers often ''feel'' what is best to do or to avoid. I call this impressionistic educational knowledge. This kind of knowing is essentially a matter of cognitive emotions. The emotions that underpin impressionistic educational knowledge are cognitive in so far as they rest on a teacher's past and present beliefs about characteristic aspects of teaching and learning that he or she has experienced. Accordingly, impressionistic educational knowledge is also situated. It is a nonverbal, affective form of knowing that develops through reflecting-in-action in genuine teaching situations. Impressionistic knowledge makes an essential contribution to a teacher's thinking-in-action because it facilitates the ability to assess, categorize, ''time,'' and ''place'' one's teaching actions. It plays a crucial role in expediting strategic judgments in action. Here again, practice teaching episodes carried out with the guidance and feedback of master teachers are the chief means of developing this situated form of knowing.

Finally, supervisory educational knowledge is the component of educatorship that informs the deployment of all other kinds of educational knowing-in-action. It is a matter of disposition: of knowing-to, knowing-when-to, and knowing-whether-to. Perhaps the most important part of a music teacher's supervisory educational knowledge is his or her *valuing* of artistic standards and traditions. Musical standards in music teachers beget musical standards in students:

> Teachers need to embody a concern with high standards; even as they support the efforts of their students, they must help these students bear in mind the importance of care, revision, reflection, discipline, regular self-examination, and sharing reactions with others. . . .Taken together, such practices can help to bring about a community in which every member cares about quality and standards—the most important catalyst in bringing about such standards.[77]

Clearly, educatorship is not learned from lectures and textbooks alone. Becoming an excellent music teacher depends heavily on learning to reflect *in* one's efforts to bring the musicianship of one's students into matching relationship with appropriate musical challenges. For this to occur, novice music teachers require music education professors who can model musicianship and educatorship through their own vivid examples. Teacher education programs ought to be organized deliberately to prepare future artist-teachers through excellent models of teaching and artistic musical materials.[78]

• *Evaluation.* There is a distinction between evaluation and assessment. The assessment of student achievement gathers information that can benefit students directly in the form of constructive feedback. Assessment also provides useful data to teachers, parents, and the surrounding educational community.[79] Building on the accumulated results of continuous assessments, evaluation is primarily concerned with grading, ranking, and other summary procedures for purposes of student promotion and curriculum evaluation.

Achieving the aims of music education depends on assessment. The primary function of assessment in music education is not to determine grades but to provide accurate feedback to students about the quality of their growing musicianship. Learners need constructive feedback about why, when, and how they are meeting musical challenges (or not) in relation to standards and traditions. As I explained in Chapter 5, feedback is important to keep students in the ''flow channel'' of self-growth and enjoyment.

Students must also learn how to assess their own musical thinking-in-action by learning what counts as competent, proficient, expert, and creative music making. To become knowledgeable and independent judges of musical excellence and creativity, students need regular opportunities to reflect on the results of their musicianship and that of their peers. It follows from this that assessment is the joint responsibility of teachers and students.

Conceived of as constructive feedback, assessments of musical achievement can be communicated via coaching, cueing, correcting, advising, discussing, modeling, approving, disapproving, and encouraging. Assessing is a natural aspect of progressive musical problem solving; it occurs continuously during the transactions of teaching and learning. It is (or should be) embedded in the processes of learning to make excellent music well as part of an ensemble and on one's own.

Musicianship cannot be assessed adequately by focusing on the results of a student's individual thinking at one moment in time.[80] The quality and development of a learner's musical thinking is something that emerges gradually. It reveals itself in the intersection of several conditions: (1) the opportunity to make music in the context of (2) an authentic musical situation that, by definition, surrounds the student with (3) musical peers, goals, and standards that serve to guide and support the student's thinking.

Unlike traditional testing, then, assessment is not a matter of two or three special events that occur outside the normal stream of teaching and learning. Assessment functions to support and advance achievement over time.[81] When learners receive regular feedback, assessment and evaluation become comfortable aspects of enjoyable learning experiences.[82]

Because musicianship differs substantially from the kinds of verbal knowledge taught in scholastic settings, there is no justification for using standardized tests in music. There is some justification for paper-and-pencil tests and for written assignments about the formal knowledge component of musicianship. Overall, however, conventional methods of evaluation are inappropriate in music education because they rely too heavily upon linguistic thinking. To be "intelligence-fair," says Gardner, assessment must be targeted directly at the student's artistic thinking-in-action. We must look at musicianship through a musical window, not a linguistic one.[83]

Lyle Davidson reminds us of a related problem.[84] Traditional notions of curriculum and evaluation tend to alternate periods of instruction with pauses for testing. Traditional procedures require teachers to freeze the teaching-learning process to examine student achievement in "stop time" and out of context. As a result, says Davidson, too little of what the student has been learning is being evaluated and too little (if any) part of the normal context of teaching and learning is taken into account.[85] Such evaluations therefore tend to misrepresent both the nature of musicianship and the musical achievements of learners.

Indeed, and more broadly, some studies indicate that even experts may fail on formal, out-of-context tests of their capacities.[86] When evaluated in the normal situations of their work, these same experts exhibit the precise thinking needed.

In musical terms, then, the true nature of a student's musicianship is unlikely to demonstrate itself reliably in the absence of appropriate contextual cues. And an essential contextual cue for many students is the ensemble context in which music teaching and learning regularly take place. As Gardner points out, different kinds of know-how are contextual in the larger sense that the knowledge needed to do something well may be distributed among people in a situation.[87] Expertise is often a team accomplishment, rather than being completely resident in the mind of one person. Thus, as experienced teachers already know, more can often be achieved by a group of music students in a chorus or an instrumental ensemble than could possibly be done by one student in the ensemble: "[S]uccessful performance of a task may depend upon a team of individuals, no single one of whom possesses all of the necessary expertise but all of whom, working together, are able to accomplish a task in a reliable way."[88]

A further word is in order about the concept of benchmarks. By "musical benchmarks" I mean excellent examples of musical thinking-in-action. Musical benchmarks can take many forms, including audio and video recordings of student performances (improvisations, composition workshops, rehearsals) and live concerts by visiting students from other classes or schools. Used wisely, musical benchmarks can assist in assessing and evaluating music students and music programs by comparing "local" results with relevant benchmarks that a school music program might reasonably be expected to achieve.

I hasten to add, however, that benchmarks should not be used to enforce rigid codes of universal behavior and achievement. In my view, benchmarks are best selected and used as inspiring models of musicianship that students can reasonably strive toward during a given period of time. Benchmark musical accomplishments should be used not as "laws" but as guideposts along the way to higher levels of achievement.

Viewed in broader terms, benchmarks provide an effective means of linking music students who are pursuing the same (or similar) musical challenges across different classes, schools, regions, and countries. (It is also possible to make such links via noncompetitive and competitive music festivals.) This kind of networking helps to induct music students (conceived of as reflective musical apprentices) into music cultures by connecting them with other experts and peer practitioners.

• *Learning context.* I suggested earlier in this chapter that a picture of the music curriculum-in-action begins to emerge toward the end of the orientation stage as teachers clarify their philosophical perspectives on each curriculum commonplace. The praxial curriculum centers on achieving self-growth and musical enjoyment in the thoughtful actions of artistic music making. Teachers and students work together to meet the musical challenges involved in realistic musical projects through reflective musical performing with frequent opportunities for related forms of music making. Music listening is directed, first, to the music being made by students themselves. Each musical work that students are learning to interpret and perform (improvise, arrange, and so on) is approached as a "full-course meal"—as a multidimensional challenge to be made artistically and listened for intelligently in all its relevant dimensions (interpretive, structural, cultural, representative, expressional). In support of artistic listening-in-context, carefully selected recordings are introduced parenthetically, in direct relation to the musical practices students are being inducted into. Similarly, formal musical knowledge is filtered into the continuous stream of authentic music making and listening as needed.

The praxial music curriculum is deliberately organized to engage learners in musical actions, transactions, and interactions that closely parallel real music cultures. The praxial curriculum immerses students in music-making projects that require them to draw upon the criteria, traditions, lore, landmark achievements, "languages," and creative strategies of the musical worlds of which their projects are a part.

From this perspective, the music teaching-learning environment is, itself, a key element in the music education enterprise. The musical actions of learners are enabled and promoted by the interactive, goal-directed swirl of questions, issues, and knowings that develop around students' efforts as reflective artistic practitioners. The praxial curriculum is, itself, informative.

In sum, when small and large performing ensembles are developed and carried out in relation to the principles I have outlined, and when performing is supplemented with improvising, composing, arranging, and conducting projects, then the music classroom becomes a reflective musical practicum, a close representation of viable music-practice situations, or music cultures. The life-like practicum context feeds back to students by revealing what counts artistically in their developing musicianship and their musical achievements.

By treating all music students (including "general" music students) as apprentice musical practitioners and by teaching all students how to find and solve musical problems in "conversation" with ongoing musical practices, music educators situate students' musical thinking and knowing. In doing so, the different kinds of knowing involved in musicianship develop and cohere. Gardner's perspective provides further support for this philosophy's emphasis on providing an artistic curriculum-as-practicum for all music students:

When students encounter the various forms of knowing operating together in a natural situation; when they see accomplished adult masters moving back and forth spontaneously among these forms; when they are themselves engaged in rich and engaging projects, which call upon a variety of modes of representation; when they have the opportunity to interact and communicate with individuals who evidence complementary forms of learning—these are the situations that facilitate a proper alignment among the various forms of knowledge.[89]

The first stage of curriculum making is complete. The result of this orientation stage can be summed in one phrase: curriculum-as-*praxis*. This praxial philosophy of music education holds that all music education programs ought to be conceived, organized, and carried out as reflective musical practicums.

Questions for Discussion and Review

1. Explain the roots of the term *curriculum*. Compare and contrast three definitions of curriculum listed in this chapter or in curriculum texts of your choice.

2. Explain the basic steps involved in technical-rational (or Tylerian) curriculum making. Locate and scrutinize examples of behavioral objectives-based music curricula. Summarize the strengths and weaknesses of this approach to music curriculum development.

3. What basic assumptions underpin the structure-of-disciplines approach to curriculum? Locate and scrutinize examples of music curricula based on the structure-of-disciplines model. Discuss the strengths and weaknesses of this approach to curriculum making.

4. Explain the term *teacher-proof curriculum*. In what ways do conventional approaches to curriculum misunderstand and deprofessionalize teachers and teaching?

5. Explain the concept of teaching as reflective action. Summarize the concept of educatorship. Do music educators require additional forms of knowing beyond musicianship and educatorship (as described here)? If so, what forms of knowing would you add?

6. Discuss this philosophy's insistence that school music programs be taught by musically qualified teachers (i.e., teachers who have achieved a proficient level of subject matter knowledge, or musicianship).

7. What differentiates practical curriculum inquiry from conventional forms of curriculum making? (Include an explanation of "curriculum commonplaces.")

8. This chapter posits a four-stage process of music curriculum making. Provide a synopsis of each stage.

9. This chapter ends by reviewing several main themes of this book's praxial philosophy in relation to seven curriculum commonplaces. In your own words,

state the most important points this philosophy makes in regard to each common-place.

Supplementary Sources

Kieran Egan. "What is Curriculum?" *Curriculum Inquiry* 8, no. 1 (1978): 65–72. A succinct introduction to curriculum.

David J. Elliott. "Rethinking Music Teacher Education." *Journal of Music Teacher Education* 2, no. 1 (Fall 1992): 6–15. A synthesis of several ideas explained in this chapter.

F. Michael Connelly and D. Jean Clandinin. *Teachers as Curriculum Planners*. New York: Teachers College Press, 1988. A critical alternative to conventional curriculum making.

Howard Gardner. *The Unschooled Mind*. New York: Basic Books, 1991. A critical perspective on the present weaknesses and future possibilities of schooling.

Renee T. Clift, W. Robert Houston, and Marleen C. Pugach, eds. *Encouraging Reflective Practice in Education*. New York: Teachers College Press, 1990. This collection of essays examines the nature of teaching as a reflective practice. Several essays offer criticisms of and alternatives to conventional curriculum making.

Lizabeth B. Wing. "Curriculum and Its Study." In *Handbook of Research on Music Teaching and Learning,* ed. Richard Colwell, pp. 196–217. New York: Schirmer Books, 1992. An extensive discussion of many important aspects of curriculum related to music education.

11

Music Teaching and Learning

How can music teachers organize music teaching and learning in ways that are true to the nature and values of MUSIC? The previous chapter ended by proposing that all music curricula ought to be organized and implemented as reflective musical practicums. The most reasonable and effective way to develop the musicianship of all music students is to structure music teaching situations as judicious models of genuine musical practices. Before discussing the next three stages of music curriculum making, let us consider the practicum concept of curriculum in broader perspective.

1. The Reflective Musical Practicum

The practicum concept of curriculum has its roots in that ancient model of education called the ''apprenticeship.'' The reflective practicum builds upon and refines several characteristics of the mentor-apprentice relationship that grounded teaching and learning in earlier times. Collins, Brown, and Newman elaborate:

> Only in the last century, and only in industrialized nations, has formal schooling emerged as a widespread method of educating the young. Before schools appeared, apprenticeship was the most common means of learning and was used to transmit the knowledge required for expert practice in fields from painting and sculpting to medicine and law. Even today, many complex and important skills, such as those required for language use and social interaction, are learned informally through apprenticeship-like methods—that is, methods not involving didactic teaching, but observation, coaching, and successive approximation.
>
> The differences between formal schooling and apprenticeship methods are many, but for our purposes, one is most important. . . . In apprenticeship learning, . . . target skills are not only continually in use by skilled practitioners, but are instrumental to the accomplishment of meaningful tasks. Said differently, apprenticeship embeds the learning of skills and knowledge in their social and functional context. . . .[1]
>
> Apprenticeship is the way we learn most naturally.[2]

The music curriculum-as-practicum is meant to *approximate* authentic music cultures. It does not attempt to duplicate real-world practices, because the aim of music education is not to educate all students for careers as professional musicians. The curricular goal is to organize music classrooms and programs as effectively and genuinely as possible by simulating the ways in which musicing and listening are carried out by artistic musical practitioners. As Donald Schön says, the practicum is a "virtual world."[3] The practicum retains the essence of actual musical practices while relieving many of the real-world pressures, risks, and distractions that could otherwise disrupt or discourage the novice. The engine that drives the practicum is productive thinking-in-action. Music students enter into a mentor-apprentice relationship with musically proficient teachers who shape the actions and interactions of the musical practicum in relation to the knowings, values, standards, and histories of carefully chosen music cultures. Schön summarizes this "induction process" and underlines a central theme of this book: "When someone learns a practice, he [or she] is initiated into the traditions of a community of practitioners and the practice world they inhabit. He learns their conventions, constraints, languages, and appreciative systems, their repertoire of exemplars, systematic knowledge, and patterns of knowing-in-action."[4]

One of the most important educational features of the curriculum-as-practicum is that it contextualizes or situates learning. The practicum is a knowledge-building community that actualizes concepts authentically so that students not only learn comprehensively, they learn *how* to learn. When teachers place productive musical actions at the center of the music curriculum, students experience the practicality of several related forms of musical knowing immediately and regularly. Students witness the reasons underlying musical procedures, criteria, and concepts and grasp these reasons concretely.[5] As Gardner points out, the practicum context is an effective learning environment because different kinds of knowing are invoked and exemplified precisely when they are needed, "rather than at some arbitrary location in a lecture, text, or syllabus"[6] or at some arbitrary location in a teacher-proof text. Students observe first-hand how their musical thinking (and the thinking of their teachers and peers) solves and reduces musical problems (or not) and locates the creative promise of musical ideas (or not). Students encounter the outcomes or "back-talk" (Schön's term) of their musical thinking straightaway and tangibly. Gardner believes that the practicum-apprenticeship model "may well be the means of instruction that builds most effectively on the ways in which most young people learn."[7]

> Such forms of instruction are heavily punctuated with sensorimotor experiences and with the contextualized use of first-order forms of symbolization, such as natural language and simple drawings and gestures. To the extent that they feature more formal notations or concepts, these are introduced to the learner directly in the context in which they are wanted, and the learner sees for himself the ways in which they may be applied.[8]

The music curriculum-as-practicum tends to be highly motivating (for students and teachers). Students get caught up in the enjoyment and excitement that surrounds their efforts to make "real music" artistically and creatively. Through induction and immersion—through "living" different musical ways of life—students connect with much more than individual works. Students bond with the musical practices and practitioners responsible for individual works. If we wish to engender a life-long involvement with (and love of) musicing and listening, then enabling students to "live" different music cultures is a reasonable and effective path to follow. A deep appreciation (in the sense of a fully informed valuing) of MUSIC and musical works is far more likely to follow from participating productively in musical practices and connecting realistically with practitioners as mentors than from the passive dabbling and "consuming" activities typical of conventional general music curricula.

As explained in Chapter 10, the curriculum-as-practicum is appropriate for all levels of schooling: early, middle, and secondary. Regardless of the age of our musical apprentices, developing musicianship and musical creativity requires the special characteristics of the practicum. This is especially important in the middle school years, which are a time for "intensive involvement in apprenticeships with knowledgeable adults and for the opportunity to heighten basic skills in the context of meaningful and rewarding projects."[9] In sum, the music curriculum-as-practicum enables and promotes the musicianship of all learners, including those among our students who may eventually decide to become professional musicians.

Clearly, there is a happy confluence between this philosophy's concept of curriculum and the professional practices of many music educators past and present. As I see it, the essential characteristics of the reflective musical curriculum are exhibited in many school choral and instrumental programs, in many excellent Kodály and Orff programs, and in many Suzuki programs. This is not surprising. For expert teachers often know more than they can explain (or have time to explain) in philosophical or psychological terms. The informal, impressionistic, and supervisory musical knowings possessed by an expert music teacher are potent. These understandings have led many music teachers to the conclusion that music teaching and learning are best carried out in a learning environment that emphasizes reflective music making. From this perspective, philosophy only reminds the expert practitioner of what he or she already knows.

At the same time, however, a critical caution is necessary. Just because a music program seems to make a prominent place for musicing does not mean it qualifies as a practical example of this philosophy or as a reflective musical practicum. First appearances can be deceiving. Teachers with insufficient musicianship or educatorship are highly prone to philosophical and practical misunderstandings. Thus, many school choral and instrumental programs squander the opportunity to educate students musically because the teachers involved are not concerned with authentic musical performing and artistic music listening, only with simplistic "sound producing." (Any valid educational premise can be distorted or invalidated by a poor teacher.) In addition, and due largely to the lingering fallacies of the aesthetic concept, some teachers still approach musical works as one-dimensional abstractions instead of multidimensional artistic-social constructions. In the absence of a grounding philosophy, many performance-based general music programs restrict students to a limited repertoire of musically unchallenging works from one or two Western musical practices. Moreover, some teachers act more like political dictators than reflective coaches and mentors.

Overall, then, there is a great deal of work to do to transform many "production-based'' programs into reflective musical practicums. This book may be taken, in part, as an attempt to map the directions that in-service teachers can take to correct the weaknesses of existing music programs and to capitalize on their potential for achieving the values and aims of music education. Curriculum renewal in this sense is particularly effective when teachers themselves have regular opportunities to connect with expert mentors in robust teaching-learning situations. Witnessing the actions of artist-teachers as they bring children's musicianship into balance with the challenges inherent in excellent works of music provides teachers with rich and inspiring concepts of music teaching expertise. In this view, music curriculum development and renewal across school districts proceeds most appropriately and effectively by creating a community of reflective music educators around exemplary teaching models and materials.

2. Stage Two: Preparing and Planning the Practicum

After the orientation stage, concrete decisions must be made about curriculum content, materials, scope, sequence, and evaluation. I suggest a seven-point approach to preparing and planning the music curriculum-as-practicum. This approach reformulates and orders the commonplaces as an interactive set of practical concerns. Although the seven decision points are presented in order, music educators should feel free to reflect back and forth among these decision points. Moreover, as explained in Chapter 10, preparing and planning involve highly complex thought processes that may or may not end up in the form of highly specific written plans. Some pre-service teachers may wish to write detailed notes next to each of the seven decision points; expert music educators may not.

In this praxial view, preparing and planning the reflective musical practicum on a daily basis can be done by drawing the familiar diagram shown in Figure 11.1, plotting the seven decision points as indicated, and making notes at each decision point as needed. Copied and used as a template each time, this seven-point diagram offers one way to bring order to the plurality of concerns that teachers will likely encounter in preparing and planning individual lessons while providing room for individual needs.

There are four reasons why it might be advantageous to prepare and plan in relation to this familiar diagram. First, its shape alone reminds teachers of several important principles: that the primary values of MUSIC and the fundamental aims of MUSIC education (self-growth, self-knowledge, and musical enjoyment) are achieved by developing students' musicianship in matching relation to significant musical challenges. Second, using this diagram as a worksheet for lesson plans provides a practical, shorthand way of reflecting, preparing, and planning on an everyday basis. Third, viewing these seven decision points together, as an interactive set of variables, serves to remind music teachers of the need to cycle back and forth among the commonplaces as they will during actual transactions in the classroom. Fourth, this approach is open and flexible. Teachers are free to add or combine decision points if they wish.

Of course, this approach is only a suggestion. It is just one way to prepare and

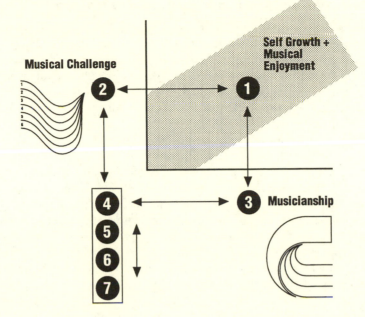

FIGURE 11.1. Preparing and Planning the Music Curriculum-as-Practicum

plan a music curriculum-as-practicum and, therefore, just one way to put this book's praxial philosophy into action.

The seven decision points in Figure 11.1 are summarized below.

1. Decide the kinds of *music making* your students will pursue. (The values of MUSIC arise in the actions of musicing and listening.)
2. Decide (a) the musical *practices* and (b) the musical *challenges* to be taught and learned in relation to your decisions at point (1) above and point (3) below.
3. Decide the components of the *musicianship* your students will require to meet the musical challenges you selected at point (2) above.
4. Decide your teaching-learning *goals* in relation to decisions made at (1), (2), and (3) above.
5. Reflect on alternative teaching-learning *strategies* in relation to your decisions at points (1) to (4) above.
6. Reflect on alternative *sequences* you may require to achieve your teaching-learning goals.
7. Decide how to *assess and evaluate* students' developing musicianship.

If you have not already done so, please draw Figure 11.1 now. As you read about each of the decision points, please relate these suggestions to your own teaching situation(s). (Please notice that there is not a one-to-one correspondence between the seven commonplaces and these seven decision points. Rather, these decision points and their interactions, taken together, include all the commonplaces.)

1. Decide the kinds of music making your students will pursue

The values and aims of music education are realized through musical actions—through musical thinking-in-action and knowing-in-action. Musicianship (which includes listenership) exhibits itself in praxis. Hence, music curricula should be organized in relation to the various ways that musical practitioners think musically in action. Just as real music cultures depend on the musicing of practitioners for their existence, continuation, and evolution, music making is the engine that powers each music curriculum-as-practicum.

Preparing and planning a music curriculum begins by deciding the kinds of artistic music making that students will pursue both in the short term and in the long term. There are five possible choices: performing, improvising, composing, arranging, and conducting. Since we cannot teach all five forms of music making at each moment to all students, we must decide which forms of musicing to select. This philosophy has argued that the music curriculum-as-practicum ought to focus primarily (but not exclusively) on music making through musical performing and (when it is appropriate) improvising. Composing, arranging, and conducting ought to be taken up with reasonable frequency (during a period of weeks and months) and in judicious relation to the musical practices and works that students are pursuing through performing.

In addition, since all forms of music making depend on artistic music listening and since artistic listening develops in relation to the five component knowings of musicianship, listening ought to be taught and learned in direct relation to the musical practices and works students are learning in and through their own active making.

This philosophy emphasizes that music making is a logical and viable educational end for all music students. Performing, improvising, composing, arranging, and conducting are rich and complex forms of cognition—they are exquisite types of human thinking and knowing. They are not mere behaviors, or skills, or means. They are not "learning activities" that students dip into now and then, here and there. Moreover, the musicianship needed to achieve self-growth and flow is not achieved through incidental and superficial dabbling. Self-growth, self-knowledge, musical enjoyment, and self-esteem depend on students' deepening involvement in musical norms and histories of practice, on the gradual, sustained, and systematic development of musicianship.

2. Decide (a) the musical practices and (b) the musical challenges to be taught and learned in relation to your decisions at points (1) above and (3) below

In curriculum terminology, musical practices and musical challenges are the curriculum *materials* of the practicum. The practicum pivots on the actions (transactions and interactions) of students and teachers in relation to carefully chosen materials. Connelly and Clandinin put it this way: "For a person, growth into the future through experience in the curriculum is . . . a process of interacting with curriculum materials."[10] Gardner makes the same point: "[M]eaningful projects taking place over time and involving various forms of individual and group activity are the most promising vehicles for learning."[11] For the music student, self-growth and enjoyment in the practicum depend on interacting with musical works or projects that embody the best musical thinking of the music cultures selected for study.

Decisions about curriculum materials relate to the *scope* of the curriculum, that is, to the long-term, horizontal organization of the practicum. To be educationally and musically valid and representative, the *scope* of a practicum ought to reflect the nature of MUSIC as a diverse human practice. MUSIC is inherently multicultural. And many music classrooms are culturally diverse. Over the long term, then, students need opportunities to "enter" a reasonably wide range of music cultures. Yet we need to be pragmatic with regard to scope. We need to decide what musical practices are most worth teaching and learning (1) in themselves, (2) in relation to the present and future musicianship of our students, (3) in relation to the cultural identities of our students, and (4) in relation to our own musicianship.

Suppose, for example, that a teacher is concerned with plotting the scope of a music curriculum-as-practicum for five meetings (or classes) with one group of students that he or she has organized and developed as a choral singing practicum. In this case, the several individual flow diagrams in Figure 11.2 might be taken to represent a teacher's preparations and plans for teaching several practices, challenges, and projects, including: (A) interpret and perform a Baroque work; (B) interpret and perform a jazz work; (C) compose and improvise melodies according to the jazz practice selected in (B); (D) interpret and perform a Zulu song; (E) return to the Baroque work in (A) above and refine the performance while learning to conduct this piece; and on and on. Depending on each teacher's circumstances, one class meeting may include several musical works (as indicated by the vertical rows of flow diagrams in Figure 11.2) or just one. Of course, in all these examples the music teacher will guide students to listen artistically and provide opportunities for students to listen to recordings of related works within the same musical practices.

In this view, the comprehensiveness of the practicum depends on making a "full-course meal" of every musical work or project by developing students' musicianship fully (in all five knowledge dimensions) in relation to the multidimensional nature of the musical works being interpreted, performed, composed, and so on. The multi-line symbols that represent musical challenges (at point 2) and musicianship (at point 3) in the flow diagrams remind us of the multidimensional nature of musical works and musicianship. Indeed, it is essential that musical works be prepared, taught, and learned in all their relevant dimensions.

A central pedagogical issue in selecting musical practices and musical challenges for the practicum is how to balance the need for musical depth with the need for teaching MUSIC as a diverse human practice. Because different students develop at different rates, it is impossible to be certain in advance about the depth and breadth of a practicum over a long period of time. Furthermore, difficulties often arise because of differences between the musical desires of students and what teachers consider musically and educationally desirable for students. Conflicts can often be resolved by engaging students in critical thinking about the selection of musical practices and challenges to be pursued in the practicum.

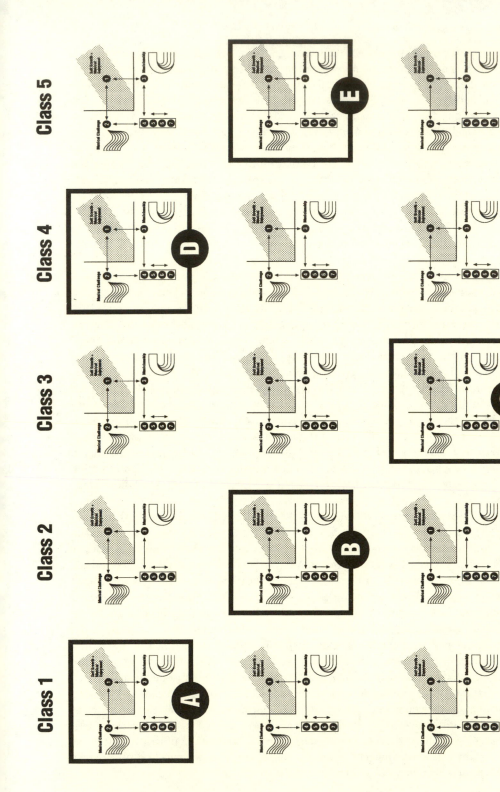

FIGURE 11.2. Long-Term Preparing and Planning

In a related vein, two ways of selecting curriculum materials are as invalid as they are common. The first way is to select practices and works purely in relation to school events, music festivals, and outside requests for public performances. Preparing and planning the practicum ought to make provisions for some performances outside the curriculum; after all, making music for others is what musical practitioners actually do, and the aims of music education and the development of student musicianship can benefit significantly by connecting the curriculum-as-practicum with the wider school community and the musical needs of the community-at-large. At the same time, however, the musical requirements of people and events outside the practicum are usually too narrow and self-serving to function as guidelines for the musical and educational needs of music students.

A second way of selecting musical practices and works is to settle for the choices of publishers. But while some music series, texts, and method books reflect excellent musical, philosophical, and educational thinking, many do not. Choosing between two music series is often like choosing between two toothpastes. Deciding what musical practices and challenges are best for music education cannot and should not be relegated to the same level as household shopping.

In sum, the educational success of the practicum depends heavily on the practices, works, and projects one decides to teach. Aside from the continuous development of our own musicianship as teachers, the most important way we can prepare materials for the curriculum-as-practicum is to perform, analyze, listen for, contextualize, and judge the musical works we intend to teach in the practicum well before we begin to teach.

3. Decide the components of the musicianship your students will require to meet the musical challenges you selected at point (2) above

In the jargon of curriculum theory, the term *curriculum content* is used interchangeably with many other terms including *subject matter knowledge, learning activities, concepts,* and *learning experiences.* In this praxial philosophy, the content of the music curriculum is musicianship. Musicianship is *what* we teach. Musicianship is a form of knowledge that is internally generated in students through their musical actions, transactions, and interactions with carefully selected musical practices and challenges. Additionally, musicianship is the subject matter knowledge that professional music teachers require to teach effectively.

As suggested in point (2) above, deciding the details of the musicianship to be taught and learned in the practicum depends on knowing the musical practices and works one intends to teach. The process of preparing our own musicianship in relation to each musical work or project we select enables us to anticipate the musical knowings that our students will require to find, solve, and reduce musical problems. In addition, preparing and planning in the short term and in the long term is also influenced by a teacher's knowledge of her students' current levels of musicianship in relation to each challenge selected.

Note, again, that decision making in the preparation and planning stage is not linear but interactive. Decision points are linked to one another. The decisions we make at point (1) (musical actions) and point (2) (musical practices and challenges) enable us to determine the curriculum content (musicianship) of the practicum at decision point (3).

Note, next, that decision points (4), (5), (6), and (7) in Figure 11.1 follow from the decisions teachers make about (1) music making, (2) musical challenges, and (3) musicianship.

4. Decide teaching-learning goals in relation to decisions made at points (1), (2) and (3) above

The short- and long-term action-goals of individual lessons follow from a teacher's understanding of the musical challenges of the practicum, the dimensions of musical meaning involved in these challenges, and the musicianship students will need to meet these demands.

Action-goals target specific details of selected musical challenges. For example, within the larger action-goal of learning to interpret and perform a selected musical work, students might focus on such subgoals as learning how to interpret the melodic expressions of sadness in a Romantic choral work or learning how to perform jazz swing authentically. Achieving these action-goals draws upon all five knowledge components of musicianship. A student's increasing ability to find, solve, and reduce musical problems is evidence that a student is achieving progressively refined levels of musical thinking.

Moment-to-moment objectives arise out of the goal-directed actions, transactions, and interactions that power the practicum. Ultra-specific instructional objectives need not be written down in advance of instruction. Similarly, verbal concepts about musical works ought not to be used to organize the practicum. Verbal information is explained and examined as needed to support musical thinking-in-action. With the action priority of the practicum firmly in mind, teachers may wish to list the verbal concepts they intend to draw upon as sidebars to decision points (2) and (3). This brings us to the topic of teaching-learning strategies.

5. Reflect on alternative teaching-learning strategies in relation to decisions made at points (1) to (4) above

As teachers reflect back and forth among decision-points (1) to (4), various teaching-learning strategies will come to mind to help students find, solve, and reduce musical problems. Six strategies are especially important to the musical practicum: modeling, coaching, scaffolding, articulating, comparative reflecting, and exploring.[12] Three of these strategies are already familiar from previous chapters. I review them now as a related set. In practice, expert music educators move in and out of these strategies in a fluid stream of teacher-student interactions.

Modeling refers to the expert carrying out of musical thinking-in-action so that students can observe, listen for, and build the practical concepts they need to think musically themselves. By "modeling" I do not mean mimicking. Modeling involves reciprocal teaching and learning. For example, a teacher performs a musical passage, develops a melodic motive, or improvises over a ii-V-I progression.

The teacher then coaches students toward the model by talking and questioning. As rapidly as possible, the teacher fades from the center of attention to allow students to continue to apply their new procedural knowledge on their own. From the students' perspective, learning from models is highly cognitive and constructive. Accordingly, as Marc Dickey observes, modeling "is an effective strategy throughout a wide age distribution" from elementary through graduate levels of music education.[13] While the music teacher is usually the primary source of modeling in the practicum, accomplished students can also be recruited to model excellent musical thinking-in-action for their peers. Of course, musical models can also be found in video- and audiotapes of expert performances, or performances by accomplished amateur musicians in the local community, visiting artists, or experts linked to classrooms through computers and "distance-education" technology.

The idea of modeling is not restricted to performing, improvising, and conducting. Teachers can also model various aspects of arranging and composing. For example, teachers can set specific arranging projects and then demonstrate how to generate and select musical solutions to specific problems of melody writing, orchestration, or rhythmic variation.

As explained in Chapter 3, *coaching* begins by diagnosing and assessing the processes and products of students' musical thinking. Coaching then proceeds by offering hints, reminders, models, or new problems designed to direct students' attention to important musical details. In these ways, coaching moves students' music making toward closer approximations of artistic and creative achievement. Collins, Brown, and Newman summarize coaching in the following way: "Coaching focuses on the enactment and integration of skills in the service of a well-understood goal through highly interactive and highly situated feedback and suggestions; that is, the content of the coaching interaction is immediately related to specific events or problems that arise as the student attempts to carry out the target task."[14]

The third strategy, called *scaffolding*, involves supporting students in various ways as they move forward in their efforts to find and solve problems themselves. Supports can take many forms, including special equipment, models, verbal suggestions, and the physical details of the learning environment itself. A clear example of the last suggestion is the way scaffolding is used to teach downhill skiing.[15] The novice skier begins on a "bunny hill," a gentle downward and upward slope in an actual ski setting. The gentle incline controls the novice's speed and eliminates the risk of injury. The gentle upward slope slows his forward momentum smoothly and safely. The novice begins on short skis that make it easy for him to turn, stop, or recover his balance in the event of a fall.

Bunny hills and short skis are support structures that are deliberately built into the ski-teaching situation. The learning context itself is responsible for a great deal of the teaching and learning that occurs. The novice skier does not begin with verbal lectures about skiing or with atomistic movements, isolated patterns, or acontextual drills. His skiing is authentic and holistic. It is far less sophisticated than Olympic-level skiing, but the novice is skiing nonetheless; he is not doing something fundamentally different in kind than the expert. From the outset, the

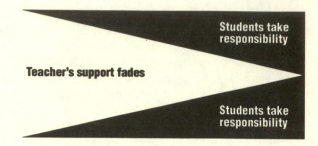

FIGURE 11.3. The "Fading" Strategy

novice is located (situated) in a natural ski situation that enables him or her to achieve enjoyment very early through a carefully planned context that matches his novice skimanship with the "bunny hill challenge."

In addition to bringing students' musicianship into balance with the fullness of musical works in situ, there are other ways that music teachers can learn from parallels between this ski example and what many music teachers already do in terms of scaffolding. Examples include the use of child-size instruments for very young instrumentalists, the use of MIDI technology to "realize" student arrangements or compositions, and the use of recorded accompaniments in teaching jazz improvisation. Clearly, successful scaffolding depends on preparing and planning the practicum in advance by diagnosing and anticipating student needs. It also depends on the ability of the teacher to assume responsibility for the more difficult aspects of a musical task that students cannot yet manage by themselves.

Fading refers to the gradual removal of supports as students become able to problem-solve on their own. As the diagram in Figure 11.3 indicates, a teacher's support can (and should) fade over time (or even during single lessons) as students take more responsibility for finding and solving musical problems.

Articulation (or verbal reflection) is an important strategy for developing supervisory musical knowledge. It includes any means of helping students express their personal approaches to musical problem solving including words, diagrams, analogies, and models. For example, to encourage the development of creative promise detectors (see Chapter 9), students might be asked to articulate different ways of approaching the dynamic markings in a new work they are learning to interpret and perform. The goal of articulation is musical self-awareness. Articulation helps students supervise (or reflect on) the processes they and their fellow practitioners are using (or not using) to find and solve musical problems.

In previous chapters I emphasized the importance of reflection in and on musical action. The music education curriculum is called a reflective practicum because several kinds of verbal and nonverbal thinking evolve *together* as students learn how to make music and listen musically. As musical actions lead to new musical circumstances and new problem solving situations, the active musical productivity of the practicum recasts what students know in more and more richly textured forms.[16]

The strategy of *comparative reflection* takes the ideas of articulation and reflection one step further. The educational power of reflecting on one's musical actions can be boosted by replaying examples of musical thinking in various ways.[17] Suppose, for example, that a teacher videotapes her students while they are solving interpretive problems in a performance rehearsal and then asks her students to analyze various aspects of the video and conduct verbal "postmortems" concerning their successes and failures. Such comparative reflecting serves to highlight the determinant features of students' effective and ineffective actions. Differences among students' reflections expose what proficient and expert students are thinking and listening for and what less knowledgeable students are overlooking.

Exploration relates to our earlier discussion of "generating and selecting" (see Chapter 9). If students are to become critical and creative musical thinkers, they must be coached toward exploring, generating, and selecting musical problems and solutions themselves. By gradually fading the supports we provide, we oblige our students to explore various decision-making routes and thereby take ownership of their musical goals and accomplishments. Suppose, for example, that a teacher divides his or her class choir (choral practicum) into several small chamber choirs. The teacher might then assign different portions of a new work to each chamber choir (directed by student conductors) with the general goal of finding and solving the musical problems involved in each assigned portion of the work. In this way, students receive opportunities to identify subproblems and subgoals and relate their solutions to the musical work as a whole.

A legitimate part of preparing for the musical practicum involves anticipating alternative teaching-learning strategies based on one's forecasts about impending transactions between particular students and the problems involved in particular musical challenges.

6. *Reflect on alternative sequences that may be required to achieve your teaching-learning goals*

Our profession's views of short-term sequencing have been powerfully influenced by the results of empirical research, especially educational psychology, "learning theory," and human development theory. These fields provide valuable perspectives on when and how to present different kinds of knowledge to students of different ages and different learning styles. Some researchers suggest, for example, that teachers should proceed from the simple to the complex or from the particular to the general. Others insist we should begin with the general (or the whole), move to the specific (parts), and then come back to the general. Some researchers say that learning sequences should begin with that material that is closest to the experience of the learners themselves.

There is utility in all of these suggestions, depending on the given situation. But neither educational psychology nor empirical research, which serves as its basis, provides conclusive evidence that supports the overall effectiveness of any particular mode of sequence. The hope for a definitive hierarchy of sequence for music teaching and learning is probably a hope for a fantasy.

As emphasized throughout this book, and as the bunny hill analogy explains, musical "wholes"—interactions with rich and authentic musical works—should precede the study and rehearsal of musical "parts" whenever possible. In deciding how to sequence lessons, my bias is toward supporting (or scaffolding) fundamental knowings to allow students to move ahead quickly and experience holistic musical achievements before working on the individual components of a work or the small details of musicianship. The point and effect of doing so is to give students the big picture (and the enjoyment) of essential musical processes before worrying about atomistic details (e.g., enabling children to sing an excellent song musically, with the aid of modeling, before focusing on their music-reading abilities). Even if students can achieve only part of a large task, having the big picture provides them with a clear musical goal-in-mind. With larger goals-in-mind, students can begin to supervise their own progress toward the whole and self-reflect on their improvements in relation to their understanding of the musical whole.

I suggest that deciding what follows moment-to-moment in any given teaching episode depends on what students require to bring their musicianship into line with a given challenge and, coincidentally, with what students require to stay centered in the musical flow channel. In the short term, there is no one way to get from point A to point B. Teachers decide in action when and how to coach, diagnose, tell, model, reflect, advise, encourage, or fade. In other words, the sequencing of events in the practicum is predominantly interactive. It depends not on following a linear script or a highly sequential set of atomistic patterns or steps but on a music teacher's moment-to-moment judgments about the quality and direction of students' musical thinking-in-action.

Of course, teachers may sometimes feel a need to depart from the practicum's focus on artistic music making in order to develop the formal knowledge component of students' musicianship. Providing that such departures are (a) relatively brief and (b) clearly linked to the artistic goals of the practicum, music history lectures, "theory lessons," and other sorts of formal learning have a legitimate place in the long-term sequencing of the practicum. In the same way that athletes benefit from verbal strategy sessions and "chalk talks," apprentice musical practitioners often benefit from taking time out to reflect historically and theoretically about their projects. In these situations, teachers may decide to sequence verbal knowledge linearly (as a linked series of questions or points), rather than interactively.

7. Decide how to assess and evaluate students' developing musicianship

Because musicianship is a multifaceted, progressive, and situated form of knowledge, music educators require a multidimensional, progressive, and situated approach to assessment and evaluation. Research efforts by Howard Gardner, Dennie Wolf, Lyle Davidson, Larry Scripp, and others[18] have produced a related set of ideas and materials that meet several of the above requirements. Gardner's term "process-folio"[19] sums up an approach to assessment and evaluation that is compatible with the requirements of the music curriculum-as-practicum. Gardner explains the essential ideas.

> In the typical art portfolio, a student or artist assembles her best works, in the hope of gaining admission to a select art school, winning a prize, or securing a showing

at a gallery or a staging at the playhouse. The emphasis falls squarely on the final product. In contrast, as the name suggests, our process-folios represent an effort to capture the steps and phases through which students pass in the course of developing a project, product, or work of art. A complete student process-folio contains initial brainstorming ideas, early drafts, and first critiques; journal entries on "pivotal moments" when ideas jelled; collections of works by others that proved influential or suggestive, in a positive or negative sense; interim and final drafts; self-critiques and critiques by peers, informed mentors, and, again, outside experts; and finally some suggestion of how one might build upon the current project in future endeavors.

I contend that creation and maintenance of a process-folio is an important, perhaps even essential phase in the development of a mature artistic practitioner in our culture. . . . [I]t is important for the aspiring creator to be able to assume some distance from his work—to be able to see where he is headed, which leads are promising, which lines of work ought to be pursued, and which ones abandoned, and to have the opportunity to submit drafts to other sympathetic but critical colleagues for feedback, suggestions, and even, on occasion, praise![20]

The musical process-folio is intended to record the development of each student's musicianship in a variety of ways over an extended period of time. The folio is a collection of musical projects-in-progress, musical projects completed to date, and feedback related to these processes and achievements. The point is not only to garner knowledge-fair evidence of student achievement for future evaluation but to create a continuing source of constructive feedback for students and teachers.

It is important to reiterate that "creating" and the concept of learning from drafts of one's work applies to all forms of music making, including performing. Student performers and performing ensembles learn from draft interpretations and performances (i.e., rehearsals) as much as composers and arrangers learn from written drafts and actual rehearsals of their works. Hence, the musical process-folio should include a selection of the following: audiotapes (and video tapes, whenever possible) of students' efforts in group rehearsals and individual practice sessions; tapes of solo, small-group, and large-group performances during class and outside class; students' self-evaluations of practice sessions, improvisations, performances, and compositions; plans and drafts of student compositions or arrangements; goals for future rehearsals; and written or recorded feedback from teachers, peers, and, when available, outside experts.

In separate discussions, Gardner, Davidson, and Scripp suggest that the contents of musical process-folios can also include the results of student-teacher interviews, student-student interviews, and student questionnaires designed to determine students' individual goals, strengths, weaknesses, fears, and hopes. Interview devices help to build the musical profiles of students in the practicum for the information of teachers, parents, and the students themselves.

The process-folio approach involves the collection, supervision, assessment, and evaluation of many items. This is both the strength and the weakness of the approach. As teachers develop ways of reducing and streamlining the administrative details of a "process-folio culture" (Gardner's term), the long-term benefits for music teaching and learning (and for the curricular status of music education) are considerable. By learning to document their progress toward musical goals, students hone their formal, informal, and supervisory musical knowings. The profiles they develop of their musical selves become the focus of student-teacher reflection and assessment. In these ways, the musical process-folio not only contributes to students' musical problem finding, problem solving, and creative achievement; it also contributes to students' self-growth and enjoyment by confirming how well they are meeting musical challenges.

From a teacher's viewpoint, the process-folio approach maps student development from multiple perspectives. These mappings help to identify the strengths and weaknesses of students' thinking and knowing. In larger perspective, the regular sharing of folio ideas, suggestions, observations, reflections, and successes helps teachers and students establish a "musical community" in the class practicum; a musical knowledge-building culture of practitioners working in common cause.

Music educators are typically masterful at educational problem reduction. Implementing a process-folio culture[21] is an educational problem that can be reduced over time through practical problem solving among teachers and music teacher educators. Perhaps one of the keys to initiating a process-folio approach to assessment and evaluation is to begin modestly by using a small number of assessment devices at first. As the teacher learns how to reduce the administrative problems involved, she can then build a richer process-folio culture.

Several scholars have proposed particular assessment devices that folios might contain. For example, Davidson and Scripp suggest that an "ensemble rehearsal critique"[22] may be used at regular intervals as students learn to interpret and perform musical works. The ensemble critique is a chart that students fill with criticisms and suggestions about the ensemble's progress as a whole and about their own efforts. After students complete a performance of a whole work (or a major section of a work), they reflect on their musicing by noting comments about the strengths and weaknesses of their thinking-in-action. As an alternative, students may write critical comments as they listen for a recording of their rehearsal.

The ensemble critique is appropriate insofar as it helps to target attention, encourage reflection, and encourage artistic music listening. But the idea is easily abused. When verbal information and reading and writing become the primary focus, the musical value of ensemble critiques is lost. Moreover, there is a tendency to conceive ensemble critiques much too narrowly, as guides to musical problem reduction (e.g., pitch error detection), rather than to musical problem finding and problem solving. To ensure the artistic use of ensemble critiques, the critique form should be constructed to relate problems of musical interpretation and performance to all relevant dimensions of the musical work being performed: its design dimension, its musical expressions of emotion (if present), its musical representations (if present), and so on (as we summarized in Chapter 8).

When properly designed and implemented, ensemble critiques support and encourage students to reflect collectively and comparatively; target their surplus attention; acquire formal, informal, and impressionistic knowledge; and share their supervisory knowledge. In all these ways, critiques help to mobilize individual students and the ensemble-practicum as a whole. In addition, by raising the level and importance of artistic musical listening, critiques help to shift the burden of reflective thinking away from teachers and toward music students.

The practice journal is a logical outgrowth of the ensemble critique. Each student keeps a personal record of plans, achievements, and self-reflections that can be shared with peers and teachers for feedback and coaching. The journal need not be limited to words. It may also include audiotapes, videotapes, practice plans, and score analyses.

The listening log takes the journal concept one more step. Each student organizes a personal listening diary using some variation on the six-dimensional model explained in Chapters 4, 6, and 8. Students note comments in relation to these dimensions as they listen for recordings during or after school or at live concerts. The log encourages students to practice listening for and reflecting on musical works as multidimensional constructions. The log also provides another means of assessing and evaluating the growth of musicianship-listenership.

Students might begin their logs by listening for recordings of works they are learning to interpret and perform in their class practicum or of related works. They might then listen more widely inside and outside the musical practices they are learning. As part of the listening log strategy at the middle and secondary school levels, teachers and students might also decide to examine reviews by professional music critics in local newspapers or in *Stereo Review, Gramophone, Fanfare, The New York Times, Downbeat,* the *Yearbook of Traditional Music,* or *The Penguin Guide to Compact Discs and Cassettes.*[23]

Once again, however, caution is advised. Listening logs cannot be allowed to overtake the artistic action-focus of the practicum. The logs are nothing more or less than supplements to artistic music making. (For students who may have difficulties with writing, teachers might find alternative ways to organize logs, perhaps as audio logs via tapes.)

Taken together, the ingredients of the process-folio concept can garner rich evidence of musical thinking and knowing over time. This evidence can be evaluated in terms of its quality, quantity, and diversity. When added to the daily assessments that music teachers make, process-folios help to clarify and verify teachers' judgments about individual and group achievements.

3. Stage Three: Music Teaching and Learning

In the third stage of curriculum making, the commonplaces come to life in the fluid interactions of music teaching and learning. This is the heart of the music curriculum: a musical teacher inducting students into musical practices through active music making. And here is where it would be best to stop talking. If I could replace this section of the book with visits to school music programs that actualize this praxial philosophy, or if I could switch from writing these words to showing videotapes of excellent practicums-in-action, I would surely do so. At this point we need to watch, reflect upon, and listen for expert music educators in action in various kinds of reflective musical practicums.

Fortunately, many school and community-based music programs in the United States, Canada, the United Kingdom, Scandinavia, and elsewhere exemplify many of the conceptual and curricular tenets of this praxial philosophy. (There are also videotaped examples of music teaching and learning that put many principles of this philosophy into practice.[24])

Unfortunately, I cannot specify the day-to-day operation of even one practicum. First, the overwhelming detail involved in verbalizing even a few moments in one school music practicum is more than I have time or space for here. Second, the praxial philosophy put forward in this book can be actualized in different formats. There are several legitimate ways to engage music students of different ages in developing the musicianship they require to meet musical challenges and many ways to operationalize the teaching-learning strategies I have suggested in relation to particular students. In short, the curriculum-as-practicum has considerable flexibility. But for me to describe one or two kinds of practicums would run counter to my emphasis on the adaptability of this approach. Third, to detail one or two musical practicums would contradict a basic principle of practical curriculum making: that the best curricula arise when teachers develop solutions to teaching-learning problems in relation to their own situations. Fourth, if you have already been imagining this book's proposals in terms of your own situation (as I suggested in Chapter 1), then whatever I might detail now would be redundant. I will therefore only flesh out the social and cooperative qualities of this kind of teaching-learning context.

A musical practicum is a social collective; it is a deliberately created community of aspiring music makers. Picture a general music class centered on choral singing. The music class becomes a reflective practicum in and through its organization and operation as a choir intent upon inducting learners into various musical practices through artistic choral singing. (Similarly, a guitar class may be patterned after the various kinds of music making done by real-world guitarists and guitar ensembles; and so on.) Recall from our discussion of musicing in Chapter Seven that musicianship is a kind of tool that can be understood and acquired only through active use in relation to the belief system of the music culture in which it is used. Learning why, how, when, and where to use musicianship as musical practitioners use it, a student, like an apprentice, must enter into that community of practitioners and its surrounding culture. Students must be immersed in the ways of thinking that propel a music culture. Thus, music teaching and learning is also a process of enculturation.

Organized and carried out as a practicum, the main musical enterprise of the school music class (for example, the class chorus, the class percussion ensemble, the class wind ensemble) is an essential ingredient in developing musicianship. The learning circumstances of these kinds of groupings provide essential parts of the structure and meaning of the knowledge we want students to grasp. In other words, the knowledge we wish to develop comes coded by and connected to the actions and practicum environment in which musicianship is developed.[25]

Achieving the aims and values of music education depends on engaging students in sustained and purposeful musical thinking that is congruent with the practices of different music cultures. This happens when elementary, middle, and secondary school music education programs are organized around the sustained development of musicianship in classroom choral and instrumental practicums that link artistic listening to all forms of music making.

As students increase their musicianship, they increase their participation in the musical community of the practicum and its "internal goods": self-growth, constructive knowledge, flow, and self-esteem; apprentice practitioners develop musicianship in the context of its application to viable musical problems; the teaching-learning context is focused on and defined by a commitment to the goals and traditions of genuine musical practices past and present; and musicianship is valued for its effectiveness and for its contribution to the effort of the classroom ensemble and its culture of emerging expertise. These features encourage positive beliefs about the nature of musical learning and expertise that fuel a student's motivation and confidence.

The *relationships* among student apprentices in a practicum play an important role in the development of musical expertise. Most practicums involve groups of students who often take on formal and informal coaching functions for and with their peers. By means of the mutually reinforcing efforts of the practicum as a social unit, students witness and test the specific ways of thinking that define a musical practice. As Schön points out, learning by exposure and immersion, or "background learning," often occurs indirectly but forcefully.[26]

Combining apprentice practitioners at various stages of musicianship with a musically educated teacher provides students in the practicum with benchmarks of musical thinking for their own development. This combination also helps students understand that music teaching and learning involve the use of multiple and cooperative resources. Collins, Brown, and Newman emphasize the broader importance of this kind of learning environment:

> [A]wareness of the distributed nature of expertise and insight is at the foundation of successful collaboration in all domains. Partly because of this key belief—that knowledge is not concentrated in any single person—skilled collaborators are more likely to be open to and seek help and input from others. As a result, they are better able to take advantage of interactions with others to construct better and more satisfactory solutions to complex problems.[27]

Many school music programs fail to qualify as reflective musical practicums because they treat students as passive audiences rather than as reflective musical apprentices-practitioners. A music class in which the ensemble director finds, solves, and reduces all musical problems himself or herself is *not* a reflective practicum. Inducting students into musical practices involves teaching students to think critically, independently, and creatively. Students need opportunities to assume multiple roles (performer, coach, critical listener, adviser, conductor) while solving musical problems.

As Dewey suggested, teachers must enable students to convert indefinite or ambiguous problems to determinate ones.[28] To do so, learners must have opportunities to experiment. Experimenting in the musical practicum is different than experimenting in the scientific context. The main difference has to do with the relationship between making musical changes and understanding these changes.

The musical performer wants to change the sounds she is making from what they are to something she understands to be more effective artistically. The performer has an interest in understanding the situation, but her interest is in the service of performing musically, not in understanding in abstraction. (The same is true for all forms of musicing.) Musical experimenting is rigorous when the student strives to achieve a musical result that meets her notion of what it should be while remaining open to possibilities that she did not predict in advance or that indicate her failure to meet her goals and standards.[29] Following Schön, I suggest that the music student plays the experimental game "in relation to a moving target," changing the musical results even as these results change with her every move.[30]

As described here, the practicum offers students opportunities to engage in "reflective conversations" with different musical practices.[31] Students apply what they already know from past experience, examples, images, understandings, and actions. New problems are seen as being similar to, yet different from, previous problems. This is what expert and creative music makers seem to do based on their informal knowledge: they *frame* a new situation in relation to something already understood. They are able to detect creative promise—to see the new in the old, and the old in the new—by using past situations as precedents or metaphors for new and unfamiliar situations. In all these ways, students learn "to practice" in a double sense: they learn to step into the stream of the musical practice they wish to learn and to practice in the sense of refining their musicianship. A few words are in order about the relationship between the practicum and student "practicing" in the sense of improving one's performing, or preparing to perform, improvise, or conduct.

Practicing is commonly thought of as mind-less repetition; one repeats movements until one "gets it right" and does not have to "think" any more. But these notions are false. They rest on a dualistic notion of action. As Vernon Howard points out, to "get it right" one must understand how and what one is doing in relation to some set of musical standards.[32] While practicing, a performer or improviser must be aware of what factors influence what. She must target her attention to a succession of musical problems in a progressive way. She must find, reduce, and solve musical problems by reflecting in and on her actions. In doing so, she listens artistically to what she is doing. As Schön suggests, when a student takes action to transform a situation into one she thinks or knows is better, there is a kind of "back talk" from the results of her actions.[33] This feedback allows the student to apprehend aspects of her musicing that go beyond her initial notion of the problem and her ability to say what she previously did and why. But the process does not go on forever, because the norms of most musical practices do not allow for just any old solution to a musical problem.

The only truth in popular notions of practicing as "getting it right" lies in this: The development of musical expertise involves proceduralizing one's thinking so that more and more of the finite energy resource called attention can be directed to more complex aspects of the musical challenge one is attempting to meet. In this view, even "drill" can be thoughtful, because developing the routine aspects of musical actions in relation to standards requires considerable attention and knowledge.[34]

Properly understood, then, practicing involves contextual repetitions: continual rethinking in relation to intended goals. Practicing is not mechanical duplication. As errors are detected and corrected and as problems are found and solved, difficulties diminish and parts are linked to larger wholes. All this requires attention, awareness, and memory. And all of this is not different in kind from what occurs in writing an essay or learning to do a scientific proof.

Writing an essay usually follows several stages. As Howard and Barton explain,[35] a writer researches ideas, generates ideas from his research, and then selects, organizes, expresses, and edits his ideas. Preparing a performance of a composition follows a similar process. A musician "researches" the composition he is attempting to interpret and perform by studying and reflecting about the composition in all its dimensions. He generates and selects musical solutions in the actions of practicing by experimenting, adjusting, correcting, and refining various parts of his performance. He organizes his interpretation in terms of dynamics, articulations, and phrasing. He then edits or polishes his performance-interpretation. Finally, the performer asserts or expresses (or "makes public") his understanding of the work as a whole. Preparing an interpretation of a composition for a performance through practicing is no less cognitive than preparing an essay for public reading through writing, even though many aspects of practicing and performing are nonverbal in essence. Knowing how to combine many of these stages by performing a composition artistically at sight (as many expert performers can do) is nothing less than an astonishing cognitive achievement.

In teaching students how to practice effectively, it is important to consider that frustration and boredom often arise from disconnected, acontextual efforts. Teachers must help students understand how their practicing leads by steps to chosen ends. Even exercises designed to help correct basic problems must be taught as "means to dreams" by linking the student's individual efforts to the larger artistic goals of the practicum.

The practicum "embodies particular ways of seeing, thinking, and doing that tend, over time, as far as the student is concerned, to assert themselves with increasing authority."[36] In other words, the curriculum-as-practicum embodies and conveys certain messages: that the musical practices taught in the practicum are worth learning and perpetuating, that musicianship is educable, and that the practicum fairly represents the kinds of musicianship it has been set up to develop.[37]

Central to the success of the musical practicum is the music educator's own commitment to being and becoming a musical mentor who inducts students into cultures by example. "Teachers," says Gardner, "must serve as role models of the most important skills and attitudes and must in a sense embody the practices that are sought."[38] The mentor-student relationship at the center of the practicum has several practical, psychological, and developmental advantages. When students are learning to make music under the guidance of teachers who are themselves musically proficient, this relationship establishes "personal bonds as well as a sense of progress toward an end."[39] This is so because the effectiveness of the teacher's musicianship is clearly recognized by his students. His musical expertise is honest and real. It has clout because it carries the weight of practical achievement. Hence, the teacher's feedback also has clout. This is why the feedback that students receive from a proficient teacher can be powerfully motivating. When musical goals and standards are clear and when teachers and students know they are meeting important musical challenges, the curriculum-as-practicum is charged with enjoyment and growth (for teachers as well as students).

4. Stage Four: A Praxial View of Curriculum Evaluation

Although there are several approaches to curriculum evaluation, the "critical" or "qualitative" approach advocated by such theorists as Eliot Eisner and J. S. Mann seems most in tune with the nature of the reflective practicum.[40] Eisner holds that the curriculum evaluation process is highly contextual and depends on gathering a wide range of data in relation to the multilayered and interactive nature of teaching-learning situations. It cannot be reduced to simpleminded tests of teacher input and student output. Critical curriculum evaluation involves interpreting collected data with a blend of qualitative judgments and concrete assessments. Of course, the effectiveness of this approach depends on evaluators who are highly critical (in the positive sense of being highly informed) about what is musically and educationally significant in the curricular context.

Although there is no one set way for teachers or external evaluators to conduct critical evaluations of music curricula, three steps seem clear enough. The first step is descriptive. The evaluator (or evaluation team) develops descriptions (including verbal, video, and audio descriptions) of the musical practicum-in-action over a reasonable slice of time. In addition to observing the quality of students' music making, data gathering also includes descriptions of students' enthusiasm and enjoyment (or lack thereof). Data from students' process-folios should have an important place in these descriptions, along with the teacher's own assessment of his or her effectiveness and the judgments of parents, principals, and community members (when possible). A curriculum description should convey both the facts and the feelings of daily life in the curriculum-as-practicum.

The second step is interpretive. Evaluators develop analyses of and explanations for the actions, transactions, and interactions described in Step 1. As Eisner, Mann, and other critical evaluators suggest, the prime function of curriculum criticism is the disclosure of meanings. Just as an artistic music maker can draw our attention to the subtle features of a performance, the critical evaluator highlights the strengths and weaknesses of a music education curriculum.

The third step is evaluative. Curriculum critics make judgments and recommendations on the basis of the results of the first two steps. Judgments and recommendations will of course vary according to the personal abilities and interests of the evaluators. But advocates of this approach view the likelihood of contrasting evaluations as one of its strengths; as well as providing educational decision makers with alternative ideas for improvement, the critical approach guards against oversimplified evaluations based on one set of criteria. In these ways, critical curriculum evaluations are more likely to reflect the complex realities of music teaching situations.

For many teachers and school systems, curriculum evaluation is a desirable but difficult task. There is often a shortage of people with the knowledge to evaluate music programs critically. Still, the results are often worth the effort, especially in political terms. If provisions for curriculum evaluation are built into the curriculum-making process and if the results can be accumulated and related to follow-up studies of student graduates, many music educators will gain exactly what they need to substantiate what they already know informally: that their music programs are, in fact, enabling children to achieve self-growth, self-knowledge, and enjoyment, three of the most important life values human beings can attain.

5. The Multicultural Music Curriculum

To end this chapter, let me connect the topic of curriculum evaluation to the multicultural nature of this philosophy. I have argued that MUSIC is inherently multicultural. It follows that any curriculum that is truly concerned with MUSIC education will be fundamentally concerned with inducting students into a variety of Musics. Curriculum evaluation should therefore consider to what extent music education programs are multicultural—whether music programs are teaching MUSIC.

What follows is a six-part typology of music curricula that may be useful in categorizing and highlighting the multicultural ideologies that music curricula can (and often do) embody and convey, whether or not the teachers involved are aware of these ideologies. This scheme is based on distinctions originally explained by Richard Pratte.[41] While I doubt that all curricula fall neatly into these six categories, the fit between theory and reality seems close enough to be useful for the purposes intended.

1. The *assimilationist* music curriculum is characterized by an exclusive concern with the central practices of the Western European classical tradition. The elevation of "taste" and the breakdown of students' affiliations with popular and minority Musics are the major preoccupations in this type of music program. The assimilationist teacher ignores or denies the musical diversity of his or her community or nation. It is also typical of this kind of curriculum that all musical works under study are approached in the same narrow way: from the Western "aesthetic" viewpoint. As a result, the assimilationist fails to recognize the cultural identity of his or her students.

2. The *amalgamationist* curriculum includes a limited range of microculture practices based on their frequency in the core repertoire of the Western classical tradition or their potential for incorporation into this tradition. Jazz, for example, is considered an acceptable practice for study by the amalgamationist because its distinctive musical features have been successfully incorporated in compositions by such "legitimate" Western composers as Ravel, Milhaud, Stravinsky, Hindemith, Copland, Ives, Gershwin, and Bernstein. Similarly, selected non-Western Musics are viewed in terms of their utility: as sources of new elements and ideas for incorporation into contemporary concert music, jazz, and pop music. At the same time, however, an amalgamationist teacher tends to view so-called world musics as having no curricular validity in and of themselves. To the amalgamationist, the

integrity of a microculture's music, like the integrity of a person's ethnic heritage, is best broken down in the interests of transmitting a society's "national culture," or macroculture. Here, music education *in* a culture becomes music education *as* culture.

3. To advocates of an *open-society* view of multiculturalism, allegiance to the traditional music of one's cultural heritage is viewed as an obstacle to social unity and the development of loyalty to the secular corporate society. In this view, all symbols of subgroup affiliation (e.g., music, literature, fashion, religious practices) are considered irrelevant to life in the contemporary nation-state.

The curricular manifestation of this ideology is the "with-it" music curriculum that places a high value on "musical relevance": the study of everything contemporary; the development of new musical forms as a means of "personal expression" in the context of "now." Tradition is scorned; "excellence" is equated with popularity.

4. The term *insular multiculturalism* applies to curricula that select musical practices exclusively on the basis of students' cultural affiliations. Like the first three types we have discussed, this approach is not multicultural in the full sense of the term. As the word *insular* implies, separateness is the real concern. This kind of music curriculum takes two common forms. One form is associated with a minority group's effort to preserve its traditional ways of life to the fullest extent within an overwhelming host culture (or macroculture). In this sense, insular multiculturalism is a kind of "circle-the-wagons" approach to life and education. The second form is associated with the majority culture's attempts to appear sensitive to children from other backgrounds. In this case, a teacher selects a token piece of, for example, Chinese music for the Chinese students in her class, a token piece of Hispanic music for the Hispanic children in her class, and nothing more. This kind of music curriculum often seems multicultural because it adds an exotic musical flavor to the conventional diet available in music programs by and for the dominant majority.

5. In the *modified* multicultural curriculum, musical practices are selected for study on the basis of local or regional boundaries of culture, ethnicity, religion, function, or race. Once selected, all music is then taught and learned from an aesthetic viewpoint. In this type of music program, students study various "styles" of music (music-as-object) with a concern for how they have been modified in reaction to, or by incorporation into, mainstream Western styles.

Examined closely, this type of curriculum is actually a particular kind of multiethnic education. The focus is on the adaptive processes undergone by various ethnic groups, the uniqueness of these adaptations, and the ongoing evolution of these microcultures within the larger host culture. As Pratte says: "The goal of multiethnic education is to make students aware of the cost of being Americanized and to extoll the virtues of cultural diversity in terms of groups being modified over time."[42]

The modified multicultural curriculum has two basic weaknesses: (1) It is biased from the outset by virtue of its insistence that the aesthetic concept of music has universal validity, and (2) the music chosen for study is often limited to the music cultures of the immediate student population. Once again, then, the ideology underlying the music curriculum obviates an essential goal of a truly multicultural curriculum: to understand the underlying musical beliefs and assumptions of various music cultures and thereby to expose ethnocentric attitudes.

This book has attempted to argue that music educators require a philosophy of music education that is conservative in its concern for preserving the integrity of all music cultures (macrocultures and microcultures), yet liberal insofar as it goes beyond local preferences and ethnocentric notions of music. Drawing on John Dewey's dictum that a great society must become a great community, Pratte suggests that we need to educate children to tackle problems willingly as a "concerned community of interest."[43] Pratte's concept of "dynamic multiculturalism"[44] emphasizes the need to convert subgroup affiliation into a community of concern through a shared commitment to a common purpose.

6. The *dynamic multicultural curriculum* overlaps our concept of the music curriculum as a reflective practicum. I have urged that music students can best achieve the values of MUSIC by learning to work together artistically (in action) in the context of familiar and unfamiliar music cultures. Such efforts inevitably include encounters with familiar and unfamiliar beliefs, preferences, and outcomes.

I shall take a leap of faith at this point and suggest that the induction of students into different music cultures may be one of the most powerful ways to achieve a larger educational goal: preparing children to work effectively and tolerantly with others to solve shared community problems. As I explained, the music curriculum-as-practicum includes a concern for developing critical perspectives on a range of music cultures. In this view, reflective musical practicums are communities of interest. Practicums are characterized by a dynamism fueled by the determination of the participants to make music well through deeper understandings of the beliefs (artistic, social, and cultural) that influence music making and listening in different practices. The productive goals of the practicum encourage students to examine the musical consequences of the beliefs underlying different music cultures. Students develop insights into the meanings and uses of various kinds of music from the inside out and from the bottom up. This approach recommends itself because it minimizes the tendency to superimpose a universal musical belief system on all music everywhere. In addition to developing students' abilities to discern the similarities and differences among and between music cultures, the praxial approach to curriculum has the potential to achieve a central goal of humanistic education: self-understanding through other-understanding.

To conclude, music education is not a neutral enterprise. Music curricula can and do function socially and culturally in powerful ways. With this in mind, I suggest that the implementation of a praxial philosophy of MUSIC education through reflective musical practicums offers the opportunity to develop students' musical understandings relative to the personhood of those who actually "live" various music cultures. In other words, by implementing a praxial philosophy of MUSIC education, teachers have a reasonable way of achieving the goals of humanistic education.

Questions for Discussion and Review

1. List five main characteristics of the practicum concept of curriculum. In what ways is the practicum similar to yet different from the venerable apprenticeship model of education? Why is the curriculum-as-practicum sometimes called a cognitive apprenticeship?

2. This chapter posits a seven-point approach to preparing and planning the music curriculum-as-practicum. What reasons are there for using the particular shape in Figure 11.1 as a template for preparing and planning the practicum? Why does the first step in this seven-point approach focus on musical actions? Why does the second decision point focus on musical practices and then on musical works?

3. What is the educational content of the music curriculum-as-practicum? How does a music teacher determine the content of individual lessons?

4. The fifth decision point in the planning process involves teaching-learning strategies. Summarize six strategies a teacher might use during a music teaching episode.

5. Explain the concepts of scope and sequence. Is there one sure way to sequence music teaching and learning? Why, or why not?

6. Explain the concept and intent of musical process-folios. Summarize the strengths and weakness of the process-folio approach to assessment and evaluation. Explain the purposes of each of the following: an ensemble critique, a practice journal, a listening log.

7. What role does experimenting have in the reflective practicum? Discuss the relationship between effective practicing and musical achievement in the practicum.

8. In terms of multiculturalism, what characteristics qualify a music curriculum as (1) assimilationist; (2) insular; (3) dynamic?

Supplementary Sources

Allan Collins, John Seely Brown, and Susan E. Newman. ''Cognitive Apprenticeship: Teaching the Crafts of Reading, Writing, and Mathematics.'' In *Knowing, Learning and Instruction: Essays in Honor of Robert Glaser*, ed. L. Resnick (Hillsdale, N.J.: Lawrence Erlbaum Associates, 1989), pp. 453–94. A discussion of the cognitive apprenticeship approach to education and related teaching-learning strategies.

Donald A. Schön. *Educating the Reflective Practitioner*. San Francisco: Jossey-Bass, 1987. A classic discussion of the reflective practicum concept.

Lyle Davidson and Larry Scripp. ''Tracing Reflective Thinking in the Performance Ensemble.'' *The Quarterly Journal of Music Teaching and Learning* 1, nos.1 & 2 (Spring 1990): 49–62. An explanation of the ensemble critique.

V. A. Howard. "And Practice Drives Me Mad; or, the Drudgery of Drill." *Harvard Educational Review* 61, no. 1 (February 1991): 80–87. A critical discussion of practicing.

David J. Elliott. "Key Concepts in Multicultural Music Education." *International Journal of Music Education* 13 (Summer 1989): 11–18. A succinct explanation of various kinds of multicultural music curricula.

12

Music Education and Schooling

In Part One of this book I proposed that if we want to think reasonably about music and music education, it is a mistake to begin with pieces of music conceived as autonomous objects. Musical works result from human actions informed by histories and standards of musical practice; they are enmeshed in and derive their nature and significance from their contexts of production and use. Even the structural properties of musical works owe their characteristic features to the reflections of practitioners and theorists who work at particular times in the history of their music cultures. Accordingly, musical works are thoroughly artistic-cultural constructions. And MUSIC, considered globally, is the multifarious human practice of making diverse kinds of music for different kinds of listeners.

In Part Two I concentrated on explaining the natures and values of musicing, listening, and musical works. I proposed that all forms of musicing depend on a multidimensional form of knowledge called musicianship. I then proposed that music listening involves the covert construction of intermusical and intramusical information, relationships, and meanings by means of the same kinds of knowing that make up musicianship: procedural, formal, informal, impressionistic, and supervisory musical knowledge. Musicianship and listenership are thus two sides of the same coin; the knowings required to listen effectively for the musical works of a given practice are the same essential knowings required to make the music of that practice.

In the next section of this inquiry I explained why some musical works can be cognized as expressional or representational and why making and listening for music always involves cultural-ideological information of some kind. In this view, making and/or listening for musical works always involves cognizing more than purely auditory information. Works of music are multidimensional "thought generators."

But what explains the existence and significance of musical practices and musical works? An examination of the tendencies of human consciousness leads to the conclusion that a central goal of each self is to order and strengthen the self. As human beings, we have an innate desire to deploy our conscious powers to bring order to consciousness and achieve self-knowledge.[1] Following the seminal work of Csikszentmihalyi, the praxial philosophy I propose suggests that when there is a match or balance between a person's musicianship and the cognitive challenges inherent in constructing musical works (overtly and covertly), musicers and listeners achieve the fundamental values, or "internal goods," of musicing and listening: self-growth, self-knowledge (or constructive knowledge), musical enjoyment (or "flow"), and self-esteem. In this view, musicianship is not only an exquisite form of knowledge, it is a unique source of one of the most important kinds of knowledge humans can achieve: self-knowledge.

In addition to these values, musicing and musical works extend the range of our expressive and impressive powers by providing opportunities to formulate musical expressions of emotions, musical representations of people, places, and things, and musical expressions of cultural-ideological meanings. When this range of opportunities for musical expression and creativity is combined with the opportunities presented by texts in vocal and choral works, music makers gain numerous ways of giving artistic-cultural form to their powers of thinking, knowing, valuing, evaluating, believing, and feeling that, in turn, challenge listeners' conscious powers and musical understandings.

On the basis of the cognitive richness of musicing and listening, this praxial philosophy argues that musical practices are also significant insofar as musical works play an important role (as memes) in establishing, defining, delineating, and preserving a sense of community and self-identity within social groups. Musical practices constitute and are constituted by their cultural contexts.

Teaching and learning a variety of Musics comprehensively as music cultures through a praxial approach amounts to an important form of multicultural education. Entering into unfamiliar music cultures activates self-examination and the personal reconstruction of one's relationships, assumptions, and preferences. Students are obliged to confront their prejudices (musical and personal) and to face the possibility that what they may believe to be universal may *not* be so. In the process of inducting learners into unfamiliar musical practices, music educators link the primary values of music and music education to the broader goals of humanistic education.

In Part Three of this book I explained why conventional forms of curriculum development are inappropriate for music teaching and learning. I argued that music educators require a systematic, flexible, and interactive way of organizing music curricula to accommodate the natures and values of MUSIC, MUSICIANSHIP, and MUSICAL WORKS. I proposed a four-stage approach to music curriculum making that attempts to explain why and how music curricula ought to be organized and carried out as reflective musical practicums.

The values of MUSIC and MUSIC education are several and profound. And they are unique to musicing, music listening, and the multidimensional nature of musical works. If this is so, then MUSIC education has a significant contribution to make to society in general and to the education of young people in particular.

The philosophy of music education developed in this text and summarized here is nearly complete; this "map" of music education is almost done. But there is at least one important region that remains uncharted: *schooling*. Before closing this inquiry, it is important to reflect critically on the relationships between music education and the context called "schooling" in which music educators practice their profession. In doing so, I hope to illuminate several ways in which schooling influences the curricular status of music education and, in turn, several ways in which music education can influence the culture of schooling.

1. Education versus Schooling

Most Western democracies hold a common set of educational expectations for their schools. These expectations (or ideals) have been stated directly in countless educational pronouncements and curriculum documents over many years. In most cases, these expectations include the following:

> to provide a comprehensive education for the whole child; to teach the young how to think critically and how to learn for themselves; to provide equality of opportunity and the means toward social equality within a democratic society; to teach social competence, character and a value system appropriate to the community and culture; to develop knowledge of the performing and nonperforming arts; to develop physical fitness; and to teach children how to lead fulfilling lives on the basis of respect for themselves and others.[2]

Given these stated ideals, it seems fair to conclude that most Western countries have a strong rhetorical commitment to a *balanced* education for the *whole* child, including a commitment to arts education, physical and health education, moral education, and the development of character.

This publicly proclaimed desire for a broadly educated populace is often echoed in less formal statements by parents, teachers, administrators, business leaders, and the mass media. For example, a cover story in *USA Today* saluted twenty high school seniors selected from 1,651 students nominated by their schools for the fifth annual "All-USA Academic First Team."[3] The selection criteria, developed in cooperation with the National Association of Secondary School Principals and the NEA, required that each "All-USA Academic" demonstrate a balance and a blend of scholarship, leadership, artistic achievement, and/or sports achievement. Singled out as "the best academic talent in the nation's high schools," these students had to be more than merely successful in math, science, or geography. Paul Jung, president-elect of the American Association of School Administrators, emphasized that the winning students were "not just eggheads" (Jung's term); of the twenty students selected for the team, ten were accomplished musical performers and twelve were varsity athletes. Jung concluded that "[i]f all Americans had the opportunity to read these kids' credentials, how good we would feel about our young people."[4]

In view of these expectations and values, and the decades of massive public funding, any reasonable person would expect to find well-balanced curricula in the schools of most Western countries, including systematic programs in music education, physical education, and moral education. One would certainly expect to find securely grounded music programs running from the elementary through the middle and secondary levels of public schooling.

Unfortunately, after several generations of research and experience in universal public education, and enormous amounts of money, most Western democracies still have difficulty developing a literate and numerate citizenry, let alone a truly educated populace. While some school systems provide excellent music education programs for all students during the first six to eight years of schooling (and, in some cases, beyond), the majority do not. Under the harsh light of reality, then, Western expectations for education seem unrealistic at best.

What explains this gap between the ideals of education and the realities of public schooling? And why is it that music is frequently less secure than many other subjects in the school curriculum? Most explanations attribute our fundamental problem to one or more of the following: a lack of time, money, qualified students, or qualified music teachers, along with our profession's own failure to make a solid case for the educational significance of music.

As Paul Lehman observes, time and money are more likely "pseudo-problems" than real explanations of music education's frequent insecurity in the school curriculum. Citing John Goodlad's *A Place Called School*,[5] Lehman suggests that there is enough time to teach a balanced educational program that includes music education (as well as physical education and other areas), providing that school schedules and administrative tasks are carried out carefully and efficiently. In terms of finances, Lehman argues the following: "A school that claims to be saving money by cutting its music program is in fact saving money by decreasing its teacher/pupil ratio. The students have to be assigned somewhere, and there can be no savings unless other classes are increased in size. This would be true no matter what was cut."[6]

Lehman continues:

> A school that dismisses or refuses to employ necessary music teachers in order to hire more teachers in other fields has probably lost sight of the true purposes of education. . . .
> The unvarnished truth is that if music is not taught, the reason is simply that it is not valued highly enough. . . . Money is not the real problem. The question is simply one of priorities.[7]

While these observations are likely correct, they still beg the questions of why schools have lost sight of the true purposes of education and why school systems generally fail to achieve society's rhetorical commitment to a balanced curriculum for the whole child.

Many school board members, administrators, and politicians believe that music education programs do not deserve support because there is only a marginal group of "talented" children in any given community who can (or should) benefit from school music instruction. Underlying this belief is the old assumption that music making is fundamentally inaccessible to most students because musical ability is something that only a few infants are blessed with and all others are not.

Considerable evidence and experience argue the contrary.[8] Given qualified music teachers, most children can achieve a competent (if not a proficient) level of musical understanding. In other words, there is nothing in the nature of human consciousness that prevents most children from learning to make and listen to music at least competently. Until many disbelievers are persuaded otherwise, the security of music in general education will likely remain in jeopardy.

In a related vein, there is no doubt that long-term parental and administrative support for music education also depends on demonstrating to skeptics that music is achievable in the sense that there is a cadre of teachers who do in fact know how to develop students' musicianship deeply and efficiently. Unfortunately, this is still not the case in many locales. In circumstances where a music teacher is unavailable or ineffective in the classroom or incapable of arguing effectively for the values of music education, unsympathetic administrators will frequently seize the opportunity to eliminate these "problems" by eliminating the school music program altogether.

Some critics place the main responsibility for music education's vulnerability on the failures of past music education philosophy. As Charles Fowler suggests, our profession has not made an effective case for music education:

> In spite of today's depressed educational marketplace, when school boards have their backs to the wall, we are still talking about the need for aesthetic education. Might we be the cause of some of our own problems? Could we be our own worst enemy?
>
> I believe that we must begin to view what we already do in different terms—in effect, to redefine ourselves.[9]

Looking back on his own considerable contributions, Charles Leonhard reaches a similar conclusion:

> I began emphasizing aesthetic education more than thirty years ago in *Education,* a now-defunct journal, with an article titled "Music Education: Aesthetic Education."
>
> At the time of publication of that article and during the intervening years, I never anticipated that the concept of aesthetic education would come to be used as the major tenet in the justification of music education. That has, however, happened. As a result, the profession has been sated with vague esoteric statements of justification that no one understands, including, I suspect, most of the people who make those statements.[10]

While the failures of past philosophy are numerous and profound, it is unrealistic to conclude that our curricular insecurity results entirely from philosophical misunderstandings about music education among ourselves or between ourselves and the public at large. This is so, I suggest, because in addition to the factors reviewed above, "security" is a two-way relationship: Something becomes secure in, or is secured by, something else. In our case, that "something else" is schooling: the context in which music educators attempt to educate children.

I suggest that underlying all the above problems and their various combinations is a more fundamental problem. The functions, principles, and corollaries of schooling are incompatible with the ideals of education in general and the values of music education in particular. As a result, a central challenge facing our profession lies not so much in music or music education but in the nature of schooling.

2. The Functions of Schooling

Western societies expect schools to fulfill several functions. Central among these are what educational researcher Mark Holmes calls the "allocative," "custodial," and "academic-vocational" functions of schooling.[11] The *allocative* function concerns jobs. In democratic societies, schools are expected to prepare young people for a wide range of vocations and professions. This function is fundamental because the school has a virtual monopoly on preparing and certifying students for employment. This function is also a societal imperative because there are few alternatives to public schools for this purpose.[12] The correlation between the amount and the type of schooling one achieves and one's future job and income is well established. As a result, schools will likely continue in their role of sifting and sorting students for future employment.

Closely allied to the allocative function of schools is their *custodial* function. Schools, says Holmes, are expected to "hold" students until they can be absorbed by employment or supported in their unemployment.[13] In fact, principals are especially concerned about the custodial efficiency of their institutions. This is not surprising; parents and communities become very alarmed when schools fail to control absenteeism, protect vulnerable children, and exercise appropriate discipline. Of course, society at large has the same concerns; if young people do not attend school, social stability can be threatened. (Indeed, drop-outs are more often found in unemployment lines than museums, churches, and concert halls.) Accordingly, the custodial function of schools is a societal imperative because communities cannot survive without the kind of "benign asylum"[14] that schools provide.

Educational rhetoric rarely mentions the allocative and custodial necessity of schools. Emphasis is placed, instead, on two functions that have become synonymous with the central purposes of public schooling during the last one hundred years or so: academic development and vocational training.

At the start of the twentieth century, Western expectations for public schooling were straightforward. Education was directed chiefly toward upper- and middle-class men seeking professional training and toward women seeking a liberal arts preparation for entry into "proper society."[15] But when the old social structure came unraveled at the outbreak of World War I, Western societies began to look for a new foundation on which to build their future. They found it in the idea of academic (formal) knowledge and vocational preparation through mass schooling. Knowledge (in the formal sense) was seen as the key to the future, and schooling was seen as the means of distributing the key. This was especially true in North America, where the idea of universal schooling meshed with the egalitarian aspirations of a classless society and a widespread popular belief in the American Dream (the belief in unlimited opportunities to those who get an education and work hard).

But while there was general agreement that the academic and vocational functions were basic to schooling, two problems arose and remain today. First, even where there is a consensus that academic studies are good for all, there is seldom a consensus about academic content, let alone the means of teaching and learning this content. Second, a long-standing tension exists between the academic and vocational functions of schooling. The vocational function goes in and out of favor in synchrony with the rise and fall of demands for a more practical, as opposed to a liberal, education.

Universal schooling has undergone fundamental changes during its evolution. Society's expectation of equal opportunities for the "good life" has caused academic and vocational offerings to change in accordance with three basic principles. Roger Clark calls these the principles of "universal accessibility," "universal achievement," and "universal application."[16]

3. The Principles of Schooling

Central to the idea of universal schooling is the principle of *accessibility*. Any domain of knowledge deemed a school subject must not only be legally accessible to all, it must be personally accessible to all. The Old-World assumption that only upper-class and "talented" children should benefit from education was eventually replaced in this century with the belief that every child deserves equal access to future success through a menu of subjects that are inherently learnable.

Closely linked to accessibility is the principle of universal *achievement*. The Old-World assumption that only upper-class and talented children were capable of achieving an education was replaced with the belief that all children are equally capable of learning and graduating from secondary school. As the twentieth century proceeded, however, the gap between society's belief in the equality of all children and the reality of individual differences (resulting from a variety of personal and social factors) began to widen. This gap has gradually shaken public confidence in the probability of equal achievement and, therefore, equal access to the good life.

To enhance the possibility of universal achievement, some communities have invested heavily in developing excellent teaching-learning situations in their schools, including recruiting a corps of excellent teachers. In many other cases, however, school systems have attempted to enhance the possibility of universal achievement by continually reformulating their standards and requirements, as reflected in trends such as nongraded schools, academic streaming, and the introduction of courses "of interest to the general school population." Thus, and not surprisingly, critics have decried what they view as a steady lowering of the demands made upon college-bound students since the 1970s.[17] In these and other ways, school systems have adopted the principle of universal achievement.

Once a society grants that all children should and can achieve an education, it becomes imperative that everything deemed a school subject meet a standard of universal *application* to all children (or be viewed as applicable to all children). Today, whatever curricular offerings are perceived to lack universal application are either eliminated or moved to the periphery of the school menu.

Public support for education peaked in the 1960s. Coincident with this peak, public schooling embraced the principles of universal accessibility, achievement, and application. At the same time, however, not all subjects had succeeded in securing the full support of administrators and the general public. In fact, ambiguity still surrounds even the most conventional subjects. For example, it is not difficult to find students and parents who question whether poetry, calculus, or chemistry are "basic" in the sense of being accessible, achievable, and/or applicable to all. Indeed, students and parents for whom the school is chiefly allocative and custodial frequently challenge the relevancy of a passing grade in a subject (e.g., poetry or European history) that does not appear directly related to a career in (say) software design, accounting, or law. Howard Gardner agrees and elaborates:

> Most students (and, for that matter, many parents and teachers) cannot provide compelling reasons for attending school. The reasons cannot be discerned within the school experience, nor is there faith that what is acquired in school will actually be utilized in the future. Try to justify the quadratic equation or the Napoleonic wars to an inner-city high school student—or his parents! The real world appears elsewhere: in the media, in the marketplace, and all too frequently in the demimonde of drugs, violence, and crime. Much if not most of what happens in schools happens because that is the way it was done in earlier generations, not because we have a convincing rationale for maintaining it today. The oft-heard statement that school is basically custodial rather than educational harbors more than a grain of truth.[18]

4. The Corollaries of Schooling

Attendance regulations, behavior codes, and grades are among the most obvious corollaries of the school's functional imperatives. This is so because schools cannot rely on students' intrinsic interest in learning to guarantee their continuous attendance and full cooperation. As Holmes observes, young people attend school partly because they want to, partly because they are obliged to, and partly because they rightly see schooling as the most direct path to future employment.[19] As a result, school authorities attempt to maintain *control* in four basic ways: through charismatic means (i.e., by means of excellent teachers who can generate, motivate, and hold students' interests in learning); through traditional means (societal norms, customs, and rules); through legal or bureaucratic means (attendance regulations, conduct codes, and grades); and through student-proof and teacher-proof curricula.[20]

When teachers are incompetent, when the charisma of principals and teachers becomes depleted, or when students are either unaware or opposed to societal norms, school authority is often reduced to a system of strict attendance regulations and conduct codes supported by explicit consequences in the form of grades and punishments (e.g., detentions, suspensions, and expulsions). Holmes develops this point in relation to secondary schools:

> As students become more and more aware of their publicly proclaimed "individual rights," they are less likely to comply with rules, customs and norms because the principal says so, or because students have always done it that way. Taught that they have equal rights and freedom in a democracy, they are sufficiently misguided to act as if it were true. What is left is legal, bureaucratic authority.[21]

Indeed (and unfortunately for students and teachers alike), the corollaries of schooling often coalesce into a culture of control that subverts the best educational efforts of teachers and administrators. Linda McNeil continues: "When the school's organization becomes centered on managing and controlling, teachers and students take school less seriously. They fall into a ritual of teaching and learning that tends toward minimal standards and minimum effort."[22]

Of course, if educators were to make school attendance voluntary, students' intrinsic interests in learning might rise. Then again, voluntary attendance would likely spell the end of universal schooling. Similarly, if schools abandoned grades, then all students would be free to pursue knowledge "for its own sake." Some nonschool approaches to education often come close to this goal; for example, grade-free apprenticeship programs are common in business and industry, and many community-based music education and athletic programs achieve extraordinary results without tests and grades. But because grading and testing are so closely tied to the allocative, custodial, and academic-vocational functions of schooling, abolishing grades would be tantamount to the abolition of public schooling itself.

5. A Fundamental Problem

A fundamental problem confronting the long-term security of music education is that while the ideals of education are primarily concerned with the whole child, including matters of self-development, integrity, social competence, cultural awareness, tolerance, and creativity, the functions of schooling are not. In addition, allocation, custody, and the academic-vocational functions of schooling are tied to mechanisms of short-term utility and control.

The upshot of these disjunctions is profound. It forces our young people to face an intolerable contradiction. On one hand, Western societies encourage children to believe that a balanced life, personal fulfillment, and enjoyment are fundamental to living the good life and working effectively. On the other hand, many school systems make it impossible for children to attain these values by failing to provide the qualified teachers, resources, and, therefore, the knowledge that students need to achieve these values.[23]

Clearly, then, the problem before us is not a practical one but a broadly philosophical one. As Holmes puts it: "The problem is not: How can the school do everything that is expected of it? Rather it is: What does society really want it to do?"[24] Diane Ravitch agrees: "Pedagogical practice follows educational philosophy, and it is obvious that we do not yet have a philosophical commitment to education that is sound enough and strong enough to withstand the erratic dictates of fashion."[25]

Put another way, the insecure circumstances of many school music programs can be traced to a social and philosophical paradox: that what teachers aspire to do because society says they should is compromised (or negated) by what schooling is obliged to do because society says it must. As a result, what schools end up doing (or not doing) is often at odds with what the general public and experts (including music educators) really want schools to do.

There is no easy way to close the gap between the ideals of education and the realities of many public (and private) schools. In an ideal world, we could do away with the school's allocative and custodial functions and their corollaries (behavior codes and grades). But our world is not ideal, and the allocative and custodial functions of schools will most likely endure. In addition, the present form of the elementary school has endured more or less intact for more than a hundred years; [26]the secondary school has survived for more than seventy years in North America and (in a more variable form) for eighty or ninety years in Western Europe. During this time, the functions of schooling have remained clear in the minds of educators and the general public. As a result, the nature of schooling will likely continue to constrain the best efforts of music teachers and sympathetic administrators, especially in situations where the functions and corollaries of schooling take extreme forms.

If this is the case, what alternatives do we have? Given our present circumstances, what can we do to further the aims and values of music education programs within the confines of public schooling?

6. Toward the Future: The Short Term

In the short term, securing the place of music in public education depends on affirming to ourselves and others that MUSIC matters and that the root of our security problem lies principally in the nature of schooling, not in the nature and significance of MUSIC. The security of music education depends upon securing the integrity of MUSIC education. The future depends on making music education more musical, more artistic, and more creative by continuing to improve our philosophical understandings of MUSIC and by continuing to improve the musicianship of pre-service and in-service teachers. The values of music education will be achieved only by deepening and broadening students' musicianship; and the achievement of these values will be demonstrated most effectively to parents, teachers, administrators, and school boards by the quality of our students' musical thinking-in-action.

Our future does not lie in schemes designed to make music education less musical. This may seem too obvious to mention until we remind ourselves that some theorists are serious when they urge music educators to "save" school music programs by teaching music as a scholastic subject[27] or by integrating music with subjects "across the curriculum" or by submerging music in multi-arts courses. These notions are based on false assumptions about the nature and values of MUSIC, about the nature of schooling, and about the nature of the problems we face. By implementing approaches that deny students the opportunity to develop musicianship (and therefore prevent students from achieving the aims of music education), these shortsighted notions jeopardize the efforts they purport to save.

In terms of what our profession can do for itself, securing the place of music education depends on preparing ourselves to explain and demonstrate to others that MUSIC is achievable, accessible, and applicable to all students. In this regard, our ongoing tasks include the following:

1. To develop and refine the critical thinking abilities of pre-service and in-service music teachers with regard to the fundamental concepts of our professional prac-

tice. Included in this primary task is the need to clarify to ourselves and others what music is and why it matters.

2. To develop and renew the musicianship and educatorship of pre-service and in-service music teachers through exemplary models of music education in action.
3. To identify excellent MUSIC education curricula and replicate these curricula across districts through models of excellent music teaching in action. Included in this task is the need to demonstrate and document how MUSIC is being taught and learned effectively as a diverse, multicultural practice.
4. To develop dynamic communities of musical interest by expanding music education horizontally and vertically beyond conventional schooling. This task includes developing ways to link school and community-based music education programs; initiate and develop links between professional music educators and the musical needs and interests of corporate employees; and develop mentor-apprenticeship relationships between senior music students and junior students in the same school system.

7. Toward the Future: The Long Term

The most essential long-term task facing our profession involves enrolling parents, colleagues, administrators, politicians, and others in the quest to make schools more *educational* in nature and, therefore, more hospitable for music teaching and learning. Closely linked to this task is the need to demonstrate to parents, colleagues, and administrators that by supporting the aims of music education, schools may also be able to fulfill their functional obligations more effectively.

Many administrators, school boards, and parents lack a realistic concept of education that embodies their expectations for children and schools. We might therefore begin by developing and advocating a concept of education that is more in line with the realities of schooling and modern life than past rhetoric understands or allows. A shared concept of education that bridges the gap between pure idealism and pure functionalism is an essential part of making schools into centers of worthwhile teaching and learning.

While "education" has come to mean many things, the essence of the word suggests that our efforts ought to focus on the full development of the young in all matters subject to deliberate action. Education, says the philosopher Clive Beck, is "any valuable human development that is more or less deliberately induced (by oneself or others)."[28] Similarly, Lawrence Cremin takes education to mean "the deliberate, systematic, and sustained effort to transmit, evoke, or acquire knowledge, attitudes, values, skills, or sensibilities, as well as any outcomes of that effort."[29]

A more direct way of expressing this is to say that education seeks to develop students as *people* rather than as mere job-fillers. As Beck maintains, *education is for life; education ought to be conceived for life as a whole,* not just for one aspect of life, such as work or schooling.[30] These thoughts point us toward a more realistic perspective on the purposes of education.

When development is discussed in the context of school—child development, student development, human development—school boards and administrators often translate this into an exclusive concern for the acquisition of formal, textbook knowledge. As I have argued throughout this book, however, and as many contemporary philosophers and psychologists also argue, schooling's myopic focus on verbal knowledge as the sole means and end of human development is the result of a long-standing misconception. Human consciousness (or "mind") is not mediated solely by linguistic or mathematical processes. Hence, it is absurd to suggest that verbal-mathematical development is the only key to worthwhile development, or even the major key.[31] Besides, scholastic knowledge is too specialized and, most often, too abstractly organized by traditional curriculum-making procedures to serve as the foundation of everyday cognition. In short, although academic achievement is necessary, it is not sufficient for an education.

The same criticisms apply to so-called liberal education. In essence, a liberal education involves gaining an understanding of the various types of formal knowledge developed in the context of the liberal arts (including literature, languages, and history), not necessarily leading or preparing students for any particular profession or vocation.

Unfortunately, the focus of many efforts in liberal education has become rather self-indulgent and, therefore, developmentally limited. A truly developmental education cannot afford such a selfish focus. Growth in formal knowledge is an important aspect of cognitive development. But education must ensure that verbal knowledge does not become an end in itself. The academic dimension of schooling has fallen into the trap that John Dewey warned us against decades ago in his *Democracy and Education:*

> There is a standing danger that the material of formal instruction will be merely the subject matter of the schools, isolated from the subject matter of life-experience. Thus we reach the ordinary notion of education: the notion which ignores its social necessity and its identity with all human association that affects conscious life, and which identifies it with imparting information about remote matters and the conveying of learning through verbal signs: the acquisition of literacy.[32]

Some amount of liberal education is essential for a rational way of life. As Clive Beck suggests, however, a large amount of liberal education for all young people is difficult to justify.[33] For people entering academia, intensive and extensive study of a wide range of academic disciplines makes sense. But we must not assume, as administrators and schools often do, that an educational program suitable for future academics is the best for all young people. (We cannot even assume that a liberal education is sufficient for future academics.)

There is much to do to free traditional schooling from its narrow agenda. To begin, it is crucial for students, parents, teachers, administrators, and the general public to recognize that much more is involved in the full and beneficial development of the individual than "the acquisition of literacy" in the reductionistic sense of academic knowledge (the so-called basics, or "readin', writin', and 'rithmetic'').

What more? Human cultures past and present pursue a fairly common set of life values goals[34] that include the following: happiness, health, enjoyment, self-growth, self-knowledge, wisdom, freedom, fellowship, and self-esteem—for oneself and for others. Most prominent, perhaps, is happiness. Happiness holds a central place in the world's philosophic traditions and in the minds of every person, young and old. But ranking is not the point. The point, says Beck, is that what these life values have in common is the fact that people seldom ask: "Why do you want . . . happiness, health, enjoyment, self-growth, self-knowledge, wisdom, freedom, fellowship, and self-esteem?"[35]

All school subjects, experiences, aims, and attainments ought to be conceived in terms of their relationship to life goals. Schooling should enable learners to achieve life goals both in school and beyond school—in working life, family life, and social life.[36] Schooling, properly conceived, is for life, both now and in the future. And a truly developmental administrator is one who plans and justifies his or her school curriculum in relation to the attainment of life values, not simply in terms of job allocation, custodial efficiency, or the goals of academic-vocational studies.

Life goals are not the only relevant goals of schooling, but they deserve more emphasis than they have received. They have been seriously neglected by school administrators. This neglect accounts for the inhumane nature of many public school systems, as well as for schooling's general lack of academic and custodial effectiveness. This is so, I suggest, because a student's pursuit of life values is inextricably linked with his or her pursuit of other goals (including academic-vocational goals) and with the goals of other people. As a result, when school boards or administrators make it impossible for students to achieve their fundamental life values during the long periods they spend in school, parents and administrators can expect to reap the results: lower-than-average levels of academic and vocational achievement and/or higher-than-average levels of custodial difficulty (i.e., disruptive or absent students). Indeed, the surprising thing about schools where life values are unimportant is not that students drop out, but that more students do not drop out.

To summarize, the pursuit of life values is natural and essential to human beings. Thus there are many good reasons for schools to pursue life values and no good reasons for schools not to pursue them. More particularly, it makes perfect educational, economic, custodial and practical sense for school boards and administrators to ensure that students are provided with the knowledge and resources they need to achieve the above-mentioned values.

If this is so, then there are many good reasons for schools to make music education a basic part of the core curriculum, kindergarten through grade 12, and no good reasons for schools not to do so. The primary values of MUSIC education are the primary values of Music: self-growth, self-knowledge, musical enjoyment, flow, and the happiness that arises from these—in short, a certain musical way of life. *MUSIC education is a unique and major source of several fundamental life values.*

Through the development of musicianship, music educators provide their students with the key to achieving several essential life goals, both now and in the future. Indeed, life goals are not distant in time. As I have emphasized, the aims of music education and the primary goals of every music teaching-learning situation are to enable students to achieve self-growth, self-knowledge, and musical enjoyment in the present by educating students' musicianship in balanced relation to authentic musical challenges. Achievement is not something that manifests itself only in high grades and that occurs only in the distant future. Achievement in the context of schooling can and should include the achievement of working understandings of one's world and an education in and for one's *life*.

In addition to the achievement of life goals, school music programs that adopt a praxial philosophy can also be seen to mitigate the negative consequences of schooling's functional imperatives. That is, if schools want and need to retain students for their own good and for the good of society and if schools are genuinely interested in students achieving success in academic or vocational studies, then the best interests of schooling lie in providing all students with opportunities to attain these life values through challenging school music education programs designed as reflective musical practicums. By actively supporting the aims of music education, school systems increase the likelihood that students will learn to *make a life as well as a living* both inside and outside school.

As a result of the multicultural nature of MUSIC, school music programs are also a primary way by which students can achieve self-identity, self-respect, and a sense of tolerance for themselves and others. Since schools today are concerned with preparing students for work and life in pluralistic societies and since schools themselves are more culturally diverse than ever, it stands to reason that schools should support the rich, cumulative, and enjoyable multicultural learning experiences that inhere in school music programs that induct children into a variety of music cultures.

8. Toward the Future: The Professional Music Educator

An excellent music curriculum, I have said, is largely an excellent music teacher in action. I might add that an excellent school music program reflects the dedication of one or more teachers who are musically, pedagogically, philosophically, psychologically, and politically savvy. Indeed, the challenges inherent in music teaching and learning are considerable.

While the professional practice of music education demands a great deal in terms of knowledge, energy, and dedication, it also gives back in very significant ways. For if we view our short- and long-term problems as *challenges* rather than as pure difficulties, and if we view our musicianship and educatorship as the know-how we need to meet these challenges, then it becomes possible to see how our participation in this professional practice called music education affords us the opportunity to achieve the internal goods of our chosen profession: self-growth, self-knowledge, enjoyment, and, perhaps, the kind of wisdom that comes from conducting one's professional career unselfishly to help others achieve the values of MUSIC for themselves.

The continuous need to improve ourselves as musicians and teachers, to improve our curricula, and to work for the long-term security of music education— all these are significant lifelong challenges that give meaning and purpose to our personal and professional lives. As such, they become an important part of our many "life themes."[37] Unlike some challenges that pivot on material rewards, the challenges of music teaching are authentic because we take them up out of deep convictions about the values of MUSIC and the importance of sharing these values with others. In all these ways, the major challenges that occupy our professional lives and the expertise we gain to meet these problems unify our lives. They give us *vita activa*:[38] a life of meaning, purpose, and intensified action. They give us access to a "certain way of life." In the process of enabling students to make a life as well as a living—in giving our students the keys to achieving their own life values and life themes—we do the same for ourselves. And in this, we are connected to a worldwide community of dedicated practitioners past and present.

The future of music education—and, perhaps, the future of education itself—lies in facing our problems as challenges, in supporting our fellow practitioners, and in inducting new music teachers into our practice so that all students in all schools can achieve the profound values of music education. It is to this, our very human practice—the "movers and shakers of the world"—that I proffer this book.

> We are the music-makers,
> And we are the dreamers of dreams,
> Wandering by lone sea-breakers,
> And sitting by desolate streams;
> World-losers and world forsakers,
> On whom the pale moon gleams:
> Yet we are the movers and shakers
> Of the world forever, it seems.
> ARTHUR WILLIAM EDGAR O'SHAUGHNESSY, "*We are the Music-Makers*"

Questions for Discussion and Review

1. Most Western countries hold a common set of educational aims. Compare the official aims of your school district with the aims of several other districts, states, provinces, and countries. To what extent is music education included in these statements? Reflect critically on the values that these documents ascribe to music education.

2. "Schools are often organized and managed in ways that contradict the purposes of education." Do you agree? If so, why? If not, why not?

3. This chapter suggests that the insecurity of music in the school curriculum is due in large part to a basic paradox. Explain this paradox.

4. This book offers several reasons why MUSIC is achievable, accessible, and applicable to all students. After reviewing this chapter and previous chapters, write a reflective critique of these reasons.

5. Summarize this chapter's concept of education and compare it to the notions of liberal education, vocational training, and the so-called basics movement. Examine other texts for alternative concepts of education. State your concept of education.

6. What do we mean by *life goals*? How are life goals related to the pursuit of academic and vocational goals? Explain the relationships between the fundamental values of music education and life values.

7. Explain the relationships between the challenges facing professional music educators and the concept of *life themes*.

Supplementary Sources

Clive Beck. *Better Schools: A Values Perspective*. New York: Falmer Press, 1990. The first three chapters of this book examine schooling, schools, and students' needs in relation to the concept of an education for life.

Carl Bereiter and Marlene Scardamalia. *Surpassing Ourselves: An Inquiry Into the Nature and Implications of Expertise*. LaSalle, Ill.: Open Court Publishing, 1993. Chapter 7 analyzes the weaknesses of conventional schooling and posits an alternative view of the school as a knowledge-building community.

Howard Gardner. *The Unschooled Mind*. New York: Basic Books, 1991. Chapters 10–13 offer many recommendations for reforming schools toward the goal of an education for understanding.

Linda McNeil. *The Contradictions of Control: School Structure and School Nature*. New York: Methuen, 1986. McNeil explains how conventional ways of organizing and managing schools compromises their educational efforts.

Mihalyi Csikszentmihalyi. *Flow: The Psychology of Optimal Experience*. New York: Harper and Row, 1990. Chapter 10, ''The Making of Meaning,'' explains the relationships between flow, meaning, purpose, and life themes.

Charles Fowler. ''Redefining the Mission of Music Education.'' In *Winds of Change: A Colloquium in Music Education with Charles Fowler and David J. Elliott,* ed. Marie McCarthy, pp. 4–20. New York: ACA Books and the University of Maryland at College Park, 1994. Fowler reflects on the curricular status of music education and outlines a value-centered paradigm for music education.

Notes

1. Philosophy and Music Education

1. Bennett Reimer, *Developing the Experience of Music*, 2d ed., (Englewood Cliffs, N.J.: Prentice Hall, 1985), p. 200.

2. Although this book acknowledges the kinds of music teaching and learning that take place in nonformal (community and other "non-school") settings and in informal (or incidental) ways, my focus here is on educational principles and procedures that are deliberately designed and formally instituted in school settings to enable and promote musical understanding. As described in the main text, the situations involving Clara Nette, Tim Pani, and Sara Band are examples of formal music education. The other two situations are examples of nonformal music education.

3. As Chapter 2 explains, James Mursell played a major role in constructing the foundations of music education as aesthetic education during the 1930s and '40s. Charles Leonhard built on Mursell's work, beginning with his seminal article, "Music Education—Aesthetic Education," *Education* 74, no. 1 (September 1953):23–26. For Leonhard's later reflections on aesthetic education, see his *A Realistic Rationale for Teaching Music* (Reston, Va.: Music Educators National Conference, 1985), p. 7.

4. For critical discussions of the MEAE philosophy, see: David J. Elliott, "Music Education as Aesthetic Education: A Critical Inquiry," *The Quarterly Journal of Music Teaching and Learning* 2, no. 3 (Fall 1991): 48–66; Wayne Bowman, "An Essay Review of Bennett Reimer's *A Philosophy of Music Education*," *The Quarterly Journal of Music Teaching and Learning* 2, no. 3 (Fall 1991):76–87; Estelle Jorgensen, "On Philosophical Method," in *Handbook of Research on Music Teaching and Learning*, ed. Richard Colwell (New York: Schirmer Books, 1992), pp. 91–101.

5. Aristotle, *Politics* (1339a15), trans. Jonathan Barnes, ed. Stephen Everson (Cambridge: Cambridge University Press, 1988), p. 189.

6. Bennett Reimer, *A Philosophy of Music Education*, 2d ed. (Englewood Cliffs, N.J.: Prentice Hall, 1989), p. 3. Similar senses appear in Charles Leonhard and Robert W. House, *Foundations and Principles of Music Education* (New York: McGraw-Hill, 1959), pp. 71–72, and Harold F. Abeles, Charles R. Hoffer, and Robert H. Klotman, *Foundations of Music Education* (New York: Schirmer Books, 1984), p. 33.

7. John Passmore, "Philosophy," in *The Encyclopedia of Philosophy*, ed. Paul Edwards (New York: Macmillan, 1967), vol. 6, p. 216.

8. Ibid.

9. Wayne Bowman, "Philosophy, Criticism, and Music Education: Some Tentative Steps Down a Less Travelled Road," *Bulletin of the Council for Research in Music Education*, no. 114 (Fall 1992):4.

10. Peter Elbow, *Embracing Contraries: Explorations in Learning and Teaching* (New York: Oxford University Press, 1986), pp. 257–63.

11. Kant is cited in Harold Entwistle. "The Relationship Between Theory and Practice," in *Philosophy of Education: Canadian Perspectives,* ed. Donald B. Cochrane and Martin Schiralli (Toronto: Collier Macmillan, 1982), p. 11.

12. Ibid., p. 12.

13. These three levels of intersection are originally described by Jonas Soltis, "Philosophy of Education," in *The Encyclopedia of Educational Research,* ed. H. E. Mitzel (New York: Macmillan, 1982), pp. 1407–11.

14. Ibid., p. 1407.

15. Chapters 10, 11, and 12 of this book make distinctions among the terms education, teaching, and schooling.

16. I am grateful to Eric McLuhan for drawing my attention to these distinctions.

17. Aristotle, *Poetics* (1450a15–24), trans. Gerald F. Else (Ann Arbor: University of Michigan Press, 1967), p. 27.

2. Toward a New Philosophy

1. Francis E. Sparshott, *The Concept of Criticism* (London: Oxford University Press, 1967), p. 7.

2. Ibid., p. 8.

3. Jerrold Levinson, *Music, Art, and Metaphysics* (Ithaca, N.Y.: Cornell University Press, 1990), p. 269.

4. Francis E. Sparshott makes this point in relation to dance. See his *Off the Ground: First Steps to a Philosophical Consideration of the Dance* (Princeton, N.J.: Princeton University Press, 1988), p. 192.

5. Ibid.

6. The other eight approaches are listed below with a brief note about the weaknesses of each. (1) The most obvious way to begin is to simply say what we think music *is* on the basis of our experience. Unfortunately, this "strategy" provides us with no method and no comprehensiveness at all. (2) We might begin by trying to say what the word *music* means. This route splits in two. One route leads us to probe the roots of the word *music*. But this is a dead end. The Greeks used *mousikē* in relation to a wide range of artistic and theoretical activities inspired by the Muses, including different kinds of singing and dancing, storytelling, poetry, and drama. The second option directs us to say what *music* means in common usage by probing what people actually do when they produce music or respond to music (as opposed to what they say they do). The problem here is that the specific means and ends of music around the world are inherently unstable. Accordingly, this approach is not so much a dead end as a circular path to nowhere. (3) A third strategy is to develop a taxonomy of music through induction. Unfortunately, the problems with induction are several and obvious. For one thing, categorizing what we collect as "music" avoids the prior question of what it is that we are categorizing in the first place. (4) A fourth way is to examine what scholars of music everywhere have said music is, past and present. Unfortunately, the concepts and practices that past and present researchers rely upon to decide what counts as music are also unstable; they change with time and cultural practice. (5) A fifth strategy is to develop a complete profile of the various aspects of meaning that music involves by gathering together all our memories of what we have ever heard, seen, experienced, and studied about music. The fatal flaw in this strategy is that there is no reasonable way of

generating such a profile or of saying how such a profile should be used. (6) A sixth strategy begins from undisputed cases of music. But what would our undisputed cases be? (7) A seventh possibility uses our understanding and experience of music as a basis for trying to decide the necessary and sufficient conditions something must meet before we call it "music." But of all the musical practices everywhere, what could we possibly find at the core of all of them that would give us anything but the most narrow and unrealistic concept? (8) The eighth strategy is a variation of the fifth and seventh. Instead of gathering together our understanding and experience of music as the basis of a profile, we could start with what we take as the key to our personal experience of music. We might then seek confirmation of our view in the writings and experiences of others. Susanne Langer follows this strategy in her seminal book *Philosophy in a New Key: A Study in the Symbolism of Reason, Rite and Art*. But while Langer's results are stirring, they are logically flawed, as I explain briefly near the end of this chapter and, in more detail, elsewhere (see my "Music Education as Aesthetic Education: A Critical Inquiry," *The Quarterly Journal of Music Teaching and Learning* 2, no. 3 [Fall 1991]: 58–64).

7. Levinson, *Music, Art, and Metaphysics,* pp. 269–70.

8. Ibid., pp. 270–71.

9. Ibid., p. 271.

10. Ibid.

11. Francis E. Sparshott, *The Theory of the Arts* (Princeton, N.J.: Princeton University Press, 1982), p. 473.

12. Ralph A. Smith, *The Sense of Art: A Study in Aesthetic Education* (New York: Routledge, 1989), p. 4.

13. Melvin Rader and Bertram Jessup, *Art and Human Values* (Englewood Cliffs, N.J.: Prentice Hall, 1976), p. 8.

14. Alexander Baumgarten, *Meditationes Philosophicae de Nonnullis ad Poema Pertinentibus* (1735), trans. and ed. Karl Aschenbrenner and William Holther (Berkeley: University of California Press, 1954).

15. As Sparshott notes, it was understood from the beginning that the intended focus of aesthetics was literary criticism. See Sparshott, *Theory,* pp. 17, 508n.

16. Sparshott, *Theory,* p.128.

17. Ibid.

18. Anthony Lord of Shaftesbury and Francis Hutcheson advanced several key ideas of aesthetics before Baumgarten provided the name. See F. Copleston, *A History of Western Philosophy* (New York: Image Books, 1964), p. 139. Moreover, as Peter Kivy points out, Hutcheson's treatise on aesthetics (noted below) may have been one of the first to address music directly. See Francis Hutcheson, *Inquiry Concerning Beauty, Order, Harmony, Design* (1725), ed. Peter Kivy (The Hague: Martinus Nijhoff, 1973).

19. Sparshott, *Theory,* p. 28.

20. According to Paul O. Kristeller, it was Charles Batteux who "was the first to set forth a clear-cut system of the fine arts in a treatise [of 1747] devoted exclusively to this subject." See Kristeller's *Renaissance Thought and the Arts: Collected Essays* (Princeton, N.J.: Princeton University Press, 1980), p. 199. Peter Kivy references this same point in his article, "Is Music an Art?," *Journal of Philosophy* 81 (October 1991): 548–49.

21. Sparshott, *Theory,* p. 103.

22. For a detailed discussion of this overlap, see Sparshott, *Theory,* pp. 102–30.

23. Terry Eagleton, *The Ideology of the Aesthetic* (Cambridge, Mass.: Basil Blackwell, 1990), p. 3.

24. Ibid., p. 23.

25. Herbert M. Schueller, *The Idea of Music: An Introduction to Musical Aesthetics in*

Antiquity and the Middle Ages (Kalamazoo, Mich.: Western Michigan University, 1988), p. 1; Lydia Goehr, *The Imaginary Museum of Musical Works: An Essay in the Philosophy of Music* (Oxford: Clarendon Press, 1992), pp. 123–31.

26. Goehr, *Imaginary Museum,* pp. 178–203. J. S. Bach was a rare exception to this rule. Although Bach was often restricted by the inferior status accorded musicians in the structure of Baroque society, he managed to achieve "an astonishing personal latitude," as Christoph Wolff explains in his *Bach: Essays On His Life and Music* (Cambridge, Mass.: Harvard University Press, 1991), pp. 32–33.

27. Goehr, *Imaginary Museum,* pp. 182–89.

28. Ibid., p. 178.

29. Ibid., pp. 185–86; 202.

30. Ibid., p. 147.

31. Ibid., pp. 173–74.

32. Ibid., p. 205ff.

33. Ibid., p. 170ff.

34. Ibid., p. 244ff.

35. Francis E. Sparshott, *The Structure of Aesthetics* (Toronto: University of Toronto Press, 1963), p. 3.

36. John Hospers, "Problems of Aesthetics," in *The Encyclopedia of Philosophy,* vol. 1, ed. Paul Edwards (New York: Macmillan, 1967), p. 35.

37. For a succinct overview of philosophical thinking about music, see Philip A. Alperson, "Introduction: The Philosophy of Music," in *What Is Music? An Introduction to the Philosophy of Music,* ed. Philip A. Alperson (New York: Haven Publications, 1987), pp. 3–9. For a more detailed discussion, see Francis E. Sparshott, "Aesthetics of Music," in *The New Grove Dictionary of Music and Musicians,* vol. 1, pp. 120–34, ed. Stanley Sadie (London: Macmillan, 1980).

38. The survey of sources in the next section of this chapter references only authors I view as central to the development of music education philosophy and, therefore, to the immediate discussion (i.e., Mursell, Broudy, Leonhard and House, Reimer). But as the interested reader will notice, the influence of the aesthetic doctrine extends to many other "foundations" texts, including the following: Thomas A. Regelski, *Principles and Problems of Music Education* (Englewood Cliffs, N.J.: Prentice Hall, 1975); Abeles, Hoffer, and Klotman, *Foundations*; Malcolm Tait and Paul Haack, *Principles and Processes of Music Education: New Perspectives* (New York: Teachers College Press, 1984). In contrast to the above, one source deserves special credit for its critical attitude toward aesthetic claims: see Christopher Small, *Music, Society, Education* (New York: Schirmer Books, 1977).

39. James Mursell, "Principles of Music Education," in *Music Education: The Thirty-Fifth Yearbook of the National Society for the Study of Education, Part Two,* ed. Guy Whipple (Bloomington, Ill.: Public School Publishing, 1936), p. 6.

40. James L. Mursell, *Human Values in Music Education* (New York: Silver Burdett, 1934), p. 35.

41. Harry S. Broudy, "A Realistic Philosophy of Music Education," in *Basic Concepts in Music Education: The Fifty-Seventh Yearbook of the National Society for the Study of Education,* ed. Nelson B. Henry (Chicago: University of Chicago Press, 1958), p. 69.

42. Leonhard and House, *Foundations,* p. 101.

43. Ibid.

44. Ibid., pp. 100–01.

45. Ibid., pp. 106–14.

46. Abraham A. Schwadron, *Aesthetics: Dimensions for Music Education* (Washington, D. C.: Music Educators National Conference, 1967), pp. 93–95.

47. Keith Swanwick, *A Basis for Music Education* (Windsor, Eng.: NFER Nelson, 1979), p. 58.

48. Ibid., p. 43.

49. Keith Swanwick, *Music, Mind, and Education* (London: Routledge, 1988), p. 101.

50. G. David Peters and Robert F. Miller, *Music Teaching and Learning* (New York: Longman, 1982), pp. 104–07.

51. Ibid., p. 15.

52. Reimer, *A Philosophy* (1989), pp. 99, 28.

53. Bennett Reimer, *A Philosophy of Music Education,* 1st ed. (Englewood Cliffs, N.J.: Prentice Hall, 1970), p. 52.

54. Reimer, *A Philosophy* (1989), p. 27.

55. Reimer, *A Philosophy* (1970), p. 86.

56. Susanne K. Langer, *Feeling and Form* (New York: Charles Scribner's Sons, 1953), p. 27.

57. Ibid., p. 40.

58. Susanne K. Langer, "The Cultural Importance of the Arts (1958)," in *Aesthetics and Problems of Education,* ed. Ralph A. Smith (Urbana: University of Illinois Press, 1971), p. 94.

59. Leonhard and House, *Foundations,* p. 100.

60. Reimer, *A Philosophy* (1989), p. 63.

61. Reimer, *A Philosophy* (1970), p. 39.

62. Swanwick, *A Basis,* p. 112.

63. Swanwick, *Music,* pp. 1, 54.

64. The arguments I have in mind include the following: Francis E. Sparshott, "Aesthetics of Music: Limits and Grounds," in *What Is Music? An Introduction to the Philosophy of Music,* ed. Philip A. Alperson (New York: Haven Publications, 1987), pp. 33–98; Philip A. Alperson, "What Should One Expect from a Philosophy of Music Education?," *Journal of Aesthetic Education* 25, no. 3 (Fall 1991): pp. 215–42; John Shepherd, Phil Virden, Graham Vulliamy, and Trevor Wishart, eds., *Whose Music? A Sociology of Musical Languages* (London: Latimer, 1977); Susan McClary, "The Blasphemy of Talking Politics During Bach Year," in *Music and Society: The Politics of Composition, Performance and Reception,* ed. Richard Leppert and Susan McClary (Cambridge: Cambridge University Press, 1987), pp. 13–62; Rose Rosengard Subotnick, "On Grounding Chopin," in Leppert and McClary, *Music and Society,* pp. 105–31.

65. Arnold Berleant, "The Historicity of Aesthetics: Part 1," *British Journal of Aesthetics* 26, no. 2 (1986): 104.

66. Landon E. Beyer, "Aesthetics and the Curriculum: Ideological and Cultural Form in School Practice" (Ph.D. diss., University of Wisconsin-Madison, 1981), p. 233.

67. Ibid., p. 248.

68. Arthur C. Danto, *The Philosophical Disenfranchisement of Art* (New York: Columbia University Press, 1986), p. 12.

69. Ibid., pp. 12–13.

70. As I have explained, the aesthetic concept of music education has been directly and indirectly endorsed in nearly every music education foundations text written during the last several decades. Although criticisms of particular aspects of MEAE have appeared occasionally, more detailed analyses are very recent, as listed in the note 4, to Chapter 1.

71. Carl Dahlhaus, *Esthetics of Music* (Cambridge: Cambridge University Press, 1982), p. 10.

72. Nicholas Wolterstorff, "The Work of Making a Work of Music," in *What Is Music?*

An Introduction to the Philosophy of Music, ed. Philip A. Alperson (New York: Haven Publications, 1987), p. 115.

73. Smith, *The Sense of Art,* p. 4.

74. Leonhard and House, *Foundations,* p. 3.

75. Ibid., p.117.

76. See Charles Fowler, ed., *The Crane Symposium: Toward an Understanding of the Teaching and Learning of Music Performance* (Potsdam: Potsdam College of the State University of New York, 1988), p. 196.

77. Ibid.

78. Ibid.

79. Reimer, *A Philosophy* (1989), p. 167.

80. Ibid., p. 169.

81. Ibid., p. 168.

82. Ibid., pp. 197–98.

83. Ibid., p. 198.

84. Bowman, "An Essay Review," pp. 84–85.

85. Swanwick, *A Basis,* p. 54.

86. Ibid., p. 53.

87. Swanwick, *Music,* pp. 42–45.

88. See Swanwick's discussion of performance in *A Basis,* p. 42ff.

89. Swanwick is an exception insofar as he rests his concept of creativity on early psychological investigations of the topic. See his *A Basis,* pp. 81–94.

90. Reimer, *A Philosophy* (1989), pp. 56–73.

91. Ibid., pp. 191–93.

92. Ibid., pp. 190–91.

93. The primary objective of the general music program, says Reimer, is "to improve every student's capacity for musical listening." See Reimer, *A Philosophy* (1989), p. 168.

94. For a prime example of a general music curriculum based on the aesthetic philosophy, see Bennett Reimer, Elizabeth Crook, David Walker, et. al., *Silver Burdett Music* (Morristown, N.J.: Silver Burdett, 1974, 1978, 1981, 1985).

95. Reimer, *A Philosophy* (1989), p. 185.

96. Ibid.

97. Jorgensen, "On Philosophical Method," p. 92.

98. Ibid.

99. Reimer, *A Philosophy* (1989), pp. 120–21.

100. Ibid. See Reimer's chart, p. 120.

101. "Immaculate perception" is not my term. I owe it to Keith Reid, a former student who improvised the term during a 1988 class discussion.

102. Reimer, *A Philosophy* (1989), p. 103.

103. S. J. Markowitz, "Art and the Tyranny of the Aesthetic" (Ph.D. diss., University of Michigan, 1983), p. 43.

104. Reimer, *A Philosophy* (1989), p. 145.

105. Markowitz, "Art and the Tyranny," pp. 34–36.

106. Cf. Goehr, *Imaginary Museum,* pp. 272–73.

107. Ibid., p. 245.

108. Reimer, *A Philosophy* (1989), p. 27.

109. Ibid.

110. Ibid., pp. 42–43, 231–32.

111. Ibid., p. 42.

112. Swanwick, *Music,* pp. 24–30.

113. Peters and Miller, *Music Teaching*, p. 103.

114. Bowman, "An Essay Review," p. 84.

115. Reimer, *A Philosophy* (1989), p. 103.

116. Ibid.

117. Alperson, "What Should One Expect," p. 231.

118. Beyer, "Aesthetics and the Curriculum," p. 364.

119. Ibid., p. 362.

120. Ibid., p. 364.

121. See Susanne K. Langer, *Philosophy in a New Key: A Study in the Symbolism of Reason, Rite and Art*, 3d ed. (Cambridge, Mass.: Harvard University Press, 1976), pp. 204–45; and Langer, *Feeling and Form*, p. 28 ff.

122. Reimer, *A Philosophy* (1989), p. 53.

123. See, for example, Iris M. Yob, "The Form of Feeling," *Philosophy of Music Education Review* 1, no. 1 (Spring 1993): 18–32; and Forest Hansen, "Philosophy of Music Education in a Slightly New Key," *Philosophy of Music Education Review* 1, no. 1 (Spring 1993): 61–74.

124. For a thorough criticism of Langer's theory, see Malcolm Budd, *Music and the Emotions: The Philosophical Theories* (London: Routledge and Kegan Paul, 1985), pp. 104–20. Additional criticisms may be found in my article "Music Education as Aesthetic Education," pp. 58–64, and in Peter Kivy, *The Corded Shell: Reflections on Musical Expression* (Princeton, N.J.: Princeton University Press, 1980), pp. 43–44, 46–49, and 60–63.

125. Reimer, *A Philosophy* (1989), p. 101.

126. See Ernest Nagel's discussion, "Review of Langer's *Philosophy in a New Key*," *Journal of Philosophy* 40 (1943): 323–29.

127. Langer, *New Key*, pp. 218, 238.

128. Ibid., p. 218.

129. Leonard B. Meyer, *Emotion and Meaning in Music* (Chicago: University of Chicago Press, 1956). Reimer neglects to note that Langer and Meyer make opposing claims. After citing Langer's central thesis that the tonal structures of musical works are analogous to the general forms of feeling, Reimer contradicts Langer (and himself) by recommending Meyer's *Emotion and Meaning in Music* for explanations of how rhythm, melody, and other qualities of music produce conditions that arouse affect. See Reimer, *A Philosophy* (1989), p. 131.

130. For a thorough criticism of Meyer's theory, see Budd, *Music and the Emotions*, pp. 151–74. See also Randall R. Dipert, "Meyer's *Emotion and Meaning in Music*: A Sympathetic Critique of Its Central Claims," *In Theory Only* 6 (1983): 3–17; and my article, "Structure and Feeling in Jazz: Rethinking Philosophical Foundations," *Bulletin of the Council for Research in Music Education*, no. 95 (Winter 1987): 13–38.

131. Meyer, *Emotion*, p. 14.

132. See Budd, *Music and the Emotions*, pp. 151–74. The frustration of an expectation is not a sufficient condition for the arousal of emotions because human beings are not billiard balls; humans do not simply react to stimuli or circumstances. Expectations are always imbued with personal intentions. For example, if my bus fails to arrive on time as I expect, I may or may not experience an emotion, depending on where, when, and why I am traveling. The frustration of an expectation is not a necessary condition for the arousal of an emotion because there are many emotions, including happiness and enjoyment, that arise because something happens exactly the way we expect it to happen.

133. James T. Borhek and Richard F. Curtis, *A Sociology of Belief* (New York: John Wiley and Sons, 1975), pp. 114–115.

134. Nicolai Listenius, *Musica* (1537), trans. Albert Seay (Colorado Springs: Colorado College Music Press, 1975).

135. Dahlhaus, *Esthetics of Music.*

136. See Sparshott, "Aesthetics of Music: Limits and Grounds"; Wolterstorff, "The Work"; Alperson, "What Should One Expect"; and David Walhout, "The Nature and Function of Art," *Journal of Aesthetics and Art Criticism* 26, no.1 (Winter 1986): 16–25.

137. Here I am thinking of many kinds (or subpractices) of jazz, country and western, rock, so-called folk music, and so on.

138. For the purposes of this book, I prefer *musicer* to *musician* because the latter tends to imply the false (Western) notion that one must be a full-time professional to make music.

139. Sparshott, "Aesthetics of Music: Limits and Grounds," p. 52.

140. Sparshott, *Off the Ground,* p. 114.

141. Both Mary Louise Serafine and Leonard B. Meyer offer recent explanations of musical "style" that concur with this concept. See Serafine's *Music as Cognition: The Development of Thought in Sound* (New York: Columbia University Press, 1988), p. 30, and Meyer's *Style and Music: Theory, History, and Ideology* (Philadelphia: University of Pennsylvania Press, 1989), p. 3.

3. Musicing

1. The original source of this idea is Walhout, "The Nature and Function of Art," pp. 18–20. Note also that Christopher Small uses the term *musicking* in his *Music of the Common Tongue: Survival and Celebration in Afro-American Music* (New York: Riverrun Press, 1987), p. 50.

2. Wolterstorff, "The Work," p. 121.

3. For a development of this point, see Sparshott, *Theory,* pp. 34–35.

4. Saul Ross, "Epistemology, Intentional Action and Physical Education," in *Philosophy of Sport and Physical Activity,* ed. P. J. Galasso (Toronto: Canadian Scholars' Press, 1988), p. 124.

5. Ibid.

6. S. Hampshire, *Thought and Action* (London: Chatto and Windus, 1965), p. 154.

7. Daniel C. Dennett, *Consciousness Explained* (Boston: Little, Brown, 1991), pp. 33, 106.

8. For the full case against dualism, see Dennett, *Consciousness,* p. 33ff.

9. Ibid., p. 33.

10. Owen Flanagan, *Consciousness Reconsidered* (Cambridge, Mass.: MIT Press, 1992), p. xi.

11. Mark Johnson develops this theme in *The Body in the Mind: The Bodily Basis of Meaning, Imagination, and Reason* (Chicago: University of Chicago Press, 1987). See also Dennett, *Consciousness,* pp. 25–39.

12. Mihalyi Csikszentmihalyi and Isabella Csikszentmihalyi, eds., *Optimal Experience: Psychological Studies of Flow in Consciousness* (Cambridge: Cambridge University Press, 1988), p. 17.

13. Mihalyi Csikszentmihalyi, *Flow: The Psychology of Optimal Experience* (New York: Harper and Row, 1990), p. 29.

14. Csikszentmihalyi, *Flow,* p. 31.

15. Csikszentmihalyi and Csikszentmihalyi, *Optimal,* pp. 17–19.

16. Ibid., p. 19.

17. Vernon Howard provides a synthesis of Aristotle's perspective and an overview of

his thinking in the "Introduction" to *Varieties of Thinking,* ed. V. A. Howard (New York: Routledge, 1990), pp. 1–14.

18. Ibid. p. 6.

19. Ibid., p. 11.

20. Howard Gardner, *Frames of Mind: The Theory of Multiple Intelligences* (New York: Basic Books, 1983).

21. R. J. Sternberg, *The Triarchic Mind: A New Theory of Human Intelligence* (New York: Viking, 1988).

22. Howard Gardner, "Symposium on the Theory of Multiple Intelligences," in *Thinking: The Second International Conference,* ed. D. N. Perkins, Jack Lockhead, and John Bishop (Hillsdale, N.J.: Erlbaum, 1987), p. 80.

23. Robert J. Sternberg, *Metaphors of Mind* (New York: Cambridge University Press, 1990), p. 266.

24. Gardner, *Frames of Mind,* p. 69.

25. Gilbert Ryle, *The Concept of Mind* (New York: Penguin Books, 1949).

26. Carl Bereiter and Marlene Scardamalia, *Surpassing Ourselves: An Inquiry Into the Nature and Implications of Expertise* (La Salle, Ill.: Open Court Publishing, 1993), pp. 43–75.

27. The concepts of reflective practice, reflective practitioner, and reflective practicum are originally presented in Donald A. Schön, *The Reflective Practitioner: How Professionals Think in Action* (New York: Basic Books, 1983), and in his *Educating the Reflective Practitioner: Toward a New Design for Teaching and Learning in the Professions* (San Francisco: Jossey-Bass, 1987).

28. Schön, *Educating,* p. 22ff.

29. Here I follow Serafine's use of the terms *simultaneous* and *successive* as explained in her *Music as Cognition,* p. 74.

30. The terms *chain, transform,* and *abstract* are original to Serafine, *Music as Cognition,* pp. 74–88.

31. Ryle, *Concept of Mind,* pp. 30–32.

32. Ibid., p. 57.

33. Ross, "Epistemology," pp. 134–35.

34. John Macmurray, *The Self as Agent* (Atlantic Heights, N.J.: Humanities Press, 1957), p. 86.

35. Schön, *Educating,* p. 31.

36. Ryle, *Concept of Mind,* p. 53.

37. Ibid., pp. 54–55.

38. Ibid., p. 55. This is a rewording of Ryle, who says: "the ability to appreciate a performance does not involve the same degree of competence as the ability to execute it."

39. Reimer's philosophy defines "a concept" in the early "classical" way. See Reimer, *A Philosophy* (1989), pp. 80–84. I argue against Reimer's outdated notion of a concept in my "Music Education as Aesthetic Education," p. 57.

40. See, for example, Edward E. Smith, "Concepts and Thought," in *The Psychology of Human Thought,* ed. Robert J. Sternberg and Edward E. Smith (Cambridge: Cambridge University Press, 1988), pp. 19–49; and, K. Nelson, *Making Sense: The Acquisition of Shared Meaning* (Orlando, Fla.: Academic Press, 1985).

41. Jean Piaget, *The Origins of Intelligence in Children* (New York: International Universities Press, 1952), p. 359.

42. Jean Piaget, *Six Psychological Studies* (New York: Random House, 1967), p. 79.

43. Hubert L. Dreyfus, *What Computers Can't Do: The Limits of Artificial Intelligence* (New York: Harper and Row, 1979), p. 190.

44. Ross, "Epistemology," p. 93.

45. Sparshott, *Theory,* p. 32.

46. Ibid.

47. Dennett, *Consciousness,* p. 243.

48. Ibid:, p. 252.

49. The concept of cultural actions is explained in two sources. See P. C. W. Van Wieringen, "Discussion: Self-Organization or Representation? Let's Have Both," in *Cognition and Action in Skilled Behavior,* ed. A. M. Colley and J. R. Beech (Amsterdam: North Holland, 1988); and A. M. Colley and J. R. Beech, *Acquisition and Performance of Cognitive Skills* (Chichester, Eng.: John Wiley, 1989), p. 174.

50. Vernon Howard explains this distinction in his *Artistry: The Work of Artists* (Indianapolis: Hackett Publishing, 1982), p. 49.

51. Schön, *Educating,* p. 25.

52. Some writers use *music literacy* as a synonym for *musical understanding* and *musicianship.* This usage is misleading on two counts. First, *literacy* gives the false impression that knowing how to read music notation is the core of what it takes to be a competent or proficient music maker. More broadly, *music literacy* gives the false impression that musical understanding is essentially a matter of formal musical knowledge. I therefore eschew the use of *musical literacy* for anything more than references to coding and decoding music notation.

53. For a detailed discussion of the "languages of craft," see Howard, *Artistry,* pp. 59–109.

54. Schön, *Educating,* pp. 25–31.

55. Ibid., p. 31.

56. Bereiter and Scardamalia, *Surpassing Ourselves,* pp. 51–54.

57. Ibid.

58. Howard, *Artistry,* p. 182.

59. Ibid.

60. Ibid., pp. 182–85.

61. John Miller Chernoff, *African Rhythm and African Sensibility* (Chicago: University of Chicago Press, 1979), pp. 102, 106.

62. Ibid., pp. 106–07.

63. Ibid., p. 114.

64. Ibid., p. 108.

65. Ibid., p. 107.

66. Ibid., p. 151.

67. See Bereiter and Scardamalia, *Surpassing Ourselves,* pp. 54–58, and Harry S. Broudy, "Types of Knowledge and Purposes of Education," in *Schooling and the Acquisition of Knowledge,* ed. Richard C. Anderson, R. J. Spiro, and W. E. Montague (Hillsdale, N.J.: Erlbaum, 1977), pp. 1–18.

68. Israel Scheffler, "In Praise of Cognitive Emotions," *Teachers College Record* 79, no. 2 (1977), pp. 171–86.

69. Paul A. Wagner, "Will Education Contain Fewer Surprises for Students in the Future?," in *Varieties of Thinking,* ed. V. A. Howard (New York: Routledge, 1990), p. 161.

70. Ibid., p. 162.

71. Ibid., p. 161.

72. *Good Night.* A Russian folk song arranged by Doreen Rao for unison treble voices and piano (New York: Boosey and Hawkes, 1990), OCTB-6631.

73. Scheffler, "In Praise of Cognitive Emotions," p. 178. Also see Wagner, "Will Education Contain Fewer Surprises," p. 164. Wagner references related writings by Nelson

Goodman and Israel Scheffler to establish the point that cognition and emotion are interdependent.

74. V. A. Howard, *Learning by All Means: Lessons From the Arts* (New York: Peter Lang, 1992), p. 14.

75. Ibid., p. 13.

76. Ibid., p. 14.

77. Ibid., p. 15.

78. Ibid., pp. 16–19.

79. R. D. Archambault, ed., *John Dewey on Education: Selected Writings* (Chicago: University of Chicago Press, 1974), p. 151.

80. Howard Gardner, *The Unschooled Mind* (New York: Basic Books, 1991), pp. 238–39.

81. D. N. Perkins, "Art as Understanding," *Journal of Aesthetic Education* 22, no. 1 (Spring 1988): 114 ff.

82. Ibid.

83. Ibid.

84. Ibid., p. 115.

85. Ibid.

86. Ibid., p. 116.

87. Ibid.

88. I am grateful to Thomas Regelski for alerting me to the following sources on these points: Andrew Harrison, *Making and Thinking: A Study of Intelligent Activities* (Indianapolis: Hackett, 1978), and Randall R. Dipert, *Artifacts, Art Works, and Agency* (Philadelphia: Temple University Press, 1993).

89. See C. B. Fethe, "Hand and Eye: The Role of Craft in R. G. Collingwood's Aesthetic Theory," *British Journal of Aesthetics* 22, no. 1 (Winter 1982): 37–51; and Arnold Whittick, "Towards Precise Distinctions of Art and Craft," *British Journal of Aesthetics* 24, no. 1 (Winter 1984): 47–52.

90. Howard, *Artistry*, p. 26.

91. Hubert Dreyfus and Stuart E. Dreyfus, *Mind Over Machine: The Power of Human Intuition and Expertise in the Era of the Computer* (New York: Free Press, 1986), p. 21ff.

92. Ibid., p. 32.

93. Bereiter and Scardamalia, *Surpassing Ourselves*, p. 125ff.

94. Here I follow a basic principle of situated cognition as explained by John Seely Brown, Allan Collins, and Paul Duguid, "Situated Cognition and the Culture of Learning," *Educational Researcher* 18, no. 1 (January–February 1989): 32–42.

95. The term *progressive problem solving* is original to Bereiter and Scardamalia, *Surpassing Ourselves*, p. 96.

96. K. Anders Ericsson and Jacqui Smith, "Prospects and Limits of the Empirical Study of Expertise: An Introduction," in *Toward a General Theory of Expertise*, ed. K. Anders Ericsson and Jacqui Smith (Cambridge: Cambridge University Press, 1991), p. 1.

97. Bereiter and Scardamalia, *Surpassing Ourselves*, pp. 77–82.

98. Ibid.

99. The ideas underlying problem finding and problem setting are discussed in Schön, *Educating*, pp. 4, 42–43.

100. Bereiter and Scardamalia, *Surpassing Ourselves*, pp. 99–101.

101. Ibid., pp. 91–98.

102. The term *reflective practitioner* is original to Schön, *The Reflective Practitioner*. The term *cognitive apprenticeship* is found in Brown, Collins, and Duguid, "Situated Cognition and the Culture of Learning."

103. Howard, *Artistry,* pp. 59–109.

104. D. N. Perkins, "Creativity and the Quest for Mechanism," in *The Psychology of Human Thought,* ed. Robert J. Sternberg and Edward E. Smith (New York: Cambridge University Press, 1988), p. 319.

4. Music Listening

1. See, for example, J. J. Gibson, *The Ecological Approach to Visual Perception* (Boston: Houghton Mifflin, 1979), and his *The Senses Considered as Perceptual Systems* (Boston: Houghton Mifflin, 1966).

2. Howard Gardner examines contrasting concepts of perception in *The Mind's New Science* (New York: Basic Books, 1985), pp. 295–322.

3. Csikszentmihalyi, *Flow,* p. 31.

4. Cognitive scientists suggest that the maximum amount of information (taken broadly as sights, sounds, ideas, feelings, and so on) that humans can process at any one time is about seven bits, or "chunks." In his *Flow* (p. 29), Csikszentmihalyi adds that "the shortest time it takes to discriminate between one set of bits and another is about $1/18$ of a second." This amounts to 126 bits of information a second. Csikszentmihalyi estimates that over a lifetime of seventy years we have the capacity to process about 185 billion bits of information (p. 29). For further discussions of attention see Csikszentmihalyi, *Flow,* pp. 28–33, and Csikszentmihalyi and Csikszentmihalyi, *Optimal,* pp. 17–19.

5. John Heil, *Perception and Cognition* (Berkeley: University of California Press, 1983), pp. 35–36.

6. Serafine, *Music as Cognition,* p. 30.

7. Gardner, *Mind's New Science,* p. 313.

8. This parallels the point I made in Chapter 3 about overt action. See Ryle, *Concept of Mind,* pp. 30–32.

9. Harold E. Fiske, "Structure of Cognition and Music Decision-Making," in *Handbook of Research on Music Teaching and Learning,* ed. Richard Colwell (New York: Schirmer Books, 1992), p. 366.

10. Ibid.

11. Serafine, *Music as Cognition,* p. 27.

12. Stephen Handel, *Listening: An Introduction to the Perception of Auditory Events* (Cambridge, Mass.: MIT Press, 1989), p. 222.

13. Ibid., p. 180.

14. C. J. Darwin, "The Perception of Speech," in *Handbook of Perception,* vol. 4 *Language and Speech,* ed. E. C. Carterette and M. P. Friedman (New York: Academic, Press, 1976), pp. 175–216.

15. Handel, *Listening,* p. 319. Spectrograms are representations of the amplitude and frequency of the vibrations that make up an oscillation.

16. Dennett, *Consciousness,* p. 111.

17. Ibid., p. 214.

18. Ibid., p. 112.

19. Ibid., p. 113.

20. Ibid., pp. 111–12.

21. Harold E. Fiske, *Music Cognition and Aesthetic Attitudes* (Lewiston, N.Y.: Edwin Mellen Press, 1993), pp. 63–65.

22. Dennett, *Consciousness,* p. 303.

23. Ibid., p. 335.

24. Ibid., pp. 392–93.

25. Harold E. Fiske, *Music and Mind: Philosophical Essays on the Cognition and Meaning of Music* (Lewiston, N.Y.: Edwin Mellen Press, 1990), p. 5.

26. Serafine, *Music as Cognition,* pp. 39ff.

27. Ibid., p. 40.

28. Ibid., p. 73.

29. Ibid., p. 70.

30. For example, see Fiske, *Music Cognition and Aesthetic Attitudes.* Although I applaud Fiske's important contributions to our understanding of music cognition, and while I cite several of his proposals in this chapter, I disagree with his claim that musical patterns are "content neutral," "nonintentional," and "merely patterns" (p. 118). For one thing, to call patterns "musical" (as Fiske does) is to acknowledge from the outset that the patterns one is discussing are not merely "neutral" patterns but patterns of a very particular kind: artistically generated, intentional, practice-specific, and culture-specific sound patterns. Fiske also claims that "it cannot be shown that music refers to anything outside itself. Rather, music is a metalanguage, limited to tonal-rhythmic self-references" (p. 52). Fiske continues: "I do not know anyone who takes referential content seriously" (p. 116). But, in fact, several contemporary philosophers offer serious reasons for believing that some musical patterns and works can and should be cognized as referring outside themselves, as I explain in Chapters 6 and 8 of this book.

31. Serafine, *Music as Cognition,* pp. 71–73. Like Fiske, Serafine excludes "nonaural material" from her concept of music listening and posits a neat distinction between aural and nonaural processes. But again, a hard and fast distinction is doubtful. For the overt generation and covert cognition of musical patterns are highly contextual processes. Thus, I suggest, the cognition of *musical* sound patterns necessarily includes more than purely acoustic data processing.

32. Ibid., p. 74.

33. Handel, *Listening,* p. 189.

34. Serafine, *Music as Cognition,* p. 72.

35. Ibid., p. 80ff.

36. Ibid., p. 83.

37. Fiske, *Music and Mind,* p. 35.

38. Serafine, *Music as Cognition,* pp. 80–83.

39. Ibid., p. 81.

40. Ibid., p. 86.

41. Handel, *Listening,* pp. 374–75.

42. For a valuable overview of musical imagery, see Fiske, *Music Cognition and Aesthetic Attitudes,* pp. 91–111.

43. Ibid., pp. 104, 107.

44. Dennett, *Consciousness,* p. 370.

45. Fiske, *Music Cognition and Aesthetic Attitudes,* p. 63.

46. Ibid., p. 64.

47. The example of a siren is used in two other discussions of music listening. See Kingsley Price, "Does Music Have Meaning?" *British Journal of Aesthetics* 28, no. 3 (Summer 1988): 208–09; and W. Jay Dowling and Dane L. Harwood, *Music Cognition* (Orlando, Fla.: Academic Press, 1986), p. 91.

48. The term *tones-for-us* is original to Sparshott, "Aesthetics of Music: Limits and Grounds," p. 48.

49. Joseph Margolis, "Music as Ordered Sound: Some Complications Affecting Descrip-

tion and Interpretation,'' in *The Interpretation of Music: Philosophical Essays,* ed. Michael Krausz (Oxford: Clarendon Press, 1993), p. 152.

50. Ibid.

51. Ibid., p. 150.

52. Lucy Green, *Music on Deaf Ears: Musical Meaning, Ideology, Education* (Manchester: Manchester University Press, 1988), pp. 28–29.

53. Sparshott, ''Aesthetics of Music: Limits and Grounds,'' p. 48.

54. For alternative views on the distinctions between aesthetic qualities and artistic qualities, see the following sources: Sparshott, *Theory,* pp. 478–479; Kivy, *The Corded Shell,* pp. 114–18; Levinson, *Music, Art, and Metaphysics,* pp. 239, 182–84; David Best, ''The Dangers of 'Aesthetic Education','' *Oxford Review of Education* 10, no. 2 (1984): 159–67; David Best, ''The Aesthetic and the Artistic,'' *Philosophy* 54 (1982): 357–72; and Dipert, *Artifacts, Art Works, and Agency,* p. 112.

55. See Levinson, *Music, Art, and Metaphysics,* p. 239n.

56. Ibid. Levinson suggests that artistic musical qualities are also generally taken to include such things as musical originality, musical expressions of emotion, and musical representations of people, places, or events (e.g., musical representations of storms).

57. Reimer makes no distinction between aesthetic qualities and artistic qualities. He claims, instead, that the terms *aesthetic* and *artistic* are essentially synonymous: ''the words 'musical' and 'artistic' and 'intrinsic' will often be used [in his book] to substitute for the word 'aesthetic' because they usually mean the same thing.'' See his *A Philosophy (1989),* p. xiii.

58. Peter Kivy, *Sound and Semblance: Reflections on Musical Representation* (Princeton, N.J.: Princeton University Press, 1984), p. 12.

59. Sparshott, ''Aesthetics of Music: Limits and Grounds,'' p. 47.

60. Alperson, ''What Should One Expect,'' p. 231.

61. Trevor Pinnock's recordings of the Bach ''Brandenburg'' Concertos are available on Deutsche Grammophone, Digital, 435 081-2.

62. Cf. Dipert, *Artifacts, Art Works, and Agency.* I owe the last part of this concept of musical works to Dipert, who says: ''Only intended events that are also intended to be regarded by another agent as intentional are performances'' (p. 197). Dipert also argues that ''[P]erformances are then artifacts that are identified with physical events rather than physical objects'' (p. 197). Unlike Dipert, however, I have attempted to emphasize that musical works conceived as performances are not copied but covertly constructed by listeners.

63. Levinson, *Music, Art, and Metaphysics,* p. 275.

64. Here I follow Meyer, *Style and Music,* pp. 14–16, 209–11. Meyer's explanation goes beyond what I can summarize here. Included in his explanation is a discussion (p. 340) of the possibilities of using nonsyntactic parameters in the manner of syntactic parameters.

65. Ibid., p. 14.

66. Ibid.

67. Ibid., p. 15.

68. Ibid., pp. 13–23

69. Ibid., p. 20.

70. Serafine, *Music as Cognition,* pp. 1–2. Serafine makes similar points with respect to musically uneducated adult listeners.

71. Sheila C. Woodward, ''The Transmission of Music into the Human Uterus and the Response to Music of the Human Fetus and Neonate'' (Ph.D. diss., University of Cape Town, 1992). Woodward's research (which includes recordings made in the intrauterine environment) suggests that the fetus may have considerable aural cognition abilities as early as five months' gestation. On the basis of the recordings accompanying this dissertation, one is tempted to speculate that the music-listening and speech-listening processes of the

fetus are forming in relation to, and by virtue of, the auditory information surrounding the daily activities (including the music making) of the pregnant mother. For a summary of research on auditory development, see John H. Flavell, Particia H. Miller, and Scott A. Miller, *Cognitive Development,* 3d ed. (Englewood Cliffs, N.J.: Prentice Hall, 1993), pp. 26–28, 276–281.

72. *Duet and Choral from Cantata 93.* Composed by J. S. Bach and edited by Doreen Rao for two-part treble voices and piano (New York: Boosey and Hawkes, 1991), OCTB-6592.

73. For examples of aesthetic call charts and perception charts, see Reimer, *Developing the Experience of Music.*

74. Peter Kivy, "Music and the Liberal Education," *Journal of Aesthetic Education* 25, no. 3 (Fall 1991): 90.

75. Ibid.

76. Cf. Edwin E. Gordon, *The Nature, Description, Measurement, and Evaluation of Music Aptitudes* (Chicago: G.I.A. Publications, 1987). Gordon's term for aural imagining is "audiation" (p. 13). Gordon holds that "audiation is the most important characteristic of music aptitude" (p. 15). A thorough consideration of Gordon's theory is beyond the scope of this discussion. Suffice it to say that whereas Gordon places audiation at the root of music aptitude and achievement, I consider it one thread (albeit an important one) in the total weave of cognitive processes that make up the procedural and supervisory dimensions of musicianship.

77. Perkins, "Art as Understanding," p. 114.

78. Kivy, "Music and the Liberal Education," p. 92.

79. Ibid., p. 91.

80. Reimer, *A Philosophy* (1989), p. 168.

81. Kivy, "Music and the Liberal Education," p. 93. Although I agree with Kivy's argument, I do not agree that knowing "first theme" and so on is merely a "parlor trick." If formal musical knowledge is part of musicianship (as I have argued in this chapter), then grasping concepts such as first theme is a legitimate part of music teaching and learning. Perhaps Kivy exaggerates here to emphasize the same point I am trying to make in different words: that formal musical knowledge is no substitute for musicianship.

82. See Doreen Rao, "Singing as Listening," forthcoming; and "Craft, Singing Craft and Musical Experience: A Philosophical Study with Implications for Vocal Music Education as Aesthetic Education" (Ph.D. diss., Northwestern University, 1988), pp. 159–73.

83. Dennett, *Consciousness,* p. 279. Dennett cites Jerry Fodor, who uses the term "isotropy" in *The Modularity of Mind* (Cambridge, Mass.: MIT/Bradford Press, 1983).

5. Musicers, Listeners, and Musical Values

1. Cf. Sparshott, "Aesthetics of Music: Limits and Grounds," pp. 51–52. Also, Nicholas Wolterstorff makes the related point that there is likely no single purpose to musical practices. See his chapter, "The Work," in Alperson, *What Is Music?,* pp. 103–29.

2. Sparshott, "Aesthetics of Music: Limits and Grounds," p. 53.

3. Aristotle, *Poetics* (1448b4-24), trans. Gerald F. Else (Ann Arbor: University of Michigan Press, 1967), pp. 21–22.

4. Dennett, *Consciousness,* p. 173.

5. Ibid., p. 177.

6. Ibid., p. 209.

7. Ibid., pp. 199–208. Dennett cites Dawkins on p. 200.

8. Ibid., p. 207.

9. Ibid., p. 206.

10. Csikszentmihalyi, *Flow*, pp. 23–24.

11. Csikszentmihalyi and Csikszentmihalyi, *Optimal*, p. 17.

12. Csikszentmihalyi, *Flow*, p. 26.

13. Ibid.

14. Ibid.

15. Ibid., p. 24.

16. Richard Dawkins, *The Selfish Gene* (Oxford: Oxford University Press, 1976), p. 215.

17. Csikszentmihalyi and Csikszentmihalyi, *Optimal*, p. 20.

18. Ibid.

19. Dennett, *Consciousness*, pp. 428–29.

20. Csikszentmihalyi, *Flow*, p. 34.

21. Perkins, "Art as Understanding," p. 114.

22. Ibid., p. 118.

23. Ibid.

24. Ibid.

25. Csikszentmihalyi and Csikszentmihalyi, *Optimal*, p. 24.

26. Ibid., p. 28.

27. Ibid., p. 24.

28. Ibid., p. 22.

29. Ibid., pp. 3–8.

30. Mihalyi Csikszentmihalyi, "Phylogenetic and Ontogenetic Functions of Artistic Cognition," in *The Arts, Cognition and Basic Skills*, ed. Stanley Madeja (St. Louis: CEMREL, 1978), p. 123.

31. Jacob Bronowski is cited in Dennett, *Consciousness*, p. 209.

32. Csikszentmihalyi and Csikszentmihalyi, *Optimal*, p. 29.

33. Ibid.

34. Csikszentmihalyi, *Flow*, p. 41.

35. Csikszentmihalyi and Csikszentmihalyi, *Optimal*, p. 27.

36. Ibid., pp. 24–27.

37. Csikszentmihalyi, *Flow*, p. 45.

38. Ibid., pp. 46–47.

39. For a concise history of the research efforts underpining the ideas in this section, see Csikszentmihalyi and Csikszentmihalyi, *Optimal*, pp. 3–14. Part 4 of *Optimal* provides measurement studies of flow in different contexts as well as a discussion of the future possibilities of the flow concept.

40. Ibid., p. 30.

41. Csikszentmihalyi, *Flow*, p. 52. Csikszentmihalyi develops these points in his notes to pp. 52–53.

42. Csikszentmihalyi and Csikszentmihalyi, *Optimal*, p. 30.

43. Ibid., p. 30, and Csikszentmihalyi, *Flow*, p. 75.

44. Csikszentmihalyi, *Flow*, p. 41.

45. Ibid., p. 61.

46. Ibid., p. 65.

47. Of course, it is not unusual to find people who receive financial rewards for doing things they enjoy. And we also find many instances of people who begin hating something and end up enjoying it.

48. Chapter 12 of this book develops the concept of life goals based on the work of Clive Beck, *Educational Philosophy and Theory* (Boston: Little, Brown, 1974).

49. R. N. Campbell, *The New Science: Self-Esteem Psychology* (New York: University Press of America, 1984), p. 7.

50. Mihalyi Csikszentmihalyi, *The Evolving Self: A Psychology for the Third Millennium* (New York: HarperCollins, 1993), pp. 194–95.

51. See, for example, Anne J. Wells, "Self-Esteem and Optimal Experience," in Csikszentmihalyi and Csikszentmihalyi, *Optimal Experience,* and S. Whalen and Mihalyi Csikszentmihalyi, "A Comparison of the Self-Image of Talented Teenagers With a Normal Adolescent Population," *Journal of Youth and Adolescence* 18, no. 2 (1989): 131–46.

52. Csikszentmihalyi, *Evolving Self,* p. 204.

53. Ibid.

54. Ibid., p. xv.

55. Sparshott, "Aesthetics of Music: Limits and Grounds," pp. 54–55.

56. Csikszentmihalyi and Csikszentmihalyi, *Optimal,* p. 30.

57. This chart is my adaptation of Csikszentmihaly's original flow diagram as it appears in his *Flow,* pp. 74–75.

58. Ibid., p. 111.

59. Cf. Reimer, *A Philosophy* (1989), pp. 103, 120–21.

60. Cf. Mihalyi Csikszentmihalyi and Rick E. Robinson, *The Art of Seeing* (Malibu, Calif.: J. Paul Getty Trust, 1990). In their study of the visual art experience, Csikszentmihalyi and Robinson suggest broadly that, in the contexts of painting and music, flow experience might also be called aesthetic experience. I disagree, for the reasons explained in Chapter 4 and in this chapter. In my view, Csikszentmihalyi and Robinson take insufficient critical account of the aesthetic concept of art and the problematic notion of aesthetic experience. In addition, their passing references to the nature of music and musical works are just that: passing references. In short, although the concepts of flow experience and aesthetic experience share the characteristics of intense absorption and concentration, the remaining characteristics of aesthetic experience do not apply to musical flow experiences.

61. Reimer, *A Philosophy* (1989), p. 103.

62. Wayne Bowman, "Sound, Sociality, and Music: Challenges to the Aesthetic Vision" (Unpublished paper presented at the Ontario Music Educators Conference, Toronto, Fall 1992), p. 4.

63. Reimer, *A Philosophy* (1989), p. 103.

64. Csikszentmihalyi, *Flow,* and Csikszentmihalyi and Csikszentmihalyi, *Optimal.*

65. Handel, *Listening,* p. xi.

66. David L. Burrows, *Sound, Speech, and Music* (Amherst: University of Massachusetts Press, 1990), p. 21.

67. Handel, *Listening,* p. 547.

68. Bowman, "Sound," p. 6.

69. Ibid.

70. Burrows, *Sound, Speech, and Music,* p. 21.

71. Ibid., p. 16.

72. Don Ihde, *Listening and Voice: A Phenomenology of Sound* (Athens: Ohio University Press, 1976), p. 75.

73. Bowman, "Sound," p. 7.

74. Ibid., p. 9.

75. For a discussion of open and closed concepts in relation to music, see Goehr, *Imaginary Museum,* pp. 90–106.

76. For examples, see the report of the National Commission on Music Education, *Grow-*

ing Up Complete: The Imperative for Music Education (Reston, Va.: Music Educators National Conference, 1991).

77. For discussions of studies in this area, see Nancy G. Thomas, "Motivation," in *Handbook of Research on Music Teaching and Learning,* ed. Richard Colwell (New York: Schirmer Books, 1992), pp. 425–36; Thomas W. Tunks, "The Transfer of Music Learning," in *Handbook,* ed. Colwell, pp. 437–47; and Karen Wolff, "The Nonmusical Outcomes of Music Education: A Review of the Literature," *Bulletin of the Council for Research in Music Education,* no. 55 (Summer 1978): 1–27.

78. Gardner, *Frames of Mind,* pp. 55–56, 124–27, 282–85.

79. Ibid., p. 126.

80. Advocacy statements often emphasize that music is a distinct form of intelligence, only to contradict the point by insisting that musical thinking overlaps with, transfers to, or integrates academic skills. See, for example, National Commission, *Growing Up Complete,* pp. 18–24.

81. Gardner, *Frames of Mind,* pp. 286ff, 316–320. For Gardner's explanation of the relationships between the self and the concept of multiple intelligences, see pp. 294–96.

82. Csikszentmihalyi, *Evolving Self,* p. 204.

83. Ibid.

84. This chart, and my discussion of its ingredients, follows Csikszentmihalyi's original version in *Flow,* pp. 74–75.

85. Ibid., pp. 83–88.

86. Ibid., p. 75.

6. Musical Works

1. Sparshott, "Aesthetics of Music: Limits and Grounds," p. 54.

2. Ibid., p. 55.

3. Peter Kivy, *Music Alone: Philosophical Reflections on the Purely Musical Experience* (Ithaca, N.Y.: Cornell University Press, 1990), p. 15.

4. Ibid., p. 30ff.

5. Sparshott, "Aesthetics of Music: Limits and Grounds," p. 71.

6. Csikszentmihalyi and Csikszentmihalyi, *Optimal Experience,* p. 33. George Herbert Mead is cited for his contribution to our understanding of how "I" supersedes "me" during flow experiences.

7. Kivy, *Music Alone,* p. 63.

8. See Jean-Jacques Nattiez, *Music and Discourse: Toward a Semiology of Music* (Princeton, N.J.: Princeton University Press, 1990), pp. 116–17; and Robert Austerlitz, "Meaning in Music: Is Music Like Language and If so, How?" *American Journal of Semiotics* 2, no. 3 (1983): 1–12.

9. Austerlitz, "Meaning in Music," p. 4.

10. Timothy F. Rice, "The Future of Music in the University" (Unpublished paper presented at the Faculty of Music, University of Toronto, November 26, 1992), pp. 8, 11–12.

11. Eduard Hanslick, *On the Musically Beautiful,* trans. and ed. Geoffrey Payzant (Indianapolis: Hackett Publishing, 1986), p. 9.

12. Kivy, *Music Alone,* pp. 184–89.

13. Eduard Hanslick, *Music Criticisms 1846–1899,* trans. and ed. Henry Pleasants (Baltimore: Penguin Books, 1950), p. 102.

14. Kivy, *Corded Shell,* p. 32.

15. B. R. Tilghman, *The Expression of Emotion in the Visual Arts* (The Hague: Martinus Nijhoff, 1970), pp. 13–14.

16. Kivy explains his theory of musical expression in *Corded Shell* and, briefly, in *Music Alone*, pp. 173–201. Sparshott gives his views on the musical expression of emotions in his "Aesthetics of Music: Limits and Grounds," pp. 56–58, and in his *Theory*, pp. 216–22.

17. Handel, *Listening,* p. 442.

18. D. L. Bolinger, "The Melody of Language," *Modern Language Forum* 40, no. 1 (1955): 19–30, cited in Handel, *Listening,* p. 442.

19. See Handel, *Listening,* pp. 443–45.

20. Johan Sundberg, "Speech, Song and Emotions," in *Music, Mind and Brain: The Neuropsychology of Music*, ed. Manfred Clynes (New York: Plenum Press, 1982).

21. Kivy, *Corded Shell,* p. 37.

22. Sparshott, *Theory,* p. 85.

23. Nelson Goodman, *Ways of Worldmaking* (Indianapolis: Hackett, 1978), p. 106, cited in Kivy, *Corded Shell,* p. 56.

24. Kivy, *Corded Shell,* p. 53.

25. Ibid., p. 55.

26. Ibid. See Chapters 6 and 7.

27. Ibid., p. 118.

28. Ibid., p. 141.

29. Ibid., p. 51. See also Kivy, *Music Alone,* pp. 181–83.

30. Kivy, *Music Alone,* pp. 182–83.

31. Sparshott, "Aesthetics of Music: Limits and Grounds," p. 58.

32. Ibid.

33. Kivy, *Music Alone,* p. 176.

34. Sparshott, "Aesthetics of Music: Limits and Grounds," p. 66.

35. Kivy, *Corded Shell,* p. 49.

36. Goodman and Kivy make similar arguments. See Nelson Goodman, *Languages of Art* (Indianapolis and New York: Bobbs-Merrill, 1968), and Kivy, *Corded Shell,* p. 49.

37. Recall my comments on Langer's theory in Chapter 2.

38. Kivy, *Corded Shell,* p. 98.

39. As Sparshott suggests in his "Aesthetics of Music: Limits and Grounds," we must admit the possibility, although it is difficult to say how it might be argued (through custom? instruction? chance? perceived congruence?) that specific musical features (e.g., rhythmic patterns, melodic patterns, timbres) of a whole musical system might come to be heard as tones and simultaneously as, for example, tones-of-joy or tones-of-anger. Deryck Cooke attempted to construct such a guide to identifying emotions in Western music by assigning emotive meanings to phrases built from intervals in the Western tonal system. Most philosophers today understand that Cooke's construction is not a serious example of what is meant by referentialism or representational music because Cooke's argument is logically flawed; it is a mere curiosity. Nevertheless, some writers (including Reimer) still cite Cooke's book as a serious discussion of referentialism on their way to discrediting the very idea (in strawman fashion). See Deryck Cooke, *The Language of Music* (London: Oxford University Press, 1959), and Reimer, *A Philosophy* (1989), p. 20.

40. Meyer, *Style and Music,* pp. 130–131.

41. See Kivy, *Sound and Semblance,* p. 28; and Jenefer Robinson, "Music as a Representational Art," in *What Is Music? An Introduction to the Philosophy of Music,* ed. Philip A. Alperson (New York: Haven Publications, 1987), p. 178.

42. Robinson, "Music as a Representational Art," pp. 179–82.

43. Ibid., p. 182.
44. Ibid.
45. Ibid., p. 185.
46. Ibid.
47. Ibid., p. 192.
48. Kivy, *Corded Shell,* pp. 147–48.
49. For an excellent explanation of musical representation in nineteenth-century Romantic music, see Meyer, *Style and Music,* Chapter 6. For further references to Meyer's recent views, see Chapter 8 of this book.

7. Musicing in Context

1. This is a variation on proposals put forth in John Seely Brown, Allan Collins, and Paul Duguid, "Situated Cognition and the Culture of Learning," *Educational Researcher* 18, no. 1 (January–February 1989): 32.
2. Alasdair MacIntyre, *After Virtue,* 2d. ed. (Notre Dame, Ind.: University of Notre Dame Press, 1984), p. 181.
3. Wolterstorff, "The Work," p. 112.
4. Ibid., p. 114.
5. Ibid., p. 125.
6. Ibid., p. 123.
7. Ibid., pp. 116–21.
8. Ibid., p. 125.
9. Thomas Carson Mark, "Philosophy of Piano Playing: Reflections on the Concept of Performance," *Philosophy and Phenomenological Research* 41 (1981): 299–324.
10. Ibid., p. 312.
11. Ibid., p. 317.
12. Sparshott, "Aesthetics of Music: Limits and Grounds," p. 82.
13. Ibid., p. 83.
14. Kivy, *Music Alone,* p. 122.
15. Alan H. Goldman, "Interpreting Art and Literature," *Journal of Aesthetics and Art Criticism* 48, no. 3 (Summer 1990): 207.
16. "Pie Jesu" from *Requiem.* Composed by Gabriel Fauré, edited and arranged by Doreen Rao for unison voices and piano (New York: Boosey and Hawkes, 1991), OCTB-6631.
17. Morris Grossman, "Performance and Obligation," in *What Is Music? An Introduction to the Philosophy of Music,* ed. Philip A. Alperson (New York: Haven Publications, 1987), p. 257.
18. These thoughts remind us again that musical sound patterns are speechlike. For just as we interpret the emphases, articulations, and expressive features needed to assert the written lines of a play or poem, we also infer what the silent notation of a musical score requires to become an articulate expression.
19. Grossman, "Performance and Obligation," p. 280.
20. Ibid.
21. Ibid., p. 261.
22. Ibid., p. 275.
23. Ibid., p. 280.
24. Philip A. Alperson, "On Musical Improvisation," *Journal of Aesthetics and Art Criticism* 43, no. 1 (Fall 1984):20.
25. Ibid., p. 26.

26. Ibid., p. 24.

27. Listen for "Giant Steps" on *Giant Steps,* Atlantic 781337-2.

28. Mark C. Gridley supports this view in his *Jazz Styles: History and Analysis,* 3d. ed. (Englewood Cliffs, N.J.: Prentice Hall, 1988), pp. 283–84.

29. Alperson, "Musical Improvisation," p. 23.

30. Ibid., p. 27.

31. Laurie Winer, "Orchestrators Are Tired of Playing Second Fiddle," *The New York Times,* Sunday, July 29, 1990, H 5–21.

32. The performance and interview by Nuclear Saxes was broadcast on National Public Radio in the United States on Sunday, August 11, 1991.

33. This view aligns with that of Dipert, *Artifacts, Art Works, and Agency* (Philadelphia: Temple University Press, 1993), pp. 203–08.

34. Israel Scheffler, "Making and Understanding," in *Proceedings of the Forty-Third Annual Meeting of the Philosophy of Education Society,* ed. B. Arnstine and D. Arnstine (Normal: Illinois State University Press, 1988), p. 65.

35. Ibid., p. 66.

36. Ibid., p. 75.

37. Ibid., p. 77.

38. The term *performative presence* is original to Howard, *Artistry,* p. 124.

39. Ryle, *The Concept of Mind,* pp. 50–51.

40. Ibid., p. 53.

41. Ibid., p. 54.

42. John Dewey, *Art as Experience* (New York: G. P. Putnam's Sons, 1934), pp. 97–98.

43. Ibid., p. 98.

44. Ibid. I have substituted the term *cognitive action abilities* for Dewey's original words "motor equipment."

45. Ibid.

46. Thomas, "Motivation," p. 428.

47. Aristotle, *Politics* (1340b20-33), trans. Jonathan Barnes, ed. Stephen Everson (Cambridge: Cambridge University Press, 1988), pp. 192–93.

48. Ibid. (1340a13-18), (1339a35-36), (1340b20-41a9).

49. Aesthetic listening charts may be found in two sources: Reimer, Crook, Walker, et al., *Silver Burdett Music,* and Reimer, *Developing the Experience of Music.*

50. Jacques Attali, *Noise: The Political Economy of Music* (Minneapolis: University of Minnesota Press, 1985), pp. 110–11.

51. Brown, Collins, and Duguid, "Situated Cognition," p. 33. D. N. Perkins makes a similar argument in his *Knowledge as Design* (Hillsdale, N.J.: Lawrence Erlbaum, 1986).

52. Brown, Collins, and Duguid, "Situated Cognition," p. 33.

53. Ibid.

54. Ibid.

55. Ibid., p. 34.

56. "Basie—Straight Ahead." Composed by Sammy Nestico. This work can be heard as performed by the Count Basie band on an LP of the same name: *Basie—Straight Ahead,* MCA Impulse 29004.

57. The concept of internal goods is explained in MacIntyre, *After Virtue,* pp. 188–189, and in Wolterstorff, "The Work," pp. 110–11.

58. Mihalyi Csikszentmihalyi, "Phylogenetic and Ontogenetic Functions of Artistic Cognition," in *The Arts, Cognition and Basic Skills,* ed. Stanley Madeja (St. Louis: CEMREL, 1978), p. 123.

59. Ibid., pp. 122–25.

60. This is not speculation. The contemporary literature of choral music and instrumental music for primary, middle, and secondary school students includes many excellent examples of works from a wide variety of musical practices. In terms of choral music, see (for example) Doreen Rao, *Choral Music for Children: An Annotated List* (Reston, Va.: MENC, 1990), and Joan Catoni Conlon, "Explore the World in Song," *Music Educators Journal* 78, no. 9 (May 1992): 46–51. For a discussion of musical diversity in the instrumental context, and a list of "world musics" for band and orchestra (by Terese M. Volk), see Will Schmid, "World Music in the Instrumental Program," *Music Educators Journal* 78, no. 9 (May 1992): 41–45. Yet another excellent resource is William M. Anderson and Patricia Shehan Campbell, *Multicultural Perspectives in Music Education* (Reston, Va.: MENC, 1989).

61. MacIntyre explores the basic idea underlying this example in relation to types and modes of excellence. See his *After Virtue,* pp. 189–190.

62. Ibid., p. 190.

63. See Sparshott, *Theory,* p. 461, and his *Off the Ground,* p. 141.

64. MacIntyre, *After Virtue,* p. 190.

65. Csikszentmihalyi, *Evolving Self,* p. xv.

66. The concept of life themes is presented in Csikszentmihalyi, *Flow,* p. 230ff.

67. This theme is implicit in Wolterstorff, "The Work."

68. See Doreen Rao, "Children and Choral Music: The Past and the Present—The Challenge and the Future," *Choral Journal* 29, no. 8 (March 1989):6–14.

69. Csikszentmihalyi, "Phylogenetic and Ontogenetic Functions," p. 125.

70. Aristotle's argument is cited in MacIntyre, *After Virtue,* p. 197.

8. Music Listening in Context

1. Reimer, *A Philosophy* (1989), p. 103.

2. Ibid., pp. 142–143.

3. Robin Barrow and Geoffrey Milburn, *A Critical Dictionary of Educational Concepts* (New York: St. Martin's Press, 1986), pp. 62–63.

4. Meyer, *Style and Music,* pp. 156–157.

5. Susan McClary, "The Blasphemy of Talking Politics During Bach Year," in *Music and Society: The Politics of Composition, Performance and Reception,* ed. Richard Leppert and Susan McClary (Cambridge: Cambridge University Press, 1987), p. 55.

6. Ibid., p. 23.

7. Ibid.

8. Ibid., p. 41.

9. Christoph Wolff, *Bach: Essays on His Life and Music* (Cambridge, Mass.: Harvard University Press, 1991), p. 391.

10. Ibid., p. 32.

11. Ibid.

12. Ibid., p. 33.

13. Ibid., pp. 391–92.

14. Ibid., p. 40.

15. Ibid., p. 83.

16. Malcolm Boyd, *Bach: The Brandenburg Concertos* (Cambridge: Cambridge University Press, 1993), pp. 15, 86–91.

17. Meyer, *Style and Music,* p. 162.

18. Ibid., pp. 166, 175–76, 180, 190.

19. Ibid., pp. 191–93.

20. Challenges to the aesthetic work-concept began with its inception and continue among musicians and theorists today. See Goehr, *Imaginary Museum,* pp. 208ff., 259–73.

21. Meyer, *Style and Music,* p. 208.

22. Ibid., pp. 311–25. Meyer offers a detailed analysis of this work.

23. Ibid., pp. 205–06.

24. Ibid., pp. 206–07.

25. Ibid., pp. 205–06.

26. Ibid., pp. 209–10.

27. Chernoff, *African Rhythm.*

28. Ibid., p. 100.

29. Ibid., p. 143.

30. Ibid., p. 126.

31. Ibid., p. 113.

32. Ibid., p. 151.

33. Ibid., p. 155.

34. Ibid., p. 162.

35. Meyer, *Style and Music,* p. 162n.

36. The concept of delineated meanings is original to Green, *Music on Deaf Ears.*

37. Sparshott, "Aesthetics of Music: Limits and Grounds," p. 58.

38. Simon Frith, "Towards an Aesthetic of Popular Music," in *Music and Society: The Politics of Composition, Performance and Reception,* ed. Richard Leppert and Susan McClary (Cambridge: Cambridge University Press, 1987), pp. 133–49. "The experience of pop music," says Frith, "is an experience of placing" (p. 139).

39. Susan McClary, *Feminine Endings: Music, Gender and Sexuality* (Minneapolis: University of Minnesota Press, 1991), p. 173.

40. Frith, "Towards an Aesthetic of Popular Music," p. 137.

41. Ibid., p. 141.

42. McClary, *Feminine Endings,* pp. 24–25.

43. Ibid., p. 25.

44. John Shepherd, "Music and Male Hegemony," in *Music and Society: The Politics of Composition, Performance and Reception,* ed. Richard Leppert and Susan McClary (Cambridge: Cambridge University Press, 1987), p. 165.

45. McClary, *Feminine Endings,* pp. 153–55.

46. Ibid., pp. 153–55.

47. Ibid., pp. 32–35.

48. Green, *Music on Deaf Ears,* p. 28.

49. Bruno Nettl, *The Study of Ethnomusicology: Twenty-Nine Issues and Concepts* (Urbana: University of Illinois Press, 1983), p. 159.

50. Ibid., p. 293.

51. Peter Kivy, *Osmin's Rage: Philosophical Reflections on Opera, Drama, and Text* (Princeton, N.J.: Princeton University Press, 1988), pp. 178–179.

52. Jeff T. Titon, James T. Koetting, David P. McAllester, David B. Reck, and Mark Slobin, *Worlds of Music* (New York: Schirmer Books, 1984), p. 1.

53. Wolterstorff, "The Work," p. 109.

54. Langer, *Feeling and Form,* pp. 109–10.

55. Philip A. Alperson, " 'Musical Time' and Music as an 'Art of Time,' " *Journal of*

Aesthetics and Art Criticism 38, no. 4 (Summer 1980): 407–17. For a more detailed discussion of the relationship between music and time, see Alperson's study, "The Special Status of Music" (Ph.D. diss., University of Toronto, 1979).

56. Alperson, "Musical Time," pp. 413–14.

57. Nattiez, *Music and Discourse,* p. 118.

58. These remarks on the communicative nature of musicing, listening, and musical works may seem too obvious to mention. Not so. For past music education philosophy denies that musical works involve communication. MEAE bases its denial on an unreasonable assumption: namely, that communication is simply a matter of unambiguous verbal message sending. See Reimer, *A Philosophy* (1989), pp. 57–63.

59. Richard S. Lazarus, "On the Primacy of Cognition," *American Psychologist* 39, no. 2 (1984): 124.

60. Richard S. Lazarus, "Cognition and Motivation in Emotion," *American Psychologist* 46, no. 4 (1991): 353.

61. Cf. Dennett, *Consciousness,* pp. 388–89.

62. Sparshott, "Aesthetics of Music: Limits and Grounds," p. 85.

63. Ibid., pp. 85–86.

64. Meyer, *Emotion.*

65. Scheffler, "Making and Understanding," pp. 65–66.

66. Richard Pratte, *Pluralism in Education* (Springfield, Ill.: Charles C. Thomas, 1979), p. 6.

67. Ibid.

68. Ibid., p. 141.

69. These selections are published by Boosey and Hawkes (New York): *Duet from Cantata No. 9,* composed by J. S. Bach, arranged by Doreen Rao (OCTB-6362); *Good Night,* arranged by Doreen Rao (OCTB-6441); *I'm Goin' Up A-Yonder,* composed by W. Hawkins, arranged by M. Sirvatka (OCTB-6451); and *The Boston Trot,* composed and arranged by David J. Elliott (OCTB-6588).

70. *Siyahamba* (New York: Boosey and Hawkes), a Zulu song arranged by Doreen Rao for three-part treble voices and piano (OCTB-6656).

71. Harold Osborne, *Aesthetics and Art Theory: An Historical Introduction* (New York: E. P. Dutton, 1970), p. 13.

72. Thomas A. Regelski, "Problems, Issues and Directions for Multiculturalism in Music Education" (Unpublished manuscript).

73. Titon, Koetting, et al., *Worlds of Music,* p. 9.

74. Sparshott, "Aesthetics of Music: Limits and Grounds," p. 86.

75. Of course, the meaning of "more distantly related" is relative. For in many North American schools today, many students (and teachers) may find dixieland, salsa, or jazz-rock fusion distant or unfamiliar.

76. Charles Taylor, *Multiculturalism and "The Politics of Recognition"* (Princeton, N.J.: Princeton University Press, 1992), p. 25.

77. Ibid.

78. Ibid.

79. Ibid., p. 26.

9. Musical Creativity in Context

1. This part of my argument parallels one by Vernon A. Howard, *Artistry.* I follow Howard in holding that "creativity comes down to a judgment of merit over the functions that works perform" (p. 125).

2. D. N. Perkins, *The Mind's Best Work* (Cambridge, Mass.: Harvard University Press, 1981), p. 245.

3. Perkins, "Creativity and the Quest for Mechanism," p. 331.

4. Mihalyi Csikszentmihalyi, "Society, Culture and Person: A Systems View of Creativity," in *The Nature of Creativity: Contemporary Psychological Perspectives,* ed. Robert J. Sternberg (New York: Cambridge University Press, 1988), p. 325.

5. Sharon Bailin, "On Originality," *Interchange* 16 (Spring 1985): 9.

6. The two recordings are: Holst, *The Planets,* Decca Digital 417-553-2; 417-553-4, Montreal Symphony Orchestra and Chorus, conducted by Charles Dutoit, and Holst, *The Planets,* EMI Digital CDD7 64300-2; ET 764300-4, Toronto Symphony Orchestra, conducted by Andrew Davis.

7. Reimer, *A Philosophy* (1989), p. 129.

8. Schafer's composition (1968) was originally intended for, and performed by, secondary school music students. It is a musical commentary on the atomic bombing of Nagasaki during World War II.

9. Bereiter and Scardamalia, *Surpassing Ourselves,* pp. 121–50.

10. Larry Briskman, "Creative Product and Creative Process in Science and Art," in *The Concept of Creativity in Science and Art,* ed. D. Dutton and M. Krausz (The Hague: Martinus Nijhoff, 1981), pp. 129–55.

11. See J. H. Holland, K. J. Holyoak, R. E. Nisbett, and P. R. Thagard, *Induction: Processes of Inference, Learning and Discovery* (Cambridge, Mass.: MIT Press, 1986); P. N. Johnson-Laird, *Mental Models* (Cambridge, Mass.: Harvard University Press, 1983), and Perkins, *The Mind's Best Work.*

12. Perkins, *The Mind's Best Work,* p. 275.

13. Reimer, *A Philosophy* (1989), pp. 56–73.

14. Ibid., p. 138.

15. Perkins, *The Mind's Best Work,* p. 247.

16. Ibid., p. 274.

17. Perkins, "Creativity and the Quest for Mechanism," pp. 330–32; Bereiter and Scardamalia, *Surpassing Ourselves;* Howard Gardner, *Frames of Mind: The Theory of Multiple Intelligences* (New York: Basic Books, 1983); Robert W. Weisberg, "Problem Solving and Creativity," in *The Nature of Creativity: Contemporary Psychological Perspectives,* ed. Robert J. Sternberg (New York: Cambridge University Press, 1988), pp. 148–76; A. H. Schoenfeld and D. J. Herrmann, "Problem Perception and Knowledge Structure in Expert and Novice Mathematical Problem Solvers," *Journal of Experimental Psychology: Learning Memory and Cognition* 8, (1982): 484–94.

18. Perkins, "Creativity and the Quest for Mechanism," pp. 332–33.

19. Perkins, *The Mind's Best Work.*

20. Perkins, "Creativity and the Quest for Mechanism," p. 323ff.

21. Ibid.

22. Ibid., pp. 332–34.

23. Bereiter and Scardamalia, *Surpassing Ourselves,* p. 125ff.

24. Ibid. The concept of a "learning-to-be-creative disposition" is also original to Bereiter and Scardamalia.

25. Sparshott, *Theory,* p. 138.

26. For developments of this point, see S. M. Kosslyn, *Ghosts in the Mind's Machine* (New York: Norton, 1983); Sam Glucksberg, "Language and Thought," in The *Psychology of Human Thought,* ed. Robert J. Sternberg and Edward E. Smith (New York: Cambridge University Press, 1988), pp. 218–19.

27. Sparshott, *Theory,* p. 139.

28. Ibid., p. 143.

29. Francis E. Sparshott, "Imagination—The Very Idea," *Journal of Aesthetics and Art Criticism* 48, no. 1 (Winter 1990): 7.

30. See Csikszentmihalyi, "Society, Culture and Person"; and Perkins, "Creativity and the Quest for Mechanism."

31. Perkins, "Creativity and the Quest for Mechanism," p. 319.

32. Ibid., p. 323.

33. See, for example, T. Z. Tardif and Robert J. Sternberg, "What Do We Know about Creativity?" in *The Nature of Creativity: Contemporary Psychological Perspectives,* ed. Robert J. Sternberg (New York: Cambridge University Press, 1988), pp. 429–40.

34. A number of studies make this same point. See the following chapters in Sternberg, *The Nature of Creativity:* Frank Barron, "Putting Creativity to Work," pp. 76–98; Csikszentmihalyi, "Society, Culture and Person," pp. 325–39; Howard Gardner, "Creative Lives and Creative Works: A Synthetic Scientific Approach," pp. 298–321; Howard Gruber and Sara N. Davis, "Inching Our Way up Mount Olympus: The Evolving Systems Approach to Creative Thinking," pp. 243–70; Tardif and Sternberg, "What Do We Know about Creativity?," pp. 429–40.

35. Frank Barron, *Creative Person and Creative Process* (New York: Holt, Rinehart and Winston, 1969); Frank Barron, *Artists in the Making* (New York: Seminar Press, 1972); Mihalyi Csikszentmihalyi and J. Getzels, *The Creative Vision: A Longitudinal Study of Problem Finding In Art* (New York: Wiley, 1976); R. Helson, "Women Mathematicians and the Creative Personality," *Journal of Consulting and Clinical Psychology* 36 (1971): pp. 210–20; R. Mansfield and T. V. Busse, *The Psychology of Creativity and Discovery* (Chicago: Nelson-Hall, 1981).

36. Perkins, "Creativity and the Quest for Mechanism," p. 328.

37. Reimer, *A Philosophy* (1989), p. 62.

38. Howard, *Artistry,* pp. 119–20.

39. See Gardner, "Creative Lives and Creative Works," and Csikszentmihalyi, "Society, Culture and Person."

40. Stephen Davies, "The Evaluation of Music," in *What Is Music?: An Introduction to the Philosophy of Music,* ed. Philip A. Alperson (New York: Haven Publications, 1987), p. 308.

41. Ibid.

42. Gunther Schuller, *The Swing Era* (New York: Oxford University Press, 1989), pp. 61–62.

43. Duke Ellington's "Daybreak Express" may be heard on the following reissue of his original recording: *Duke Ellington and His Orchestra 1933–1935,* Classics 646 CD.

44. For a formal outline and analysis of this work, see Schuller, *The Swing Era,* p. 64.

45. Reimer, *A Philosophy* (1989), p. 133.

46. Schuller, *The Swing Era,* p. 64.

47. Ibid., p. 61.

48. Ibid., pp. 148–52.

49. Ibid., p. 141.

50. Sparshott, "Aesthetics of Music: Limits and Grounds," p. 54.

51. Ibid.

52. Ibid., p. 76.

53. For Howard Gardner's comments, see "Symposium on the Theory of Multiple Intelligences," in *Thinking: The Second International Conference,* ed. D. N. Perkins, Jack Lockhead, and John C. Bishop (Hillsdale, N.J.: Erlbaum, 1987), pp. 97–98.

10. Music Education and Curriculum

1. The concept of reflective practicum is original to Schön, *Educating.*
2. Kieran Egan, "What is Curriculum?" *Curriculum Inquiry* 8, no. 1 (1978): 65.
3. Ibid., pp. 64–71.
4. Ibid.
5. Ibid., p. 69.
6. Hilda Taba, *Curriculum Development: Theory and Practice* (San Francisco: Harcourt, Brace and World, 1962), p. 11.
7. Arthur W. Foshay and Lois A. Beilin, "Curriculum," in *Encyclopedia of Educational Research,* 4th ed., ed. R. I. Ebel (New York: Macmillan, 1969), p. 275.
8. Daniel Tanner and Laurel N. Tanner, *Curriculum Development: Theory into Practice* (New York: Macmillan, 1975), p. 45.
9. John P. Miller and Wayne Seller, *Curriculum: Perspectives and Practice* (New York: Longman, 1985), pp. 3–4.
10. George J. Posner and Alan N. Rudnitsky, *Course Design* (New York: Longman, 1986), pp. 7–8.
11. Floyd G. Robinson, John A. Ross, and Floyd White, *Curriculum Development for Effective Instruction* (Toronto: OISE Press, 1985), p. 3.
12. Decker F. Walker and Jonas F. Soltis, *Curriculum and Aims* (New York: Teachers College Press, 1986), p. 67.
13. Ibid. Along with most curriculum theorists, Walker and Soltis hold that the approach put forth in Ralph Tyler's *Basic Principles of Curriculum and Instruction* is "by far the most influential set of ideas about how to make curriculum" (p. 45). In their text, *Curriculum Development: Theory into Practice,* 2d ed. (New York: Macmillan, 1980), Tanner and Tanner affirm that Tyler's concept of curriculum making has become the dominant way of thinking about curriculum development (p. 90).
14. Ralph W. Tyler, *Basic Principles of Curriculum and Instruction* (Chicago: University of Chicago Press, 1949), p. 38.
15. Ibid., p. 28.
16. In fairness, Tyler's original thinking was broader and more flexible than most behavioristic adaptations of his procedures.
17. William H. Schubert, *Curriculum* (New York: Macmillan 1986), pp. 172, 188.
18. See, for example, R. D. Greer, *Design for Music Learning* (New York: Teachers College Press, 1980). For a broad discussion of behavioral-instructional objectives and examples of their influence on State Music Guides, see J. David Boyle, ed., *Instructional Objectives in Music: Resources for Planning Instruction and Evaluating Achievement* (Vienna, Va.: MENC, 1974).
19. Abeles, Hoffer, and Klotman, *Foundations,* pp. 213–14.
20. Reimer, Crook, Walker, et al., *Silver Burdett Music.*
21. Reimer, *A Philosophy* (1989), p. 150.
22. Schön, *The Reflective Practitioner,* p. 21.
23. Reimer, *A Philosophy* (1989), p. 161.
24. Jurgen Habermas, *Knowledge and Human Interests,* trans. Jeremy J. Shapiro (Boston: Beacon Press, 1971).
25. Shirley Grundy, *Curriculum: Product or Praxis* (London: Falmer Press, 1987), p. 28.
26. Ibid., p. 31.
27. Michael W. Apple, "Curricular Form and the Logic of Technical Control," in *School-*

ing, Ideology and the Curriculum, ed. L. Barton, R. Meighan, and S. Walker (London: Falmer Press, 1980), p. 16.

28. Reimer laments that "music education in the past has . . . failed to demonstrate that it is capable of becoming a genuine curriculum" (Reimer, *A Philosophy* [1989], p. 149). But this is not a failure for music education. The failure lies in Reimer's unexamined assumption that music education should strive to be a "genuine curriculum" as defined by dubious curriculum theory. The fact that many music educators have resisted the reductionism of technical rationality and the mistakes of the structure-of-disciplines approach should be counted as a triumph of wise practice (especially informal educational knowledge) over weak theoretical pronouncements.

29. Brown, Collins, and Duguid, "Situated Cognition," p. 41.

30. Ibid., p. 33.

31. For an uncritical endorsement of the structure-of-disciplines notion, see Reimer, *A Philosophy* (1989), pp. 218–19. For his application of these principles, see pp. 167–70. Reimer continues his uncritical praise of 1960s curriculum "reform" and the structure-of-disciplines notion in his article "Would Discipline-Based Music Education Make Sense?," *Music Educators Journal* 77, no. 9 (May 1991): 21–28.

32. Reimer, *A Philosophy* (1989), p. 170.

33. See Tanner and Tanner, *Curriculum Development* (1980), pp. 60, 66, 518–67, 774.

34. David Tanner and Laurel N. Tanner, *History of the School Curriculum* (New York: Macmillan, 1990), pp. 177–178, 276. For Jerome Bruner's own reflections and reversals, see his article "The Process of Education Revisited," *Phi Delta Kappan* 53, no. 1 (September 1971): 18–21.

35. Schubert, *Curriculum,* pp. 218–19.

36. Clive Beck, *Educational Philosophy and Theory* (Boston: Little, Brown and Company, 1974), pp. 141–42.

37. Swanwick, *Music,* pp. 146–47.

38. Ibid., p. 147.

39. Arthur D. Efland, "The Arts and Physical Education in General Education: A Canonical Interpretation," in *Cultural Literacy and the Idea of General Education: Eighty-Seventh Yearbook of the National Society for the Study of Education,* ed. Ian Westbury and Alan C. Purves (Chicago: University of Chicago Press, 1988), p. 144.

40. Tanner and Tanner, *Curriculum Development* (1980), p. 60.

41. Reimer, *A Philosophy* (1989), p. 219. In the absence of a critically reasoned position on the nature of music performance, Reimer wants to claim that performance in and of itself "is inadequate as a mode for general education in music." If performing were simply a matter of producing sounds, then Reimer might have a point. But this is not the case. As I have argued in this book, performing (properly understood) always includes critical listening and always offers many possibilities for creative achievement through artistic interpretation. All of this, in turn, involves several forms of thinking and knowing, as explained in chapters 3 and 4 of this book.

42. David Best, "The Dangers of 'Aesthetic Education'," *Oxford Review of Education* 10, no. 2 (1984): 164.

43. Stanley S. Madeja, "Reflections on the Aesthetic Education Program," *Journal of Aesthetic Education* 20, no. 4 (Winter 1986): 89.

44. Ibid.

45. Ibid.

46. Ibid., p. 88.

47. Support for this view is available in several sources, including the following: Virginia Richardson, "The Evolution of Reflective Teaching and Teacher Education," in *Encour-*

aging Reflective Practice in Education, ed. Renee T. Clift, W. Robert Houston, and Marleen C. Pugach (New York: Teachers College Press, 1990), pp. 3–19; David L. Smith, "On the Curriculum Planning Processes of Teachers," *Curriculum Perspectives* 6, no. 2 (October 1986): 1–7; Robert J. Yinger, "A Study of Teacher Planning: Descriptions and Theory Development Using Ethnographic and Information Processing Methods" (Ph.D. diss., Michigan State University, 1977); and C. Clark and R. Yinger, "Research on Teacher Planning: A Progress Report" *Journal of Curriculum Studies 11*, no. 2 (1979): 175–77.

48. Walker and Soltis, *Curriculum and Aims*, p. 50. Further support for this point may be found in the following sources: Decker F. Walker, "The Process of Curriculum Development: A Naturalistic Model," *School Review* 80 (November 1971): 51–65; Yinger, "A Study of Teacher Planning"; Clark and Yinger, "Research on Teacher Planning"; J. A. Zahorik, "Teachers' Planning Models," *Educational Leadership* 33 (1975): 134–39; D. F. Walker, "Curriculum Development in an Art Project," in *Case Studies in Curriculum Change*, ed. W. A. Reid and D. F. Walker (London: Routledge and Kegan Paul, 1975); and L. Brady, "An Educological Analysis of Curriculum Design," *International Journal of Educology* 3, no. 1 (1989): 81–91.

49. See John Dewey, *The Child and the Curriculum* (Chicago: University of Chicago Press, 1902), and his *Democracy and Education: An Introduction to the Philosophy of Education* (New York: Macmillan, 1916).

50. See Yinger, "A Study of Teacher Planning"; Clark and Yinger, "Research on Teacher Planning"; and Smith, "On the Curriculum Planning Processes of Teachers."

51. See A. Tom, "Teacher Reaction to a Systematic Approach to Curriculum Implementation," *Curriculum Theory Network II* (1973), pp. 86–93; R. Toomey, "Teachers' Approaches to Curriculum Planning," *Curriculum Inquiry* 7, no. 2 (1977): 121–29; Zahorik, "Teachers' Planning Models"; and Reid and Walker, *Case Studies in Curriculum Change*.

52. Allen T. Pearson, *The Teacher: Theory and Practice in Teacher Education* (New York: Routledge, 1989), p. 63.

53. Ibid., p. 65.

54. By "changes" jazz musicians usually mean "chord changes."

55. MENC, "The Music Specialist in the Elementary School," *Music Educators Journal* 59, no. 3 (November 1972):60.

56. See, for example, Brown, Collins, and Duguid, "Situated Cognition."

57. Schubert, *Curriculum*, p. 287ff.

58. Walker and Soltis, *Curriculum and Aims*, p. 50.

59. Aristotle, *Topica*, trans. W. A. Packard-Cambridge, in *The Basic Works of Aristotle*, ed. R. McKeon (New York: Random House, 1941), pp. 187–206. My source for this strategy is F. Michael Connelly and D. Jean Clandinin, *Teachers as Curriculum Planners* (New York: Teachers College Press, 1988), pp. 83–86.

60. See J. J. Schwab, "The Teaching of Science as Enquiry," in *The Teaching of Science*, ed. J. J. Schwab and P. Brandwein (Cambridge, Mass.: Harvard University Press, 1962).

61. This concept combines the idea of curriculum commonplaces with the view put forth by Connelly and Clandinin, *Teachers as Curriculum Planners*, p. 6.

62. Robert J. Yinger, "The Conversation of Practice," in *Encouraging Reflective Practice in Education*, ed. Clift et al., p. 89.

63. Ibid.

64. Ibid., p. 88.

65. Ibid., p. 93.

66. A useful overview of curriculum evaluation is found in Miller and Seller, *Curriculum: Perspectives and Practice*.

67. Howard Gardner, *Art Education and Human Development* (Los Angeles: J. Paul Getty

Trust, 1990), p. 42. Although Gardner explains his ideas in terms of visual art education (according to the Getty interest), the sweep of his comments and his frequent references to "arts education" make it clear that the principles he urges in this context apply equally (but with modifications of course) to music education.

68. Ibid.

69. Ibid.

70. Gardner, *The Unschooled Mind*, p. 239.

71. Gardner, *Art Education and Human Development*, p. 40.

72. Note, again, that Gardner's concepts apply to "arts education" in general. See note 65.

73. Tanner and Tanner, *Curriculum Development* (1980), pp. 62–63.

74. Gardner, *Art Education and Human Development*, p. 42.

75. Ibid., p. 49.

76. Ibid.

77. Gardner, *The Unschooled Mind*, p. 242.

78. Gardner, *Art Education and Human Development*, p. 41. For a discussion of music teacher education, see my "Rethinking Music Teacher Education," *Journal of Music Teacher Education* 2, no. 1 (Fall 1992):6–15.

79. Howard Gardner, "Assessment in Context: The Alternative to Standardized Testing," in *Report of the Commission on Testing and Public Policy*, ed. B. Gifford (np: 1991), pp. 13–17.

80. Ibid., pp. 11–12. Gardner makes the same point in broader terms.

81. Ibid., pp. 14–17.

82. Ibid., p. 17.

83. Ibid., p. 15. See also Gardner, *Art Education and Human Development*, p. 42.

84. Lyle Davidson, "Too Often We Test Too Little, Too Narrowly—or We Don't Test at All," in *Special Research Interest Group in Measurement and Evaluation*, no. 11 (Winter 1991), ed. Richard Colwell and Robert Ambrose (Boston: Boston University and Music Educators National Conference): 1.

85. Ibid.

86. Gardner, "Assessment in Context," pp. 11–13.

87. Ibid.

88. Ibid.

89. Gardner, *Art Education and Human Development*, pp. 31–32.

11. Music Teaching and Learning

1. Allan Collins, John Seely Brown, and Susan E. Newman, "Cognitive Apprenticeship: Teaching the Crafts of Reading, Writing, and Mathematics," in *Knowing, Learning and Instruction: Essays in Honor of Robert Glaser*, ed. L. Resnick (Hillsdale, N.J.: Erlbaum, 1989), pp. 453–54.

2. Ibid., p. 491.

3. Schön, *Educating*, p. 37.

4. Ibid., pp. 36–37.

5. Gardner, *The Unschooled Mind*, p. 203.

6. Ibid., p. 124.

7. Ibid.

8. Ibid. For Gardner's overview of the apprenticeship model, see pp. 121–25.

9. Ibid., p. 204.

10. Connelly and Clandinin, *Teachers as Curriculum Planners*, p. 137.

11. Gardner, *The Unschooled Mind*, p. 204.

12. Collins, Brown, and Newman, "Cognitive Apprenticeship," pp. 481–83.

13. Marc R. Dickey, "A Review of Research on Modeling in Music Teaching and Learning," *Bulletin of the Council for Research in Music Education*, no. 113 (Summer 1992): 36.

14. Collins, Brown, and Newman, "Cognitive Apprenticeship," pp. 481–82.

15. Richard R. Burton, John Seely Brown, and Gerhard Fischer, "Skiing as a Model of Instruction," in *Everyday Cognition: Its Development in Social Context*, ed. Barbara Rogoff and Jean Lave (Cambridge, Mass.: Harvard University Press, 1984), pp. 139–50.

16. Brown, Collins, and Duguid, "Situated Cognition," p. 33.

17. The concepts of replay and postmortems are original to Collins, Brown, and Newman, "Cognitive Apprenticeship," p. 483.

18. The majority of ideas explained in this section are originally presented in the following sources: Gardner, *The Unschooled Mind*, pp. 238–43; Lyle Davidson and Larry Scripp, "Tracing Reflective Thinking in the Performance Ensemble," *The Quarterly Journal of Music Teaching and Learning* 1, nos. 1 & 2 (Spring 1990): 49–62; Dennie Wolf, "Artistic Learning: What and Where Is It?" *Journal of Aesthetic Education* 22, no. 1 (Spring 1988): 143–55; Davidson, *Too Often We Test Too Little*; Larry Scripp, *Transforming Teaching Through Arts Propel Portfolios: A Case Study of Assessing Individual Student Work in the High School Ensemble* (manuscript, 1990); Larry Scripp, "Establishing a Portfolio Culture in Music Education: Future Directions for Arts Propel" in *Special Research Interest Group in Measurement and Evaluation*, no. 11 (Winter 1991), ed. Richard Colwell and Robert Ambrose (Boston: Boston University and Music Educators National Conference): 12–17.

19. Gardner, *The Unschooled Mind*, p. 240.

20. Ibid., pp. 240–41.

21. Ibid., p. 241.

22. Davidson and Scripp, "Tracing Reflective Thinking," pp. 49–62.

23. Ivan March, Edward Greenfield, and Robert Layton, *The Penguin Guide to Compact Discs and Cassettes: New Edition* (London: Penguin Books, 1992).

24. Examples include Doreen Rao, *ACDA on Location, Vol. 1: The Children's Choir* (Lawton, Okla.: American Choral Directors' Association, Educational Videotape Series, 1988). Rao puts many of the themes of this praxial philosophy into action in ways that have been replicated in many school and community music programs. See also John Feierabend, *Music and Early Childhood*, Connecticut Public Television, 1991. Feierabend's interactions with the very young children in this program offer another demonstration of many principles in this praxial philosophy.

25. Brown, Collins, and Duguid, "Situated Cognition," p. 36.

26. Schön, *Educating*, p. 38.

27. Collins, Brown, and Newman, "Cognitive Apprenticeship," p. 486.

28. Cited by Schön, *Educating*, p. 42.

29. Ibid., p. 74.

30. Ibid., pp. 68–75.

31. Ibid., p. 36.

32. Howard, *Artistry*, pp. 160–76. See also his article "And Practice Drives Me Mad; or, the Drudgery of Drill," *Harvard Educational Review* 61, no. 1 (1991): 80–87.

33. Schön, *Educating*, p. 33.

34. Howard, *Artistry,* p. 162.

35. V. A. Howard and J. H. Barton, *Thinking on Paper* (New York: William Morrow, 1986).

36. Schön, *Educating,* p. 37.

37. Ibid., p. 38.

38. Gardner, *The Unschooled Mind,* p. 204.

39. Ibid., p. 124.

40. See E. W. Eisner, *The Educational Imagination: On the Design and Evaluation of School Programs* (New York: Macmillan, 1979), and J. S. Mann, "Curriculum Criticism," *Curriculum Theory Network* 2 (Winter 1968–69):2–14.

41. Pratte, *Pluralism.*

42. Ibid., p. 79.

43. Ibid., pp. 147–56.

44. Ibid.

12. Music Education and Schooling

1. Csikszentmihalyi and Csikszentmihalyi, *Optimal,* p. 28.

2. This list is an adaptation of one proposed by Mark Holmes in "The Secondary School in Contemporary Western Society," *Curriculum Inquiry* 15, no. 1 (1985): 7.

3. Pat Ordovensky, "Cover Story: Scholars Who Shine Beyond Schoolrooms," *USA Today,* May 17, 1991, D-1.

4. Ibid., pp. D-2, D-4.

5. John Goodlad, *A Place called School* (New York: McGraw-Hill, 1983), pp. 127–28, 134, 286–87.

6. Paul R. Lehman, *Music in Today's Schools: Rationale and Commentary* (Reston, Va.: Music Educators National Conference, 1987), pp. 7–8.

7. Ibid., pp. 7–8.

8. See, for example, Howard Gardner, "Symposium on the Theory of Multiple Intelligences," in *Thinking: The Second International Conference,* ed. D. N. Perkins, Jack Lockhead, and John Bishop, (Hillsdale, N.J.: Lawrence Erlbaum, 1987), p. 77–101. Gardner argues that music is a form of intelligence and not a "talent" in the sense of something that some people are "given" innately and other people are not.

9. Charles Fowler is cited in Marie McCarthy and Bruce Rodger, "Winds of Change: A Colloquium in Music Education," *Maryland Music Educator* 39, no. 3 (February 1993): 41.

10. Charles Leonhard, *A Realistic Rationale for Teaching Music* (Reston, Va.: Music Educators National Conference, 1985), p. 7.

11. These distinctions are original to Holmes, "The Secondary School in Contemporary Western Society," pp. 16–25.

12. Ibid., p. 24.

13. Ibid., pp. 19–20.

14. Ibid., p. 27.

15. Roger A. Clark, "Aesthetic Self-Disclosure in Visual Arts: Factors Affecting the Creative Impulse in Secondary Schools," (Ph.D. diss., Ontario Institute for Studies in Education, University of Toronto, 1987).

16. Ibid.

17. See, for example, Daniel J. Singal, "The Other Crisis in American Education," *The Atlantic Monthly*, November 1991, pp. 59–74.

18. Gardner, *The Unschooled Mind*, p. 202.

19. Holmes, "The Secondary School in Contemporary Western Society," p. 25.

20. Ibid.

21. Ibid.

22. Linda McNeil, *The Contradictions of Control: School Structure and School Nature* (New York: Methuen, 1986), p. xviii.

23. Holmes, "The Secondary School in Contemporary Western Society," p. 30.

24. Ibid., pp. 26–27.

25. Diane Ravitch, "Why Educators Resist a Basic Required Curriculum," in *The Great School Debate*, ed. Beatrice Gross and Ronald Gross (New York: Simon and Schuster, 1985), p. 203.

26. Holmes, "The Secondary School in Contemporary Western Society," p. 30.

27. See, for example, Harry S. Broudy, "The Role of Music in General Education," *Bulletin of the Council for Research in Music Education*, no. 105 (Summer 1990):23–43.

28. Beck, *Educational Philosophy*, p. 2.

29. Lawrence A. Cremin, *Traditions of American Education* (New York: Basic Books, 1977), p. 134.

30. Beck, *Educational Philosophy*, p. 41.

31. Ibid., p. 42.

32. John Dewey, *Democracy and Education* (New York: Macmillan, 1916), pp. 9–10.

33. Beck, *Educational Philosophy*, pp. 50–54.

34. The concepts of education for life and life goals that I draw upon here are originally explained by Beck, *Educational Philosophy*, p. 21ff.

35. Ibid.

36. Ibid., pp. 22–24.

37. Csikszentmihalyi, *Flow*, p. 230.

38. Ibid., p. 226.

Bibliography

Abeles, Harold F., Charles R. Hoffer, and Robert H. Klotman. *Foundations of Music Education*. New York: Schirmer Books, 1984.

Alperson, Philip A. "The Special Status of Music." Ph.D. diss., University of Toronto, 1979.

———. " 'Musical Time' and Music as an 'Art of Time'." *Journal of Aesthetics and Art Criticism* 38, no. 4 (Summer 1980): 407–17.

———. "On Musical Improvisation." *Journal of Aesthetics and Art Criticism* 43, no. 1 (Fall 1984): 17–29.

———. "Introduction: The Philosophy of Music." In *What Is Music? An Introduction to the Philosophy of Music*. Edited by Philip A. Alperson. New York: Haven Publications, 1987.

———. "What Should One Expect from a Philosophy of Music Education?" *Journal of Aesthetic Education* 25, no. 3 (Fall 1991): 215–42.

Anderson, William M., and Patricia Shehan Campbell. *Multicultural Perspectives in Music Education*. Reston, Va.: Music Educators National Conference, 1989.

Apple, Michael W. "Curricular Form and the Logic of Technical Control." In *Schooling, Ideology and the Curriculum*. Edited by L. Barton, R. Meighan, and S. Walker. London: Falmer Press, 1980.

Archambault, R. D., ed. *John Dewey on Education: Selected Writings*. Chicago: University of Chicago Press, 1974.

Aristotle. *Politics*. Translated by Jonathan Barnes. Edited by Stephen Everson. Cambridge: Cambridge University Press, 1988.

———. *Poetics*. Translated by Gerald F. Else. Ann Arbor: University of Michigan Press, 1967.

———. *Topica*. In *The Basic Works of Aristotle*. Translated by W. A. Packard-Cambridge. Edited by R. McKeon. New York: Random House, 1941.

Attali, Jacques. *Noise: The Political Economy of Music*. Translated by Brian Massumi. Minneapolis: University of Minnesota Press, 1985.

Austerlitz, Robert. "Meaning in Music: Is Music Like Language and If So, How?" *American Journal of Semiotics* 2, no. 3 (1983): 1–12.

Bailin, Sharon. "On Originality." *Interchange* 16 (Spring 1985): 6–13.

———. "Creativity and Skill." In *Thinking: The Second International Conference*. Edited by D. N. Perkins, Jack Lockhead, and John Bishop. Hillsdale, N.J.: Erlbaum, 1987.

———. *Achieving Extraordinary Ends: An Essay on Creativity*. Boston: Kluwer Academic Publishers, 1988.

Barron, Frank. *Creative Person and Creative Process*. New York: Holt, Rinehart and Winston, 1969.

———. *Artists in the Making*. New York: Seminar Press, 1972.

———. "Putting Creativity to Work." In *The Nature of Creativity: Contemporary Psychological Perspectives*. Edited by Robert J. Sternberg. New York: Cambridge University Press, 1988.

Barrow, Robin, and Geoffrey Milburn. *A Critical Dictionary of Educational Concepts*. New York: St. Martin's Press, 1986.

Barwell, Ismay. "How Does Art Express Emotion?" *Journal of Aesthetics and Art Criticism* 44, no. 2 (Winter 1986): 175–81.

Batteux, Charles. *Les Beaux Arts réduits à un même principe*. Paris: 1746.

Baumgarten, Alexander. *Meditationes Philosophicae de Nonnullis ad Poema Pertinentibus*. Translated by Karl Aschenbrenner and William Holther. Berkeley: University of California Press, 1954.

Beck, Clive. *Educational Philosophy and Theory*. Boston: Little, Brown, 1974.

———. *Better Schools: A Values Perspective*. New York: Falmer Press, 1990.

Bereiter, Carl, and Marlene Scardamalia. *Surpassing Ourselves: An Inquiry Into the Nature and Implications of Expertise*. La Salle, Ill.: Open Court Publishing, 1993.

Berleant, Arnold. "The Historicity of Aesthetics: Parts 1 and 2." *British Journal of Aesthetics* 26, no. 2 & 3 (1986): 101–11; 195–203.

Bernstein, Richard. *Beyond Objectivism and Relativism: Science, Hermeneutics and Praxis*. Philadelphia: University of Pennsylvania Press, 1983.

Best, David. "The Dangers of 'Aesthetic Education'." *Oxford Review of Education* 10, no. 2 (1984): 159–67.

———. "The Aesthetic and the Artistic." *Philosophy* 54 (1982): 357–72.

Beyer, Landon E. "Aesthetics and the Curriculum: Ideological and Cultural Form in School Practice." Ph.D. diss., University of Wisconsin-Madison, 1981.

Beyer, Landon E., and Michael W. Apple, eds. *The Curriculum: Problems, Politics and Possibilities*. Albany: State University of New York Press, 1988.

Bolinger, D. L. "The Melody of Language." *Modern Language Forum* 40, no. 1 (1955): 19–30.

Borhek, James T., and Richard F. Curtis. *A Sociology of Belief*. New York: John Wiley and Sons, 1975.

Bowman, Wayne. "An Essay Review of Bennett Reimer's *A Philosophy of Music Education*." *The Quarterly Journal of Music Teaching and Learning* 2, no. 3 (Fall 1991): 76–87.

———. "Philosophy, Criticism, and Music Education: Some Tentative Steps Down a Less Travelled Road." *Bulletin of the Council for Research in Music Education*, no. 114 (Fall 1992): 1–19.

———. "Sound, Sociality, and Music: Challenges to the Aesthetic Vision." Paper presented at the Ontario Music Educators Conference, Toronto, October 1992.

———. "The Problem of Aesthetics and Multiculturalism in Music Education." *Canadian Music Educator* 34, no. 5 (May 1993): 23–30.

Boyd, Malcolm. *Bach: The Brandenburg Concertos*. Cambridge: Cambridge University Press, 1993.

Boyle, J. David, ed. *Instructional Objectives in Music: Resources for Planning Instruction and Evaluating Achievement*. Vienna, Va.: Music Educators National Conference, 1974.

Brady, L. "An Educological Analysis of Curriculum Design." *International Journal of Educology* 3, no. 1 (1989): 81–91.

Briskman, Larry. "Creative Product and Creative Process in Science and Art." In *The Concept of Creativity in Science and Art*. Edited by D. Krausz and M. Dutton. The Hague: Martinus Nijhoff, 1981.

Broudy, Harry S. "A Realistic Philosophy of Music Education." In *Basic Concepts in Music Education: The Fifty-Seventh Yearbook of the National Society for the Study of Education*. Edited by Nelson B. Henry. Chicago: University of Chicago Press, 1958.

———. "Types of Knowledge and Purposes of Education." In *Schooling and the Acquisition of Knowledge*. Edited by Richard C. Anderson, R. J. Spiro, and W. E. Montague. Hillsdale, N.J.: Erlbaum, 1977.

———. "The Role of Music in General Education." *Bulletin of the Council for Research in Music Education*, no. 105 (Summer 1990): 23–43.

Brown, John Seely, Allan Collins, and Paul Duguid. "Situated Cognition and the Culture of Learning." *Educational Researcher* 18, no. 1 (January–February 1989): 32–42.

Bruner, Jerome. "The Process of Education Revisited." *Phi Delta Kappan* 53, no. 1 (September 1971): 18–21.

Budd, Malcolm. *Music and the Emotions: The Philosophical Theories*. London: Routledge and Kegan Paul, 1985.

Burrows, David L. *Sound, Speech, and Music*. Amherst: University of Massachusetts Press, 1990.

Burton, Richard R., John Seely Brown, and Gerhard Fischer. "Skiing as a Model of Instruction." In *Everyday Cognition: Its Development in Social Context*. Edited by Barbara Rogoff and Jean Lave. Cambridge, Mass.: Harvard University Press, 1984.

Calvin, William. *The Cerebral Symphony: Seashore Reflections on the Structure of Consciousness*. New York: Bantam, 1989.

Campbell, R. N. *The New Science: Self-Esteem Psychology*. New York: University Press of America, 1984.

Carterette, E. C., and R. A. Kendall. "Human Music Perception." In *The Comparitive Psychology of Audition*. Edited by R. J. Dooling and S. H. Hulse. Hillsdale, N.J.: Erlbaum, 1989.

Chernoff, John Miller. *African Rhythm and African Sensibility*. Chicago: University of Chicago Press, 1979.

Clark, C., and R. Yinger. "Research on Teacher Planning: A Progress Report." *Journal of Curriculum Studies* 11, no. 2 (1979): 175–77.

Clark, Roger A. "Aesthetic Self-Disclosure in Visual Arts: Factors Affecting the Creative Impulse in Secondary Schools." Ph.D. diss., Ontario Institute for Studies in Education, University of Toronto, 1987.

Clift, Renee T., W. Robert Houston, and Marleen C. Pugach, eds. *Encouraging Reflective Practice in Education*. New York: Teachers College Press, 1990.

Cohen, Sara. *Rock Culture in Liverpool: Popular Music in the Making*. New York: Oxford University Press, 1991.

Colley, A. M, and J. R. Beech. *Acquisition and Performance of Cognitive Skills*. Chichester, Eng.: John Wiley, 1989.

Collins, Allan, John Seely Brown, and Susan E. Newman. "Cognitive Apprenticeship: Teaching the Crafts of Reading, Writing, and Mathematics." In *Knowing, Learning and Instruction: Essays in Honor of Robert Glaser*. Edited by L. Resnick. Hillsdale, N.J.: Erlbaum, 1989.

Conlon, Joan Catoni. "Explore the World in Song." *Music Educators Journal* 78, no. 9 (May 1992): 46–51.

Connelly, F. Michael, and D. Jean Clandinin. *Teachers as Curriculum Planners*. New York: Teachers College Press, 1988.

Cooke, Deryck. *The Language of Music*. London: Oxford University Press, 1959.

Copleston, F. *A History of Western Philosophy*. New York: Image Books, 1964.

Cremin, Lawrence A. *Traditions of American Education*. New York: Basic Books, 1977.

Csikszentmihalyi, Mihalyi. "Phylogenetic and Ontogenetic Functions of Artistic Cognition." In *The Arts, Cognition and Basic Skills*. Edited by Stanley Madeja. St. Louis: CEMREL, 1978.

———. "Society, Culture and Person: A Systems View of Creativity." In *The Nature of Creativity: Contemporary Psychological Perspectives*. Edited by Robert J. Sternberg. New York: Cambridge University Press, 1988.

———. *Flow: The Psychology of Optimal Experience*. New York: Harper and Row, 1990.

———. *The Evolving Self: A Psychology for the Third Millennium*. New York: Harper-Collins, 1993.

Csikszentmihalyi, Mihalyi, and J. Getzels. *The Creative Vision: A Longitudinal Study of Problem Finding In Art*. New York: John Wiley, 1976.

Csikszentmihalyi, Mihalyi, and Isabella Csikszentmihalyi, eds. *Optimal Experience: Psychological Studies of Flow in Consciousness*. Cambridge: Cambridge University Press, 1988.

Csikszentmihalyi, Mihalyi, and Rick E. Robinson. *The Art of Seeing*. Malibu, Calif.: J. Paul Getty Trust, 1990.

Dahlhaus, Carl. *Esthetics of Music*. Translated by William W. Austin. Cambridge: Cambridge University Press, 1982.

Danto, Arthur C. *The Philosophical Disenfranchisement of Art*. New York: Columbia University Press, 1986.

Darwin, C. J. "The Perception of Speech." In *Handbook of Perception. Vol. 4. Language and Speech*. Edited by E. C. Carterette and M. P. Friedman. New York: Academic, 1976.

Davidson, Lyle. "Too Often We Test Too Little, Too Narrowly—or We Don't Test at All." In *Special Interest Group in Measurement and Evaluation*, no. 11 (Winter 1991): 1–4. Edited by Richard Colwell and Robert Ambrose. Boston: Boston University and Music Educators National Conference.

———. "Portfolio Assessment: Tracing Learning from Recall to Reasoning." *Holistic Education* 6, no. 2 (1993): 45–51.

Davidson, Lyle, and Larry Scripp. "Tracing Reflective Thinking in the Performance Ensemble." *The Quarterly Journal of Music Teaching and Learning* 1, no. 1 & 2 (Spring 1990): 49–62.

Davies, Stephen. "The Evaluation of Music." In *What Is Music?: An Introduction to the Philosophy of Music*. Edited by Philip A. Alperson. New York: Haven Publications, 1987.

Dawkins, Richard. *The Selfish Gene*. Oxford: Oxford University Press, 1976.

Dennett, Daniel C. "Memes and the Exploitation of Imagination." *Journal of Aesthetics and Art Criticism* 48, no. 2 (Spring 1990): 127–35.

———. *Consciousness Explained*. Boston: Little, Brown, 1991.

Dewey, John. *The Child and the Curriculum*. Chicago: University of Chicago Press, 1902.

———. *Democracy and Education: An Introduction to the Philosophy of Education*. New York: Macmillan, 1916.

———. *Art as Experience*. New York: G. P. Putnam's Sons, 1934.

Dickey, Marc R. "A Review of Research on Modeling in Music Teaching and Learning." *Bulletin of the Council for Research in Music Education*, no. 113 (Summer 1992): 27–40.

Dipert, Randall R. "Meyer's Emotion and Meaning in Music: A Sympathetic Critique of Its Central Claims." *In Theory Only* 6 (1983): 3–17.

———. *Artifacts, Art Works, and Agency.* Philadelphia: Temple University Press, 1993.

Dowling, W. Jay, and Dane L. Harwood. *Music Cognition.* Orlando, Fla.: Academic Press, 1986.

Dreyfus, Hubert L. *What Computers Can't Do: The Limits of Artificial Intelligence.* New York: Harper and Row, 1979.

Dreyfus, Hubert L., and Stuart E. Dreyfus. *Mind Over Machine: The Power of Human Intuition and Expertise in the Era of the Computer.* New York: Free Press, 1986.

Eagleton, Terry. *The Ideology of the Aesthetic.* Cambridge, Mass.: Basil Blackwell, 1990.

Efland, Arthur D. "The Arts and Physical Education in General Education: A Canonical Interpretation." In *Cultural Literacy and the Idea of General Education: Eighty-Seventh Yearbook of the National Society for the Study of Education.* Edited by Ian Westbury and Alan C. Purves. Chicago: University of Chicago Press, 1988.

Egan, Kieran. "What Is Curriculum?" *Curriculum Inquiry* 8, no. 1 (1978): 65–72.

Eisner, E. W. *The Educational Imagination: On the Design and Evaluation of School Programs.* New York: Macmillan, 1979.

Elbow, Peter. *Embracing Contraries: Explorations in Learning and Teaching.* New York: Oxford University Press, 1986.

Elliott, David J. "Structure and Feeling in Jazz: Rethinking Philosophical Foundations." *Bulletin of the Council for Research in Music Education,* no. 95 (Winter 1987): 13–38.

———. "Key Concepts in Multicultural Music Education." *International Journal of Music Education* 13 (Summer 1989): 11–18.

———. "Music as Culture: Toward a Multicultural Concept of Arts Education." *Journal of Aesthetic Education* 24, no. 1 (Spring 1990): 147–66.

———. "Music as Knowledge." *Journal of Aesthetic Education* 25, no. 3 (Fall 1991): 21–40.

———. "Music Education as Aesthetic Education: A Critical Inquiry." *The Quarterly Journal of Music Teaching and Learning* 2, no. 3 (Fall 1991): 48–66.

———. "Rethinking Music Teacher Education." *Journal of Music Teacher Education* 2, no. 1 (Fall 1992): 6–15.

———. "When I Sing: The Nature and Value of Choral Music Education." *Choral Journal* 33, no. 8 (March 1993): 11–17.

Elliott, David J., and Doreen Rao. "Musical Performance and Music Education." *Design for Arts in Education* 91, no. 5 (1990): 23–34.

Ericsson, K. Anders, and Jacqui Smith. "Prospects and Limits of the Empirical Study of Expertise: An Introduction." In *Toward a General Theory of Expertise.* Edited by K. Anders Ericsson and Jacqui Smith. Cambridge: Cambridge University Press, 1991.

Fethe, C. B. "Hand and Eye: The Role of Craft in R. G. Collingwood's Aesthetic Theory." *British Journal of Aesthetics* 22, no. 1 (Winter 1982): 37–51.

Fiske, Harold E. *Music and Mind: Philosophical Essays on the Cognition and Meaning of Music.* Lewiston, N.Y.: Edwin Mellen Press, 1990.

———. "Structure of Cognition and Music Decision-Making." In *Handbook of Research on Music Teaching and Learning.* Edited by Richard Colwell. New York: Schirmer Books, 1992.

———. *Music Cognition and Aesthetic Attitudes.* Lewiston, N.Y.: Edwin Mellen Press, 1993.

Flanagan, Owen. *Consciousness Reconsidered.* Cambridge, Mass.: MIT Press, 1992.

Flavell, John H., Particia H. Miller, and Scott A. Miller. *Cognitive Development*. 3d ed. Englewood Cliffs, N.J.: Prentice Hall, 1993.

Fodor, J. A. *The Modularity of Mind*. Cambridge, Mass: MIT/Bradford Press, 1983.

Foshay, Arthur W., and Lois A. Beilin. "Curriculum." In *Encyclopedia of Educational Research*. 4th ed. Edited by R. I. Ebel. New York: Macmillan, 1969.

Fowler, Charles. "Redefining the Mission of Music Education." In *Winds of Change: A Colloquium in Music Education with Charles Fowler and David J. Elliott*. Edited by Marie McCarthy. New York: ACA Books and the University of Maryland at College Park, 1994.

——, ed. *The Crane Symposium: Toward an Understanding of the Teaching and Learning of Music Performance*. Potsdam: Potsdam College of the State University of New York, 1988.

Frith, Simon. "Towards an Aesthetic of Popular Music." In *Music and Society: The Politics of Composition, Performance and Reception*. Edited by Richard Leppert and Susan McClary. Cambridge: Cambridge University Press, 1987.

Gardner, Howard. *Frames of Mind: The Theory of Multiple Intelligences*. New York: Basic Books, 1983.

——. *The Mind's New Science*. New York: Basic Books, 1985.

——. "Symposium on the Theory of Multiple Intelligences." In *Thinking: The Second International Conference*. Edited by D. N. Perkins, Jack Lockhead, and John Bishop. Hillsdale, N.J.: Erlbaum, 1987.

——. "Creative Lives and Creative Works: A Synthetic Scientific Approach." In *The Nature of Creativity: Contemporary Psychological Perspectives*. Edited by Robert J. Sternberg. New York: Cambridge University Press, 1988.

——. *Art Education and Human Development*. Los Angeles: J. Paul Getty Trust, 1990.

——. "Assessment in Context: The Alternative to Standardized Testing." In *Report of the Commission on Testing and Public Policy*. Edited by B. Gifford. Np: 1991.

——. *The Unschooled Mind*. New York: Basic Books, 1991.

Gibson, J. J. *The Senses Considered as Perceptual Systems*. Boston: Houghton Mifflin, 1966.

——. *The Ecological Approach to Visual Perception*. Boston: Houghton Mifflin, 1979.

Glucksberg, Sam. "Language and Thought." In *The Psychology of Human Thought*. Edited by Robert J. Sternberg and Edward E. Smith. New York: Cambridge University Press, 1988.

Goehr, Lydia. *The Imaginary Museum of Musical Works: An Essay in the Philosophy of Music*. Oxford: Clarendon Press, 1992.

Goldman, Alan H. "Interpreting Art and Literature." *Journal of Aesthetics and Art Criticism* 48, no. 3 (Summer 1990): 205–14.

Goodlad, John. *A Place Called School*. New York: McGraw-Hill, 1983.

Goodman, Nelson. *Languages of Art*. Indianapolis and New York: Bobbs-Merrill, 1968.

——. *Ways of Worldmaking*. Indianapolis: Hackett, 1978.

Gordon, Edwin E. *The Nature, Description, Measurement, and Evaluation of Music Aptitudes*. Chicago: G.I.A. Publications, 1987.

Green, Lucy. *Music on Deaf Ears: Musical Meaning, Ideology, Education*. Manchester: Manchester University Press, 1988.

Greer, R. D. *Design for Music Learning*. New York: Teachers College Press, 1980.

Gridley, Mark C. *Jazz Styles: History and Analysis*. 3rd ed. Englewood Cliffs, N.J.: Prentice Hall, 1988.

Grossman, Morris. "Performance and Obligation." In *What Is Music? An Introduction to the Philosophy of Music*. Edited by Philip A. Alperson. New York: Haven Publications, 1987.

Gruber, Howard, and Sara N. Davis. "Inching Our Way up Mount Olympus: The Evolving Systems Approach to Creative Thinking." In *The Nature of Creativity: Contemporary Psychological Perspectives.* Edited by Robert J. Sternberg. New York: Cambridge University Press, 1988.

Grundy, Shirley. *Curriculum: Product or Praxis.* London: Falmer Press, 1987.

Habermas, Jurgen. *Knowledge and Human Interests.* Translated by Jeremy J. Shapiro. Boston: Beacon Press, 1971.

Hampshire, S. *Thought and Action.* London: Chatto and Windus, 1965.

Handel, Stephen. *Listening: An Introduction to the Perception of Auditory Events.* Cambridge, Mass.: MIT Press, 1989.

Hansen, Forest. "Philosophy of Music Education in a Slightly New Key." *Philosophy of Music Education Review* 1, no. 1 (Spring 1993): 61–74.

Hanslick, Eduard. *Music Criticisms 1846–1899.* Translated and edited by Henry Pleasants. Baltimore: Penguin Books, 1950.

———. *On the Musically Beautiful.* Translated and edited by Geoffrey Payzant. Indianapolis: Hackett Publishing, 1986.

Harris, Michael W. *The Rise of Gospel Blues: The Music of Thomas Andrew Dorsey in the Urban Church.* New York: Oxford University Press, 1992.

Harrison, Andrew. *Making and Thinking: A Study of Intelligent Activities.* Hassocks, England: Harvester Press, 1978.

Heil, John. *Perception and Cognition.* Berkeley: University of California Press, 1983.

Helson, R. "Women Mathematicians and the Creative Personality." *Journal of Consulting and Clinical Psychology* 36 (1971): 210–20.

Hoffer, Charles. *Teaching Music in the Secondary Schools.* 4th ed. Belmont, Calif.: Wadsworth Publishing, 1991.

Holland, J. H., K. J. Holyoak, R. E. Nisbett, and P. R. Thagard. *Induction: Processes of Inference, Learning and Discovery.* Cambridge, Mass.: MIT Press, 1986.

Holmes, Mark. "The Secondary School in Contemporary Western Society." *Curriculum Inquiry* 15, no. 1 (1985): 7–36.

Hospers, John. "Problems of Aesthetics." In *The Encyclopedia of Philosophy,* vol. 1. Edited by Paul Edwards. New York: Macmillan, 1967.

Howard, V. A. *Artistry: The Work of Artists.* Indianapolis: Hackett Publishing, 1982.

———. "Introduction." In *Varieties of Thinking.* Edited by V. A. Howard. New York: Routledge, 1990.

———. "And Practice Drives Me Mad; or, the Drudgery of Drill." *Harvard Educational Review* 61, no. 1 (1991): 80–87.

———. *Learning By All Means: Lessons from the Arts.* New York: Peter Lang Publishing, 1992.

Howard, V. A., and J. H. Barton. *Thinking on Paper.* New York: William Morrow, 1986.

Hunt, Morton. *The Story of Psychology.* New York: Doubleday, 1993.

Hutcheson, Francis. *Inquiry Concerning Beauty, Order, Harmony, Design* (1725). Edited by Peter Kivy. The Hague: Martinus Nijhoff, 1973.

Ihde, Don. *Listening and Voice: A Phenomenology of Sound.* Athens: Ohio University Press, 1976.

Johnson, James R. "Joy and Process: A Philosophical Inquiry." *The Quarterly Journal of Music Teaching and Learning* 2, no. 3 (Fall 1991): 22–29.

Johnson, Mark. *The Body in the Mind: The Bodily Basis of Meaning, Imagination, and Reason.* Chicago: University of Chicago Press, 1987.

Johnson-Laird, P. N. *Mental Models.* Cambridge, Mass.: Harvard University Press, 1983.

Jorgensen, Estelle. "On Philosophical Method." In *Handbook of Research on Music Teaching and Learning*. Edited by Richard Colwell. New York: Schirmer Books, 1992.

Kivy, Peter. *The Corded Shell: Reflections on Musical Expression*. Princeton: Princeton University Press, 1980.

———. *Sound and Semblance: Reflections on Musical Representation*. Princeton: Princeton University Press, 1984.

———. "How Music Moves." In *What Is Music? An Introduction to the Philosophy of Music*. Edited by Philip A. Alperson. New York: Haven Publications, 1987.

———. *Osmin's Rage: Philosophical Reflections on Opera, Drama, and Text*. Princeton, N.J.: Princeton University Press, 1988.

———. *Music Alone: Philosophical Reflections on the Purely Musical Experience*. Ithaca, N.Y.: Cornell University Press, 1990.

———. "Is Music an Art?" *Journal of Philosophy* 81 (October 1991): 544–54.

———. "Music and the Liberal Education." *Journal of Aesthetic Education* 25, no. 3 (Fall 1991): 79–93.

———. "Live Performers and Dead Composers: On the Ethics of Musical Interpretation. In *The Fine Art of Repetition: Essays in the Philosophy of Music*. Edited by Peter Kivy. New York: Cambridge University Press, 1993.

Kosslyn, S. M. *Ghosts in the Mind's Machine*. New York: Norton, 1983.

Kristeller, Paul O. *Renaissance Thought and the Arts: Collected Essays*. Princeton, N.J.: Princeton University Press, 1980.

Lamb, Roberta. "Aria Senza Accompagnamento: A Woman Behind the Theory." *The Quarterly Journal of Music Teaching and Learning* 4, no. 4, and 5, no. 1 (Winter 1994): 5–20.

Langer, Susanne K. *Feeling and Form*. New York: Charles Scribner's Sons, 1953.

———. "The Cultural Importance of the Arts" (1958). In *Aesthetics and Problems of Education*. Edited by Ralph A. Smith. Urbana: University of Illinois Press, 1971.

———. *Philosophy in a New Key: A Study in the Symbolism of Reason, Rite and Art*. 3rd ed. Cambridge, Mass.: Harvard University Press, 1976.

Lave, Jean. *Cognition in Practice*. Cambridge: Cambridge University Press, 1988.

Lazarus, Richard S. "On the Primacy of Cognition." *American Psychologist* 39, no. 2 (1984): 124–29.

———. "Cognition and Motivation in Emotion." *American Psychologist* 46, no. 4 (1991): 352–67.

Lehman, Paul R. *Music in Today's Schools: Rationale and Commentary*. Reston, Va.: Music Educators National Conference, 1987.

Leonhard, Charles. "Music Education—Aesthetic Education." *Education* 74, no. 1 (September 1953): 23–26.

———. *A Realistic Rationale for Teaching Music*. Reston, Va.: Music Educators National Conference, 1985.

Leonhard, Charles, and Robert W. House. *Foundations and Principles of Music Education*. New York: McGraw-Hill, 1959.

Levinson, Jerrold. *Music, Art, & Metaphysics*. Ithaca, N.Y.: Cornell University Press, 1990.

———. "Musical Literacy." *Journal of Aesthetic Education* 24, no. 1 (Spring 1990): 17–30.

———. "Music." In *Handbook of Metaphysics and Ontology*. Edited by Hans Burkhardt and Barry Smith. Munich: Philosophia Verlag, 1991.

Listenius, Nicolai. *Musica* (1537). Translated by Albert Seay. Colorado Springs, Colo.: Colorado College Music Press, 1975.

McCarthy, Marie, and Bruce Rodger. "Winds of Change: A Colloquium in Music Education." *Maryland Music Educator* 39, no. 3 (February 1993): 40–41.

MacIntyre, Alasdair. *After Virtue*. 2d ed. Notre Dame, Ind.: University of Notre Dame Press, 1984.

Macmurray, John. *The Self as Agent*. Atlantic Heights, N.J.: Humanities Press, 1957.

Madeja, Stanley S. "Reflections on the Aesthetic Education Program." *Journal of Aesthetic Education* 20, no. 4 (Winter 1986): 86–91.

Mann, J. S. "Curriculum Criticism." *Curriculum Theory Network* 2 (Winter 1968–69): 2–14.

Mansfield, R., and T. V. Busse. *The Psychology of Creativity and Discovery*. Chicago: Nelson-Hall, 1981.

March, Ivan, Edward Greenfield, and Robert Layton. *The Penguin Guide to Compact Discs and Cassettes*. New edition. London: Penguin Books, 1992.

Margolis, Joseph, "Music as Ordered Sound: Some Complications Affecting Description and Interpretation." In *The Interpretation of Music: Philosophical Essays*. Edited by Michael Krausz. Oxford: Clarendon Press, 1993.

Mark, Thomas Carson. "Philosophy of Piano Playing: Reflections on the Concept of Performance." *Philosophy and Phenomenological Research* 41 (1981): 299–324.

Markowitz, Sally J. "Art and the Tyranny of the Aesthetic." Ph.D. diss., University of Michigan, 1983.

McClary, Susan. "The Blasphemy of Talking Politics During Bach Year." In *Music and Society: The Politics of Composition, Performance and Reception*. Edited by Richard Leppert and Susan McClary. Cambridge: Cambridge University Press, 1987.

———. *Feminine Endings: Music, Gender and Sexuality*. Minneapolis: University of Minnesota Press, 1991.

McNeil, Linda. *The Contradictions of Control: School Structure and School Nature*. New York: Methuen, 1986.

Music Educators National Conference. "The Music Specialist in the Elementary School." *Music Educators Journal* 59, no. 3 (November 1972): 60–62.

Meyer, Leonard B. *Emotion and Meaning in Music*. Chicago: University of Chicago Press, 1956.

———. *Style and Music: Theory, History, and Ideology*. Philadelphia: University of Pennsylvania Press, 1989.

Miller, John P., and Wayne Seller. *Curriculum: Perspectives and Practice*. New York: Longman, 1985.

Mursell, James. "Principles of Music Education." In *Music Education: The 35th Yearbook of the National Society for the Study of Education, Part Two*. Edited by Guy Whipple. Bloomington, Ill.: Public School Publishing, 1936.

———. *Human Values in Music Education*. New York: Silver Burdett, 1934.

Nagel, Ernest. "Review of *Philosophy in a New Key*." *Journal of Philosophy* 40 (1943): 323–29.

National Commission on Music Education. *Growing Up Complete: The Imperative for Music Education*. Reston, Va.: Music Educators National Conference, 1991.

Nattiez, Jean-Jacques. *Music and Discourse: Toward a Semiology of Music*. Princeton, N.J.: Princeton University Press, 1990.

Nelson, K. *Making Sense: The Acquisition of Shared Meaning*. Orlando, Fla.: Academic Press, 1985.

Nettl, Bruno. *The Study of Ethnomusicology: Twenty-Nine Issues and Concepts*. Urbana: University of Illinois Press, 1983.

Ordovensky, Pat. "Cover Story: Scholars Who Shine Beyond Schoolrooms." *USA Today,* May 17, 1991, D-1.

Ornstein, Allan C., and Francis P. Hunkins. *Curriculum: Foundations, Principles and Issues.* Englewood Cliffs, N.J.: Prentice Hall, 1988.

Osborne, Harold. *Aesthetics and Art Theory: An Historical Introduction.* New York: E. P. Dutton, 1970.

O'Shaughnessy, Arthur William Edgar. "Ode." In *Music and Moonlight: Poems and Songs.* London: Chatto and Windus, 1874.

Page, Christopher. *Discarding Images: Reflections on Music and Culture in Medieval France.* Oxford: Clarendon Press, 1993.

Palmer, Anthony J. "World Musics in Music Education." *International Journal of Music Education* 19 (1992): 32–40.

Passmore, John. "Philosophy." In *The Encyclopedia of Philosophy,* vol. 6. Edited by Paul Edwards. New York: Macmillan, 1967.

Pearson, Allen T. *The Teacher: Theory and Practice in Teacher Education.* New York: Routledge, 1989.

Perkins, D. N. *The Mind's Best Work.* Cambridge, Mass.: Harvard University Press, 1981.

————. *Knowledge as Design.* Hillsdale, N.J.: Erlbaum, 1986.

————. "Art as Understanding." *Journal of Aesthetic Education* 22, no. 1 (Spring 1988): 111–131.

————. "Creativity and the Quest for Mechanism." In *The Psychology of Human Thought.* Edited by Robert J. Sternberg and Edward E. Smith. New York: Cambridge University Press, 1988.

Peters, G. David, and Robert F. Miller. *Music Teaching and Learning.* New York: Longman, 1982.

Piaget, Jean. *The Origins of Intelligence in Children.* Translated by Margaret Cook. New York: International Universities Press, 1952.

————. *Six Psychological Studies.* Translated by Anita Tenzer. New York: Random House, 1967.

Posner, George J., and Alan N. Rudnitsky. *Course Design.* New York: Longman, 1986.

Pratte, Richard. *Pluralism in Education.* Springfield, Ill.: Charles C. Thomas, 1979.

Pressing, Jeff. "Improvisation: Methods and Models." In *Generative Processes in Music: The Psychology of Performance, Improvisation and Composition.* Edited by John Sloboda. Oxford: Clarendon Press, 1987.

Price, Kingsley. "Does Music Have Meaning?" *British Journal of Aesthetics* 28, no. 3 (Summer 1988): 208–09.

Rader, Melvin, and Bertram Jessup. *Art and Human Values.* Englewood Cliffs, N.J.: Prentice Hall, 1976.

Rao, Doreen. "Craft, Singing Craft and Musical Experience: A Philosophical Study with Implications for Vocal Music Education as Aesthetic Education." Ph.D. diss., Northwestern University, 1988.

————. *ACDA On Location. Vol. 1: The Children's Choir.* Lawton, Okla.: American Choral Directors' Association, Educational Videotape Series, 1988.

————. "Children and Choral Music in ACDA: The Past and the Present—The Challenge and the Future." *Choral Journal* 29, no. 8 (March 1989): 6–14.

————. *Choral Music for Children: An Annotated List.* Reston, Va.: Music Educators National Conference, 1990.

Ravitch, Diane. "Why Educators Resist a Basic Required Curriculum." In *The Great School Debate.* Edited by Beatrice Gross and Ronald Gross. New York: Simon and Schuster, 1985.

Regelski, Thomas A. *Principles and Problems of Music Education.* Englewood Cliffs, N.J.: Prentice Hall, 1975.

———. "Problems, Issues and Directions for Multiculturalism in Music Education." Manuscript.

Reese, W. L. *Dictionary of Philosophy and Religion: Eastern and Western Thought.* Atlantic Highlands: Humanities Press, 1980.

Reimer, Bennett. *A Philosophy of Music Education.* Englewood Cliffs, N.J.: Prentice Hall, 1970, 1989.

———. *Developing the Experience of Music.* 2d ed. Englewood Cliffs, N.J.: Prentice Hall, 1985.

———. "Would Discipline-Based Music Education Make Sense?" *Music Educators Journal* 77, no. 9 (May 1991): 21–28.

Reimer, Bennett, Elizabeth Crook, and David Walker. *Silver Burdett Music.* Morristown, N.J.: Silver Burdett, 1974, 1978, 1981, 1985.

Reimer, Bennett, and Jeffrey E. Wright, eds. *On the Nature of Musical Experience.* Niwot, Colo.: University Press of Colorado, 1992.

Rice, Timothy F. "The Future of Music in the University." Paper presented at the University of Toronto Symposium on the Future of Music in the University, Toronto, November 26, 1992.

Richardson, Virginia. "The Evolution of Reflective Teaching and Teacher Education." In *Encouraging Reflective Practice in Education.* Edited by Renee T. Clift, W. Robert Houston, and Marleen C. Pugach. New York: Teachers College Press, 1990.

Robinson, Floyd G., John A. Ross, and Floyd White. *Curriculum Development for Effective Instruction.* Toronto: OISE Press, 1985.

Robinson, Jenefer. "Music as a Representational Art." In *What Is Music? An Introduction to the Philosophy of Music.* Edited by Philip A. Alperson. New York: Haven Publications, 1987.

Rosenberg, Jay F. *The Practice of Philosophy: A Handbook for Beginners.* Englewood Cliffs, N.J.: Prentice Hall, 1984.

Ross, Saul. "Epistemology, Intentional Action and Physical Education." In *Philosophy of Sport and Physical Activity.* Edited by P. J. Galasso. Toronto: Canadian Scholars' Press, 1988.

———. "Skill Execution: Knowledgeable Movement." In *Philosophy of Sport and Physical Activity.* Edited by P. J. Galasso. Toronto: Canadian Scholars' Press, 1988.

Ryback, Timothy W. *Rock Around the Bloc: A History of Rock Music in Eastern Europe and the Soviet Union, 1954–1988.* New York: Oxford University Press, 1990.

Ryle, Gilbert. *The Concept of Mind.* New York: Penguin Books, 1949.

Schaareman, Danker, ed. *Balinese Music in Context.* Frankfurt: Amadeus Verlag, 1992.

Scheffler, Israel. "In Praise of Cognitive Emotions." *Teachers College Record* 79, no. 2 (1977): 171–86.

———. "Making and Understanding." In *Proceedings of the Forty-third Annual Meeting of the Philosophy of Education Society.* Edited by B. Arnstine and D. Arnstine. Normal: Illinois State University Press, 1988.

Schoenfeld, A.H., and D.J. Herrmann. "Problem Perception and Knowledge Structure in Expert and Novice Mathematical Problem Solvers." *Journal of Experimental Psychology: Learning, Memory and Cognition* 8 (1982): 484–94.

Schön, Donald A. *The Reflective Practitioner: How Professionals Think in Action.* New York: Basic Books, 1983.

———. *Educating the Reflective Practitioner: Toward a New Design for Teaching and Learning in the Professions.* San Francisco: Jossey-Bass, 1987.

Schubert, William H. *Curriculum*. New York: Macmillan Publishing, 1986.

Schueller, Herbert M. *The Idea of Music: An Introduction to Musical Aesthetics in Antiquity and the Middle Ages*. Kalamazoo, Mich.: Western Michigan University, 1988.

Schuller, Gunther. *The Swing Era*. New York: Oxford University Press, 1989.

Schwab, J. J. "The Teaching of Science as Enquiry." In *The Teaching of Science*. Edited by J. J. Schwab and P. Brandwein. Cambridge, Mass.: Harvard University Press, 1962.

————. *The Practical: A Language for Curriculum*. Washington, D.C.: National Education Association, 1970.

Schmid, Will. "World Music in the Instrumental Program." *Music Educators Journal* 78, no. 9 (May 1992): 41–45.

Schwadron, Abraham A. *Aesthetics: Dimensions for Music Education*. Washington, D.C.: Music Educators National Conference, 1967.

Scripp, Larry. "Establishing a Portfolio Culture in Music Education: Future Directions for Arts Propel." *Special Research Interest Group in Measurement and Evaluation*, no. 11 (Winter 1991): 12–17. Edited by Richard Colwell and Robert Ambrose. Boston: Boston University and Music Educators National Conference.

————. *Transforming Teaching Through Arts Propel Portfolios: A Case Study of Assessing Individual Student Work in the High School Ensemble*. Manuscript.

Serafine, Mary Louise. *Music as Cognition: The Development of Thought in Sound*. New York: Columbia University Press, 1988.

Shavelson, R., and P. Stern. "Research on Teachers' Pedagogical Thoughts, Judgements, Decisions and Behavior." *Review of Educational Research* 52, no. 4 (1981): 455–90.

Shepherd, John. "Music and Male Hegemony." In *Music and Society: The Politics of Composition, Performance and Reception*. Edited by Richard Leppert and Susan McClary. Cambridge: Cambridge University Press, 1987.

Shepherd, John, Phil Virden, Graham Vulliamy, and Trevor Wishart, eds. *Whose Music? A Sociology of Musical Languages*. London: Latimer, 1977.

Singal, Daniel J. "The Other Crisis in American Education." *The Atlantic Monthly* (November 1991): 59–74.

Small, Christopher. *Music, Society, Education*. New York: Schirmer Books, 1977.

————. *Music of the Common Tongue: Survival and Celebration in Afro-American Music*. New York: Riverrun Press, 1987.

Smith, David L. "On the Curriculum Planning Processes of Teachers." *Curriculum Perspectives* 6, no. 2 (October 1986): 1–7.

Smith, Edward E. "Concepts and Thought." In *The Psychology of Human Thought*. Edited by Robert J. Sternberg and Edward E. Smith. Cambridge: Cambridge University Press, 1988.

Smith, Ralph A. *The Sense of Art: A Study in Aesthetic Education*. New York: Routledge, 1989.

Soltis, Jonas F. "Philosophy of Education." In *The Encyclopedia of Educational Research*. 5th ed. Edited by H. E. Mitzel. New York: Macmillan, 1982.

————. *An Introduction to the Analysis of Educational Concepts*. Lanham, Md.: University Press of America, 1985.

Sparshott, Francis E. *The Structure of Aesthetics*. Toronto: University of Toronto Press, 1963.

————. *The Concept of Criticism*. London: Oxford University Press, 1967.

————. *The Theory of the Arts*. Princeton, N.J.: Princeton University Press, 1982.

————. *Off the Ground: First Steps to a Philosophical Consideration of the Dance*. Princeton, N.J.: Princeton University Press, 1988.

————. "Imagination—The Very Idea." *Journal of Aesthetics and Art Criticism* 48, no. 1 (Winter 1990): 1–8.

————. "Education in Music: Conceptual Aspects." In *The New Grove Dictionary of Music and Musicians,* vol. 6. Edited by Stanley Sadie. London: Macmillan, 1980.

————. "Aesthetics of Music: Limits and Grounds." In *What Is Music? An Introduction to the Philosophy of Music.* Edited by Philip A. Alperson. New York: Haven Publications, 1987.

————. "Portraits in Music—A Case-Study: Elgar's 'Enigma Variations.' " In *The Interpretation of Music: Philosophical Essays.* Edited by Michael Krausz. Oxford: Clarendon Press, 1993.

Stenhouse, Lawrence. *An Introduction to Curriculum Research and Development.* London: Heinemann, 1975.

Sternberg, R. J. *The Triarchic Mind: A New Theory of Human Intelligence.* New York: Viking, 1988.

————. *Metaphors of Mind.* New York: Cambridge University Press, 1990.

Sternberg, Robert J., and John Kolligian, Jr., eds. *Competence Considered.* New Haven: Yale University Press, 1990.

Stubley, Eleanor V. "Philosophical Foundations." In *Handbook of Research on Music Teaching and Learning.* Edited by Richard Colwell. New York: Schirmer Books, 1992.

Subotnick, Rose Rosengard. "On Grounding Chopin." In *Music and Society: The Politics of Composition, Performance and Reception.* Edited by Richard Leppert and Susan McClary. Cambridge: Cambridge University Press, 1987.

Suchman, L. A. *Plans and Situated Actions.* Cambridge: Cambridge University Press, 1987.

Sundberg, Johan. "Speech, Song and Emotions." In *Music, Mind and Brain: The Neuropsychology of Music.* Edited by Manfred Clynes. New York: Plenum Press, 1982.

Swanwick, Keith. *A Basis for Music Education.* Windsor: NFER Nelson, 1979.

————. *Music, Mind, and Education.* London: Routledge, 1988.

Taba, Hilda. *Curriculum Development: Theory and Practice.* San Francisco: Harcourt, Brace and World, 1962.

Tait, Malcolm, and Paul Haack. *Principles and Processes of Music Education: New Perspectives.* New York: Teachers College Press, 1984

Tanner, Daniel, and Laurel N. Tanner. *Curriculum Development: Theory into Practice.* New York: Macmillan, 1975, 1980.

————. *History of the School Curriculum.* New York: Macmillan, 1990.

Tardif, T. Z., and Robert J. Sternberg. "What Do We Know About Creativity?" In *The Nature of Creativity: Contemporary Psychological Perspectives.* Edited by Robert J. Sternberg. New York: Cambridge University Press, 1988.

Taylor, Charles. *Multiculturalism and 'The Politics of Recognition'.* Princeton, N.J.: Princeton University Press, 1992.

Thomas, Nancy G. "Motivation." In *Handbook of Research on Music Teaching and Learning.* Edited by Richard Colwell. New York: Schirmer Books, 1992.

Tilghman, B. R. *The Expression of Emotion in the Visual Arts.* The Hague: Martinus Nijhoff, 1970.

Titon, Jeff T., James T. Koetting, David P. McAllester, David B. Reck, and Mark Slobin. *Worlds of Music.* New York: Schirmer Books, 1984.

Tom, A. "Teacher Reaction to a Systematic Approach to Curriculum Implementation." *Curriculum Theory Network II* (1973): 86–93.

Toomey, R. "Teachers' Approaches to Curriculum Planning." *Curriculum Inquiry* 7, no. 2 (1977): 121–29.

Tunks, Thomas W. "The Transfer of Music Learning." In *Handbook of Research on Music*

Teaching and Learning. Edited by Richard Colwell. New York: Schirmer Books, 1992.

Tyler, Ralph W. *Basic Principles of Curriculum and Instruction.* Chicago: University of Chicago Press, 1949.

Van Wieringen, P. C. W. "Discussion: Self-Organization or Representation? Let's Have Both." In *Cognition and Action in Skilled Behavior.* Edited by A. M. Colley and J. R. Beech. Amsterdam: North Holland, 1988.

Wagner, Paul A. "Will Education Contain Fewer Surprises for Students in the Future?" In *Varieties of Thinking.* Edited by V. A. Howard. New York: Routledge, 1990.

Walhout, David. "The Nature and Function of Art." *Journal of Aesthetics and Art Criticism* 26, no. 1 (Winter 1986): 16–25.

Walker, Decker F. "The Process of Curriculum Development: A Naturalistic Model." *School Review* 80 (November 1971): 51–65.

———. "Curriculum Development in an Art Project." In *Case Studies in Curriculum Change.* Edited by W. A. Reid and Decker F. Walker. London: Routledge and Kegan Paul, 1975.

Walker, Decker F., and Jonas F. Soltis. *Curriculum and Aims.* New York: Teachers College Press, 1986.

Weber, William. *The Rise of Musical Classics in Eighteenth-Century England: A Study in Canon, Ritual, and Ideology.* New York: Oxford University Press, 1992.

Weisberg, Robert, W. "Problem Solving and Creativity." In *The Nature of Creativity: Contemporary Psychological Perspectives.* Edited by Robert J. Sternberg. New York: Cambridge University Press, 1988.

Weiss, Piero, and Richard Taruskin. *Music in the Western World.* New York: Schirmer, 1984.

Wells, Anne J. "Self-Esteem and Optimal Experience." In *Optimal Experience: Psychological Studies of Flow in Consciousness.* Edited by Mihalyi Csikszentmihalyi and Isabella Csikszentmihalyi. Cambridge: Cambridge University Press, 1988.

Whalen, S., and Mihalyi Csikszentmihalyi. "A Comparison of the Self-Image of Talented Teenagers with a Normal Adolescent Population." *Journal of Youth and Adolesence* 18, no. 2 (1989): 131–46.

Whittick, Arnold. "Towards Precise Distinctions of Art and Craft." *British Journal of Aesthetics* 24, no. 1 (Winter 1984): 47–52.

Wilson, Blake. *Music and Merchants: The Laudesi Companies of Republican Florence.* New York: Oxford University Press, 1992.

Winer, Laurie. "Orchestrators Are Tired of Playing Second Fiddle." *The New York Times.* July 29, 1990, H-5.

Wing, Lizabeth B. "Curriculum and Its Study." In *Handbook of Research on Music Teaching and Learning.* Edited by Richard Colwell. New York: Schirmer Books, 1992.

Wolf, Dennie. "Artistic Learning: What and Where Is It?" *Journal of Aesthetic Education* 22, no. 1 (Spring 1988): 143–55.

Wolff, Christoph. *Bach: Essays on His Life and Music.* Cambridge, Mass.: Harvard University Press, 1991.

Wolff, Karen. "The Nonmusical Outcomes of Music Education: A Review of the Literature." *Bulletin of the Council for Research in Music Education,* no. 55 (Summer 1978): 1–27.

Wolterstorff, Nicholas. *Art in Action.* Grand Rapids, Mich: William B. Erdmas Publishing, 1980.

———. "The Work of Making a Work of Music." In *What Is Music? An Introduction to the Philosophy of Music.* Edited by Philip A. Alperson. New York: Haven Publications, 1987.

Woodward, Sheila C. "The Transmission of Music into the Human Uterus and the Response to Music of the Human Fetus and Neonate." Ph.D. diss., University of Cape Town, 1992.

Yinger, Robert J. "A Study of Teacher Planning: Descriptions and Theory Development Using Ethnographic and Information Processing Methods." Ph.D. diss., Michigan State University, 1979.

———. "Learning the Language of Practice." *Curriculum Inquiry* 17, no. 3 (1987): 295–318.

———. "The Conversation of Practice." In *Encouraging Reflective Practice in Education.* Edited by Renee T. Clift, W. Robert Houston, and Marleen C. Pugach. New York: Teachers College Press, 1990.

Yinger, R., and C. Clark. "Research on Teacher Planning: A Progress Report." *Journal of Curriculum Studies* 11, no. 2 (1979): 175–77.

Yob, Iris M. "The Form of Feeling." *Philosophy of Music Education Review* 1, no. 1 (Spring 1993): 18–32.

Zahorik, J. A. "Teachers' Planning Models." *Educational Leadership* 33 (1975): 134–39.

Author Index

Subject Index

Abbado, Claudio, 164, 204
Absolute music, 139
Absolutism, 154–55, 176, 193
Academic achievement. *See* Music education
Action. *See also* Musicianship: and procedural
    musical knowledge
  vs. activity, 50
  and consciousness, 51, 55, 58, 78–79, 103
  contexts of, 41, 117–18
  covert and overt, 80–81, 86
  as cultural, 57, 59, 124
  descriptions of, 60–62
  and dualism, 51, 55
  vs. movement, 50, 59, 62
  and musicianship, 53–71
  and music, 49–50
  and praxis, 14, 69, 209
  problems of, 61, 173
  thinking and knowing in, 53–71, 80, 85, 86,
    95, 97, 101, 274
  and verbal concepts, 57–58, 60–62, 95–97, 173
Activity
  vs. action, 50
  and music, 39–42, 45, 50
Advocacy. *See* Music education philosophy
Aesthetic, 21, 84
Aesthetic concept. *See also* Aesthetic
    experience; Aesthetic object; Aesthetic
    perception; Aesthetic qualities; Music
    education as aesthetic education; Work-
    concept
  of art, 22–26
  of composers, 25
  criticisms of, 29–38, 90–91, 124–25
  decline of, 29
  ethnocentricity of, 33–34
  and European society, 23–24
  as ideology, 23–24, 33
  of music, 23–26, 30–38, 124–25

  of music making, 25, 30–33
  of musical works, 22–38, 84, 97
  and structural properties, 84, 90–92, 97
Aesthetic experience
  concept of, 22–23, 25, 36–38
  and music education, 27–28, 36–38
  vs. musical experience, 124–25
  problems of, 29, 36–38, 124–26
Aesthetic object. *See also* Work-concept
  as autonomous, 22–26, 103, 140, 162, 188,
    195, 296
  concept of, 22–26
  and music education, 27–28, 30–33, 91, 103,
    296
  problems of, 29–33, 91, 296
Aesthetic perception
  concept of, 22–26, 33
  and music education, 27–28, 32–36, 175, 220
  and musical worth, 184
  problems of, 29, 33–36, 98, 102, 124–26, 220
Aesthetic qualities. *See also* Artistic qualities
  concept of, 22–23, 25, 90
  and music education, 27–28, 32, 33
  problems of, 90, 125, 193
Aesthetic sensitivity, 32, 249
  problems of, 249
Aesthetics
  axioms of, 22–23
  and beauty, 21–23
  concepts of, 26
  decline of, 29
  doctrine of, 26, 33
  and fine art, 22–26
  and literary criticism, 315n.15
  and music education philosophy, 26–38
  origins and development of, 21–26
  and the philosophy of music, 26
  and poetry, 22
  and the work-concept, 24–26